ON BENDED KNEE

The Press and the Reagan Presidency

ALSO BY MARK HERTSGAARD

Nuclear Inc.: The Men and Money
Behind Nuclear Energy

MARK HERTSGAARD

ON BENDED KNEE

The Press and the Reagan Presidency

FARRAR STRAUS GIROUX

NEW YORK

LIBRARY OF CONGRESS CATALOGING-IN-PUBLICATION DATA
Hertsgaard, Mark.
    On bended knee.
    Includes index.
    1. Press and politics—United States—History—20th
century.   2. Reagan, Ronald—Relations with journalists.
3. United States—Politics and government—1981–
    I. Title.
E876.H46   1988   973.927'092'4   88-7179

Portions of this book first appeared, in slightly different form,
in *Esquire* and in *The Village Voice*

Contents

Author's Note

The overwhelming majority of the direct quotes contained in this book come from some one hundred and seventy-five interviews the author conducted with top officials of the Reagan administration and senior journalists and news executives throughout the press. (A complete list is included in Appendix A.) Where this is not the case, the original source is generally noted in the text itself. Judgments expressed about news coverage are based on a comprehensive analysis of hundreds of newspaper articles and television stories, mainly from the three major commercial networks, *The Washington Post*, *The New York Times*, *Newsweek* and *Time*. Definitive sources for all material can be found in the Notes section.

One of the most extraordinary things about England is that there is almost no official censorship, and yet nothing that is actually offensive to the governing class gets into print, at least in any place where large numbers of people are likely to read it. If it is "not done" to mention something or other, it just doesn't get mentioned. The position is summed up in the lines by (I think) Hilaire Belloc:

> You cannot hope to bribe or twist
> Thank God! The British journalist:
> But seeing what the man will do
> Unbribed, there is no reason to.

—GEORGE ORWELL

ON BENDED KNEE

The Press and the Reagan Presidency

1

"ALL THESE KILLERS"

"WE HAVE BEEN kinder to President Reagan than any President that I can remember since I've been at the *Post*."

So said Benjamin C. Bradlee, executive editor of *The Washington Post*, some four months before the November 1984 re-election of Ronald Reagan. Three years later, after the Iran-contra affair had shattered Mr. Reagan's previous image of invincibility, I asked the legendary editor if he still stood by his statement. He did. Stressing that this was "all totally subconscious," Bradlee explained that when Ronald Reagan came to Washington in 1980, journalists at the *Post* sensed that "here comes a really true conservative. . . . And we are known—though I don't think justifiably—as the great liberals. So, [we thought] we've got to really behave ourselves here. We've got to not be arrogant, make every effort to be informed, be mannerly, be fair. And we did this. I suspect in the process that this paper and probably a good deal of the press gave Reagan not a free ride, but they didn't use the same standards on him that they used on Carter and on Nixon."

Even with all that eventually went wrong—the Iran-contra scandal, the stock-market crash, the seemingly endless series of criminal investigations of former top White House officials—the overall press coverage of the Reagan administration was extraordinarily positive. It is rare indeed for public officials to express satisfaction with their press coverage—in the words of NBC News White House correspondent Andrea Mitchell, "Politicians always say they want a fair press, when what they really want is a positive press"—but the men in charge of media and public relations in the Reagan White House were, almost unanimously, quite pleased with how their President was treated.

James Baker, White House chief of staff during the first term and Secretary of the Treasury during the second, told me, "There were days and times and events we might have some complaint about, [but] on balance and generally speaking, I don't think we had anything to complain about in terms of first-term press coverage."

David Gergen, former White House director of communications, confirmed shortly after leaving the administration in January 1984 that President Reagan and most of his advisers had come to believe that the basic goal of their approach to the news media—"to correct the imbalance of power with the press so that the White House will once again achieve a 'margin of safety' "— had finally been attained.

Most expansive of all was Michael Deaver, the first-term deputy chief of staff and a virtual surrogate son to the Reagans. Deaver wrote in his memoirs that up until the Iran-contra scandal broke, "Ronald Reagan enjoyed the most generous treatment by the press of any President in the postwar era. He knew it, and liked the distinction."*

How Reagan managed to elude critical news coverage for so long baffled many political observers, not least news executives and journalists themselves.

"I don't know how to explain why he hasn't been as vulnerable to the onslaught of the American press as some previous Presidents; it is a hard subject for me," said ABC News executive vice president David Burke. Agreeing with Ben Bradlee about the extraordinary kindness of Reagan's press coverage, he continued, "I wonder why. It isn't because he intimidates us. It isn't that he blows us away with logic. So what the hell is it?"

Burke, a former top aide to Senator Edward Kennedy, finally settled on a variation of the Great Communicator theory, long favored by journalists and White House aides alike for explaining Reagan's positive public image. The key, in this view, was Reagan himself. His personal gifts—an amiable personality, sincere manner, perfect vocal delivery and photogenic persona—made him the television era equivalent of the Pied Piper of Hamelin; he

---

* Even traditional right-wing press bashers were apparently not displeased with Reagan news coverage during the first six years of his presidency. A Gallup poll conducted in June 1985 found that only 21 percent of respondents who described themselves as "strong conservatives" felt that news organizations had been unfair to their President. Even during the Iran-contra scandal, that figure increased only to 42 percent.

played a tune so gay and skipped ahead so cheerily that others could not help but trust and follow him. To attack such a man was unthinkable. "You just can't get the stomach to go after the guy," explained Burke. "It's not a popularity thing, it's not that we're afraid of getting the public mad at us. I think it is a perception that the press has in general of Reagan, that he is a decent man. He is not driven by insecurities, by venality, by conspiracies and back-room tactics."

Tom Brokaw, anchor and managing editor of the *NBC Nightly News*, also felt that Reagan got "a more positive press than he deserves," a feat for which Brokaw credited the White House staff as well as the President. "In part it goes back to who he is," said Brokaw, "and his strong belief in who he is. He's not trying to reinvent himself every day as Jimmy Carter was. . . . Ronald Reagan reminds me of a lot of CEOs I know who run big companies and spend most of their time on their favorite charitable events or lunch with their pals and kind of have a broad-based philosophy of how they want their companies run. Reagan's got that kind of broad-based philosophy about how he wants the government run, and he's got all these killers who are willing and able to do that for him."

The "killers" primarily responsible for generating positive press coverage of Reagan were Michael Deaver and David Gergen, and if they did not exactly get away with murder, they came pretty close. Deaver, Gergen and their colleagues effectively rewrote the rules of presidential image-making. On the basis of a sophisticated analysis of the American news media—how it worked, which buttons to push when, what techniques had and had not worked for previous administrations—they introduced a new model for packaging the nation's top politician and using the press to sell him to the American public. Their objective was not simply to tame the press but to transform it into an unwitting mouthpiece of the government; it was one of Gergen's guiding assumptions that the administration simply could not govern effectively unless it could "get the right story out" through the "filter" of the press.

The extensive public relations apparatus assembled within the Reagan White House did most of its work out of sight—in private White House meetings each morning to set the "line of the day" that would later be fed to the press; in regular phone calls to the television networks intended to influence coverage of Reagan on the evening news; in quiet executive orders imposing extraordinary new government secrecy measures, including granting the FBI and CIA permission to infiltrate the press. It was Mike Deaver's special responsibility to provide a constant supply of visually attractive, prepackaged news stories—the kind that network television journalists in particular found irresistible. Of course, it helped enormously that the man being sold was an ex-Hollywood actor. As James Lake, press secretary of the Reagan-Bush '84 campaign, acknowledged, Ronald Reagan was "the ultimate presidential commodity . . . the right product."

The Reagan public relations model was based on a simple observation, articulated to me by longtime Reagan pollster Richard Wirthlin: "There's no question that how the press reports [on] the President influences how people feel about the President. People make up their minds on the basis of what they see and hear about him, and the press is the conduit through which they get a lot of their information." Because the news media were the unavoidable intermediary between the President and the public, Wirthlin, Deaver, Gergen, Baker and their colleagues focused their talents on controlling to the maximum extent possible what news reports said about the President and his policies. The more influence they could exercise over how Reagan's policies were portrayed in the press, the greater were the White House's chances of implementing those policies without triggering widespread disaffection or endangering Mr. Reagan's re-election chances.

To be sure, Reagan's was hardly the first administration to establish a public relations apparatus within the White House. But few, if any, administrations had exalted news management to as central a role in the theory and practice of governance as Reagan's did. Leslie Janka, a deputy White House press secretary, who resigned in protest after the administration excluded the press from the Grenada invasion, went so far as to say, "The whole thing was PR. This was a PR outfit that became President and took over the country. And to the degree then to which the Constitution forced them to do things like make a budget, run foreign policy and all that, they sort of did. But their first, last and overarching activity was public relations."

What made relations with the press especially vital to the success of Reagan's presidency was the fact that much of his agenda was at odds with popular sentiment. On the basic political issues of his day, Ronald Reagan was much farther to the right than the majority of his fellow citizens. (Contrary to the widely accepted conventional wisdom of the time, American mass opinion in the late 1970s and early 1980s was not galloping to the right. As political economists Thomas Ferguson and Joel Rogers have demonstrated, public opinion was shifting, if anything, slightly leftward during that period, with Reagan's policies themselves apparently providing some of the impetus.)

Reagan's 1981 economic recovery program, for example, combined significant cuts in social spending and federal regulations with fantastic tax reductions aimed overwhelmingly at the very wealthiest Americans. In the name of free enterprise, the administration advocated a massive subsidy program for America's corporations and rich citizens—not an easy thing to sell to average working- and middle-class Americans. Yet Reagan emerged from his first presidential summer gloriously triumphant, with Capitol Hill Democrats and Washington reporters alike convinced— falsely, as it happened—that he was the most popular President in decades.

The Reagan model worked so well that the relationship between the White House and the press will never be the same again. Long after Ronald Reagan has left the White House, the model of news management introduced during his tenure will remain behind, shaping press coverage and therefore public perception. Republican and Democratic candidates alike are relying on elements of the Reagan model in their respective quests for the presidency in 1988, and it is virtually certain to inform the media strategy of whoever succeeds Reagan as President in 1989.

David Gergen was so proud of what the Reagan apparatus accomplished that he told me it would be "worthwhile to institutionalize some of the approaches Reagan has taken toward press events, in order to make it work" for future Presidents. Jody Powell, President Carter's press secretary, and a man who knew a thing or two himself about manipulating the press, was convinced that future administrations would indeed copy the Reagan strategy of news management, but argued that the American people would be the poorer for it.

"There are a lot of people going to school on this administration," said Powell, "and one of the lessons is that the press's bark is much worse than its bite. They'll huff and puff around, but in the end you can cut severely into the flow of information and manage it with a much firmer hand than we were able or willing to do. . . . If you as much as say to the administration, which is what the press is doing, 'Look, you can do this and there's not a damn thing we can do about it,' they're damn sure going to do it. It's too much of a temptation for frail mortals to bear."

Understanding the Reagan propaganda operation is essential if Americans are to make sense of what happened to their country and their politics during the Reagan era. But there is more to the story than slick skulduggery on the part of power-hungry politicos. Precisely because the Reagan PR model seems destined to become an enduring feature of presidential politics in this country, it is crucial to examine how the American press responded to it. After all, in the U.S. system, it is the job of the press to find and present the truth despite officially erected obstacles. As Tom Brokaw commented, "I can't point my finger at [the Reagan White House]. I think they're doing what they need to do, and if there's a failure, it's ultimately the press's failure."

Most of the more than one hundred and fifty journalists and news executives interviewed for this book rejected the idea that Ronald Reagan had gotten a free ride from U.S. news organizations, even as they hastened to add that neither had the press been too tough on him. Like the baby bear's porridge in the children's fairy tale, press coverage of Reagan had been not too hot, not too cold, but just right. If Reagan was popular, argued members of the press, it was because the American people liked him, not because the press had not done its job.

But this self-absolution by members of the press was contradicted by none other than the Reagan men themselves. Proud as they were of their efforts on President Reagan's behalf, more than one of his senior advisers believed that the taming of the press was less the doing of the White House than of the press itself. "I think a lot of the Teflon came because the press was holding back," said David Gergen. "I don't think they wanted to go after him that toughly."

This book tells the story of how top officials in the Reagan White House went about taming the supposedly savage beast known as the press and using it for their own political purposes. But it also tells how leading journalists and news organizations, with honorable individual exceptions, *allowed* themselves to be used. As much through voluntary self-censorship as through government manipulation, the press during the Reagan years abdicated its responsibility to report fully and accurately to the American people what their government was really doing. The result was not only a betrayal of American journalism's public trust but also an impoverished democracy. If these twin tragedies are to be reversed, we must begin by understanding how they came to pass.

2

THE GANG OF FOUR

WHEN HE first settled into Washington and the White House, Michael Deaver felt uncommonly lucky. More than lucky, really: amazed. Suddenly the most influential figures in Washington were seeking him out, treating him with deference, hanging on his every word. Soon after Reagan's January 1981 inauguration, Deaver and his wife, Carolyn, found themselves the guests of honor at a dinner party "with all these cave dwellers [in] their salon in Georgetown." By official Washington standards, it was a smallish affair, with only a dozen or so guests. But they were "cave dwellers"—a slang term for the high-and-mighty of Washington society: a collection of federal officials past and present, Georgetown hostesses, patrons of the arts, lawyers and businessmen and certain influential journalists who comprised a permanent elite in the nation's capital. Presidents came and went, but the cave dwellers remained. It was customary at their gatherings for the guest of honor to speak at dinner's end. And so that night, once the servants had cleared the tables and served the coffee, Katharine Graham, publisher of *The Washington Post*, gently brought the group to attention by asking Deaver, "What do you find the most surprising thing now that you've been in Washington awhile?" After a moment, the new White House deputy chief of staff replied, "The most surprising thing to me is that I'm actually sitting here and you people think I'm important and interesting."

What Deaver couldn't figure out about Washington's society's rush to embrace him, he later explained, was "why all these people who'd been through the Kennedy, Roosevelt, Truman and all these other administrations would find this kid from Bakersfield interesting." It did not take him long to realize that it was the new President's closest aide, not the kid from Bakersfield, who really interested them. "They were fascinated by anyone who's around any President, I guess." Still, it amazed him that the two had become one, that a lower-middle-class kid from a small California valley town had risen to become, at forty-two, the right-hand man to the President of the United States.

He had been granted, he felt, two natural talents with which to make his way in life. As a child, he was never much of an athlete, a failing he now blames on the nephritis (a not uncommon kidney disorder) he contracted at age nine. "Because I could never achieve in athletics, I ran for every office of student politics there was. And I could get attention by playing the piano."

Young Deaver studied piano for over ten years, impelled by a special auditory gift, the musical equivalent of photographic memory. "When I was about six or seven, I realized I could play anything I heard," said Deaver. "I just had an ear." When learning a difficult étude, a task usually accomplished at the rate of a page and a half of sheet music per week, Deaver would be sure to have his instructor play the piece once completely through at the close of the lesson. Then he would race home, the music still in his head, and reproduce the instructor's performance note for note.

The piano remained a source of aid and comfort throughout Deaver's life. No fraternity chose Deaver when he rushed the first time at San Jose State; he later played the piano one night after dinner for one of the brothers, and a week later he was in. On afternoons when the stress of White House life became too much, Deaver would occasionally wander into the East Room, where there stood, in his words, "probably the finest Steinway ever built," a gift from Franklin Roosevelt. With his only audience a couple of White House guards, he would sit down and play for an hour or so, classical selections mainly, until he felt able to face the world again.

Music never became more than an avocation for Mike Deaver; his path to fame and fortune followed a different route; the creativity that might have expressed itself in beautiful concerts and recordings was instead applied to stage-managing the public appearances of Ronald Reagan. But then politics had been an interest of Deaver's for almost as long as music had. He had majored in political science in college (after toying with the idea of becoming a journalist) and shortly after graduating took a field job with the Republican party state apparatus in Santa Barbara. Privately, he favored Reagan's more moderate opponent for the gubernatorial nomination in 1966, but after Reagan won both the primary and general elections, aide William Clark recruited Deaver, then twenty-eight, for the transition team. Several months after Governor Reagan took office, Clark was jumped from cabinet secretary to chief of staff, with Deaver accompanying him as deputy. It was then that he first became involved in the scheduling of Ronald Reagan's public appearances as well as in press work. The former activity in particular brought him into close personal contact with the Reagans, and a mutual fondness soon developed.

Even after Reagan's second term expired in 1974, Deaver remained at his side, loyally and skillfully managing his political affairs and public image. In partnership with a colleague from Sacramento days, Peter Hannaford, Deaver opened a public relations company whose primary client was Ronald Reagan. According to Reagan biographer Lou Cannon, "Reagan became Deaver and Hannaford's meal ticket. Within three months of leaving office, Reagan was making eight to ten speeches a month at an average fee of $5,000 a speech. His column was appearing in 174 newspapers, and his commentaries on more than 200 radio stations." The association continued throughout the 1970s. When Reagan announced his candidacy in 1980, his official headquarters were in the Deaver & Hannaford office on Wilshire Boulevard in Los Angeles.

Just as he had scarcely needed a teacher at piano, Deaver claimed not to require any instruction in political communication and image-making. When I asked who had first taught him the basic tricks of the trade, he seemed almost offended: "Nobody taught me. It was instinct, just a God-given talent."

That talent could not fully blossom, however, until Ronald Reagan attempted his first full-fledged run for the U.S. presidency in 1976. "I never understood the so-called management of news until the '76 campaign," remarked Deaver. "That's when I really got into . . . staging things and planning issues and that sort of thing. . . . [In California] you didn't have the constant media attention to everything he did or you did or said, [so daily news management] just wasn't a necessity."

If the news media's constant, voracious presence took some getting used to, it was also, like the unexpected show of friendship and respect from the Georgetown cave dwellers, a tangible sign of just how high Michael Deaver had risen in the world. The skill which had lifted him there—managing the public presentation of Ronald Reagan—had, by his own account, come to him as easily as playing the piano had nearly forty years ago in Bakersfield. Now, as he and his client prepared to stage their act upon the world's ultimate stage, he would continue to be guided above all by instinct. Partly this was a function of simple experience. In one manner or another, he had been marketing Ronald Reagan to the public for fourteen years now, including eight years of the California governorship and two national presidential campaigns; the right moves now mostly came automatically. Besides, his success as Ronald Reagan's backstage director had always rested mainly on his visceral understanding of and personal affection for the man. Explaining their mutual chemistry, Deaver himself said, "You know yourself, you probably have a friend, or a family member, where you instinctively know what their feelings are. You don't have to second-guess that because of the relationship. That's a hard thing to develop, and Reagan and I had developed that."

His attachment to Reagan elevated Michael Deaver to the pinnacle of earthly power, but very early in his White House tenure he was warned not to let his exalted new status go to his head. On January 20, 1981, the day of Reagan's inauguration, Deaver found himself in the back seat of a long black limousine, being chauffeured to one or another of the day's celebratory events, when, out the window, he suddenly spied former President Carter's press secretary, Jody Powell, his head down, hands jammed in his pockets, walking alone and unnoticed down Pennsylvania Avenue. For four years, Powell had been to Carter as Deaver was to Reagan: an alter ego, a virtual son, his closest and most trusted aide. Now, in the space of a single day, he had been cast down like Lucifer from heaven and made once again to inhabit the world below like other mortals. Deaver was haunted by the image. As the limousine drove on, he silently vowed never to forget it.

• • •

As DIFFERENT as earth and fire in most respects, David Gergen and Michael Deaver nonetheless shared one peculiarity in their

personal histories: each had gotten into the field of political propaganda by a fluke, and, stranger still, each had done so in his
twenty-ninth year. For Gergen, Deaver's junior by four years,
that was 1971. On the cusp of leaving young manhood, he was
thinking seriously about returning to his native North Carolina
for a quiet life as a university professor (his recently deceased
father had chaired the math department at Duke for nearly thirty
years) when fate propelled him through the gates of Richard
Nixon's White House to meet a man named Ray Price who would
change his life forever.

Price, the President's chief speechwriter, was looking to hire
a new assistant. A White House job is seen as the ultimate plum
by young men come to Washington seeking to make a name for
themselves, but the idea of working there had never occurred to
Dave Gergen. The only reason he was in the capital in the first
place was that the Navy had stationed him there for the final year
of his tour of duty, and the only reason he knew about the job
with Price was that an old roommate from his undergraduate years
at Yale happened to work in the White House and suggested he
apply for it. "On a lark," as he later recalled, he did so, but with
no expectation of success. He had never written a political speech
in his life, and to make matters worse, he was still a registered
Democrat. (Growing up in the South, Gergen said with a grin
during one of our interviews, "I never met a Republican until I
was free, white and twenty-one.") But once he arrived in Ray
Price's office, it was apparent that the benefits of his Yale connection had yet to exhaust themselves. It turned out that Price,
too, had gone to Yale, about ten years before Gergen did. As
they quickly fell to reminiscing about New Haven days, the two
men, in Gergen's words, "hit it off very well," and the old school
tie became the basis of "a very good relationship."

In Price, Gergen had stumbled upon a mentor who ranked as
one of the pioneers of media politics. Price knew the news business from the inside; he had written editorials for the *New York
Herald Tribune* for years before entering government. He had
also been a member of the 1968 Nixon campaign team whose
innovative applications of modern television advertising techniques were chronicled in Joe McGinniss's *The Selling of the
President 1968*. It was Price who had argued most persuasively
that to win the election Nixon's image had to be changed. In a

key strategy memo that years later remained a brilliant primer on media politics, Price wrote: "Get the voters to like the guy and the battle's two-thirds won. [The voter's] response is to the image, not to the man. . . . It's not the man we have to change, but rather the received impression."

Originally Gergen planned on spending only a year in the White House, but "then the [1972 re-election] campaign started up, and it became much more interesting." Among other tasks, he was charged with scripting the Republican National Convention. Because the convention "was essentially a coronation of Richard Nixon" where no real decisions would be made, Gergen and his colleagues were afraid that, in his words, "it was going to be a downer politically. So the real question was, 'How do you make it interesting for television, and put some drama into it, some excitement, a little entertainment, some pizzazz?' And that was my first exposure to that kind of thinking."

Gergen was promoted after the 1972 election to chief of the White House research and writing team, but there was considerably less fun to be had during the second term as the Nixon presidency lurched inexorably toward the self-destruction of Watergate. Loyalist that he was, Gergen stayed until the bitter end, then resurfaced in the Ford administration. A notch or two upward on the organizational flow chart, his official title there was the same as he would later attain under President Reagan: director of White House communications.

A number of those who observed Gergen during both periods noticed a mellowing of his views regarding the press after the sour Nixon-Ford experience. Indeed, throughout his years of service to Reagan, Gergen was attacked by right-wingers, inside and outside the White House, for being more loyal to the press than to the President. In particular, he was criticized for speaking too freely with journalists.

"I don't think anybody who went through the Watergate experience and was as seared by that as some of us were could believe anything but that you have to be very straightforward [and] candid about what's going on," said Gergen. "In the long run, you're better served with a relationship of trust."

Gergen's prescription for good government-press relations was broadly shared by chief of staff James Baker and presidential assistant Richard Darman, two other Reagan officials who were frequent targets of right-wing wrath. In fact, because they exercised greater influence over administration policy, Baker and Darman were denounced even more often and bitterly than Gergen was, as "pragmatists" who were betraying the conservative revolution by refusing to "let Reagan be Reagan." The three men had first come to know one another while working in the Nixon and Ford administrations; later, Baker brought the younger two into the Reagan White House with him. According to Gergen, the Watergate experience had made all three of them aware of the dangers of extreme partisanship.

"All of us came out of the Watergate years feeling *very* strongly about the importance of trust in government, of developing relationships in this town that stood on something more than simply power, because the titles can change so quickly. I knew a lot of people who went to jail, people whose careers crashed, people who were at the top who went to the bottom. . . . The people I saw who went down were either highly partisan or extremely ambitious. The White House was the main chance for them, they grabbed it, and they grabbed too high and the whole thing collapsed on them."

The right-wing critics were right in one respect: Gergen's primary allegiance was not to the triumph of the Republican party, or the so-called conservative agenda. His concern, rather, was with the future viability of the American system. To be sure, he was a conservative, but his basic loyalties went deeper than that. He had spent the Carter years as a resident fellow at the American Enterprise Institute, a conservative Washington think tank, watching from the sidelines as yet another administration floundered into mediocrity. Seeking a greater understanding of how Americans felt about their government and why, he conceived and edited the monthly magazine *Public Opinion* at AEI. Gergen despaired over the growing popular cynicism in the 1970s toward the government and other established institutions; a nation that stopped believing in itself was a nation in danger of disintegration and decline.

Gergen returned to what he "knew would be a cauldron" in the White House not out of any ideological commitment to Ronald Reagan; his preferred candidate in 1980 had actually been George Bush. Doubtless the chance to return to the Washington power game had its attractions, for Gergen was an ambitious man, but on a philosophical level apparently what motivated him to join the Reagan team was the opportunity to work from within to break the string of failed or interrupted presidencies that in his view stretched from Carter back to Kennedy. For a man so distrustful of ideologues, it was ironic that the vehicle for his quest would be the most ideologically conservative, indeed reactionary, President to govern the United States in decades—a President who before leaving office would oversee a blatant assault on the constitutional system of government that Gergen held dear.

• • •

DRAWN TOGETHER by circumstance, Deaver and Gergen stayed together, and flourished, on the basis of their common appreciation of the supreme importance of good propaganda to a modern presidency. Neither man would put it quite that way, of course. The word "propaganda" had long ago been banished from respectable discourse in the United States (except when describing doings behind the Iron Curtain). "Public relations," a harmless-enough-sounding term, was one widely used substitute, and recently the even more innocuous concept of "communications" had gained great favor as well. Yet "propaganda," despite the pejorative connotations acquired over the years, was still a perfectly good word, and aptly described the endeavor at which Deaver and Gergen labored. As defined by *The Random House Dictionary of the English Language*, it referred to "information, rumors, etc., deliberately spread widely to help or harm a person, group, movement, institution, nation, etc." What did Deaver, Gergen and their White House colleagues do if not select certain information and deliberately spread it widely to help the government of Ronald Reagan?

As illustrated by Deaver's pithy summary of contemporary American politics—"Television elects Presidents"—the men around Reagan saw television as the path to power, the ultimate technical fix, the modern American King Maker. More than most of their peers in the politics business, they appreciated that without a sophisticated knowledge of how to exploit television, any politician's hopes of wielding power on a national scale were doomed. Whether candidate or incumbent, a politician desiring a successful presidency had to be able to communicate to the electorate his goals and vision for the country; in that process, television was the unavoidable intermediary.

But it was not enough merely to project one's own message.

Television was the proverbial double-edged sword, King Slayer as well as King Maker. As Democratic presidential candidate Gary Hart discovered to his dismay in 1987, when the press decided to go after a politician, the effects could be lethal. To men like Deaver and Gergen it was a truism that no man could gain the Oval Office or govern effectively once there without mastering TV. The corollary of that point was that television exercised something very close to veto power over the running of the presidency. If it could not out-and-out dictate the winner of the election or the agenda of an incumbent, it nevertheless could condemn would-be Presidents to oblivion and sitting ones to impotence. And while the networks' normal posture was one of deference to established authority (especially the federal authorities in Washington who licensed them to operate and profit), their potential to influence what the populace thought about a given issue at a given time was so immense that on those occasions when they did break from routine, the consequences for those on the receiving end could be troublesome indeed.

Jimmy Carter had learned this truth the hard way during the Iranian hostage crisis, and the lesson was not lost on the men in charge of managing the public presentation of Ronald Reagan. Like lions in a circus show, the press could be tamed rather more easily than outsiders might think, for there was a part of them inclined toward obedience from the start. On the other hand, they only had to pounce once in the space of four years to leave their master bloodied if not buried. So the lion tamer had to approach his task with a delicate blend of wariness and self-confidence, exhibiting not only a willingness to crack the whip but also a polite respect for an adversary who was quite capable of tearing his head off.

Aram Bakshian, chief White House speechwriter from November 1981 to October 1983, offered a revealing glimpse of how top Reagan administration officials regarded news media bosses when he explained why David Gergen was never entirely trusted by many of his White House colleagues. "Jim Baker trusted him," began Bakshian. "But just about everybody else there was never quite sure how much Dave might have been saying to people on the outside, and how much of it might have been about them. They knew that every day as part of his job, even if he wasn't being in the least bit indiscreet, he might be talking to several senior network people . . . and with major papers, maybe *Time* or *Newsweek*. So the attitude was, even if he's totally trustworthy, this guy is handling dynamite."

Dynamite which, in the Reagan men's view, had blown up in the faces of their predecessors. Most recently they had seen what the relentless press coverage of the Iranian hostages had done to President Carter's chances for re-election. Before that, Presidents Ford and especially Nixon had encountered their own problems with press coverage. Vietnam, Watergate, the illegal and otherwise scandalous CIA activities uncovered in 1975—it seemed to much of the governing elite in the 1970s that the press could not find enough negative things to report about what the U.S. government was doing. Only a few years before, it had been routine for Walter Cronkite to deliver two-minute verbatim recitations of statements made by the President or Secretary of State without any suggestion that the information needed to be balanced at all. That was how the system was supposed to work: government-issued propaganda, unfiltered, injected straight into the popular consciousness. But as Vietnam and then Watergate gradually unfolded, the deceptions became too obvious to ignore, and self-respect, if nothing else, demanded of journalists a more skeptical attitude toward what they were told.

This had a predictable effect on day-to-day working relations between reporters and government officials. From his vantage point as President Reagan's communications director, David Gergen looked back in near-horror at how combative White House reporters were during the Watergate period: "One of my strongest beliefs is that the degree of cynicism which cropped up in the Vietnam period and the Watergate period and the almost animalistic spirit which cropped up and grew in the [White House] pressroom [were] very destructive of decent press relations. . . . It was extraordinarily difficult, on occasion, to get out information, just straight information in the pressroom, in . . . a way which was productive for anybody. It became a shouting match."

Re-establishing a positive professional working relationship with the White House press corps was a top priority for Gergen and Deaver. How could the President lead the country if he could not communicate with it? Both Deaver and Gergen recognized that to engineer mass consent in the modern media age, the government had to be able to present its version of reality to the public over and over again. Neutralizing the press, by limiting journalists' ability to report politically damaging stories, was necessary but not sufficient. The press had to be turned into a positive instrument of governance, a reliable and essentially non-intrusive transmitter of what the White House wanted the public to know.

The most visible member of the Reagan propaganda apparatus was Larry Speakes, the deputy press secretary, who usually handled the daily briefings of the White House press corps. Speakes became the administration's principal spokesman after James Brady, the original White House press secretary, was incapacitated after being shot in the head during the March 1981 assassination attempt on President Reagan. Like so many other members of the Reagan apparatus, Speakes had first learned about news management while working in the Nixon White House. Although he had worked first as a journalist in his native Mississippi, Speakes soon jumped to the other side of the fence; he would spend the bulk of his professional life seeking to influence the press on behalf of powerful politicians and private interests. As White House point man, Speakes inevitably caught flak from reporters dissatisfied with the quality of information and access they received; indeed, it often seemed that a good part of his job was to draw such fire and thus divert antagonism from his superiors, who actually set policy. Speakes liked to boast that there were a thousand different ways to say "no comment" to a reporter, and he had used 999 of them. But that was not all he did. After leaving the White House in February 1986, Speakes wrote a book called *Speaking Out* in which he revealed that on at least two occasions he had outright manufactured quotable quotes and passed them off as President Reagan's own words. The admission caused an uproar in Washington and led to Speakes's resignation from a $400,000-a-year job as chief public spokesman for Merrill Lynch, the Wall Street investment firm.

Although not on the government payroll, another key figure in the Reagan propaganda apparatus was pollster Richard Wirthlin. Reagan had been a client of Wirthlin's on and off since 1968, and his readings of the electorate's moods were vital to Reagan's success in 1980. Wirthlin's surveys detailed the contours of the political landscape on which the apparatus would battle to shape public opinion. Specifically, his surveys pinpointed which issues were causing Reagan trouble with which constituencies, suggested ways to calibrate his message to ameliorate those concerns and finally tested whether the alterations had worked. Polls did not necessarily dictate policy—"If you get numbers back saying 70 percent are really being hurt by inflation or unemployment, you take that very seriously; if the numbers are 53–47, you know the public is mixed," according to Gergen—but, properly interpreted, they were crucial to a successful media operation. If one is trying to influence the public mind, "you need," in Gergen's words, "to know what the public is thinking about."

Richard Darman was another central figure. Among the forces behind the throne in the Reagan White House, few wielded as much influence, as quietly, as did Darman. He played a key role in many administration initiatives, including the 1981 tax and budget cuts, the re-election campaign and the 1986 tax-system overhaul. He had volunteered early on to monitor the paper flow into and out of the President's office, a task that experienced White House hands recognized as far less mundane than it appeared, since it gave him effective control over every document that went to the President or was publicly issued on his behalf. His undeniable abilities gave rise to a self-confidence, and self-importance, that struck some colleagues as arrogance. "Where would you put Dick Darman in the organizational chart?" went one White House joke. "Well, here's God," answered the joke teller, drawing an imaginary box in the air, "and here," drawing an identical box right next to the first, "is Dick."

Darman had an intellectual's disdain for public relations work. In an interview for this book, he made a point of minimizing the importance of the White House media apparatus to President Reagan's accomplishments. "The key to success," he declared, "is not communications policy but policy policy."

Much as Darman may have, in Deaver's words, "felt it beneath him," he nevertheless helped to shape the public image of Ronald Reagan in countless ways. As one of the people in the White House who, in Deaver's words, "understood the importance of that story every night," he regularly attended the "line of the day" and various other meetings where communications policy was set. Deaver added that he found it especially valuable to "pick [Darman's] brains" for ideas on how to get the most political bang for the public relations buck in the regular "Friday Group" meetings where long-term communications strategy was set.

And while he rarely agreed to speak to reporters on the record, Darman nevertheless exercised considerable indirect influence over their reporting about the Reagan administration. David Gergen viewed Darman's ability to "articulate what this presidency is all about" as crucial to establishing a good rapport with the Washington press corps. "That's what happened to the Carter administration in the end," added Gergen. "There was really only one person—[pollster] Pat Caddell—who could philosophize about the nature of the administration. A President needs people around him who can talk in a language that is both precise and deep. One of the reasons the Kennedy administration was successful with the press was that they had people who enjoyed schmoozing with the press, and they were good at it; they liked to talk about things. Dick Darman was very good at that."

Presiding over the entire Reagan communications apparatus was the White House chief of staff, James Baker. Born into a wealthy Texas family, Baker made plenty of additional money as a partner in one of Houston's major law firms before turning his attention to politics. He served on President Ford's campaign staff in 1976, and again opposed Reagan when he ran George Bush's campaign for the presidency in 1980. But Baker was careful, once the ultimate outcome became apparent, not to let Bush fight on too long or stridently, thus preserving the candidate's chances for the vice presidential spot, as well as his own hopes of joining the Reagan camp. Along with Reagan campaign manager (and subsequent Central Intelligence Agency director) William Casey, it was Michael Deaver who argued most strongly after the election that Reagan should choose Baker over longtime adviser Edwin Meese as his White House chief of staff. From what he had seen of Baker during the campaign, explained Deaver, "I thought he had the street smarts for getting around Washington, dealing with the press and the Hill, and in fact he was much more along my line on how to handle the press."

What Baker understood above all was how to connect media strategy and political strategy. He was, in David Gergen's words, "the maestro . . . who brought it all together." Not only did Baker grasp intellectually that political and media strategy had to reinforce one another, he had the political skills to manage the much more delicate task of turning the trick in practice. First he made sure he had the necessary elements under his control: the White House communications office, the Legislative Strategy Group, and the political and outreach shops. He then adroitly coordinated their individual actions into a powerful collective force. One result was that, in Gergen's words, "for the first time in any presidency, we molded a communications policy around our legislative strategy."

Baker himself attributed his skill in such matters to his experience at running national political campaigns. "Implementing policy depends on getting your media operation and your political operation together, but so does running a successful political campaign," he told me. "A, you've got to have a message, and B, you've got to be able to sell that message. The only thing added to that once you move into the White House is that you've got to be able to sell it not just to the public but also on the Hill. But the key to selling it on the Hill is to sell it publicly."

Although he had joined the Reagan bandwagon relatively late, Jim Baker was no less committed to good public relations than any of the California veterans were. Indeed, his selection as chief of staff reinforced the public relations ethos in the White House with a Washington political sophistication that proved crucial to Reagan's many first-term successes. In the words of former assistant deputy press secretary Leslie Janka: "The President, Deaver, Baker and those guys, when they do something, it's not an afterthought [to decide] who gets on the *Today* show, who are our spokesmen. This group understands that a policy, no matter how good it is, is not going to succeed if it isn't sold well."

Thus, communications strategy in the Reagan White House was controlled by a Gang of Four consisting of Baker, Darman, Gergen, and Deaver—three "pragmatists" plus the President's closest aide. But it was Gergen and Deaver who managed the PR apparatus on a daily basis. Their skills complemented one another nicely: Gergen handled the reporters, Deaver the pictures. While Gergen spent his days on the phone talking with journalists, Deaver spent his masterminding the events they would cover.

Deaver neither cared nor knew enough about substantive matters to push specific policy proposals, but he wielded what came close to tacit veto power over Reagan policy—or at least those parts of Reagan policy that required the President's public sales skills to succeed, a category which included most major initiatives. Partly this was because he had, in the envious words of President Carter's image packager Gerald Rafshoon, "total control of the body." But Deaver also enjoyed a very close personal relationship with Nancy Reagan. Keeping the First Lady happy required untold hours of figurative hand-holding and telephone chitchatting on Deaver's part, but the reward for his patience was enormous additional bureaucratic clout. For Mrs. Reagan was an awesomely powerful force behind the scenes of the Reagan White House, and she was not shy about acting in her husband's interests. Thus, whatever its substantive merits, if a proposed course of action struck Michael Deaver as politically dangerous to Ronald Reagan, chances were it died aborning.

Deaver was acknowledged by White House reporters and colleagues alike as a "master" at staging flattering photo and television shots of the President. It was a skill he had been honing since he first went to work for Reagan, and over the years the older man had given him a number of valuable tips. Having never been around a celebrity before, Deaver used to enjoy passing the time traveling between appearances by asking his boss what certain favorite movie stars were really like.

"One day Dick Powell died, and I asked him, 'Was he really as good a guy as I think he was?' " recollected Deaver. "And Reagan said, 'You know, you keep asking me about these actors. There's one thing you've got to understand, Mike. The camera doesn't lie. Eventually you are what you are.' And that is so true."

Or is it? Two breaths later, Deaver concluded the thought by relating a second lesson Reagan taught him about cameras: there are some you *can* fool, if you know what you're doing. "When I first went to work for him, when you brought a television camera in, he was fine. He'd sit there and work at his desk, whatever. Bring a still camera in, and the back of his neck would stiffen up. I asked him finally, 'Does it bother you when I bring stills in?' He said, 'It's funny you ask that. I can always recover on a moving camera, but you can never recover from a still shot.' "

On top of his fifteen years of working closely with Reagan, Deaver gained one additional, enormous advantage when he followed his boss into the White House in early 1981. It was true of all Presidents, but of none (except perhaps Kennedy) so much as Reagan: the news media and especially the television networks loved good pictures of the Commander-in-Chief, and the more the better; it was the visual equivalent of "good copy." After Reagan visited the demilitarized zone separating North and South Korea in November 1983 (fresh from his triumph in Grenada), the evening news shows, newspapers and newsweeklies across the country were filled with inspiring photos of the Leader of the Free

World, dressed in a flak jacket, staring down the Communists through field glasses. As was their habit whenever Reagan made a foreign trip, Deaver and his aides visited the site in advance, accompanied by representatives of the major networks, to plan the media event down to the smallest detail.

"I saw the toe marks for him," Andrea Mitchell of NBC later recalled. Terming the DMZ visit "one of the great advanced events of all time," Mitchell added, "When he didn't stand on his toe mark he was signaled by one of the advance men to move over into the sunshine."

"It was great television," David Gergen said of the DMZ event in an interview with *Broadcasting* magazine. "I think every White House would rather see its President in what amounts to a heroic situation . . . and it sure is a hell of a lot better picture than a guy like Carter, stumbling up in Camp David when he's jogging around up there, falling down. One picture builds support for the President. The other, I think, destroys him."

Sam Donaldson said both Deaver and Gergen understood "a simple truism about television: the eye always predominates over the ear when there is a fundamental clash between the two." Donaldson illustrated his point by recalling Reagan's appearance at a ceremony in February 1984, the day after he had reversed policy and withdrawn the U.S. Marines from Beirut. Donaldson paraphrased the report he broadcast, to the effect that the President was trying to put the best face on his crumbling Lebanon policy by appearing before a carefully screened crowd of Republican loyalists in his old hometown, and concluded, "That's my script. Tough, right? Wrong. Because the *pictures* are of your old friend and mine, Ronald Reagan, before a cheering crowd of people . . . and it's what people see that counts."

Asked in an interview about the eye predominating over the ear, and the related notion that 60 to 70 percent of the total message a viewer gets from television is what he or she sees, Deaver enthusiastically concurred. "Exactly. Oh, exactly. In the 1984 campaign the Defense Department and the Air Force continually wanted us to do a rollout on the B-1 bomber. And of course one of the negatives on Reagan was that he was more likely to get us into a war, so I was always shying away from military kinds of events. But jobs were just as important during the campaign in California, and the B-1 accounted for something like 40,000 jobs in southern California, so I agreed to do a stop at the Rockwell plant in Palmdale. But I said, across the B-1 I want the biggest sign you can make saying 'Prepared for Peace.' So you never really saw the B-1. All you saw was the President with this big sign behind him."

There were limits, of course, to the power of compelling pictures, though Deaver himself sometimes seemed unaware of them. During one of our interviews, for example, he bragged about arranging a Reagan visit to a working-class bar in Boston. This was in January 1983, at the depth of the recession, when a majority of Americans believed that the President's economic policies were not fair and not working, and Deaver figured that a photo opportunity of Reagan hoisting a few beers with the boys would show he was just a regular guy. "It may sound cynical," explained Deaver, "but you can do a lot of things cutting programs, but a picture of an Irish President in an Irish pub at two o'clock in the afternoon raising his glass with a bunch of blue-collar workers and an Irish priest—that will last you for a long, long time." What Deaver failed to mention, and indeed did not even recall after it was pointed out to him, was that while the pub pictures had indeed made all three network newscasts that night, they had been overshadowed by the day's main story: that Reagan had called for abolishing the corporate income tax, thus reinforcing the already widespread impression that he was a rich man's President. Deaver nonetheless continued to maintain that over the long run it was the image, not the news story, that lingered in voters' minds.

William Greider, the assistant managing editor of *The Washington Post* during 1981, credited clever visuals with one of the foremost accomplishments of the Reagan propaganda apparatus: "They have managed to create the sense, which is known by anybody at all close to the White House not to be true, that this is an activist President. The reality, to put it mildly, is that he is a very passive man. . . . The real combat of decisions is not within Ronald Reagan so much as the people around him fighting for his mind. Yet the public image of him is quite the opposite: of a forceful, take-charge man, who is willing to plunge into uncharted territory. It's a theme they peddle that is implicit in all those images, because what the public *sees* of him is an activist President."

"You don't tell us how to stage the news, we won't tell you

how to cover it," read a small sign Larry Speakes kept on his desk throughout his tenure as White House deputy press secretary. While it was true that not even the most skillful staging of news could give the White House *complete* control over subsequent coverage, it could profoundly influence that coverage, if only by determining what it would *not* be. In Donaldson's words: "They are very good at directing the news by making available something on a story that they want out and withholding from sight—remember television—something they aren't prepared to discuss."

"This administration, more than any other, has closed off access to the West Wing [of the White House], to the real goings-on behind the development of an issue," noted Saul Friedman, White House correspondent for the Knight-Ridder News Service. "Things are more tightly held by a few people, and unless you can get access to those people—Baker, Deaver, Meese, McFarlane, [presidential assistant Craig] Fuller and Darman—you don't know what's going on, you can only guess."

Access to Reagan himself was even more tightly controlled. Indeed, the President's inaccessibility became a standing joke within the press corps. "Covering this President," went the gag, "means you never have to say you saw him." Reagan held press conferences less frequently than any other modern President, for example, a policy that Donaldson ascribed to the fact that "he displays abysmal ignorance about current events. That's why Deaver doesn't want him talking." It is also why, according to Donaldson, "working journalists like me don't have access to him on a day-to-day basis, or to his top people. They serve up what they want, and also deny us the opportunity to do anything else. So our options are, do nothing or do it their way. The apparatus uses him—now be careful, I'm not calling him a stooge—but they use him as you would a puppet. When you want coverage, you put him out there."

Reagan's aides had perfected the art of controlling the conditions under which Reagan appeared before reporters long before they entered the White House. After unleashing a number of politically damaging statements, candidate Reagan was made virtually inaccessible to the press during the last two months of the 1980 campaign, for example. Questioned about it later, campaign press secretary Lyn Nofziger defended the policy heartily.

"I will take as much blame as anyone wants to give for keeping the candidate from the press," said Nofziger. "I believe that if you're running for office, you ought to do the things that will help you win. You ought not to do the things that are not going to help you win. . . . If you can control the access of the press to the candidate, you have a hell of a lot better chance of him not screwing up and [of] keeping your campaign on track. Why let the press at the candidate to distract us by talking about things that don't help our campaign?"

The March 1981 assassination attempt gave White House aides a reason for further isolating President Reagan physically from the press. "There was nothing that gave them a better reason to keep people away from Reagan," recollected David Kaplan, producer of Sam Donaldson's White House stories for ABC News. "It had begun even before that, during the campaign, so by the time Reagan got in the White House, everybody was used to it and just tolerated the fact that you were farther away from Reagan than you were from Jimmy Carter, because they didn't think there was anything they could do about it."

What Kaplan's boss Donaldson did about it was simply to ask his questions in a louder tone of voice, a practice which earned him the ire of some viewers but which he defended as journalistically necessary. Blaming his shouted questions on the White House staff's distancing of President Reagan from reporters, Donaldson observed, "I didn't have to yell questions at Jimmy Carter. He was close. We [reporters] could walk along with him and ask questions, and he would answer them, quite often to his detriment. . . . I never see this President."

Of all the officials in the Reagan White House, David Gergen was the one most sympathetic to reporters' pleas for greater access. In fact, Gergen often acted as a "back channel" for reporters frustrated by the obstacles the administration erected between the press and key policymakers. One of Gergen's foremost responsibilities as White House communications director was convincing network officials to make airtime available when the White House planned a nationally televised presidential speech. During the first two years of the Reagan presidency, he also often handled the formal daily briefings of the White House press corps. But perhaps his most important dealings with the press were in private, one-on-one telephone conversations with reporters eager for a relatively more candid and expansive explanation of administration policy than the pablum ladled out at the daily news briefings.

"While Gergen was there," said Knight-Ridder correspondent Saul Friedman, "Gergen was the interpreter in the West Wing. If you had access to Gergen, you were still able to find out something about *why* something was happening, even though they tried to put their own spin on it."

Gergen's position as the reporters' gatekeeper to the West Wing gave him a finger on the pulse of the White House press corps. His back-channel conversations also gave him considerable potential influence over reporters' news stories. Any story implicitly told the audience how to understand the pictures and information it contained. How a report was framed, which facts it contained and emphasized and which it ignored, and in what context, were as important to shaping opinion as the bare facts themselves. These were the very decisions Gergen attempted to influence during his many phone conversations with White House reporters.

Gergen acknowledged in an interview that he made "frequent" calls to reporters working on stories. "I tried to call them back late in the afternoon, after they had their information and wanted to put it in some kind of context. That's what everybody referred to as 'spin control,' but I thought it was important, if they were way off base, to draw them back, or if they had something to make sure . . . they had some sense of what the White House view on it was."

One senior White House official was quoted in a January 1984 story in *The National Journal* as saying that Gergen routinely had "called all three major networks about an hour and a half before their final deadline to find out what they were going with. And then, for the next hour and a half, there was a flurry around here trying to influence what they were doing." The same story quoted Michael Deaver (who had by then assumed the just-resigned Gergen's communications responsibilities) as saying that the practice was "absolutely necessary" and still continued.

Jeff Gralnick of ABC denied ever receiving such calls during the thirty months he spent as executive producer of the *World News Tonight* broadcast, but NBC Washington bureau chief Robert McFarland said he spoke to Gergen often, at least once a day when the news schedule was hectic.

"Gergen would call and say, 'The President's going to speak at the Hilton today. You should know that he's probably going to make some news.' And I would say, 'How?' He'd answer, 'He's going to talk about the Middle East.' 'Well, what about the Middle East?' [He would say,] 'I can't tell you any more than that.' " Concluded McFarland wistfully, "We used to play an interesting game."

Asked about the late-afternoon calls, McFarland replied, "Gergen might have done that with our correspondents, but very seldom with me. I can recall maybe a couple of occasions where he would call and say, 'We're going to be putting out a statement here in the White House in the next ten minutes that will lead your nightly news.' [My response was] 'David, tell me what it says, we'll make the decision whether it will lead our nightly news.' But that was rare. It wasn't crass. There would be a note of urgency in his voice, as if to say, this is big. And if he hadn't said it would lead the news, I would immediately have asked him, 'David, could this lead the news? Give me some guidance, David! How big is this thing?' "

By virtually all accounts, the network most often contacted by the White House was CBS. Anchor Dan Rather acknowledged in a 1983 interview with *The New York Times* that calls from White House officials had had some effect, and referred to them as a form of "pressure."

"It is designed to have us think twice," said Rather. "I don't care how good you are, in some ways, on some days, it is bound to work on your subconscious. We are better at resisting it, but we are not perfect at resisting it."

Gergen's former deputy Joanna Bistany confirmed separately that "Gergen made a very conscious effort at the start to concentrate on the networks," and that the "on deadline" calls had been placed "five, maybe ten times, or maybe fifteen."

That estimate sounded about right to Tom Bettag, a senior producer of the *CBS Evening News* during the first Reagan term who later was promoted to be the show's executive producer. "The phone calls more often than not went to the Washington bureau," said Bettag, "but there were maybe five and no more than ten in the whole Reagan presidency that came to us. Usually the tone is, 'We know we should go through the Washington bureau, but we think you're headed someplace that we have to straighten you out in a hurry.' " Bettag said such calls were usually taken by the executive producer, and agreed that a mere five or ten such calls went a long way: "A call even from a Gergen is no small thing. It's a sort of subtle reminder, usually over relatively small details. There was no 'Don't run that story!' They understand how much we brace at anything smacking of overt control. Usually it was more like 'We wonder if you realize that . . .' "

Gergen himself, when asked about Rather's comment, said that "Dan's views were taken a little out of context," and that on the occasions when the two men did speak it was usually at Rather's initiative. But he added, "If a story comes out that puts a bad spin on things or really distorts the news from our point of view, if it was really egregious, particularly on facts, I had no hesitation about calling them up and saying, 'We've got a real problem with this story,' or Larry [Speakes] had no problem calling. . . . I learned it was better to call the correspondent who had done the piece than to call the bureau chief. Or if you couldn't reach the correspondent or were at loggerheads [with him or her], you would call the bureau chief. I might tell Lesley Stahl, 'I'm going to need to talk to [CBS Washington bureau chief] Jack Smith about this.' "

Gergen further confirmed that "CBS was the network we had the most problems with," an ironic counterpoint to the fact that he and Smith became personal friends during his years in the Reagan White House. In a March 1984 interview, Gergen said of Smith, "I have a good relationship with Jack Smith, great respect for him. In fact, he's coming up to teach my class at Harvard [Gergen taught a semester in the Kennedy School of Government after leaving the White House], and we see each other from time to time. I enjoy his company a lot, and we used to play tennis together occasionally." When the White House would call Smith's bureau to complain about a CBS story, said Gergen, "they took it seriously. They would check into it, and if they thought they were wrong, they'd correct it." Gergen claimed CBS even made corrections in time to insert them into the second "feed" of its newscast, the one transmitted to local affiliates at 7 p.m. "We would call at, say, 6:43 p.m., and if they checked into it, they could change it for the seven o'clock. They were good about it. I came out with a lot of respect for CBS as a news organization."

3

"MANIPULATION BY INUNDATION"

In a White House whose chief spokesman was named Speakes, it was somehow fitting that the director of communications had begun his professional life as a damage-control officer in the United States Navy. Dave Gergen himself saw the irony in the situation, and cheerfully admitted that his naval training had "served me well over a lot of administrations." As important as good damage control was, though, Gergen recognized it was no substitute for avoiding troublesome situations in the first place. As a student of the American presidency, he had carefully investigated the press operations of previous administrations in search of lessons he could apply in the Reagan White House. His hero and role model was President Eisenhower's legendary press secretary, James Hagerty. Gergen particularly admired Hagerty's success at shielding Eisenhower from the daily cross fire between the administration and the press.

"I think it is terribly important that the President not be out on the line every day, particularly on bad news," said Gergen. "Eisenhower was the last President to do that, to ride above the storm. They kept him out of harm's way. My theory on that is that you only have one four-star general in battle, but you've got a lot of lieutenants who can give blood. And if the going is getting hot and heavy, it is far better to have your lieutenants take the wounds than your general. Because once that happens to your President, it is very difficult to recover from it. One of the most destructive aspects of the Carter administration was that they continually let him go out there and be the point man, on everything! A lot of our strategy had to do with *not* having the President out answering questions every day. . . . So on the budget issue, we intentionally put Stockman out front. On environmental issues, as controversial as [Interior Secretary James] Watt was, it was better to have Watt out talking about environmental issues than the President. Watt did become the lightning rod, and he knew that when he came in. It was a conscious policy in terms of shaping the news."

The lightning-rod theory was applied, according to Gergen, even as Watt was leaving the administration. Apparently the White House had been planning to have President Reagan deliver a major environmental speech around the time of Watt's spring 1983 resignation, "but we decided to hold back from that because it would shift the attention to the President," explained Gergen. Instead, Reagan merely appeared at the swearing-in ceremony of Watt's successor, William P. Clark, and urged him to proceed with all deliberate speed toward a solution of the nation's acid-rain problem. "The idea was, 'Get it over there [in the Interior Department],' " added Gergen. "When we have something developed that we can go out and talk about in a positive way, then bring it back to the White House."

His repeated reliance on military metaphors notwithstanding, Gergen, when asked the question directly, denied viewing relations between the press and the White House as a battle. "I don't see it as a battle, but I certainly see it as a very major struggle to govern well in this country. To govern successfully, the government has to set the agenda; it can't let the press set the agenda for it."

Controlling the political agenda and setting the terms of debate was, in the eyes of supporters and opponents alike, one of the greatest successes of the Reagan White House, and the key to many of its policy triumphs. "If you ask the Reagan people, they'll say his greatest success has been in changing the framework of debate on issues," said Juan Williams, a *Washington Post* reporter who covered the White House in 1983. "Now we no longer ask how the federal government can help people who need it, but why should the government have to support these people at all." Williams went on to argue that the perspective of right-wing social scientist Charles Murray (best known for his book *Losing Ground*, which charged that the Great Society programs of the 1960s had hurt rather than helped poor people) "has insinuated itself into our coverage here and especially that of *The New York Times* and the networks. . . . Once you win that argument in an editor's mind, you undermine a lot of stories before they're ever assigned or written."

One way that Reagan and his men helped to set the terms of

debate was by applying the following basic news management principles:

- plan ahead
- stay on the offensive
- control the flow of information
- limit reporters' access to the President
- talk about the issues *you* want to talk about
- speak in one voice
- repeat the same message many times

Planning was the key to all the rest. Joanna Bistany, Gergen's deputy (who left the White House in 1983 to become a top executive at ABC News), said in an interview that from the start "Gergen was very much of the mind that if you don't coordinate you are always going to have a disaster on your hands, you will always be in damage-control mode."

For his part, Deaver was very much aware upon arriving at the White House that the previous four Presidents had endured nasty tangles with the press; his PR man's faith in planning gave him hope that Reagan might avoid their fates. "The two things always uppermost in my mind were, if you were going to be successful at this, you had to stay ahead of the press in planning, and you had to deal with them in a candid but professional way," he recalled. It was Deaver who initiated the so-called Blair House or Friday Group meetings, weekly lunches among a half dozen or so senior White House aides to determine overall communications strategy. According to one official who attended them, these lunches were "the big-picture meeting, where you discuss things like the impact of Grenada, where are we on relations with the Soviets after Andropov's death, should we send Reagan or Bush to Moscow for the funeral, how do we want to position ourselves for the upcoming summit?"

Tactics were decided at meetings of the White House communications group. Blair House members "may see the smoke beginning, or the opportunity available down the road," said one former White House aide, "but at the communications meeting we talk about how we will sell our story. Do we put the President on television, have a few reporters over for cocktails in the residence on a background basis, use the Saturday-afternoon radio address?"

The White House schedule during the first term began most mornings with a 7:30 breakfast meeting of the so-called Troika—Baker, Deaver and Meese—where the President's three top aides discussed overnight developments, news coverage, legislative priorities and the like. Marching orders were handed out at the eight o'clock meeting of the senior staff, including the dozen or so assistants to the President, which Baker chaired. Then came the "line of the day" meeting at 8:15, again usually chaired by Baker, with Gergen, Darman and Speakes the other principal participants. At 8:30 Deaver chaired the communications meeting, where he and his staff reviewed the day's planned event(s) and coordinated preparations for short-term future activities.

" 'What are we going to do today to enhance the image of the President?' is the dominant question," said one participant in these meetings. " 'What do we want the press to cover today, and how?' "

CBS News White House correspondent Bill Plante downplayed the importance of devising a line of the day intended to tilt news coverage in a desired direction. "They do do that among themselves, and then bring it out to us," said Plante. "And we say on occasion, 'Awwwright, whaddaya got today? What's the line today?' Everybody laughs about it. It's a known quantity."

Nevertheless, the strategy meetings illustrated a point made by ABC's Sam Donaldson: that one reason the Reagan administration was so much better at running a propaganda machine than its predecessors was that "it seems to believe it has a divine right to do whatever it wants in the way of manipulation. . . . The people around Reagan, and perhaps Reagan himself, really have contempt for the press as an institution. They believe they were born to rule, their ideology was born to prevail, that they somehow are the upper class."*

The very devising of a line of the day was a tacit admission that what the White House told the press was not so much the

---

* According to Michael Deaver, Donaldson nonetheless felt a grudging respect for what Deaver and his colleagues had accomplished. "Sam never fraternized, but I remember when I [was leaving] the White House and we were on the road someplace, he came up and said, 'Can I buy you a drink?' " recalled Deaver. "I said, 'Sure.' And he said, 'I just want to tell you that I don't agree with what you've done, but you've done it well.' He was the guy who shouted one time, when he got back on the press bus, 'You know, I think Deaver could have saved the Edsel!' "

truth as a carefully calculated and sanitized version of it. Yet
Deaver did not apologize for this; he was in fact quite candid
about the line's purpose: "It's to make sure we're all saying the
same thing."

And not just within the White House but throughout the executive branch. The line of the day was immediately made available via computer to other senior administration officials; a
cabinet official could punch into his office terminal and get the
line before a luncheon interview. It was handed down to press
spokespersons throughout the rest of the federal bureaucracy in
two separate conference telephone calls every morning, one involving foreign policy agencies and the other domestic. David
Gergen recognized that the spokespersons would be far more
persuasive if they had in-depth knowledge of the issues they were
promoting, so he arranged substance seminars for them. Thurs-
days in the morning Treasury Secretary Donald Regan briefed
press aides on economics, and in the late afternoon national security adviser Robert McFarlane discussed current foreign policy
issues; Gergen co-chaired the meetings and stressed the communications implications of the policies under discussion.

The White House representative tended to run the conversation
during the morning conference calls, according to one official who
participated in them. "It was like, 'Okay, what do we say about
Lebanon today?' We'd go through the newspapers and see a story
about South Africa, say, and figure out how we wanted to handle
that. 'Well, no-comment it,' we'd decide, or 'That's a Pentagon
story, we will shut up. State, you've got the lead today on George
Shultz's press conference in Brazil.' Now, the White House may
say, 'Look, the President's got a statement tomorrow, so shut up
today, goddammit, just shut up, don't pre-empt the President,
[we'll] cut your nuts off if you leak anything out on this one,' that
kind of guidance. Other times we would say, 'Here's what we're
going to say, everybody just say it at once. I don't care if you're
asked the question or not, everybody in the administration today
praises Gemayel's leadership,' or Mubarak's leadership, or whatever it is."

Reporters would hear the line of the day first at the 9:15 a.m.
White House press mini-briefing, then again at the regular noon
briefing. The real importance of the 9:15 event, however, was to
point television reporters toward a story for that night. Thus the

President's official spokesman, usually Speakes, would begin by announcing Mr. Reagan's scheduled activities for the day and informing reporters which one(s) they would be able to cover and under what conditions. According to Speakes, it often seemed that the network correspondents were more interested in the logistics of coverage than in the substance of what Reagan would be doing. "Their first question," Speakes recalled, "was always 'Can we get pictures? Can we get pictures?' " Although conducted only sporadically early in the administration, 9:15 briefings proved such an effective device that they gradually became part of the daily routine at the Reagan White House.

Journalists who served America's heartland were a special target of the Reagan apparatus. "How do you get your message out to the grass roots? You go to the people who write for the grass roots," explained Joanna Bistany. "You go to *The Arkansas Gazette*, to *The Memphis Sentinel*, because those are the people who are going to report to the people you want to vote for you."

One White House official confirmed that more than 150 special White House briefings were organized during Reagan's first three years in office. "You'd bring in eighty or ninety [journalists], maybe from a certain part of the country, maybe from all around the country, depending on what you were trying to accomplish, and invite anchormen or news directors from major markets and the editors of major newspapers," explained the official. "And this is how some press people from a little town in North Dakota or somewhere like that come to these things. And they're thrilled to come. We take them up to our main briefing room and have maybe twenty-five camera crews from local stations, and then put on a real good program for them—usually cabinet officers or maybe just below that. . . . Then we take them over to the state dining room for a nice lunch with the President, and they are all very pleased to come to the White House, it's a nice touch. . . . They're served well, and they tell us about the contrast with the previous administration, when they got served cheese sandwiches in the basement."

Many of the communications techniques used by the Reagan propaganda apparatus were, as David Gergen freely admitted, not new. Gergen was fond of stressing his admiration for the job James Hagerty did managing news during the Eisenhower years, but in fact the administration that he and his Reagan colleagues borrowed from most heavily was Richard Nixon's. The so-called line of the day, for example, the morning conference calls among foreign and domestic agency press officers, the heartland journalist program, the weekly long-range communications strategy meetings—these were just some of the news management techniques introduced during the Nixon years that reappeared under Reagan.

But the resemblance went deeper than mere technique. The erecting of such an extensive propaganda apparatus within the White House was a Nixon invention; no previous administration had devoted so many resources to managing the news or approached the task with so much calculation. The staffing of the Reagan apparatus as well bore an almost eerie resemblance to that of Nixon, especially at the top. H. R. Haldeman, the man in charge of the Nixon machine, was, like Michael Deaver, a former advertising and public relations man from California. And as director of communications in the Nixon White House, Herbert Klein had some of the same responsibilities that David Gergen later had.

But the most important legacy of the Nixon years was not a matter of technique but one of attitude. It was Nixon, or, more accurately, the men around him, who first grasped the applicability of mass-marketing techniques to national electoral politics, who saw that the same advertising gimmicks used to sell Americans breakfast cereals and automobiles could also be used to sell them politicians. Public relations alone was not enough. But melding PR principles—control your message, keep it simple, repeat it many times over—into an overall political strategy had been important to Nixon's triumph in 1968, just as it would be to Reagan's successes in the White House over a decade later. Politics was selling, and selling was done through the media. It was a simple enough equation, but Jimmy Carter, for one, never mastered it.

"The difference between Reagan and Carter is that Reagan fundamentally understands that politics is communication with leadership, and he probably puts communication above substance," argued former Reagan press aide Leslie Janka. "Carter was just the flip side of that. He put substance ahead of politics."

Gerald Rafshoon, Carter's image manager, agreed: "Over there at the [Reagan] White House there is one voice, one apparatus devoted to selling the President's programs, one President devoted to selling his programs. Carter wasn't. He was devoted to his programs. . . . He got into office and began thinking that good substance alone was enough, that style didn't matter."

The Reagan people learned from the mistakes as well as the successes of the Nixon apparatus. That different individuals drew different conclusions from the Nixon experience was evident from the recurring split among top Reagan strategists over whether to adopt a conciliatory or a confrontational stance toward the press. Hard-liners—personified by presidential counselor and later Attorney General Edwin Meese and national security adviser and later Interior Secretary William Clark—harbored a distrust of the news media based on the traditional conservative conviction that all journalists were political liberals eager to do in Republicans. They pushed for tough restrictions on press access and for polygraph testing of suspected news leakers, and urged that Reagan sell his policies by going "over the head of the press" and appealing directly to Americans in television speeches and radio addresses, just as President Nixon and his aides had tried to do.

The pragmatists, Gergen and Baker, argued for cordial relations with the press and warned of the dangers of restricting information too tightly. Gergen, who as a Nixon press aide had seen firsthand how an attitude of belligerence and secrecy had backfired in the disaster of Watergate, attempted to establish good relations with key members of the news media. To abuse the press, according to this view, only made it that much harder to use it, and invited retaliation that otherwise would not occur. Or, as Baker reportedly advised his colleagues: "Don't get paranoid and draw the wagons around the White House. It's hard to win an all-out shoot-out with the press, whatever the provocation."

The critical swing vote in such matters often belonged to Michael Deaver: "I felt you should deal openly and honestly and candidly, but there should be ground rules." In the name of establishing what he referred to as "a professional relationship" between the White House and the press, he therefore was more willing to stiff-arm the press than Gergen and Baker were; in fact, after leaving the White House, he cited questions of reporters' access to be the one significant difference he had with his two colleagues over communications policy. "The only time Jim and I would get into arguments," Deaver said of Baker, "was, I really felt the press had gotten too much a part of the government and there had to be restrictions on how you dealt with them, mainly mechanical and procedural kinds of things. He didn't agree with me." As for Gergen, "Dave wanted to keep the press happy at any cost, and that included giving them information I felt we shouldn't be giving them."

At the same time, Deaver seemed to evince less hostility toward news coverage that departed from the White House's conception of what should be reported than many of his erstwhile California colleagues did. Some of them had particularly little patience with the notion that reporters were surrogates of the public and as such deserved answers when they questioned a politician.

"That surrogates of the public stuff is bullshit, it's total crap," exclaimed Lyn Nofziger. "The only reason [reporters] say that is because they want a story. They talk about the public's right to know. I say, show me. Here's the Constitution, you show me anywhere in there about the public's right to know, that you have a right to answers to questions. . . . It ain't there."

Such antipathy toward the First Amendment's guarantee of freedom of the press was anathema to men like Baker and Gergen; Deaver, when asked about it, laughed and said, "I don't agree with that necessarily. I think [the press has] a role to play, and I think we worked out the best professional relationship anybody's had in a long time with the media." In the eyes of hardliners, this was virtual appeasement of the enemy, and so Deaver was continually under bureaucratic attack from Meese and Clark for not being tough enough toward the press. Lyn Nofziger, after leaving the White House, accused Deaver of having been "coopted" by the pragmatist Baker, a charge to which there may be some truth. Deaver himself suggested that his relatively more open dealings with the press were motivated at least as much by pragmatism as by morality.

"I never, ever lied to the press, and I took great pride in that," recalled Deaver. "Others chose not to understand that, like Ed Meese. He thought there were things they shouldn't know, and would stonewall them. Which I didn't agree with—didn't agree with because I didn't think it was right, but also because I didn't think you'd get away with it. I thought you'd get into bigger trouble."*

But Deaver was positively reticent compared to David Gergen; even some of the pragmatists felt Gergen often gave away too much in his frequent back-channel conversations with reporters. Gergen conceded he eventually was "discouraged from talking about who said what at the meetings," but he tried to remain as accessible to reporters as possible. It was all part of keeping up the rapport that he believed was so critical to a positive relationship between the White House and the press. "There were some people on the inside, like Meese, who thought what we were doing was leaking," recollected Gergen, "when instead the goal was to talk it through, to give us a historical context and some background to *why* things were going the way they were and what the President was trying to accomplish."

What emerged from the internal White House struggle between the hard-liners and the pragmatists was a sort of good cop–bad cop approach to dealing with the news media. The hard-liners won their share of skirmishes—President Reagan was convinced, for example, to sign an executive order in March 1983 that made all federal employees with access to classified information subject to lie-detector tests—but Michael Deaver recalled one particular battle he lost.

"I still think the greatest mistake Richard Nixon made was not Watergate but moving the press into the West Wing," said Deaver. "The President of the United States cannot walk from his office to his home without passing the White House press corps. That's not right. I tried [to have them moved out of there], but Baker and the rest of them, Gergen in particular, said, 'They'll kill us. They'll kill us.' "

Providing reporters with a pleasant working environment was important to Gergen and other pragmatists. "If you give some-

---

* A story Deaver told in a separate interview showed how narrowly he defined lying: "I remember one Sunday afternoon [then CBS White House correspondent] John Feruggia, who's a friend, called me at home and there was some secret meeting the President had had with a Soviet official and he asked me, 'Did [Soviet ambassador Anatoliy] Dobrynin go in to see the President today?' And I said, 'Dobrynin? No.' And he said, 'Goddammit, I know Dobrynin was in there.' Well, he had the name wrong. And I wasn't going to offer him any advice at all." Mr. Deaver did not confirm it, but it seems likely that the Soviet official in question was Dobrynin's deputy, whose name was Dubynin.

body a comfortable place to work, good facilities, provide food because you know they can't take time to go to a restaurant ten miles away to eat, and in general provide the creature comforts, how then can someone turn around and bite the hand that feeds him?" explained Joanna Bistany. "I had reporters [at the 1983 Western economic summit meeting] in Williamsburg tell me, 'Jesus Christ, how can I write a nasty story? Every time I need something, somebody is there to provide it for me. I got two phones right in front of me, food over there, it's really hard to write a nasty story.' "

Catering to journalists' occupational needs and whims became especially important to the Reagan apparatus during the hectic days of the 1984 election campaign. "The Democrats would never talk to you until the last minute, but Republicans would talk to you about logistics from the start because they want that picture out as much as you do," recalled CBS News Washington producer Susan Zirinsky. The apparatus took as much toil and trouble out of the job of covering Reagan's campaign speeches as possible. Walter Robinson of *The Boston Globe* had broken his thumb shortly before being transferred to the Reagan beat, "but [I] learned during Reagan's [late October whistle-stop train] trip through Ohio I didn't have to take notes. They gave you, within twenty minutes, the remarks, as delivered, with punctuation, pauses, etc. And within thirty seconds after each train stop, they had sixty phones set up [for reporters]."

Although they did not always manage to practice what they preached, the pragmatists also argued against engaging in self-destructive flailing at journalists and news corporations who had produced negative stories. "There is a remarkable lack of animus in this White House," said Andrea Mitchell of NBC. "I have been as adversarial as the next person . . . but I have not found that people get personally hostile."

This stood in marked contrast to the sort of aggressive attacks the Nixon administration had staged against the press. "Haldeman didn't like the press, didn't trust them," recalled Lyn Nofziger. "He used to call them the snakes. One reason the press went after them was because they could sense that hatred, kind of like how a dog senses fear. That was never the case in the Reagan administration. Ronald Reagan likes everybody. He never had this feeling that the press as a group was out to get him."

For the most part, Reagan officials made a genuine and conscious effort to cultivate friendly relations with leading journalists, especially early in the administration. Of course, they were already on friendly terms with some journalists, such as ABC anchor Frank Reynolds. "Frank was loved by the Reagans and by me personally," said Michael Deaver. Deaver recalled "a wonderful piece" Reynolds broadcast after the 1976 Republican convention, where Reagan failed to wrest the presidential nomination from Gerald Ford. Over pictures of the Reagans' jet taking off, Reynolds intoned, according to Deaver, that "regardless of what comes next, Ronald Reagan has had an impact on politics in this country. And then he says, 'Goodbye, Rawhide. Goodbye, Rainbow.' " (Rawhide and Rainbow were the Secret Service code names for the Reagans.) It was a commonly held view within the Reagan White House that ABC was the kindest of the three networks. Said Deaver, "I think a lot of the ABC good-feel was because of Frank Reynolds."

"The idea of making the press part of your inner circle, or making them *believe* they were part of the inner circle, was something that hadn't happened in a long time in Washington," noted Sanford Socolow, the executive producer of the *CBS Evening News* for years during the Cronkite era and for the first ten months of the Reagan administration. "Reagan, during the inaugural period, made it a point to attend Washington parties, Georgetown parties. George Will gave him a party. Jimmy Carter thought . . . it was okay for [his chief of staff Hamilton] Jordan and [Jody] Powell to pose as ragamuffins on the cover of *Rolling Stone* but thought it was terrible to go to Georgetown parties. That's an index of what we were dealing with." Asked whether Reagan's greater affection for the Georgetown crowd had helped him with the press, Socolow affirmed, "Oh, I think tremendously, yes. The press is always hungry for affection, for recognition."

"It was a very smart move," agreed Lyn Nofziger, "and you can thank Mike Deaver, Jim Baker, Nancy Reynolds and those people for that. They began meeting with people right after the election. . . . They were determined to work *with* the Washington establishment, including the press, and not against it. That sensibility came from having operated in the big-league world of California politics and not the boonies of Georgia like the Carter people had."

Nancy Reynolds was a longtime close personal friend of Rea-

gan's wife, Nancy, as well as an accomplished political organizer
who had done advance work for Reagan back in his California
days. In September 1980 she took a five-month leave of absence
from her Washington public relations and political consulting firm
to assist her old friends in their time of need. She thought it
important that the President-elect and his wife meet and charm
the right people in Washington—"[once] personal links have been
established, it doesn't mean everything will be fine, but it can be
helpful later on"—and she took it upon herself to arrange a number of gatherings large and small for that purpose.

"It's like marrying into a new family when you move to Washington," explained Reynolds. "So many of the Carter people were
invited places and never went. . . . They alienated the establishment so much the establishment went after them. And that creeps
into reporting. . . . [T]he impression people had was that the
Carters were hicks. In fact, they entertained very well and were
well educated. You never read that, though, because the Washington establishment had already made up its mind about them."

"We made every effort to have Mrs. Graham and [*Washington
Post* editorial-page editor] Meg Greenfield get to know Nancy
Reagan better," added Reynolds. "Mrs. Graham and she had
lots of common friends already. Baker and Deaver made themselves very available for the social circuit. They were very friendly
and very popular at parties. They realized you had to get to know
your new neighbors."

"I think we were conscious of coming in after an administration
that disliked the Washington media, the Washington aura and
ambiance, and jumping right in and enjoying it and becoming a
part of it," said Deaver. "I think that made a big difference."

"In a previous time, reporters may have viewed themselves as
outsiders. They didn't belong to the inner circle to the degree
they do now, when relatively well-paid reporters and government
officials can move in the same social circles," observed ABC News
Washington bureau chief George Watson. "I went to a dinner
party with a reporter [of ours] in early 1985 where there was the
Attorney General, the Israeli ambassador, a prominent senator.
That happens more than it used to. Today as never before our
reporters are part of the town's elite, which seems a reasonable
factor in explaining why there is less of an adversarial tone in the
coverage [of Washington]."

"This used to drive me nuts, I thought it was just a waste of time, but they *want* to have cabinet officers and important political types in the White House to lunch," said William Greider of his former colleagues and superiors at *The Washington Post.* "It's a perfect Washington symbiosis—those people *want* to come to lunch." Greider recalled that such power lunches were usually held in a conference room just down the hall from Katharine Graham's office at *Post* headquarters on 15th Street. The guest was seated at the middle of a long table, flanked by either Mrs. Graham or son Donald or both, and surrounded by perhaps twenty *Post* editors and reporters. One could gauge the cachet of the day's guest not only by whether both Grahams attended but also by which grade of menu was served; only the highest officials were favored with the Triple-A meal. Although most power lunches were "on the record," Greider emphasized that such sessions were "not about getting news stories. It's about getting to know those people and getting a feel for who they are. . . . The talk may be bullshit, but it takes on a different meaning when said over the intimacy of the luncheon table. The ambiance is, 'We're all insiders here.' "

• • •

DAN RATHER, back in 1972 when he was still the White House correspondent for CBS, once offered a theory for why the Nixon administration was more successful at manipulating the media than its predecessors had been. President Kennedy, argued Rather, had had the knowledge but not the will to manipulate the press, President Johnson had had the will but not the knowledge, whereas Nixon and his advisers had plenty of both.

The rising CBS star was overly romantic about Kennedy's press dealings—JFK was in fact occasionally embarrassingly overt about ordering a reporter replaced or a news story suppressed—but he was right about the combination of skill and attitude that animated the Nixon propaganda apparatus. The Nixon experience showed just what manner of miracles sound technique, relentlessly applied, could perform. Even someone as thoroughly untelegenic as Richard Nixon—a man who looked uncomfortable at best on television, who smiled at all the wrong times and much too obviously, whose every tone and gesture unwittingly proclaimed how *forced* the show of honesty and sincerity was—could be saved from his personal excesses and sold to the American public (at least temporarily), provided he was presented properly.

But what if all that technical expertise and calculated determination were focused on promoting someone with a *winning* personality? What then could be achieved? The Reagan presidency offered an answer. To rephrase Mr. Rather's formulation, while Nixon had the technique and Kennedy had the personality (and Johnson had neither), Ronald Reagan had both, in abundance. As Gergen would enthuse after spending three years as his director of communications, here was a man whose "sense of humor and smile, when dealing with the press on television, are worth a million votes."

In a country where politics had increasingly become a contest of images rather than ideas, there was a certain bizarre inevitability about a B-grade movie star finally being elected President. Administration officials usually played down Reagan's acting abilities, conceding at most that his personality was what made him such a good salesman. But in a not-for-attribution interview, one former White House aide made a rare admission: "He's an actor. He's used to being directed and produced. He stands where he is supposed to and delivers his lines, he reads beautifully, he knows how to wait for the applause line. You know how some guys are good salesmen but can't ask the customers to give them the order? This guy is good at asking for the order, and getting it."

If Reagan was the star, Mike Deaver was the director who knew just what it took to inspire the best possible performance from his man. Such relationships, at their best, are a product of a certain delicate chemistry between the two individuals involved, and thus are virtually impossible to replicate. After leaving the White House, Deaver noticed the difference in Reagan's public persona, particularly during his disastrous November 19, 1986, press conference about the administration's arms sales to Iran. "He wasn't well prepared for that," he remarked. "Particularly on an issue like that, the last thing you want to do is brief him or cram him full of answers, because the answers were all there. Reagan is basically a performer. What you really need to do is what a director would do, and that is set the stage and get his mind in the right position. He should have *bounced* into that press conference. [Instead] he *walked* down that hall. Somebody probably told him, 'Now, be serious tonight.' Absolutely wrong coaching!"

Perhaps Reagan's strongest communications attribute was his image as a nice guy. "A lot of what we've done [was] because of Ronald Reagan and his warm personality," observed Joanna Bistany. "You can get away with a lot, because he can then come up and defuse the antagonism." And not just among the public, one might add, but among the press. Although the President harbored a certain condescension toward reporters—"He thinks of the press as poor souls who can be saved by the redemption of his superior knowledge," commented Reagan speechwriter Kenneth Khachigian—his bantering friendliness toward them paid off.

"Jimmy Carter you felt sorry for, but he was aloof and hard to get to know," said Susan Zirinsky. "But Reagan always made you laugh. It was hard not to like him."

"I would agree that Reagan has gotten the breaks in terms of press coverage," acknowledged Maynard Parker, editor of *Newsweek*, "for the reason that most reporters covering him genuinely like the man and find it difficult to be as tough as they might like."

John Sears, Reagan's (and Nixon's) former presidential campaign manager, thought that journalists' fondness for Reagan was what encouraged gentle press coverage of the so-called gaffe problem—the President's frequent practice of unburdening himself of statements that were demonstrably false, silly or otherwise politically unwise. "If Jimmy Carter were making these mistakes, he would be treated much worse," said Sears. "The press didn't like Carter on the level of a personal human being. But they like Reagan, and this affects their intensity factor."

Mr. Reagan's personal strengths and abilities were such that two of the closest observers of his political career argued that the White House propaganda apparatus deserved but marginal credit for his presidential achievements. "I don't [think] the White House press apparatus has anything to do with what Reagan has accomplished," declared *Washington Post* correspondent Lou Cannon, who was widely acknowledged by colleagues and competitors alike as the single most knowledgeable reporter about Reagan. Cannon, who had covered Reagan since the beginning of his political career in California, added, "Ronald Reagan was able to shift the direction of the debate when he didn't have Mike Deaver and he didn't have the White House. . . . The fact is that Reagan himself is the guy who does this."

"One reason we were so good at [managing news] is we had a candidate who just comes across a hell of a lot better," explained Lyn Nofziger. "You could have put the Reagan staff in there with Jimmy Carter and Jimmy Carter still wouldn't have come out good. You can't make a silk purse out of a sow's ear. . . . Ronald Reagan is the best candidate. I'm not talking about ability to govern, but the best candidate from the standpoint of understanding instinctively what you have to do to get favorable coverage for the kind of media we have today—my mother could have run his campaign and he'd still have been elected President. . . . I don't mean to belittle Mike Deaver, he did a fine job, but I would like to have seen him working with Ford or Carter or Nixon and then come back and tell me."

In response, Deaver said that "90 percent of [Reagan's] success is the man himself," but he maintained that the apparatus had nonetheless played a vital role: "What we did was strategize for periods of time what we wanted the story [about the administration] to be and [we then] created visuals to go with that story. I don't think television coverage will ever be the same. We really did something to change that.

"We would take a theme, which we usually worked on for six weeks—say, the economy," Deaver explained. "The President would *say* the same thing, but we had a different visual for every one of those stops. They see the President out at an auto plant because imports are down and American cars are up. They see the President at a high-tech plant in Boston because high-tech means jobs. Pretty soon it begins to soak in, pretty soon people begin to believe the economy *is* getting better."

One striking example of the way the White House public relations machinery—from the Blair House strategists down to press officers and event organizers—operated in nearly perfect synchronization was the public relations blitz on the theme of education that Deaver directed in 1983. In response to polls indicating a two-to-one public disapproval of Reagan's cutbacks in federal aid to education, the Blair House group ordered a communications offensive that emphasized "excellence in education," merit pay for teachers and greater classroom discipline. The end result was to reverse the polling figures to a two-to-one *support* for Reagan, without the actual Reagan *policy* changing at all.

"The President himself made some twenty-five-odd appearances on the issue of education," recalled Knight-Ridder correspondent Saul Friedman. "They understood that to shift the fulcrum of the debate, you have to do it with repetition, which the President is very good at."

Repetition was necessary because, in a modern electronic society, the messages that actually pierce the static and register on people's consciousness are those which are repeated over and over again. According to Deaver, this was one requirement of his salesman's job that Reagan groused about. "It used to drive the President crazy, because repetition was so important," said Deaver. "He'd get on that airplane and look at that speech and say, 'Mike, I'm not going to give this same speech on education again, am I?' I said, 'Yeah, *trust* me, it's going to work.' And it did."

Reagan apparently let boredom get the better of him on at least one such occasion, and he was caught at it by NBC White House correspondent Chris Wallace. After delivering a speech in Illinois, Reagan was asked a basic question about administration policy. Clearly ignorant of the correct answer, the President referred the query to Education Secretary Terrel Bell, who was seated beside him. Wallace showed the episode to viewers, and concluded his report by noting that Reagan had traveled halfway across the country to make political points with his speech, and then could not remember his own education policy.

Questioned about the incident later, Deaver was remarkably blasé, for reasons which reveal much about the tactical considerations behind such PR blitzes. He conceded that Wallace's was "a pretty negative story," but countered that "the total impact was very positive. I mean, there he is in the classroom with a bunch of kids when he gets the picture taken. . . . The visual, and repetition, overcome that kind of twist Chris put on it, because you've got one bad story and twenty good ones."

Twenty good ones? According to Deaver, the primary news media targets in such a PR blitz were not the networks but the local evening newscasts.

"We were playing to local markets," he explained. "We plotted it out to overlay [what were] key political states for us with major media markets: Atlanta, Dallas, Los Angeles, Chicago, St. Louis, Boston. You'd have two days of stories before the President arrived, about the security and logistics and all that, then they'd cover the actual day of the President's visit. And then many times we'd give the local anchor guy a half-hour interview, which they'd often run five nights in a row, five minutes each night on the local news. And of course with the local anchor, you had a much stronger bargaining position to tell him, 'You can ask questions about these topics and nothing else,' because for them to have a chance to interview the President was a very big deal. A lot of times their network White House correspondent might tell the anchor to ask [Reagan] such and such, which was the question they needed for their story that night, but that's part of the game. So he got that one shot, but we got four nights on the local news with something positive to us in a major media market."

So, how much of the credit belonged to Reagan and how much to the apparatus behind him? Tom Shales, one of the most perceptive and certainly the wittiest mainstream television critic writing during the Reagan years, observed that it was in the joining of the two that the danger lay: "It is potentially a very sinister combination—this enormously charismatic President, this figurehead that everyone loves, and this [collection] of aides who are terribly cunning about how to put their boy across. . . . These guys understand television so much better, and they understand that television is what you *have* to understand. Nothing else matters much, really."

Deaver and his colleagues were fortunate to occupy the White House at a time when television had utterly transformed Washington journalism. During the Reagan years, it was the rare network evening newscast that did not include at least one White House story. It had not always been so; Washington coverage during previous presidencies had featured a more varied diet of stories, with some originating on Capitol Hill, some in the State Department, some elsewhere in the federal bureaucracy. The trend toward telling a given Washington story through the prism of the White House could be traced back to the Nixon years, but it was greatly stimulated by the arrival of the Reagan administration, with its prowess as a supplier of attractive visual images.

"This is the only time in history when a major medium had a section regularly fenced off just for the President to speak," complained Christopher Matthews, former press secretary to Democratic Speaker of the House Thomas P. "Tip" O'Neill. "They know the presidency is ideally suited for the television age, because it is one person, there is all the *People* magazine aspect— what is he like, what is Nancy like? It is amazing how the monarchy translates so well into the television age and legislatures do not."

"Five years ago there was not every day a story from the White House, no matter what. I think there is today, partly due to television," said Robert Kaiser of *The Washington Post*. "[The President] is the political figure that the whole country has in common. If you start with that presumption, which is understandable sociologically but bizarre journalistically, you're giving it away to this guy to begin with. You're saying, 'Anything you do or say in public, Mr. President, is going to be news.' "

"They understand the mechanics and they know we're not going to go on the air and criticize it as pure theater if Reagan stands on the Great Wall of China," said Robert Frye, executive producer of ABC's *World News Tonight* in 1983. "How do you say, 'We're not going to put that stuff on the air'? You don't. If you tallied the score every day, the Rose Garden appearances that have nothing to do with policy would be about 95 percent of Reagan's appearances, so [if you excluded them] you wouldn't have much to put on the air."

The networks' appetite for pictures of the President was apparently ample enough to cause Deaver and his cohorts to conclude that the balance of power within the relationship favored the White House. Deaver himself phrased it more bluntly: "They had to take what we were giving them." He could afford to be so cavalier because he was, in effect, a monopolist operating in a seller's market. Television's demand for White House stories was, it seemed, virtually inexhaustible, and Deaver was the man who controlled the sole source of supply. As Lyn Nofziger explained, there existed "kind of a mutual back-scratching" arrangement between television and the Reagan communications apparatus: "It's an unsaid thing. You need each other. Television needs Deaver to make sure they get something out of the White House today. Deaver needs television to make sure the President is presented in a good light."

The symbiotic relationship between the White House and the

press, especially television, encouraged a subtle form of media complicity in the selling of the President. Television, for its own professional and commercial reasons, wanted to broadcast the most visually appealing pictures of the President possible. But it was difficult to do that without at the same time producing a presidential puff piece. In Robert Frye's words: "TV becomes a witting or unwitting participant in the formation of the image. I've been on Air Force One, and it's heady. There *is* no back of the bus on Air Force One. You become part of 'What's going to make it look good?' And then we try to deal with it editorially, but it's questionable whether that can work, even with a reporter like Sam Donaldson who keeps away from the party line, [because] television presenting the President is such a part of the governing process."

"As opposed to Kissinger and Haldeman and that crowd, whose view was that you control the media by giving them bits and pieces [of information], the Reagan White House came to the totally opposite conclusion that the media will take what we feed them," explained Leslie Janka, who worked as a press officer in both administrations. "They've got to write their story every day. You give them their story, they'll go away. As long as you come in there every day, hand them a well-packaged, premasticated story in the format they want, they'll go away. The phrase is 'manipulation by inundation.' You give them the line of the day, you give them press briefings, you give them facts, access to people who will speak on the record. . . . And you do that long enough, they're going to stop bringing their own stories, and stop being investigative reporters of any kind, even modestly so."

"I think that's true," added Deaver. "The only day I worried about was Friday, because it's a slow news day. That was the day that always bothered me the most, because if you didn't have anything, they'd go *find* something."

Central to Deaver's success was his recognition of something journalists were loath to admit about their business: that news was, to the corporations that produced it, primarily a commodity to be bought and sold. Whatever their journalistic merits, White House stories in particular were regarded (albeit largely unconsciously) as valuable commercial products, especially by the television networks. The secret of Deaver's "manipulation by inundation" approach—and what made it vastly superior to

Haldeman's "manipulation by withholding"—was that, like the Japanese self-defense method jujitsu, it was based on using the adversary's own strength against him. Rather than resist the networks' desire for saturation coverage of the President, the Reagan propaganda apparatus would cater to it. The networks wanted visuals of the President? Fine. But they would be visuals carefully designed to promote the Reagan agenda.

Next to the night-and-day difference between the two men at the top—"the talent," as ex-PR man Deaver sometimes referred to Mr. Reagan—this was the second major difference between the Nixon and Reagan propaganda apparatuses. The Nixon people had specifically chosen *not* to cater to the White House press corps. Their strategy of "going over the press's head" had instead stressed speeches and other tightly controlled television appearances by the President, as well as a major effort to service the so-called hinterlands press. The Reagan apparatus employed these techniques as well, but their appreciation of how to exploit network television's insatiable appetite for good visuals gave them an immeasurable added advantage. Like a double-threat running back in football, blessed with the strength to power his way up the middle as well as the speed to sweep the end, the Reagan apparatus projected its messages to the American public not only by going over the top of the press but also by going right through it.

4

A PALACE COURT PRESS

"IF THERE IS anything deficient about press coverage of the Reagan administration, and there of course is, it has to do simply with our own deficiencies and laziness, and no especial cleverness, or blandishments, or seductions, or threats on their part," asserted Meg Greenfield, the editorial-page editor of *The Washington Post*. "I think we in this newspaper are situated in an absolutely blessed position," she added. "We have a very supportive, journalistically minded management. We have a lot of dough. We have a lot of resources. We have a lot of really smart people. And we have the commanding newspaper position in the [nation's] capital. We can do any damn thing that is important that we have the wit to see and pursue. . . . I really think that anyone who works for this newspaper has every chance imaginable in journalism to go out and get the Story."

"The odds against us [in the press] are not overwhelming," declared *Washington Post* executive editor Ben Bradlee. "Their weapons are enormous, but we're not unarmed in this struggle, we're not unarmed." Beyond the extraordinary array of resources and the journalistic license mentioned by Ms. Greenfield, there was above all the simple fact that, collectively, the press exercised perhaps the greatest power there was in politics: the power to define reality, to say what was—and what was not—important at any given time. The three major television networks in particular could cause big trouble for the White House virtually anytime they wanted simply by focusing sustained attention on any of the scandals, inequities, dangerous or bankrupt policies or other shortcomings common to every Washington administration. True, they usually didn't, but the threat was always there.

All this made the news media a force to be reckoned with for any administration. Yet at the same time, the press's freedom to operate as an independent force within the American political system was constrained by the environment in which mainstream journalists lived and worked. Adversarial behavior was discouraged by certain basic facts of journalistic life. For instance, as employees of some of the largest and most profitable corporations in the land, journalists and news executives ultimately answered to superiors whose individual and collective self-interest mitigated against strong or consistent criticism of a government as pro-corporate as Ronald Reagan's. There was also the age-old challenge of maintaining good and reliable sources without becoming a captive of them.

According to the old journalistic truism, a reporter was only as good as his sources. For White House reporters, this raised a troubling dilemma. Most news organizations' definition of proper White House coverage stressed reporting the views and actions of the President and his aides above all else. Thus the officials with whom reporters were, in theory, supposed to have an adversarial relationship were the very people upon whom they were most dependent for the information needed to produce their stories. As Lee Lescaze, who covered the White House for *The Washington Post* in 1981, explained, "There are only six or seven real sources in the White House who know anything. So you can't write a tough story if you're one of the 90 percent of the press corps who can be frozen out. . . . [Jim] Baker has three hundred phone message slips waiting for him, and he's going to call back the ones he likes or needs."

For obvious reasons, the White House propaganda apparatus concentrated its efforts on the big-circulation outlets: the major networks, the wire services and the big papers. "Anybody else," noted CBS White House correspondent Bill Plante, "can whistle 'Dixie.' "

White House officials recognized that television's commercial imperatives gave them a strategic edge. "I think by temperament, by inclination, by desire, [White House reporters] are highly adversarial," said one senior Reagan aide. "They are very smart. They are hardworking, by and large, the good ones. They simply have an extraordinarily difficult problem, because their subject, the President, is what the network wants to run."

The great demand for White House news stories meant that the Reagan media apparatus could sharply restrict reporters' access, and thereby gain greater control over coverage, without inhibiting its own access to the nation's airwaves and newspapers. It meant that top White House officials could mount the stage in the West Wing pressroom and brief the entire press corps on a "background" basis—that is, their names would not be attached to any quoted statements—without eliciting a peep of protest from the journalists gathered below. It meant that President Reagan could be made available to cameras only under the most carefully controlled conditions but with utter confidence that his remarks would nonetheless be widely printed and broadcast.

"What the Reagan White House does is say you can't have access to the President and his principal aides; you'll write what we want you to," said Juan Williams of *The Washington Post*. "And instead of the press saying this is bullshit and pushing for more press conferences, more access of all kinds, they compete with one another to get that one interview or that one scoop."

"The reason this can go on is that the reporters on the White House beat have been deadened," said Vicki Barker, a United Press International Radio general assignment reporter who covered the White House during the summer of 1985. "It's like that scene in *A Clockwork Orange* where the droog is strapped into a chair with Beethoven blasting away at him and he's being reprogrammed. That's the White House beat. [The administration] keeps up a steady drip-drop of [what is] barely news, and you have to scramble to keep up with it, because otherwise your editors ask why the competition has it."

"A lot of reporters recognized that they were dealing not with real news but pseudo-news," said Rich Jaroslovsky, a White House reporter for *The Wall Street Journal*. "[In private] network correspondents complain that a lot of it is bilge, but they still want that story to go on. They don't sit around on Air Force One asking why they're writing these stories. They know how the system works, and they accept it." As George Watson, Washington bureau chief of ABC News, commented, "We aren't consciously sitting around saying, 'How can we be more adversarial?' "

White House reporters were occupied with a much more immediate and pressing concern: getting the story, getting it first, and getting on the air or in the paper with it. As they had to be, one might add, if they were to keep their high-profile jobs. Why should their bosses keep them on the beat and pay them strong five-figure salaries—in the case of TV reporters, strong *six*-figure salaries—if they did not produce plenty of stories, or if they consistently got "beaten" by their competitors? There was also the goad of ego, which in the case of most White House correspondents was a powerful goad indeed. One did not rise as high within the journalistic profession as these reporters had if one did not really want to be—indeed, *have* to be—number one. Appearances on the evening news and the morning front page were a large part of keeping score in that contest.

Perhaps because he tended to be in the direct path of the stampeding herd, White House spokesman Larry Speakes complained that this collective urge on the reporters' part led to "distortion of the news. The correspondents never go back to their desk and say, 'There's no story here today.' . . . If Chris [Wallace of NBC] gets a piece for the evening news, then Andrea [Mitchell] has to find another angle on it to get it on the air [the next morning on the *Today* show]. And in some cases, the story gets distorted looking for that other angle. The next afternoon, Chris is looking to Sam [Donaldson] and Lesley [Stahl], so he's trying to figure out how he can hype it more and more and make sure he's got something a little bit more than they have."

Michael Deaver, on the other hand, believed that the pack mentality of the White House press corps played into his hands—it meant they tended to come to him and take what stories he offered. "You know, they'd be much better off if they were in offices scattered all over town," said Deaver. "But they beat on each other, and if they don't have a story, sure, they're going to take [ours]. Whereas if they were out on their own, they'd be hustling and digging and getting their own stories."

To be sure, the White House needed the major outlets as much as vice versa, but that did not necessarily embolden reporters at such news organizations. There was enough competitiveness on the White House beat so that even reporters with audience clout had to worry about being discriminated against. Coverage too sharply or consistently critical could well provoke White House officials into favoring one's rival with the next inside tip.

Lou Cannon, the White House correspondent for *The Washington Post*, was the journalist widely regarded as enjoying the closest contacts with high Reagan officials. Appropriately enough,

his stock-in-trade was stories revealing the inner workings of the
Reagan White House. As Cannon's former editor William Greider explained, "What Lou lives for is that exclusive story that he
gets not just twenty-four hours before anybody else but weeks
before anybody else." Maintaining the kind of access that yielded
such leaked stories, however, exacted a cost. Cannon's regular
Monday column on the Reagan White House often contained
wonderful inside stuff and useful insights available nowhere else.
Unfortunately, it just as often was marred by an "on the one
hand, on the other hand" point of view that greatly diluted the
power of Cannon's information. Comments critical of the President were invariably balanced by an equal dose of approving
remarks, resulting in essays that sounded eminently fair-minded
to most of the reading public even as they preserved the author's
special relationship with the Reagan White House.

According to Lee Lescaze, who said he "got on extremely well"
with Cannon when they covered the White House together for
the *Post* in 1981, Cannon was "very sympathetic" toward Reagan.
"If [a reporter assigned to work with Cannon] began by saying
to Lou, 'Look, you like Reagan, I don't. So you can write all the
puff you want, but I'll still be tearing the lid off of it,' Lou would
think he was dealing with a wild man. He'd want to keep control
over the major pieces and make sure they were written with what
he'd call the right sensitivity."

"As all my former and present editors know," responded Cannon, "I've got two imperatives in covering the White House: to
be critical and to be fair." Noting that he spent most of 1981 on
a leave of absence to complete his biography of Reagan, Cannon
defended his toughness by recalling that his first story upon returning to the White House beat in January 1982 "ended by saying
that the question about Ronald Reagan was the same that it was
when he became President a year earlier: is he up to the job?"
Cannon went on to complain that he had a hard time covering
the Reagan administration precisely because he was so critical.
And it was true: his coverage was relatively critical. But the emphasis belongs on the word "relatively." Lou Cannon ranked a
notch above his peers because he occasionally engaged in what
should have been standard practice: stating (albeit in carefully
qualified language) the obvious about Ronald Reagan.

"It's hard to avoid the analogy of the White House press corps as a bunch of caged hamsters thoroughly dependent on their masters for their daily feeding," remarked *The Boston Globe*'s Walter Robinson, who was assigned to the beat in 1985. "There is so little real information there that people really do end up competing for crumbs. And they consider it a badge of honor to get one of the crumbs, even though most of them turn out to be not as nourishing as advertised."

In reaction to the intense competition, said Robinson, "people lower their standards [and] take single-source things that you'd never take in another kind of environment. . . . It's a generally held view within the press corps that the *New York Times* coverage of the White House is shameless. It's so important for the *Times* to be first that they throw their standards out the window. There's general resentment among other print reporters of the *Times* and the *Post* because of their access. It's so much easier for [second-term White House chief of staff] Donald Regan to drop something in there as a trial balloon, and then everybody else will pick it up." Beyond the front-page scoops, added Robinson, "the *Times* is also shameless with the fawning profiles of White House officials who will later be leaking stories [to the authors of said profiles]."

Tom Oliphant, Robinson's predecessor as the *Globe*'s White House reporter, agreed that reporters at "second tier" news corporations were afforded less access to officials, but asked, "So what if you can't get Don Regan on the phone twice a week? I prefer this in some ways to being a *New York Times* reporter with official sources which produce official stories that are beside the point."

Fame and fortune, whether in the form of being read by the Washington power elite or perhaps being invited to join the Sunday talk-show panels, were powerful temptations to which White House reporters were especially susceptible. After all, they were members, in former NBC White House correspondent Emery King's words, of "the most pampered press corps in the world." And their position of privilege inevitably, if subtly, shaped their reporting. "There are no whores in the [White House] press corps," declared Tom Oliphant. "They're all independent journalists. They work hard. None of them want to report just what the White House says is true. But there is subtle entrapment. . . . The perks, the trips, the *life*, as they say, are more than any

human being should be expected to withstand. There are too many
tender traps to report strongly there for long."

To be sure, some White House reporters resisted these traps
more vigorously than others. Sam Donaldson of ABC, for example, was not one to pull punches for reasons of decorum. When
White House press aides prevented reporters from getting close
enough to the President to ask questions, Donaldson was not shy
about shouting loud enough so that even the hard-of-hearing Mr.
Reagan couldn't ignore the question. Donaldson was the man
right-wing press bashers loved to hate, yet he was just as willing
to hound Democrats as Republicans.

Yet not even Donaldson, probably the best television reporter
covering the White House during the Reagan years, was genuinely
as adversarial as commonly supposed. True, he was not afraid of
challenging the official line, but he hardly made a habit of it. As
befit a television journalist, his image as a mad dog was more a
function of form than substance; the bark was much worse than
the bite. Often, what was interpreted as hard-nosed reporting on
his part had more to do with Donaldson's aggressive manner and
nettlesome appearance than with the actual content of his reports,
which usually were only marginally more adversarial than those
of his colleagues.

Stan Opotowsky, director of political operations at ABC News
and a man who worked closely with Donaldson years before he
became a star, told me that to understand Sam Donaldson one
had to bear in mind that he was really two persons: the loudmouth
maverick of his public persona and the shrewd professional who
is very much part of the establishment. *Hold On, Mr. President!*,
Donaldson's 1987 autobiography, confirmed that analysis. For all
his apparently outrageous behavior and growling aggressiveness,
Sam Donaldson held to rather conventional opinions about news,
politics and the connection between them. Which perhaps helps
explain an apparent paradox: of the network correspondents on
the White House beat, Donaldson was unanimously considered
by the top Reagan press aides interviewed for this book to be the
fairest of them all.

The sources dilemma was not quite as acute for reporters on
beats other than the White House, if only because they tended
to have a larger pool of potential sources on which to draw. Still,
if they were to provide the kind of daily stories most desired by

their editorial and executive superiors, maintaining cordial relations with top government officials was an occupational necessity. As a foreign policy reporter, "you need to be on speaking terms with the Secretary of State and the Assistant Secretary of State for Latin American Affairs, or Soviet Affairs," said ABC national security correspondent John McWethy. But how likely was a reporter to stay on speaking terms with such officials if he was consistently engaged in full-bore adversarial journalism? President Reagan's Assistant Secretary for Inter-American Affairs, Elliott Abrams, actually refused to take questions from or appear on talk shows or in public debates with certain journalists and policy analysts because he considered them politically biased. "It is time we begin to define what constitutes the borders of responsible criticism," Abrams told the *Columbia Journalism Review* in defending his refusal to grant an interview to CBS's Jane Wallace, who contributed some of the most aggressive reporting on Central America to appear on network television during the Reagan years. Because she was not restricted to the Central America beat, Ms. Wallace was not greatly harmed by Abrams's ban. But for journalists who did do the bulk of their reporting on that beat, such a blacklisting would have amounted to a significant competitive handicap.

"How do you develop sources on a beat without becoming captive to them? I don't know. It's one of the real dilemmas for any reporter," said Stephen Engelberg of *The New York Times*. Commenting on press coverage of the Iran-contra affair, Engelberg added, "That's why the people who have done the best on this story are those who came out of left field. [*Miami Herald* reporter Alfonso] Chardy didn't have to make the White House like him. Neither did [*Los Angeles Times* reporter Michael] Wines. . . . Ollie North was a Pulitzer waiting to happen for anybody on the White House or national security beat, but reporters are human beings. The fewer sources there are, the more you think about how they'll react to your story. You'll gore somebody's ox if you have to, but you'll think about it carefully beforehand."

• • •

DURING the late 1960s Jeff Gralnick was one of Walter Cronkite's favorite young producers at CBS News. When Cronkite made his famous fact-finding journey to Vietnam following the Tet offensive of 1968, Gralnick had already been "in-country" seven or eight weeks, trying to figure out, as he later recalled, "whether I should be in front of the camera or behind it." It was in the latter capacity that he assisted in preparing what would be one of Cronkite's most important broadcasts ever: a special prime-time report in which Cronkite, who, like most other dominant news media voices in the United States, had thus far been quite supportive of the war, contradicted the Johnson administration's claims that the war was being won and suggested that the United States think about withdrawing. It was a half hour of television regarded by war supporters and critics alike, and indeed by Johnson himself, as a clear sign that mass American opinion was turning irreversibly against the war. And it was remarkable for another reason as well: Walter Cronkite, the man thought to embody objective journalism, had expressed a clear opinion in the broadcast; he had taken a stand *against* the government.

Fifteen years later, a mature Jeff Gralnick held one of the most powerful jobs in American television news: executive producer of ABC's *World News Tonight*. Naturally he answered to executive superiors in that job, but on a day-to-day basis it was he who exercised ultimate control over what stories appeared on *World News Tonight* and which correspondents and producers were assigned to report them, and over the length, emphasis and general tone of those stories. As the man who controlled the broadcast from September 1979 until July 1983, Gralnick decided what approximately twelve million Americans learned about their government and the world five nights a week during the first two and a half years of Ronald Reagan's presidency.

The journalistic philosophy he brought to the job differed considerably from that which had informed Cronkite's Vietnam broadcast years before. For example, when asked how he as executive producer responded to Reagan administration efforts to restrict journalists' access to Reagan, he replied, "It's not my job to respond to it. . . . It is not my position to say, 'For shame, Public Agency.' It's my job to take the news as they choose to give it to us and then, in the amount of time that's available, put it into the context of the day or that particular story." Later in the same interview, Gralnick declared, "The evening newscast is not supposed to be the watchdog on the government. It never was, never will be. We are a national front page, five days a week."

When asked about Lou Cannon's belief that President Reagan had gotten "a fairer press than he deserves," Gralnick shot back, "I wouldn't consider talking about what the President does or does not deserve. It's a political, subjective judgment."

"Aren't those kinds of judgments made in anyone's journalism?"

"Better not be. *The Village Voice* may make those kinds of judgments, but I sure as hell don't."

Asked finally whether he was saying that *The Village Voice* had a point of view while such mainstream news organizations as *The New York Times* and ABC News did not, the network vice president seemed suddenly impatient. Grabbing that morning's *Times* from under a pile of papers on his desk, he held it up with both hands, nodded toward the fully extended front page and in a schoolteacher tone explained, "On its front page the only point of view exhibited by *The New York Times* is the view of what stories are on the right-hand lead, the left-hand lead, above and below the fold." He then ripped through the paper's front section, flung it open to the opinions and editorials page, smacked the page with the back of his hand and announced, "*That* is where *The New York Times*'s point of view is."

"He is either very naïve or a real liar," responded television critic Tom Shales of *The Washington Post.* "For Jeff Gralnick to say no political judgments go into those broadcasts is just silly."

"*The New York Times* is a very good newspaper with lots of good reporters, but to say it's value-free I think is wrong," offered Bill Wheatley, then senior (and later promoted to executive) producer of the *NBC Nightly News.* "There are values expressed just by what stories are placed on the front page, by what facts lead the story and what facts are in the middle of the story."

" 'Objectivity' contradict[s] the essentially subjective nature of journalism," wrote former *Post* editor Ben Bagdikian in his landmark 1983 study, *The Media Monopoly.* "Every basic step in the journalistic process involves a value-laden decision: Which of the infinite number of events in the environment will be assigned for coverage and which ignored? Which of the infinite observations confronting the reporter will be noted? . . . Which story will be prominently displayed on page 1 and which buried inside or discarded? . . . 'Objectivity' place[s] overwhelming emphasis on established, official voices and tend[s] to leave unreported large areas of genuine relevance that authorities choose not to talk about."

Objectivity also prohibited reporters from exercising much intelligence and judgment on behalf of their readers, according to author and former *New York Times* reporter David Halberstam. Reflecting on news coverage of the 1972 presidential campaign, Halberstam once wrote: "Despite all the fine talk of objectivity, the only thing that mildly approached objectivity was the form in which the reporter wrote the news, a technical style which required the journalist to appear to be much dumber and more innocent than in fact he was. So he wrote in a bland, uncritical way which gave greater credence to the utterances of public officials, no matter how mindless these utterances. . . . Thus the press voluntarily surrendered a vast amount of its real independence; it treated the words and actions of the government of the United States with a credence that those words and actions did not necessarily merit."

Notwithstanding such criticisms, objectivity remained the dominant journalistic philosophy in the United States throughout the Reagan years. True, few articulated so extreme a version of that philosophy as did Jeff Gralnick. In the aftermath of Vietnam and Watergate, objectivity had come under sufficient criticism from within the profession so that now most journalists, if pushed, would concede that perfect objectivity was impossible; explicitly or implicitly, every news story unavoidably expressed a point of view. As NBC News Washington bureau chief Robert McFarland pointed out: "Do you lead your newscast with the story of how inflation is falling, or how unemployment is still 14 percent in Detroit? That's a value judgment."

The value judgments American journalists made in reporting the news were inevitably influenced by their own backgrounds. "Even as an objective journalist, you're an American first and a journalist second," observed *CBS Evening News* Washington producer Susan Zirinsky. "You come from a framework to every story, and I'm an American, that's where I come from." Former ABC Pentagon correspondent Dean Reynolds made a similar point when I asked why the press had generally refrained from highlighting the obvious potential of President Reagan's Strategic

Defense Initiative space weapons system to function as a first-strike nuclear weapon. Reynolds said that he and other reporters had asked Defense Secretary Caspar Weinberger about this possibility. "And he ultimately falls back on 'Well, you have to look at the two systems [the United States versus the Soviet Union]. Which one do you believe?' That's a pretty fundamental question. And I believe this administration and this Defense Secretary [when they] say we are not attempting to build a first-strike weapon."

Even journalists who rejected simplistic notions of value-free news nevertheless usually embraced more refined versions of the doctrine of objectivity. If it was impossible to avoid a point of view entirely, they would do their best to minimize it. As much as possible, they would leave explanations and interpretations to others. They would strive for "fairness" and "balance" (the two buzzwords that had arisen to replace "objectivity" in the journalistic lexicon). They would, above all, remain politically neutral.

In accordance with their avoidance of partisanship, many journalists seemed to regard strenuous challenging of the government as an improper violation of the rules of objectivity. Honest adversarial journalism they equated with, and often dismissed as, "advocacy" journalism. NBC's Tom Brokaw was but one of those who argued that it was not the press's job to protect the public from White House efforts to manipulate opinion; rather, the press was to share with the public "the biggest, most thorough picture of what [the White House] is up to in the policy and the manipulation, and let the public respond to that."

As much as any other constraint, it was this allegiance to objectivity that put the press at such a strategic disadvantage vis-à-vis the Reagan White House. Whatever it promised in theory, in practice objective journalism was far from politically neutral, largely because of its overwhelming reliance on official sources of information. In fact, in its own way, it was no less slanted than the advocacy journalism that mainstream reporters and editors so self-righteously shunned. It was just that its slant was in deference, rather than opposition, to the reigning conventions and authorities of the day.

"Objectivity is fine if it's real," said independent journalist I. F. Stone. "Every society has its dogmas, and a genuinely objective approach can break through them. But most of the time objectivity is just the rationale for regurgitating the conventional wisdom of the day. If what you're saying challenges the stereotypes of the day, it's hard to get it printed."

It was an article of faith within the American press that everyone was free to say whatever they liked; there were no limits on opinion, and all serious views were given fair representation. In fact, however, subtle but definite limits were imposed on the nation's political debate by the press's definition of who constituted responsible, and thus quotable, news sources. As a practical matter, the definition of who was worth listening to was limited to official Washington: administration officials (past and present), members of Congress, the occasional well-connected academic specialist. "What you see are the people who are the movers and shakers, who have the power to change things in the short term," explained Sanford Socolow, former executive producer of the *CBS Evening News.* "They're the ones you see on the news."

Emphasizing the statements and actions of officials above all else often resulted in woefully one-sided reporting and reduced the press to little more than a nominally independent mouthpiece of the government, a stenographer to power. Especially on the White House beat, so-called objective reporting tended to produce news stories comprised largely of information reflecting the White House's own point of view—what (unnamed) official X thought about issue Y, what the President planned to tell foreign leader Z next week. Occasionally these views would be balanced by alternative voices, but in most cases, only marginally so. In the words of venerable *New York Times* Washington columnist James Reston: "What we do most of the time is, we really are a transmission belt." Noting that the White House would "like us to be even more of a transmission belt than we already are," he added, "Probably we should be analyzing more than we do."

Or at least relying on a more politically diverse range of sources. "Serving as a stenographer to power isn't real objectivity," argued Robert Parry, a reporter who worked for the Associated Press and *Newsweek* during the Reagan years. "Real objectivity means listening to all sides of the debate. Many reporters won't deal with certain kinds of information because of where it comes from—say, from people who are sympathetic to the Sandinistas. I've been accused of being non-objective for that reason. But I think I'm being truly objective. I think you deal with *all* sides equally, evaluate their information, and if it checks out, you print it."

Former *Washington Post* assistant managing editor William Greider argued that the tendency of the press to serve as "more conduit than critic of the government" was due to an "ingrown quality of deference which makes the press unwilling to challenge presidential announcements. As a result, the press will print and broadcast reams and reams of rhetoric they themselves know to be wrong. Sure, they'll challenge him if he's got his facts 180 degrees wrong, but otherwise they're very reluctant."

"In the media at large there is no intellectual center of gravity," explained Robert Kaiser of the *Post*. "The practicing Washington press corps lacks intellectual self-confidence; [it] is most uncomfortable standing up and saying, 'Hey, naked, not so, stupid policy, dumb idea, whatever. If you talked to Lebanon experts about [the 1983 Reagan policy of] using U.S. marines as part of a peace-keeping mission, you knew it was a stupid policy from day one. But reporters don't do that. They cover it as a spectacle, as a political event: What are they saying up on the Hill?"

Presidential assistant Richard Darman told me that the so-called Teflon phenomenon—the fact that blame never seemed to stick to President Reagan, even after such disasters as the Beirut suicide bombing that claimed the lives of 241 marines—was directly related to journalists' tendency to emphasize personality over substance. "It doesn't ever say this explicitly," said Darman, "but what their [journalistic] culture tells them is: Your job, when a proposal is launched, is to talk about who did what to whom making it get launched, who's fighting with whom now that it has been launched, how is it being received here, there and such and such a place; in other words, what are its bureaucratic origins and what are its larger political prospects. The tendency is to concentrate on who did shoot John, who might shoot John, who wants to shoot John but doesn't have a gun.

"I don't think we consciously used [this tendency]," Darman continued, "[but] the President benefited [from it]. The Teflon phenomenon is a function of the fact that when there's a problem with substance, the press doesn't say there's something wrong with Reagan's policies. They say party A in the White House is fighting with party B *about* the policy. It tends to insulate the

President from substantive criticism and convert it into personality stories about conflicts between individuals within the administration beneath the level of the President."

One other related but rarely acknowledged consequence of objective journalism's sourcing habits was to make the press in effect a hostage to the debate within the Washington political elite. Lesley Stahl, who covered the White House for CBS for the first six years of the Reagan presidency, alluded to this dynamic in a February 1987 interview on PBS's *MacNeil-Lehrer Newshour*. Conceding that the press had been slow to pick up on the Iran-contra scandal, Stahl laid part of the blame on the Congress, "which is often a source for these kinds of stories." Indeed, she added, one reason press coverage of Mr. Reagan had not been more aggressive throughout the course of his presidency was that the Congress "ha[d] not been a source for the press in the whole Reagan administration. They don't want to criticize this beloved man."

The press's overwhelming reliance on official sources meant that news coverage of Washington by and large reflected and reinforced the assumptions, opinions and general worldview of official Washington. Venturing beyond the boundaries of the Democrat-to-Republican spectrum was rare in the extreme. However valid a given political position might be on an intellectual level, if it was not forcefully articulated by a significant part of the Washington establishment, it received little or no attention from the mainstream press.

"It's a little harder for the boys in the White House to keep the troops in line than it is for the boys in the Kremlin," investigative reporter Seymour Hersh observed during a May 1987 seminar at the Institute for Policy Studies in Washington, "but it is true that *Pravda* and *The Washington Post* and *The New York Times* are alike in the sense that they don't report reality so much as what a small group of top leaders *tells* them is reality."

Thus did numerous journalists argue that if Ronald Reagan did get off easy, it was less the fault of the press than of the Democratic party. Not only did Democrats fail to project a compelling alternative to Reaganism, they often seemed either afraid or unwilling even to criticize it.

"Look at defense, it's the perfect example," exclaimed David Hoffman of *The Washington Post* in a July 1985 interview. "Ronald Reagan will have doubled the defense budget in five years.

Doubled. That's a lot of dollars every year they didn't have before. In *The Washington Post* as an editorial voice and even in our headlines and our stories in a certain sense, you see that the debate is now not over whether we should go back to half of what we have now. It's whether we should go back to zero growth. So Reagan has achieved a doubling of the defense budget, and as long as the public supports that [sic] and the public debate is over zero growth or 3 percent growth, that's where our debate is. Now, if next week every Democrat came out and said, 'We're going back to the Carter budget, back to half of what we have now,' we would start writing stories about that. But we're not going to write those until those politicians start to make those noises. We follow in that respect. . . . We fill the paper with stories on the margin of issues, not sweeping overviews. If you went through the paper and stamped every story whether it was 2 degrees, 5 degrees or 360 degrees [off the center of the debate], you would see a lot of 2-degree stories."

Hence the importance of the opposition party to Washington press coverage. The doctrine of objectivity meant that the press was, quite simply, only as adversarial as the opposition party allowed it to be. "I don't think the coverage has been terrible," remarked Jonathan Kwitney, author and investigative reporter for *The Wall Street Journal.* "There has been some good reporting. But there is no opposition within the political system, and that's partly why the stories don't keep running on page one."

Indeed, part of the reason Ronald Reagan was able to pull the political debate so far to the right during his presidency was that there was no countervailing presence on the left in the Washington political arena. In the United States, where anti-Communism had been injected into the collective consciousness so relentlessly for so many years, "soft on Communism" was the last thing any politician—or journalist, for that matter—could afford to have thought about him. Thus criticisms of the nuclear arms race had to be prefaced with declarations of not liking or trusting the Russians any more than the next fellow, and backed up by a voting record that looked favorably on at least some of the big-ticket weapons systems that the Pentagon and its nominally private sector allies ceaselessly put forward as additional necessary deterrence to the Soviet threat. Likewise, if a member of Congress disagreed with President Reagan's policy of making war on Nicaragua, that member invariably first made sure to emphasize that he detested the Sandinista government as much as Reagan did before voicing any preference for negotiations over bloodshed.

As *New York Times* correspondent R. W. "Johnny" Apple commented: "To come back from Europe [where Apple spent nearly ten years as London bureau chief]—where the parliamentary tradition is alive and the spectrum of acceptable political debate stretches from non-Communist Marxists and Trotskyists and Eurocommunists on the left to neo-fascists on the right—to Washington was striking. I had a broader range of opinion represented around my dinner table in London than you could find in official Washington. . . . My wife and I were sitting around thinking one night of who was the leading left-wing politician in Washington and we came up with Teddy [Kennedy]. Now, Teddy would feel very comfortable in the left wing of the [British] Tory party. He could be quite comfortably accommodated within the Christian Democratic party in West Germany. If he happened to be a socialist, he would be in the far, far right wing of the Socialist party in Spain. That says a lot."

"As a working journalist you have to talk to people and quote them," said Robert Parry. "Normally you go to the opposition party. But what we ran into during that period [of extreme Sandinista bashing from 1983 onward] was that no one would defend the Sandinistas, even to say they weren't the worst things on earth. No one would put them in perspective—by saying that this and this may be true about the Sandinistas, but this and this isn't—because even putting it in perspective was considered defending the Sandinistas. So it was very hard to write stories raising questions about Reagan's policy, because the Democrats weren't playing the role of an opposition party." Parry and his partner at the Associated Press, Brian Barger, responded by visiting Miami, where "the debate going on inside the Nicaraguan exile community was much more honest and broad-based than the debate going on in Washington. We were talking to people who were all anti-Sandinista . . . and they would talk about how artificial the contra movement was and about the corruption [within it]. They were very upset about it. . . . We got a lot more truth out of Miami than we did in Washington."*

---

* A reporter covering the Middle East could have said the same thing about Jerusalem and Washington. The official debate was considerably broader in Jerusalem than it was in Washington, where, prior to the widespread Palestinian unrest of late 1987, administration and congressional officials alike rarely criticized the actions of the Israeli government.

But reporters like Parry and Barger were the exception. Most Washington journalists focused exclusively on doings in the capital, and thus tended to internalize, if only unconsciously, the basic premises underlying U.S. policy. In foreign policy, for example, the United States was presumed to act from an essentially defensive posture and with benevolent intent; recall, for example, Dean Reynolds's trust that the Reagan administration would not develop a first-strike nuclear weapon. And while the United States was by any historical definition an empire of extraordinary reach and power, with hundreds of overseas military bases and a long record of military and economic interventions aimed at toppling or propping up foreign governments, it was rarely referred to as an empire in mainstream news accounts, nor were its actions evaluated from such a perspective. Likewise, only official U.S. enemies practiced "terrorism"; U.S. allies like El Salvador that engaged in widespread and systematic violence against their civilians were called "democracies" and forgiven their excesses on the grounds that they were resisting "Communist subversion."

Human rights coverage provided perhaps the clearest illustration of the ideological double standard embraced by the U.S. press. While the media showered attention on physicist Andrei Sakharov and other dissidents living in the Soviet sphere of influence, dissidents from the U.S. sphere were usually all but ignored.

Consider, for example, the parallel cases of Lech Walesa and Oscar Romero. Both men suffered abuse at the hands of state authorities for leading struggles of poor and working people for social justice, Walesa as the head of the Solidarity movement in Poland, Romero as a Catholic archbishop in El Salvador. Walesa was repeatedly harassed and imprisoned by the Soviet-backed regime in Poland; Romero was harassed and ultimately assassinated in March 1980 by death squads working for the U.S.-backed regime in El Salvador. Yet while Walesa became a virtual household name in the United States, Archbishop Romero remained a stranger to the American public. In the same manner, the U.S. news media lavished coverage on the Solidarity uprising in December 1981, even as it completely ignored the concurrent terror campaign then underway in Guatemala, where a U.S.-backed military government was engaged in a repression of the civilian population that was substantially more brutal than what was taking place in Poland.

"You're supposed to see El Salvador on one set of terms and Nicaragua on an entirely different set of terms," charges Robert Parry. "I raised this once with Elliott [Abrams] over dinner, and he said, 'I hope you're not going to get into this question of moral equivalency.' . . . [Their] thinking is that when we invade a country, it's okay, but when the Soviets invade a country, it's not." (Repeated attempts to interview Mr. Abrams were rebuffed.) Parry complained that government officials applied a similar double standard to news coverage: "The difference is, if you're writing a story the way they want you to, you could make as many mistakes as you want and not be criticized for it. But if you're writing something that goes against the grain, you had to be perfect. If you had the slightest error, they would latch on to that and use it to come after you."

Journalists who refused to adopt the preferred double standard risked censure not only from U.S. officials but from their colleagues in the press. Parry himself was subjected to a "whisper campaign" in which administration officials, including Elliott Abrams's press secretary, Gregory Lagana, attempted to discredit him as a Sandinista sympathizer to at least two other reporters, according to interviews with those reporters. One Reagan official even tried to convince Parry that his partner, Barger, was politically suspect. "And if you don't succumb to all that," noted Parry, "you get the line from your editors that maybe they should take you off the story, since you seem to be pursuing a political agenda. When the government attacks you, even your colleagues begin to doubt your credibility, when it should be just the opposite."

Compared with the imprisonment and worse risked by journalists elsewhere in the world who dared dissent from official orthodoxy, smearing of reputations and derailing of careers was relatively tame stuff. But in the American context, such tactics generally proved an effective form of coercion. The more a journalist strayed beyond acceptable bounds of discussion, the less likely he was to see his reporting printed or broadcast. As I. F. Stone explained: "There is a palpable range of discourse, and if you stray outside it—either to the right or to the left, but especially to the left—you're not in Siberia or *samizdat*, but you're in *The Nation*, or *In These Times*, or *The Progressive*, and not much read. A young journalist in the mainstream press doesn't have to be told this, he can see it all around him."

"It isn't very easy to try to respect the American tradition of journalistic fairness—'objectivity' is a strange word, I don't know exactly what it means, but 'fairness' is more operative—and it depends on your own perspective," acknowledged CBS News White House correspondent Bill Plante. "You can say it is all pablum, wire service straight down the middle, report the facts, serve as a conduit for the government, when you should be taking a point of view. I won't argue that it can't be bland, or that we are terribly successful in pointing out the inconsistencies, but I do think the American tradition of journalistic fairness is an important element in allowing freedom of opinion. It may also have helped homogenize thought."

Here Plante expressed the fundamental contradiction inherent in the reigning definition of journalistic fairness: although in theory it was supposed to encourage freedom of opinion, in practice it usually tended to limit the range of political discourse and encourage homogenized political thinking.

Plante's suggested solution to the problem? Teach courses on attribution in the nation's classrooms. Although he resisted the notion that television provided "a point of view that resembles the government's more than anything else," he did admit that "you have to read or listen very carefully to understand what's really being said." Asked to comment on *Boston Globe* political reporter Tom Oliphant's view that the press corps "conveyed Reagan's version of reality" in its 1984 campaign coverage, he replied, "Do you convey Reagan's version of reality, or do you convey what Reagan *says* is reality? We certainly conveyed what he *said* was reality. . . . Now, it may be true that most people don't make that distinction. They should. We ought to start off in grammar school, or junior high, with a course on reading the newspaper and watching television: how to understand attribution."

In the meantime, one alternative was for the press to devote as much time and space to White House critics as it did to the White House itself. The problem was, contradicting the President raised the issue of press neutrality. That did not mean it could never be done, but there were limits; one had to be fair about it. And what was fair? "I have the feeling, and we, meaning the establishment, have the feeling," explained ABC News senior vice president Richard Wald, "that you can say the President is wrong, and you can repeat it once, but after that it becomes a crusade. And television doesn't do crusades. Nor do news-papers."

This self-imposed restraint was the ideal definition of responsible journalism for the Reagan White House, for Ronald Reagan was nothing if not shameless about repeating statements and stories shown to be false or misleading. Since news organizations tended to consider almost anything a President said or did to be news, and since they were nowhere near as stingy about letting a President make his case as they were about correcting him, simple arithmetic meant that over time the public tended to get far more exposure to the President's than to competing versions of reality.

The political advantages for the White House in this were obvious. Especially during the first six years of his presidency Mr. Reagan time and again shifted the framework of debate simply by repeating the same dubious assertions over and over until they became accepted as political facts of life. On May 9, 1984, for example, Reagan delivered a nationally televised speech about Central America filled with enough accusations of Communist subversion to make one wonder if the White House had hired Joe McCarthy's ghost as a speechwriter. The President charged that "Sandinista rule is a Communist reign of terror" and that Nicaragua was engaged in an unjustified military buildup in order to "export terror to every other country in the region." All this was part of "a bold attempt by the Soviet Union, Cuba and Nicaragua to install Communism by force throughout the hemisphere." While the United States wanted only "to promote democracy and economic well-being" in Central America and would "never be the aggressor," the Communists were shipping tons of weapons to guerrillas in El Salvador who "want to shoot their way into power and establish totalitarian rule." If the United States did not act, quickly and resolutely, "our choice will be a Communist Central America with additional Communist military bases on the mainland of this hemisphere and Communist subversion spreading southward and northward."

Now, it would seem important for Americans to realize that many of the things their President had just told them were at best unproved assertions or one-sided interpretations and at worst demonstrably false statements. Yet not one of the network commentators pointed this out in their post-speech summaries. Neither did the next day's account in *The New York Times* or *The Washington Post*. To do so would have implied that the President was either a liar or a fool, hardly a politically neutral message. Instead, objectivity prevailed over accuracy, Reagan's statements were reported uncritically, just as Senator McCarthy's were, and the American people were left not merely uninformed but misinformed.

Had news stories given prominent if not equal weight to countervailing views, Reagan would not have been able to impose his often mistaken premises on the political debate so easily. It should have been a simple matter of standing up for truth and accuracy, but in the eyes of objective mainstream journalists such behavior smacked of partisanship and thus violated the sacred vow of neutrality.

James Reston, for example, though he lamented the press's tendency to serve as a "transmission belt" for the official government line of the moment, nonetheless argued that "it would be very dangerous, I think, for us to spend 50 percent of our reports announcing their statements and decisions and then using the other 50 percent to say what liars they are." And even Sam Donaldson, certainly one of the most aggressive reporters in Washington, made a similar point when he cautioned, "My mission is not to blow them out of the water every day. I think it would be very dangerous if I took that attitude."

All of which suggests the conclusion that during the Reagan years the Washington and especially the White House press corps functioned less as an independent than as a palace court press. Journalists were extremely adept at discovering and detailing the intrigues of palace politics—who were the powers behind the throne, what were the King and his men up to, what factions within court society opposed them and how strongly, what decisions were made and what effects they would have. This was valuable information, and often the press reported more of it than some, particularly the King and his men, would have liked. The press in this sense was the bad boy of palace court society. But the press tended to confine its naughtiness within relatively narrow limits. It was not inclined to step outside the mind-set of the authorities it covered, or to challenge in any fundamental way the policies they formulated or the assumptions and values that gave rise to those policies. As Robert Kaiser explained, journalists and news organizations "are members of this class, this governing, political class." As such, their coverage inevitably reflected the values, beliefs and interests of that class. Although formally independent, in practice the American press functioned more often than not as an arm of the American state.

5

"A GREAT CAPITALIST INSTRUMENT"

A. J. LIEBLING's wonderfully acute observation that "freedom of the press is guaranteed only to those who own one" was never more true than in the 1980s. As ABC's Sam Donaldson acknowledged in his autobiography: "The press, myself included, traditionally sides with authority and the establishment." It is hard to see how it could do otherwise; the press was itself a central part of the American establishment.

According to Ben Bagdikian's *The Media Monopoly*, a mere fifty large corporations owned or controlled the majority of media outlets in the United States—newspapers, radio and television stations, magazines, books and movies—when Ronald Reagan came to power in 1981. By the time Bagdikian published a new edition of his book in 1987, mergers and acquisitions had shrunk the previous fifty down to twenty-nine. Half of these media moguls ranked among the Fortune 500—itself an elite club whose members, while numbering less than 1 percent of all industrial corporations in the United States, nevertheless accounted for 87 percent of total sales. The parent corporations of nine of the most influential national news organizations—ABC, CBS, NBC, *The New York Times*, *The Washington Post*, *The Wall Street Journal*, the *Los Angeles Times*, *Newsweek* and *Time*—were all Fortune 500 members. Moreover, through interlocking directorates—sharing members on boards of directors—and lines of credit and other financial relationships, these parent corporations were themselves linked with dozens of others of the largest corporations and banks in the United States. Contrary to right-wing mythology, the press was not an institution dominated by leftists but a creature of the very richest of the rich and mightiest of the mighty in American society.

The rising profitability of news as a commodity was what

spurred large corporations to buy up monopoly positions within the news business. From 1960 to 1985, newspaper chains increased their share of total daily newspaper circulation in the United States from 46.1 percent to 77 percent. The actual number of daily papers in existence remained roughly the same during this period (approximately 1,700), as did the number of individual copies sold daily—59 million in 1961 versus 63 million in 1985. But the revenues generated by these newspapers *doubled*, from $12.7 billion to $25.5 billion (in 1986 dollars). By 1987, very few Americans had the luxury of choosing between two competing local newspapers; monopoly reigned in 98 percent of cities with a daily newspaper.

As for television, the combined pretax profits of the three major networks nearly *quadrupled* during this period, from $268 million in 1961 to $1,035 million in 1985 (in 1986 dollars). "I don't know anybody who has less interest in undermining capitalism than the people who work in television," chuckled critic Tom Shales of *The Washington Post* in a May 1985 interview with ABC News. "They all make oodles and tons of money, and tons of money is made from television. It's a great capitalist instrument."

Although it was an unwelcome truth within the profession, there was no denying that commercial considerations had long played a central role in the behavior of U.S. news organizations. Indeed, the very introduction of "objective" journalism in the 1920s and 1930s had been driven largely by newspaper publishers' desire for greater sales and profits.

"The introduction of mass circulation papers is when you see newspapers leave their partisan, sectarian, regional [or] religious identities behind and become what we think of as quote objective," explained William Greider. "The economics of that are quite direct. If you're going to be a mass circulation journal, that means you're going to be talking simultaneously to lots of groups that have opposing views. So you've got to modulate your voice and pretend to be talking to all of them."

Modern television, as the greatest mass communications instrument in history, operated according to the same principle, only more so. One result was a numbing uniformity among network news broadcasts. The discerning viewer could detect certain differences in the three main evening newscasts—ABC, for example, tended to give international news more play than did its competitors—but these were minor compared to the many similarities in format, content and political perspective among the shows. The single most noticeable difference among the three, of course, the difference at the anchor position, had less to do with news than with personal style and appearance. However much pride Peter Jennings, Tom Brokaw and Dan Rather took in their skill as reporters, they could not change the fact that at this point in network television history to be an anchorman meant that one was a celebrity first and a journalist second.

The same critique applied to the national news magazines, where the tendency toward homogenization had been accelerating since the early 1960s. In 1961, *Time* and *Newsweek* had identical cover subjects four weeks out of fifty-two; in 1985, their covers were alike sixteen times, nearly once in every three issues. The reason was not, as some laypersons seemed to suspect, a conspiracy between the two magazines; staffers high and low at each publication genuinely considered themselves to be in sharp competition with their rival. It was simply that the journalists in charge of the two magazines increasingly shared similar views of the world and thus similar perspectives on what was important to discuss, and how.

Diversity seemed an almost frightening concept to many news media managers. A high-level producer on one of the three network evening newscasts was reminded of this the day that U.S. fighter jets performed a successful aerial interception of the alleged hijackers of the Italian cruise ship *Achille Lauro*. Before the newscast, this producer argued against colleagues who wanted to open the show with a video of President Reagan declaring that the interception had "sent a message to terrorists everywhere: You can run but you can't hide," claiming that it would make the network a party to administration propaganda. The producer was overruled and the video was used. As it happened, the other two networks also opened *their* broadcasts with the identical piece of Reagan video. In the postmortem meeting after the broadcast, the producer's colleagues pointed to their competitors' leads as evidence that their initial news judgment had indeed been correct.

A second and related commercial consequence of objectivity was a definite preference for conventional values and thinking. As longtime *Philadelphia Daily News* reporter Frank Dougherty said in an interview with the *Columbia Journalism Review*: "No

matter what editors say, I think they do want conventional think-
ers and they don't want people off-center anymore. . . . The
people they're hiring respond more to corporate manipulation."
Washington Post foreign correspondent Loren Jenkins made a
similar point about the post-1960s generation of reporters (referred to by Dougherty as SYJs—Serious Young Journalists):
"They have a less broad interest than we had. I find them very
directed, intense, total workaholics, totally devoted to their publication. A lot view being a foreign correspondent not as an ultimate career to aspire to but as a ticket to be punched. A lot
say, 'I'll take one or two tours and then get back to Washington
or New York. I want to be an editor.' There's much more ambition
now to move up the ladder."

"Compared to twenty years ago, a lot of the fun has gone out
of journalism," remarked Johnny Apple of the *Times*. "This used
to be a business that attracted a lot of nonconformists, oddballs
and unusual characters, in terms of interest, background and appearance. A lot of that seems to have been leached out of the
business somehow. I look out around the *New York Times* newsroom [now], it looks like a law firm. . . . My hunch is that this
more conventional behavior and dress and attitude probably car-
ries over into more conventional thinking about events and issues
of the day."

As Tom Yellin, one of the original producers on ABC's *Nightline* show and later the senior producer of CBS's *West 57th* news
magazine, explained: "The political sensibilities of people in network television are mainstream, traditional and conservative; neither far left nor far right. . . . We share the same basic assumptions
of bankers, lawyers and the rest of the establishment. You ain't
going to see a bunch of radicals coming in here."

Salary levels alone made sure of that. Television paid better
than print and those in front of the camera earned more than
those behind it, but none of the top journalists and news executives at major U.S. news organizations were anything less than
upper-middle-class, and most were considerably more than that.
Network news anchors in particular ranked among the country's
economic royalty. Dan Rather of CBS made a reported $2.3
million a year, Tom Brokaw of NBC $1.7 million and Peter Jen-
nings of ABC $1.8 million. Key Washington correspondents might
have to struggle along on a quarter as much. Executive producers

of evening newscasts earned in the neighborhood of $200,000 to $250,000 a year. Star print reporters on major Washington beats for such prominent newspapers as *The Washington Post* and *The New York Times* could earn $60,000 to $80,000 a year.

It is useful to bear in mind here that less than 10 percent of the rest of the American population earned as much as $60,000 a year during this period. In other words, even the lowest-paid members of the journalistic elite earned more money than did 90 percent of the public as a whole. Tom Dooley, a mythical character created around the turn of the century by Chicago newspaperman Finley Peter Dunne, once declared that the role of the press should be to "comfort the afflicted and afflict the comfortable." But with journalists no longer living among or even nearby society's afflicted, how could they know or much care about comforting them? And what would motivate them to afflict their new neighbors in the comfort class?

"It's not that these guys come out for Reagan's tax plan, as they selfishly should," said Stan Opotowsky of ABC News. "They just don't come in contact with people not in their [income] bracket. They've lost touch with their constituency." Or as Dougherty of the *Philadelphia Daily News* put it: "They don't know people who make water go through your pipes."

Nevertheless, for the sake of ratings, network anchors in particular were encouraged to project an Everyman identity on the air—to look like someone viewers at home would like and trust, and therefore watch. Thus viewers of the December 10, 1985, edition of the *CBS Evening News* were treated to the spectacle of multimillionaire anchor Dan Rather asking Capitol Hill correspondent Phil Jones how proposed changes in the tax law would "affect my pocketbook and the pocketbooks of other Americans." At the time, Rather and Jones were engaged in what was called "cross-talk"—a live interview by the anchor of his own correspondent, which audience surveys indicated helped to boost ratings by making viewers feel closer and more engaged with the faces they were watching. The phrasing of Rather's question was likewise designed to encourage the sense that he and the viewers were all in this together. An honest answer by correspondent Jones—"Well, Dan, as someone who makes over two million dollars a year, your tax bill could be reduced by as much as a couple hundred thousand dollars, but average wage earners should expect to save hundreds or at most a few thousand dollars"—would have punctured the illusion, but it also would have gotten Jones fired.

The fact that network journalists ranked in the top 2 percent of the nation's population by income, argued longtime CBS News vice president Robert Chandler, was not easily squared with the supposition that the media were an institution dominated by liberals. Offering a personal anecdote to illustrate the point, he recalled watching one of President Reagan's nationally televised speeches one night with his wife. As the President stressed the need to cut domestic spending in order to trim the federal deficit, Chandler's wife, whom he described as "a genuine liberal," burst out, "Oh, why not just tax the rich!" Chandler looked over at her. "Hey, schmuck," he growled. "That's us."

In addition to their wealth, top journalists and news executives also resembled the rest of the American establishment in age, gender and racial identity. Overwhelmingly, the top ranks of U.S. news organizations were populated by white, middle-aged men. A study for the American Society of Newspaper Editors found that minorities accounted for just 5.72 percent of the nation's newsroom employees in 1984. (By contrast, minority groups constituted some 20 percent of the total U.S. population.) A survey by *Los Angeles Times* reporter David Shaw found that while "the vast majority of editorial writers are white males in their 40s and 50s [there were] only about 24 blacks on newspaper editorial boards across the country."

Moreover, because superiors tended to surround themselves with and promote those with whom they felt most comfortable, women, blacks and other minorities who did have journalism jobs often found it difficult to rise within their respective organizations.

"It's an awful struggle, being repeatedly passed over," said George Strait, medical correspondent for ABC News. As the senior black correspondent at ABC, Strait helped to organize a minority caucus in 1985 to pressure management to change employment and assignment practices. One indication of the attitude confronting the caucus, according to Strait, was references to it in the hallways of ABC as "the watermelon caucus." Strait also recalled how veteran black correspondent Carole Simpson, arriving at a colleague's farewell party, was asked by a man who could be termed one of her bosses, "Are you here to serve?"

Top female journalists at ABC had organized a similar caucus earlier in 1985, complaining that women were underrepresented on the editorial and management staffs and on the air. The minority grouping echoed those charges; not one of ABC News's seven executive producers was black, and only two of its seventeen senior producers were black. But the minority caucus also went a significant step further, arguing that the lack of blacks had resulted in inadequate coverage of important news stories.

"After *Nightline* [spent a week covering the racial situation in South Africa in 1985], which was wonderful, we were all appalled by how regularly we were being beaten by particularly CBS on the coverage of South Africa," Strait explained. "We were appalled at the way the Reagan Justice Department was not being covered. . . . We were appalled that the only black stories *20/20* had were stories about Lionel Ritchie and Kareem Abdul-Jabbar. We were appalled that not only do there continue to be no senior blacks on a management track, but no mid-level or junior ones either." When ABC News president Roone Arledge and five of his lieutenants were confronted with such arguments at a February 1986 meeting, added Strait, "it hadn't crossed their minds. . . . We told Roone that one of the problems was that *This Week With David Brinkley* was more like *This Week With Middle-Aged White Men.*"

(ABC News senior vice president Richard Wald, who attended the February meeting, conceded in a subsequent interview that "the minority caucus had some good points." Although he denied that ABC had neglected hiring young black journalists, he did say that the network had not done enough and that improvements would be made.)

"Until blacks get in the editorial decision-making mix, none of these things are going to change more than sporadically," said Strait. "One problem with blacks making it into senior management is that we can't break through to that upper level in the social scene. We're not seen at the cocktail parties or at the country clubs, and, frankly, they don't want us there."

The fact that the American news media were dominated by white, well-off, middle-aged men did not, however, deter right-wing critics from charging that the media were populated largely by anti-establishment liberals out to undermine the American way of life. The accusation came originally from the Nixon White

House. In the midst of their campaign of wiretapping and spying against perceived domestic political opponents, Nixon officials continued to be incensed by the "nattering nabobs of negativism" in the liberal news media, whom they viewed as the real enemies of truth and freedom in the United States. Vice President Spiro Agnew led the attack, delivering speeches crafted by Patrick Buchanan, the right-wing ideologue who would resurface in the White House some fifteen years later as the director of communications during Ronald Reagan's second term. The press was too powerful, the Nixon indictment charged, too critical of the government, too out of touch with "real" Americans.

It was all part of the broader Nixon campaign to intimidate the press, and, crude though it was, it had considerable lasting effect. Well into the Reagan era, the press remained very sensitive to accusations of so-called liberal bias in news coverage. Ironically, it was the news organizations themselves which, unwittingly or not, gave the idea sufficiently wide circulation and respectability to turn it into conventional wisdom. Though one rarely heard the press criticized for being too cozy with the powers that be, journalists and news executives did take the contrary idea seriously enough to spend considerable time and news space ventilating it. To be sure, the charge of liberal bias was usually denied, but in the process the right-wing critique gradually came to be regarded as the standard, indeed virtually the only, public criticism of the press.

The consequences could be comical. Reporting the results of a public opinion poll about the news media in August 1981, *The Washington Post* seemed surprised that "the complaints aired by the public are at variance with complaints repeatedly voiced by the growing corps of professional media critics." For example, while such critics liked to argue that the press "tries to tear down the government in Washington," a 40 percent plurality of the public had exactly the opposite complaint: that major news organizations were "not critical enough" of the government. Likewise, in coverage of politics and politicians, noted the *Post*, "the public sees bias but perhaps not in the same terms as the critics. The press and TV networks were unfair to Jimmy Carter, a Democrat, but are treating Republican Ronald Reagan fairly, according to the survey."

A 1985 study conducted by the Gallup Organization for Times

Mirror (the huge media conglomerate whose holdings included the *Los Angeles Times* and *Newsday*) and advertised as "the most comprehensive study ever conducted of public attitudes toward the press" yielded similar conclusions. Although 41 percent of those questioned did see news organizations as liberal, only 22 percent believed news reporting was liberally biased. Moreover, a majority of respondents seemed to feel that the press was not too hard but too soft on the powers that be; 53 percent thought that the press was too "often influenced by powerful people and organizations," including the federal government, big business, labor unions and the military. In a phrase, most Americans saw the press as "a sheep in wolf's clothing."

At the same time, there did exist a number of individuals within the press, some holding positions of genuine authority, whose views placed them on the left side of the American political spectrum. Exactly how sizable this proportion was—and what that implied about news coverage—were contentious issues. Corporate and right-wing spokesmen, early in the Reagan administration, hailed two studies in particular as evidence that journalists held extreme liberal views and were thus "out of step" with the rest of the populace. Stanley Rothman of Smith College, S. Robert Lichter and Linda Lichter, both of George Washington University, published the studies in 1981 and 1982. Among many other findings, their interviews with a random sample of 240 journalists at the nation's major news organizations suggested that 54 percent described themselves as "liberals," while only 17 percent were "conservatives." The remaining 29 percent were "middle of the road."

Serious questions were later raised about the scholarly integrity of the Rothman-Lichters study; its conclusions ran counter to a Brookings Institution study, for example, that found that 58 percent of Washington press corps members considered themselves either "conservative" or "middle of the road." The deeper flaw in the liberal-press thesis, however, was that it completely ignored those whom journalists worked for. Reporters could be as liberal as they wished and it would not change what news they were allowed to report or how they could report it. America's major news organizations were owned and controlled by some of the largest and richest corporations in the United States. These firms were in turn owned and managed by individuals whose politics were, in general, anything but liberal. Why would they employ journalists who consistently covered the news in ways they did not like?

To the class of super-rich and powerful businessmen who ultimately controlled the U.S. news media, Ronald Reagan was the most ideologically congenial President in living memory. Like most of their corporate brethren, the parent companies of America's major news organizations did very well under Ronald Reagan. The 1981 Reagan tax cuts in particular were a veritable bonanza for corporate America. The President's old employer (and, as of 1986, owner of the NBC television network) General Electric, for example, made nearly $10 billion in profits during the first Reagan term, yet paid not a penny in tax. According to a study by Citizens for Tax Justice, a tax reform organization, forty-four large corporations paid no tax on $57 billion of profits generated during Reagan's first term. Indeed, corporate tax subsidies tripled, from $40 billion to $120 billion, in the five years following passage of the 1981 tax cuts.

What ABC correspondent George Strait said about his own executive superiors by and large held true for the bosses of other major news organizations as well: "Clearly, the people who run Capital Cities and ABC are very comfortable with the people who are senior in the Reagan administration. Their basic values and approaches to the world are not dissimilar."

In theory, of course, that should not have mattered much; according to the ideology of mainstream American journalism, the owners and corporate overseers of news organizations exercised no power over news decisions; journalists were free to say and write whatever they wished. True, they did answer to executive superiors who in turn answered to corporate superiors, but it was the journalists themselves who made the hundreds of decisions large and small that went into producing each day's newspaper or broadcast. As Sam Donaldson once boasted: "People ask, Do your bosses at ABC tell you what to say? The answer is no."

In fact, the answer was not so clear-cut, as Donaldson himself discovered early in the Reagan administration when a sharp disagreement with Roone Arledge, according to Donaldson, "almost cost me my job." In November 1981, President Reagan did ABC the favor of helping to dedicate its new Washington news bureau.

Apparently ABC management had privately agreed to a White House demand that there be no questions from reporters at the event. Donaldson (along with United Press International White House correspondent Helen Thomas) unwittingly questioned Reagan anyway, provoking Arledge to snap, in front of scores of observers, "I was only joking when I said the first question would be by Sam Donaldson." To which Donaldson replied in what he hoped was a lighthearted tone, "So, fire me." "You know," responded Arledge, "that's not a bad idea." Ironically, Donaldson survived the face-to-face confrontation thanks in part to an intervention on his behalf by Ronald Reagan.

It was true that superiors rarely interfered overtly in the news-gathering and reporting process; nor did they often tell journalists what to say, at least not directly. The system of ideological control usually worked more subtly than that. In particular, it told journalists (again, generally implicitly) not so much what *to* say as what *not* to say. Like the most important rules in any bureaucracy, the news business commandments were not written down anywhere, or even acknowledged to exist by most members of the community. Nor could they be, if collective belief in the ideal of total journalistic freedom was to be preserved. Rather, journalists learned the unwritten rules as they went about their daily routine and pursued their career path. They discovered the limits on expression when they bumped up against them, and they accepted those limits or they got out. As Ben Bagdikian wrote: "Some intervention by owners is direct and blunt. But most of the screening is subtle, some not even occurring at a conscious level, as when subordinates learn by habit to conform to owners' ideas."

Management did not, for example, have to circulate memos or post notices on the newsroom bulletin board to remind journalists that advertising revenues paid the news organization's bills. As Walter Cronkite wrote in a 1977 article in *Chief Executive* magazine, there existed a "symbiotic" relationship between U.S. journalists and U.S. business leaders. "Journalism can thrive only as long as the business community remains healthy enough to provide the funds. Business, on the other hand, depends on journalism to foster its own growth—through the dissemination of information through news and advertising."

"I've heard of cases where executives come down on reporters because of their criticism of Ronald Reagan, but that's rare," said

Saul Friedman of Knight-Ridder. "What is more the problem, and it's more subtle, is that editors and publishers around the country are in a milieu in which Reagan is liked. They go to the country club or the cocktail parties or the Rotary Club lunches; that's the way it works. If you want to be classical about it, newspapers in many of our cities are edited these days for the people who do vote, who do buy, who do advertise, who have profited a great deal from Ronald Reagan's presidency, for what I call the Bloomingdale's part of town and not necessarily the K Mart part of town."

Veteran Washington reporter James Deakin described in his book *Straight Stuff* the subtle process by which the limits on discussion got passed from the top of news organizations down the hierarchy to the reporters who actually went out and gathered and reported the news. The following passage refers to the Eisenhower era, but corresponds with what a number of journalists said privately about their own news organizations during the Reagan years:

> Most newspaper publishers were Republicans. Their editors were salaried employees. . . . The reporters knew this. They tried sporadically but they could not demonstrate a full-scale alternative to the official line. And they knew that if they somehow succeeded in doing this, they would find it virtually impossible to get it into print. So they did not try too hard. [Eisenhower press secretary James] Hagerty knew this, too. It was what you call an atmosphere, a climate.

The owners, after all, were the ones who decided (either directly or through their board of directors) who would be appointed to run their news organizations. The power to appoint a newspaper's or a magazine's top editor or a television network's president was basic to the character and performance of the organization, for that individual would in turn decide who would be hired to fill the organization's other key jobs. And it was only human nature for owners to pick someone they trusted not to offend their interests and sensibilities. As Bagdikian wryly noted: "It is a rare corporation that appoints a leader considered unsympathetic to the desires of the corporation." At the same time, it was a rare editor or news executive who did not wish to maintain at least the appearance of editorial independence. He thus was often torn between obedience to his superiors and loyalty to his crew. As former CBS News president William Leonard explained: "As president of the news division, your fundamental responsibility is to the people and mission of the news division. On the other hand, you are subject to orders. You have a boss, you have to fight for and husband your money, fight for your [air]time, think about ratings. Because if you don't, in the long run they're going to get another boy. It's like a ball club; if the team drops from first to eighth place, they fire the manager. You try to protect everybody else in the division from thinking those corporate thoughts as much as possible, [and] keep the corporate people off your people's backs so they can do their jobs."

But increasingly during the 1980s the newspaper editor or network president was himself becoming one of "the corporate people." The change was evident at the 1985 annual meeting of the American Society of Newspaper Editors. A report on the meeting in *The New York Times* noted that "one of the traditional pleasures of being a newspaper editor has been the role of defending the sanctity of the paper's news operation from encroachments by the business side of the paper, represented by the publisher." But the "adversarial atmosphere" this had engendered at previous ASNE meetings had now "almost completely disappeared. . . . As newspapers have been consolidated into chains and the chains have grown into communications conglomerates, editors have increasingly become key executives in a corporate structure whose product is news," the report explained. "The editor's role now often includes participating in such corporate functions as strategic planning and marketing."

Even in previous decades, unbridled editorial independence had been a myth. If he was to keep his job, the editor, or network president, had to obey and enforce at least the most insistent of his corporate superiors' orders—though sometimes, for appearance' sake, he did so surreptitiously. For example, in his memoirs of his many years as managing editor of *The New York Times*, Turner Catledge revealed that he used to pass on the suggestions of publisher Arthur Hays Sulzberger to reporters and editors as if they were Catledge's own so they would not feel that "the publisher was constantly looking over their shoulders. In truth, however, he was."

Of course, the journalists on the receiving end of such signals were usually quick to recognize if not internalize them. After all, failure to do so made rising within the organization and even getting on the air or into print all but impossible. What evolved, then, was an insidious form of self-censorship, wherein journalists modified their behavior according to the perceived (if rarely stated) desires of superiors and rationalized it according to the catchall doctrine of objectivity. "You get to know the [senior producers'] and executive producer's idiosyncrasies," explained *CBS Evening News* producer Richard Cohen, "and you choose to cross them or not, and most people didn't."

"They don't tell you directly what to do, they don't have to," one former very senior network journalist unwilling to be identified said about the higher-ups in his organization. At weekly editorial meetings with his executive superiors, this man recalled, "there wasn't a direct mandate politically to cover a story in a certain way. It was always [phrased], 'Shouldn't we be doing this?' " The roundabout manner in which such editorial direction was given meant that "in most cases it's very difficult to put fingerprints on the decisions." Proving political motivation was particularly difficult, since "you never talk about a correspondent's politics. It's 'I don't like how he's addressing the story,' or something like that." Noting that "the first impact is who they put in the job, and second, people are conditioned to respond and think in certain ways," this source drew a parallel between what journalists gave up in editorial independence in order to have such high-status jobs and "a politician and what he's sold by the time he's gained office." And should any journalist who had risen that high still be inclined to exceed the limits of appropriate news coverage, he would find himself blocked by barriers invisible to the naked eye but impenetrable nonetheless. "If you go outside the parameters, it's like bumper cars," this source explained. "You hit the wall and get bounced back."

• • •

IF THE NEWS MEDIA'S rules of conduct and corporate identity made it such a reliable articulator and enforcer of governing-class perspectives, why did the Reagan (or any other) administration have to worry about taming it in the first place?

Partly because news reporting was by nature a threat to authority. The founding purpose and tradition of journalism was to pursue and report the truth, to describe things as they were, even if that meant, as it usually did, challenging, angering, or otherwise offending powerful interests and individuals. As much as the press had been co-opted over the years and diverted from its original adversarial course, there still beat in the journalistic heart, admittedly more faintly at some times than others, an instinctive resistance to consistently reporting what was not true.

Moreover, most journalists prided themselves on being no one's fool or political errand boy. As Robert Kaiser of *The Washington Post* said: "A good editor in this or any other newsroom would much rather embarrass the President than make him look good. That is in the journalistic ethos, I think, provided it is fair." Although his colleagues in the press often did not live up to Kaiser's boast, it was true that in most journalists a commitment to objectivity coexisted with a strong reformist impulse and a sense of responsibility to serve as (loyal) critics of government. They were not disposed to radical criticism of the American system per se, but they did believe in making the system work better. Like early-twentieth-century Progressives, they believed in exposing at least certain forms of incompetence, corruption and injustice. In the words of the *Post*'s David Hoffman: "Reporters and editors, because they are reformers, like to see government that works. We're always begging for it, and writing about it when it doesn't."

Yet another potential cause of friction between the news media and the government was the modern media's insatiable appetite for information. Because information was what the press sold to make its money, it wanted lots of it, and squawked when it didn't get it. Michael Deaver's "manipulation by inundation" strategy effectively quelled such complaints during most of the first Reagan term. But shortly after Deaver departed came the Beirut hostage crisis of June 1985, when hijackers seized control of TWA flight 847 in midair and diverted it to Beirut, where they killed one American and held another thirty-nine hostage for some seventeen days. The U.S. networks broadcast round-the-clock coverage of the situation, and were harshly criticized for it. By elevating the story in the American mass consciousness to a level where domestic pressure to obtain release of the hostages became virtually irresistible, such saturation coverage unquestionably made things more difficult for the Reagan White House. It both forced the administration to negotiate with the kidnappers and weakened its hand in the negotiations themselves.

The Beirut story was a case where the major networks' usual

allegiance to officialdom clashed with the one force capable of overwhelming it—the networks' desire to attract the largest possible audiences. TV journalists realized that what made the story gripping television was the human drama of the thirty-nine Americans held hostage. Who could forget the image of TWA pilot John Testrake answering a reporter's questions through the cockpit window, then ducking back inside when his captor waved an automatic pistol in front of his face? The networks wanted film of such moments, the more the better, and they wanted it before their competitors. If that meant broadcasting pictures that had been staged by hijackers, or cramping the negotiating position of the United States government, those were secondary concerns.

But the single most important reason why a press disposed toward reporting and reflecting the views of the governing class could make trouble for a President was that there were usually important disagreements within that class over how the nation should be governed. Republicans and Democrats alike, for example, agreed that the United States should maintain a global military posture to protect overseas interests and oppose Communism, but they frequently disagreed over such specifics as how large a force, what interests it should protect, when it should do so and how.

During the Reagan years, the debate over Central America was a perfect example. Official Washington disagreed over means, not ends, when it came to U.S. policy toward the region. Nearly everyone concurred that the Sandinista government in Nicaragua was a menace to U.S. interests; Communism and Soviet expansionism had to be resisted. There was also strong elite consensus against sending U.S. combat troops to fight there. But should the Sandinistas be pressured to alter their behavior through diplomacy and negotiations (many Democrats' preference) or should a CIA-created mercenary army be used to overthrow the government outright (the Reagan position)? The disagreement was over tactics, but the contending positions were deeply held and strongly argued, and were reflected as such in mainstream news coverage. Thus the Reagan administration found the press a compliant enough instrument when it came to demonizing Nicaragua as a dangerous Communist tyranny; few if any voices in official Washington disagreed with Reagan on that score. But the administration was less successful at generating uniformly positive coverage of its preferred policy, supporting the contras, because much of the rest of the Washington elite had strong reservations about such a course.

All of which recalls the point that the doctrine of objectivity often made the press a hostage to the political debate within official Washington. When strong disagreement existed within the establishment over a given policy, journalists could do story after story questioning the policy. But on issues where the elite consensus was broad and firm, dissent by the press was sporadic at best.

News media scholar Daniel Hallin offered a useful way of thinking about this phenomenon in his book on news coverage of the Vietnam War, *The "Uncensored War."* The journalist's world, he suggested, was divided into three separate regions, each governed by different journalistic standards. Those three regions he represented with a drawing of three concentric circles, in a figure resembling a doughnut. The innermost region, the "hole" of the doughnut, was the Sphere of Consensus. This was motherhood-and-apple-pie territory, encompassing values and beliefs neither journalists nor society as a whole regarded as controversial—the superiority of American democracy over Soviet Communism, for example, or the need for a strong national defense. "Within this region journalists do not feel compelled either to present opposing views or to remain disinterested observers," wrote Hallin. "On the contrary, the journalist's role is to serve as an advocate or celebrant of consensus values."

Nor did journalists feel bound to impartiality in the outermost region, the Sphere of Deviance. This region—"outside" the doughnut—was "the realm of those political actors and views which journalists and the political mainstream of the society reject as unworthy of being heard"—the Ku Klux Klan or the Communist Party U.S.A., to cite two extreme examples. Here, according to Hallin, "journalism becomes, to borrow a phrase from [social theorist] Talcott Parsons, a 'boundary-maintaining mechanism': it plays the role of exposing, condemning or excluding from the public agenda those who violate or challenge the political consensus. It marks out and defends the limits of acceptable political conflict."

Finally, the middle region was the Sphere of Legitimate Controversy. "The limits of this sphere," Hallin argued, "are defined primarily by the two-party system—by the parameters of debate between and within the Democratic and Republican parties—as well as by the decision-making process in the bureaucracies of the executive branch." In other words, the limits were defined by the official Washington debate. It was only within this charmed region that journalists actually practiced the objectivity and balance they preached, and their virtue in this regard depended largely on where within the Sphere of Legitimate Controversy the issue they were covering was located. Near the border of the Sphere of Consensus, wrote Hallin, "objectivity involves a straight recitation of official statements. Farther out, as the news deals with issues on which consensus is weaker, the principle of balance is increasingly emphasized" and coverage featured more criticism of official policy.

Vietnam, the subject of Professor Hallin's book, was a good example of how, over time, the official consensus on a major public issue could shift, and with it, mainstream news coverage. Early in the 1960s, elite consensus was strong that the United States was right to fight in Vietnam and certain to win; as an issue, Vietnam fell just on the border between the Spheres of Consensus and Legitimate Controversy. Accordingly, news coverage, especially by journalists based in Washington, contained few criticisms of U.S. policy. The view that the United States did not belong in Vietnam was at this stage still considered part of the Sphere of Deviance and excluded from the news.

As time passed without any clear progress toward U.S. victory, doubts about the conduct (though not the rightness) of the war grew within officialdom, and Vietnam as an issue began drifting toward the middle of the Sphere of Legitimate Controversy. Proclamations by administration officials continued to dominate news coverage, but conflicting stories from reporters on the ground in Vietnam slowly began to increase in number and prominence. Although a grass-roots anti-war movement had risen up across the country, the idea of U.S. withdrawal from Vietnam continued to be ignored or dismissed by the mainstream press.

Not until Senator Eugene McCarthy's initially promising challenge to President Johnson for the 1968 Democratic presidential nomination did the anti-war position cross the threshold between the Spheres of Deviance and Legitimate Controversy and begin to be taken seriously. Shortly after, the Tet offensive of 1968 brought to ruin the U.S. elite consensus that the war could be won. As Walter Cronkite's special prime-time broadcast both indicated and hastened, the center was turning against the war. As more and more American GIs came home in body bags, and as the anti-war movement grew in strength and influence, popular support for the war deteriorated further. Reaction among the elite was confused. Increasingly, official Washington split between "hawks," who believed in continuing and if necessary intensifying the war, and "doves," who urged various forms of disengagement. Just as the lack of dissent within the formal political system had made for uniformly positive press coverage of the war effort early on, rupture of the bipartisan consensus now made for relative turbulence. It is inconceivable, for example, that the press would have dared to publish the Pentagon Papers had not many "responsible" members of the American establishment—in the Congress, in business, in the academy—begun questioning the war by 1971. (Even so, all three television networks were apparently sufficiently intimidated by the Nixon administration's war on the press that they rejected the chance to break the story. And as Harrison Salisbury described in his book *Without Fear or Favor*, *The New York Times* nearly lost its nerve at the last minute as well.)

U.S. withdrawal from Vietnam eventually became the mainstream position in Washington. By 1972, the debate within the elite no longer centered on whether to pull out, but on when and under what conditions. Thus, in the space of approximately ten years, U.S. withdrawal from Vietnam went from being a "fringe" view that the press ignored to a mainstream view that the press implicitly endorsed. Whereas in the early 1960s the assumption animating U.S. news coverage was that the war in Vietnam should and could be won, by the early 1970s it was that the war was a quagmire from which the United States somehow had to extricate itself. Which is not to say that the press became a champion of the anti-war movement. Although the movement's goal of stopping the war was eventually embraced by politicians and hence the press, the analysis underlying that position, and in particular the view that the war was not just unwinnable but morally wrong, remained forever excluded from serious consideration, a permanent exile in the Sphere of Deviance.

Although news coverage clearly followed rather than led the

shift in opinion against the war, the press nonetheless soon came to be blamed for "losing" Vietnam. A similar myth grew up around the Watergate scandal. Each for their own reasons, right-wing press bashers and members of the press alike preferred to believe that Richard Nixon had been driven from office by a vigilant Washington press corps that refused to rest until all the facts about the bugging of Democratic headquarters and the subsequent attempted cover-up were brought before the public. In fact, with the exception of *The Washington Post*, the American press was scandalously late in coming to the story—for months, Carl Bernstein and Bob Woodward of the *Post* were the only reporters pursuing it—and timid in its coverage. Moreover, as Robert Kaiser of the *Post* subsequently remarked, "Woodward and Bernstein would have died on the vine were it not for the official investigations they set off." In that sense, Watergate was a further illustration of how press coverage tended to follow elite opinion and action in Washington; not until Congress set up special committees to investigate did the rest of the press get fully involved in reporting the Watergate story.

Watergate and Vietnam nonetheless were seized upon by right-wing critics as further evidence that Nixon, Agnew and Company had been right all along: the national news media were too powerful, too negative, too aggressive, too liberal, too much. With Nixon now gone, the threat of the federal government's stripping news corporations of their broadcasting licenses had receded, but attacks on the freedom and independence of the press intensified from another quarter. A national press corps which seemed no longer to assume that the government was basically good and trustworthy posed a threat not only to politicians but to the stability of the broader social order. Those individuals and institutions who worried about such matters quickly mobilized in opposition.

"The most important new source of national power in 1970, as compared to 1950, was the national media," Samuel Huntington, a Harvard professor of political science and frequent government consultant, wrote in 1975. Huntington was one of dozens of scholars hired to explore the theme of "the governability of democracy" for the Trilateral Commission, a private group founded by banker David Rockefeller and composed of highly influential business, political and academic figures from the United States,

Western Europe and Japan. It was the Trilateral Commission's view that the United States suffered from an "excess of democracy" which prevented the country from making the difficult and painful choices needed to set things right again. On the specific topic of the press, Huntington asserted, "There is . . . considerable evidence that the development of television journalism contributed to the undermining of governmental authority."

Backed by large corporate foundations, right-wing think tanks and other representatives of the American power structure, the attack on the press seemed aimed at convincing both the press itself and the public at large that journalists were out of step with the rest of the country. Toward that end, countless studies were commissioned, seminars convened and articles written. The misleadingly named pressure group Accuracy in Media was formed to campaign against alleged anti-business and pro-Communist bias within the press. The perspective and the intent of right-wing forces were made clear in an article, "The Power of the Press: A Problem for Our Democracy," published in 1977 by Max Kampelman, an adviser to conservative Democratic senator Henry Jackson who later was appointed President Reagan's chief nuclear arms negotiator. Accusing members of the press of not sharing the values of American society—"Journalists are reported to have an instinctive suspicion and distrust of authority, particularly governmental authority"—Kampelman argued that the time had come to limit the "relatively unrestrained power of the media."*

A number of press bosses seemed to agree. Fresh from her Watergate triumph, *Washington Post* publisher Katharine Graham called for a retreat from the journalistic aggressiveness that had earned the *Post* its Pulitzer. The press assumed an increasingly conservative hue through the 1970s as more and more columnists with right-of-center politics began appearing in major newspapers. As David Gergen noted in a 1981 interview with *Public Opinion* (the magazine he edited for the American Enterprise Institute during the Carter years): "In terms of the syndicated columnists, if there is an ideological bias, it's more and more to the right." Other signs of a shift to a form of journalism more accommodating to political and corporate authority were also in

---

* In a November 1987 interview, Mr. Kampelman asserted that the problem had only gotten worse over the intervening ten years.

evidence, most notably a steep decline in investigative reporting.

The assault on the press was in fact but a part of a broader rightward shift within the American power elite during the 1970s. Although the corporate agenda would not be fully implemented until President Reagan took office, its political ascendancy was clear even during the Carter administration. By the end of his term, President Carter had acceded to most of big business's demands, often reversing his previous stands in the process. On taxes, for example, he had promised progressive reform but ended up signing a law that, among other regressive features, cut the top capital-gains rate by more than 40 percent. He beat a similar retreat from his initial policy of aggressive enforcement of federal regulatory laws. But it was not only Carter who bowed to the political strength of corporate forces; Congress was an equal and eager partner. Unsatisfied with the 5 percent real increase in military spending proposed by the Carter White House in 1980, for example, Congress added more funds on its own, eventually enacting a 1981 defense budget with 9 percent real growth built into it.

With occasional individual exceptions, the news media joined in encouraging the pro-corporate economic policies, the arms buildup and the more aggressive foreign policy. As press historian James Boylan later wrote in the *Columbia Journalism Review*,

> Starting with the seizure of the Teheran embassy late in 1979 and the Russian occupation of Afghanistan the press had both reported and joined what George Kennan called the greatest "militarization of thought and discourse" since World War II. Roger Morris wrote in 1980: "American opinion this winter bristled with a strident, frustrated chauvinism—and, from sea to shining sea, American journalism bristled with it." . . . [T]he press, led by television, played the patriot, obsessively focusing on crisis and suggesting that America, not individuals, had been held hostage. At the same time, the press thus cannily painted itself as being as loyalist as the jingo in the street.

News coverage of Carter grew suddenly kinder immediately after the embassy seizure, but as months passed without the hostages being released, and as the domestic economy continued to deteriorate, the press seemed to turn on Carter with a vengeance. True to its habit of reflecting the thoughts and actions of official Washington, press coverage early in the administration had often portrayed Carter as weak, indecisive and incompetent. At the time, such charges had been based largely on his failures on Capitol Hill. Now they were being revived, with the added complaint that Carter seemed unwilling or unable to defend American honor around the world.

Contrary to the liberal press thesis, Carter was criticized by the news media by and large from the right, not the left. He was not, for example, attacked for agreeing to admit the brutal and widely hated Shah of Iran to the United States for medical treatment, thus precipitating the embassy seizure that proved his undoing, nor for sharply cutting federal aid to the poor, blacks and cities in 1980. He was denounced instead for not being tough enough, either abroad or at home.

One *New York Times* political reporter remembered hearing just such an attack on Carter from *Times* editor A. M. Rosenthal at the 1980 Democratic National Convention. "I was sitting in the stands waiting for a speech to start," this reporter said, "when suddenly Abe walks up and sits down next to me and launches into this incredible diatribe against Carter, all about how he despised Carter for his weakness, how he'd been a terrible President, and on and on. As I sat there listening to him, I thought to myself, 'I can't believe it—Abe's voting for Ronald Reagan. This New York Jew who grew up poor in the Depression, went to City College, and spent his life at a newspaper thought of as a bastion of liberalism is going to vote for Ronald Reagan.' "

(Mr. Rosenthal recalled no such conversation. He did say that he considered Carter "an ineffective President. But I'll always have a soft spot in my heart for Jimmy Carter," he added, "because he made human rights a major political issue.")

To a press already rapidly, if largely unconsciously, shifting to the right, the 1980 presidential election was the proverbial coup de grace. William Greider of *The Washington Post* called the election "quite traumatic for the press, editors and reporters. Not on a partisan level, as conservatives imagine, but because it seemed to confirm the message of the critics [that the press was out of touch with the rest of the country]. The general aura and dimensions of Reagan's victory were far beyond what the press imagined might happen. It was a sense of 'My God, they've elected this guy who nine months ago we thought was a hopeless clown.' Similar trauma went on in Congress, and throughout 1981 they were reacting in a similar way: 'Hey, there's something going on here we don't understand and we don't want to get in the way.' It was a semi-conscious kind of feeling that I know existed but never gets articulated, but was in everybody's head.''

But if Reagan's victory startled many working journalists, it left some of their superiors positively overjoyed. In a speech delivered a week after inauguration day 1981, Associated Press president and general manager Keith Fuller enthusiastically welcomed the arrival of Ronald Reagan and all he represented. Asserting that Americans were ready to throw off the oppressive, degenerate legacy of the 1960s, Fuller interpreted the November election results as evidence that a nation was saying, "We don't believe that the union of Adam and Bruce is really the same as Adam and Eve in the eyes of creation. We don't believe that people should cash welfare checks and spend them on booze and narcotics. We don't really believe that a simple prayer or a pledge of allegiance is against the national interest in the classroom. . . . But most of all, we're sick of your self-perpetuating, burdening bureaucracy weighing ever more heavily on our backs.''

For all the talk during the 1970s about the press being too powerful and aggressive for the nation's good, its gradual shift back to the traditional posture of deference suggested rather that it was indeed a sheep in wolf's clothing—a sheep that, consciously or not, ended up following the lead of its corporate superiors. As William Greider said about the major news organizations: "They're powerful institutions. Their own sensibility is that they do share in the governing process; whether that's right or wrong, that's how they look at themselves; therefore, they have to be responsible within that governing elite. . . . They perceived over a period of years that the sensibilities and direction of the governing elite were shifting, and they'll not long be out of step with that.''

6

"JELLY-BEAN JOURNALISM"

WHEN Ronald Reagan arrived in January 1981 to begin his term as the fortieth President of the United States, he was blessed to inherit a national press corps that had long since abandoned the mildly adversarial posture of the late Nixon years in favor of a more deferential attitude toward conservative ideology and authority. After a decade in which it had occasionally exposed wanton abuse of state power, and absorbed the political pressure and discomfort such behavior entailed, the American press seemed to welcome a chance to prove its patriotism and get back on the team. In David Gergen's words, as Reagan came to power "there was a consensus within the press" toward returning to the traditional posture of deference that the press had exhibited toward the government in the days before Vietnam and Watergate. "I think there was a feeling on the part of the press corps when Reagan came in that somehow they had been a participant in a lot of presidential hangings and that they wanted to stand back from the rope this time," continued Gergen. "There is no question in my mind there was more willingness to give Reagan the benefit of the doubt than there was [for] Carter or Ford."

"The return to deference," explained Ben Bradlee of *The Washington Post*, "was part of the subconscious feeling we had . . . that we were dealing with someone this time who really, really, really disapproved of us, disliked us, distrusted us, and that we ought not give him any opportunities to see he was right." Bradlee added, "You know, initially after Watergate the public was saying about the press, 'Okay, guys, now that's enough, that's enough.' The criticism was that we were going on too much, and trying to make a Watergate out of everything. And I think we were sensitive to that criticism much more than we should have been, and that we did ease off."

A docile press was not Ronald Reagan's only piece of good fortune. Over the previous several years, consensus had been building among the nation's political and economic elites for vast increases in military spending and, in economic policy, a virtual class war involving reduced social spending, repeal of federal environmental, labor and health regulations and massive new tax reductions for corporations and the well-to-do. The substantive arguments advanced to support these policies were flimsy retreads of previously discredited notions of "trickle-down economics" and "The Russians Are Coming," and if judged on their merits would have been laughed out of the political arena. But partly as a result of immense organized pressure from business interests, partly because of losses incurred at the polls the previous November, the Democratic party that faced Reagan in January 1981 was in shambles. Dispirited, divided, torn between fealty to their corporate constituency and loyalty to their working-class base, the ostensible opposition party was, to put it mildly, indisposed to mount vigorous resistance to the Reagan agenda.

But the most dramatic piece of luck to fall into Reagan's lap was Iran's decision to release the American hostages on the very day he was inaugurated. The optimism and good cheer that permeated every presidential inaugural was magnified a hundredfold in Reagan's case by the news that the human symbols of America's apparently declining global power were at last coming home. Though it was President Carter who had secured their release, it was Reagan who found himself basking in a national outpouring of relief, patriotism and gratitude.*

What made the hostage release an extra windfall for Reagan was the chance it gave him to lay claim, virtually overnight, to the kind of mass public support he had been unable to earn at the polls in November. Although little attention was paid to the figure at the time, a mere 27 percent of the eligible voting public— barely one in four registered adult Americans—had cast their

---

* In fact, it may have been more than just luck that brought the hostages home on the very day Reagan became President. Persuasive evidence was later uncovered suggesting that 1980 Reagan campaign advisers may have cut a deal with Iran to delay the hostage release until Reagan's inauguration day. Indeed, this alleged deal may well have been the genesis of the Iran-contra affair that eventually crippled the Reagan presidency: the quid pro quo for the delay was reportedly a guarantee of future U.S. arms deliveries to Iran, which had just come under attack by Iraq. See Notes section for details.

ballots for Reagan in the 1980 election. That did not, however, deter White House and other conservative spokesmen from later pointing to Reagan's more impressive margin in the electoral college and proclaiming that he had been given a "mandate" by the American people to pursue his extreme policies. Nor, for that matter, did it deter many journalists from swallowing and repeating that line often enough to turn it into conventional wisdom. Part of the reason the body politic found this misrepresentation so easy to digest was the ground swell of patriotic affection that engulfed Reagan as he took office—a ground swell that in all likelihood would have engulfed whoever was President when the hostages returned.

Exploiting the window of opportunity presented by the hostages' return and building upon the national euphoria it generated were critical to the political prospects of the Reagan White House. Obviously, the cooperation of the press would be vital to that effort. If Reagan had been lucky to inherit a press already shifting to the right, it nevertheless remained up to him and his media massagers to keep it moving in that direction. Michael Deaver, David Gergen and the rest of the Reagan communications apparatus were acute enough to recognize the shift in mood and temper then underway within the press and, in subtle ways, to encourage it. Asked whether he had encouraged among the press the idea of stepping back from the hanging rope this time, Gergen replied, "Of course. . . . I brought it up in various conversations; it'd been a persistent theme of mine for a long time. There was a gentlemen's . . . there was a consensus within the press," Gergen corrected himself, that Reagan should be given a fair chance.

The press also had more concrete motives for treating Reagan well. Richard Cohen, an associate producer on the *CBS Evening News* during Reagan's first term, later coined a phrase for television's coverage of the Reagan White House: "jelly-bean journalism" he called it, and he was not proud of it. The phrase derived, of course, from the new President's much-remarked fondness for jelly beans, but it had a broader, more profound meaning as well. In Cohen's view, when Reagan came to power, network news operations were so tickled by the ability of the new White House media apparatus to provide visually appealing images of the President that they seemed to lose their journalistic bearings. Either not seeing or not minding the manipulation inherent in the process, they eagerly broadcast pictures carefully staged by Michael Deaver to project an endearingly positive image of Reagan as a man who wished harm to no one. White House control over television's portrayal of President Reagan was so pervasive early in the administration, Cohen felt, that "Deaver should have been listed as the executive producer on all the political stories we broadcast.

"Much more than newspapers, it was the institution of the evening news that would make it or break it for Reagan," Cohen added. "I think it was obvious to the Reagan people that if they gave us pictures of Ron kissing Nancy or giving a wink to the camera, it would get on the air. We were slow to realize we were being suckered, and when we did we didn't care much about it. It may just be too much to ask an executive producer to pass up a great picture."

Looking back on it four years later, Cohen was convinced that the first six months of Ronald Reagan's presidency were the key to understanding his relationship with the press. "You know how in child psychology they say that the first three to four years of someone's life lock in behavior patterns and character traits that last a lifetime?" he asked rhetorically. "I think Reagan's relationship with the media was established that first year in the same way."

It is hard to say whether White House cajoling or news media self-censorship was the stronger goad in producing the extremely friendly news coverage that greeted the Reagan administration in 1981. Both factors clearly were at work, and in many instances the players themselves probably could not say why they did what they did. In the very first weeks of his presidency, for example, an ABC News camera crew visited Reagan in the Oval Office for a routine interview. Three-by-five index cards in hand, the President eloquently delivered the statements his staff had prepared, and in short order the interview was over. But no sooner had Reagan finished speaking than he strode over to his desk, reached into a drawer and happily pulled on a small green finger monster. Grinning and providing his own sound effects, he wagged his fierce little friend at the camera crew three times, winked broadly and left the room, chuckling. The ABC producer in charge of the event remembered that a White House "elbow grabber" quickly approached him and nervously asked, "You weren't rolling on that, were you?" Inexplicably, the producer assured the aide, falsely, that no, they had not been. Later, in an illustration of the obverse of Richard Cohen's "jelly-bean journalism" theory, the videotape in question was buried in the ABC archives, never to be broadcast.

Squelching embarrassing pictures or highlighting flattering ones, it was all part of getting the new President off to a good start. One of David Gergen's pet theories about news management held that a White House could not hope to govern successfully unless it could get *its* version of reality through the "filter" of the press and out to the American public. But especially during the early months of the Reagan administration, the press resembled less a filter than a clear pane of magnifying glass. The ability of the White House media apparatus to project through that glass virtually whatever images it wished would prove a powerful weapon indeed during the campaign that spring and summer to gain congressional approval of Reagan's radically regressive tax and budget cuts.

While top Reagan officials later affirmed that press coverage of the administration had been fair and balanced throughout the first term, both Gergen and Deaver cited these first six months as an especially friendly time. It was not until August, they later said, that the press began to turn critical. By that time, of course, Reagan and "the fellas," as the President liked to refer to his aides, had, with lots of Democratic help, already gotten their astonishing economic package passed on Capitol Hill and thereby set in motion one of the greatest government-engineered transfers of wealth in modern U.S. history.

Equally if not more important, they had transformed the landscape of American politics. Through skillful manipulation of the public dialogue in the press and adroit insider maneuvering, they had elevated Reagan to near-godlike status in official Washington and nurtured the already gathering climate of timidity and reactionary conformity. With Reagan increasingly perceived as a leader one dared not challenge, the rightward shift in the premises underlying U.S. public policy that began in the late 1970s sharply accelerated, ensuring a more hospitable reception for other items on the Reagan agenda as well. In this sense, the successes of the first six months of 1981 were perhaps the most crucial of the entire Reagan presidency. For not only did they include the administration's single most important domestic policy achievement, the tax and budget cuts, they also laid the foundation for Ronald Reagan's continued domination of American political thought and action for years to come.

• • •

NOTWITHSTANDING their public claims of a Reagan mandate, the core group of strategists who made things happen in the Reagan White House were keenly aware from the very start of how delicate, even fragile, their political situation really was. Reagan had been catapulted into office less on the virtues of his own candidacy than on the strength of mass disappointment with Jimmy Carter and a vague sense that, as most Reagan voters had told exit pollsters, it was simply "time for a change." His advisers furthermore recognized that Reagan's extreme views put him well to the right of the majority of the American people and that he therefore lacked the breadth of popular support necessary to sustain a successful presidency. These shortcomings could be finessed in the short term—the return of the Iranian hostages and the traditional honeymoon period with the press would give the White House some much-needed breathing room and maneuvering space—but something would have to be done, and fairly quickly, if the President's right-wing agenda was to have any chance of becoming reality.

The strategy settled on by Reagan's advisers was a virtual monument to the elevation of image over substance. Recognizing that their strongest card was Reagan himself, the White House apparatus concentrated on two basic tactics. First, Mr. Reagan's public appearances would be carefully staged and controlled to emphasize his attractive persona and winning personality to television viewers. Second, he would be promoted not on the basis of his philosophy or his program but rather as a decisive, can-do leader who promised to get the country moving again after a period of turmoil and doubt.

"I always believed that if people got to see him, the other part of him besides what the media had written for years, people would like him," explained Mike Deaver. "I don't think that's true of every President. Johnson didn't care if he was liked. Carter couldn't be liked. We knew instinctively the qualities were there for Reagan, though, and all you had to do was manage it in such a way that those good qualities were emphasized, whether in the staging or the words."

"The whole theory going in was, if we go to the country and just try to sell conservatism straight up, it's not going to work," commented Gergen. "You don't have the kind of [political] base in the country to do that. What you do is start out with the base of, say, 35 percent [sic], people who believe in Reagan, mostly conservatives, and the question is, how do you build on that core base? The point was, if Reagan can be successful, and show that he is effective, people would come to believe in Reagan. And as they believe in Reagan, they would eventually come to agree with him on issues, and see him as sensible, and eventually his philosophy would have a lot more impact."

"The key to a successful presidency is that he be seen to be a leader—somebody who can convert his philosophy into policy goals," agreed James Baker. "And the way you do that is to pick your issues carefully, and make sure that once you pick them you win them. And also not to have the focus too diffuse. . . . If we had any success in those early years, it was because we were single-minded in our concentration on the economy in that first year."

"One of the critical points of that first year was to learn from the mistakes of the Carter administration, which had set a diverse initiative for the country when it sent up several legislative initiatives [right away]," explained Kenneth Duberstein, the Reagan administration's chief lobbyist in the House of Representatives in 1981. "If you can rivet public attention on one or two things, you have a less difficult time focusing the congressional mind-set. So the economic recovery program became *the* agenda. When Ronald Reagan spoke to the nation on television, or did a photo opportunity, or met with members of Congress, it was always on the economic recovery program."

As Michael Deaver was the man who controlled the President's personal schedule, his cooperation with this scheme was essential. It was also easily acquired, for as a former public relations executive, he knew instinctively that marketing a product required repeating the same simple message over and over again. "In 1981 and through the first half of '82 I would not allow anything to be put on the [President's] schedule that didn't have to do with economic reform," recalled Deaver. "I just said, 'That's all we're going to do.' " Asked whether he didn't encounter flak from officials elsewhere in the administration with different agendas, Deaver grinned. "Yes. But I prevailed, because it was working."

Managing the news flow was essential not just to selling Reagan to the public but, by extension, to selling his economic program on Capitol Hill. "The linkage between legislative priorities and communications priorities was exceedingly close that first year," confirmed Ken Duberstein. And the two officials most responsible for that achievement were James Baker and his chief deputy, Richard Darman.

"The critical element of the Baker stewardship, and it was very different from previous administrations, was that he was the only person in the White House who brought it all together," said David Gergen. "For one of the first times I'm aware of, we molded a communications strategy around a legislative strategy. We very carefully thought through what were the legislative goals we were trying to achieve, and then formulated a communications strategy which supported them."

The mechanism through which the administration's political and press strategies were coordinated was the Legislative Strategy Group. Credited by Gergen as "more responsible than any other group around there for the operational success of the Reagan presidency," the LSG was a brainchild of Richard Darman. The purpose of the LSG was to bring together in one small group all the relevant power points within the administration—connecting tactics with strategy and politics with substance. As Duberstein explained: "A high degree of coordination came out of there regarding our messages to the media, to the public, and so forth. . . . That's where the major linkages came together."

The Legislative Strategy Group became, in effect, the primary White House within the White House, and thus a principal means by which chief of staff James Baker managed to establish himself as the dominant power broker within the Reagan administration. It was quite a coup for a man who, just a year before, had been the campaign manager for candidate Reagan's chief rival, and it did not sit well with many of the President's most right-wing supporters, who thought Ed Meese was more disposed to "let Reagan be Reagan." Late in 1980, Reagan had relented to pressure from Deaver and campaign manager William Casey to name the more organized and efficient Baker as the White House chief of staff. In typical fashion, however, Reagan tried to split the difference by naming Meese as "counselor" to the President. Baker and Meese then met and drew up a written agreement specifying their respective areas of responsibility, which Reagan approved. As longtime Reagan aide Lyn Nofziger recalled: "When I looked at what Ronald Reagan assigned to Meese on the same day he appointed Jim Baker chief of staff, I said, 'Ed, you have just stolen the federal government.' It literally gave Meese control of everything except the White House staff. Ed is a nice man, he never took advantage of that. Jim Baker took advantage of what he had and tried very hard to relegate Meese into a secondary position. I don't know a better in-house politician than Jim Baker. . . . Baker brought in Gergen and Darman and kind of co-opted Deaver, and they really formed a clique within the White House that kind of took charge."

Although it got off to a promising start with two well-received nationally televised presidential addresses, the apparatus's grand plan for promoting President Reagan and his economic program was almost immediately sidetracked when Secretary of State Alexander Haig unilaterally launched his *own* propaganda campaign to build support for U.S. military action and other forms of aggression in Central America.

Haig and his aides began in early February to leak stories portraying Cuba and the Soviet Union as the source of revolution and turmoil in Central America. One of the first fruits of their labors was a February 6 *New York Times* article reporting that "the Soviet Union and Cuba agreed last year to deliver tons of weapons to Marxist-led guerrillas in El Salvador." The *Times* based its charge on "secret documents reportedly captured from the insurgents by Salvadoran security forces" and not only placed the story on the front page but made it the day's lead article. Such prominent placement in the nation's leading newspaper ensured that the story would be widely picked up in the rest of the U.S. press. This piggyback effect, combined with continued background briefings and public statements by Haig about "drawing the line" against so-called Soviet expansionism in El Salvador, quickly made Central America the hottest story of the day. Fortunately for Secretary Haig, most other news organizations displayed the same ferocious skepticism the *Times* did. At CBS, for example, former Richard Nixon personal aide-turned-television reporter Diane Sawyer told viewers on February 12 that "U.S.

officials say the evidence is unmistakable that the Cubans are resupplying the guerrillas in El Salvador under the direct sponsorship of the Soviet Union."

The campaign of carefully orchestrated leaks culminated February 23 in the highly publicized release of a State Department White Paper entitled "Communist Interference in El Salvador." By that time, the idea that foreign Communists were behind the unrest in Central America had been circulating through the news media long enough to take on a virtual life of its own; the claim had been repeated so often that few thought anymore to ask for proof. Most reporters, for example, apparently did not bother to examine the nineteen documents released in support of the paper (all of which were in Spanish anyway) and opted instead to file reports based on the eight-page summary provided by the State Department. It was routine procedure, and it resulted in a fantastic public relations coup for the State Department as reporters in effect reduced themselves to human transmission belts, disseminating propaganda that would later be revealed to be false.

The major news organizations ended up endorsing the White Paper claim that the Salvadoran insurgency was a "textbook case of indirect armed aggression by Communist powers through Cuba" virtually without dissent, with only fig leaves of perfunctory attribution clauses protecting their journalistic integrity. Typical was the report by NBC News State Department correspondent Bernard Kalb. Displaying the same allegiance to official U.S. pronouncements that would win him the job of official State Department spokesman in Reagan's second term, Kalb raised not a single question about the White Paper's veracity or relevance. The closest he came to skepticism was to note in introducing his story that the administration had "kept up its orchestrated campaign to focus attention on charges of Communist bloc involvement in El Salvador." Brandishing the White Paper on camera, Kalb added that it "contains almost two hundred pages of what are described as documents demonstrating Communist support of the Salvadoran insurgency. A second document refers to definitive evidence of the clandestine military support given by the Soviet Union, Cuba and their Communist allies to Marxist-Leninist guerrillas now fighting to overthrow the established government of El Salvador." To Kalb, the key question was not whether all this was true but what the United States was going to do about it. Specifically: "Is the Reagan administration contemplating any military action against Cuba, including a naval blockade to try to cut off military hardware going to the guerrillas?" And Kalb was almost restrained in comparison with his ABC News counterpart Barrie Dunsmore, whose gushing declaration that "this phone-book-sized report . . . firmly establishes the links between the leftist insurgents in El Salvador and Communist governments worldwide" was dramatized with an animated map showing the countries of Central America turning red, one by one.

The State Department's propaganda campaign was spectacularly successful. It directed the gaze of the press onto the issue it wished and, equally important, it set thè terms in which that issue would be discussed. True, the White Paper was eventually exposed as disinformation—reports by the Pacific News Service and, later, *The Wall Street Journal* and *The Washington Post* would reveal its key claims to be misleading distortions—but that was months in the future. And besides, those rebuttals would be given far less prominence in the media than the White Paper itself. Meanwhile, with very few exceptions, reports in the nation's major newspapers and on the three television networks trumpeted the new administration's claims about the dangers of Communist intervention in the United States' backyard.

Considering the situation on the ground in Central America and the actual U.S. role in the region, this parroting of Washington's self-serving claims by the American press was nothing short of shameful. If anyone, it was the United States, not Cuba or the Soviet Union, who was behind the hideous violence that racked El Salvador. Although Secretary Haig and the rest of the Reagan administration talked piously about defending democracy in El Salvador, the military junta which ruled that country was one of the most murderously repressive in the world. In March 1980, Archbishop Oscar Arnulfo Romero, who a month earlier had criticized the armed forces for human rights abuses and pleaded with President Carter not to send them more military aid, was assassinated while saying mass. In all, some 10,000 civilians were murdered in 1980, causing Archbishop Romero's successor to condemn the armed forces' "war of extermination and genocide against a defenseless civilian population." Not only was the United States supporting the El Salvador government as it slaughtered thousands of its own people; it was actively abetting that slaughter. By the time Reagan came to power in 1981, the United States had provided over $20 million in military aid to El Salvador and trained some 2,000 of its elite officers. Worse still, U.S. officials from the State Department, the CIA and other agencies had helped to establish and maintain the widely feared death-squad apparatus, whose hired hands had tortured and killed so many Salvadorans over the years. And now Haig and his colleagues in the Reagan administration wanted to increase U.S. backing of the junta.

But if Secretary Haig found it easy to promote his analysis of the situation in Central America through the press, he ran into trouble when he began pushing his preferred solution. At a news conference on February 27, four days after the release of the White Paper, Haig told reporters that the problem was "emanating first and foremost from Cuba and that it is our intention to deal with this matter at its source." By this time, there was not even a show of detachment in the media's reporting of Haig's accusations; Cuba was simply guilty as charged. Walter Cronkite, for example, on the night of Haig's news conference, did not bother to go through the motions of including a perfunctory denial of the charges by the Cuban government. He instead led off his broadcast by focusing on the U.S. response, reporting that "the Reagan administration today threatened to step up pressure against Cuba to stop that Communist nation's military assistance to leftist guerrillas in El Salvador." From the State Department's standpoint, this was fine as far as it went, but as soon as news organizations began exploring the implications of Haig's idea of going to the source, trouble started. Virtually overnight, a new theme emerged in news coverage: Was the United States getting involved in another Vietnam?

It was the last question that a President like Reagan, who had been plagued with a warmonger image for years, wanted to have raised, but as February turned into March he repeatedly found himself denying that he planned to send U.S. troops to Central America. Mr. Reagan seemed almost to resent the Vietnam parallels, but in an interview for this book, Robert McFarlane, the State Department counselor in 1981 and later Reagan's national security adviser, came to the media's defense. Referring to Cuban-Soviet involvement and a possible repeat of Vietnam, the twin themes that dominated U.S. press coverage of Central America, McFarlane commented that they "contribute to a very reasonable framework for press treatment of the issue. Evoking a recollection of Vietnam is a very legitimate point to make, because it simply exposes the reality of difficulty you will have in sustaining popular support for your policy. That's a valid criticism. You may not like it, but it's real."

The result was seemingly schizophrenic news coverage that warned of the potential for another Vietnam even as it endorsed Secretary Haig's indictment of Communist interference in Central America. ABC's *World News Tonight* broadcast of March 3 was a perfect example. An opening report by White House correspondent Sam Donaldson described President Reagan's efforts "to head off criticism that in Central America he is headed down the same road that led to U.S. military involvement in Vietnam." Then Capitol Hill correspondent Charles Gibson showed excerpts of the congressional debate over Haig's request for more military aid to El Salvador, noting that Senate Majority Leader Howard Baker did not believe such aid would lead the United States into a "quagmire." Then the news frame shifted back to Communist intervention with a long piece by Barrie Dunsmore, which Frank Reynolds introduced by declaring that the conflict in El Salvador was no longer merely a civil war but had "become in fact an East-West confrontation by proxy." Mr. Dunsmore was good enough to mention in closing that the security forces there were "very repressive," but the bulk of his report concerned U.S. efforts to counter "direct Cuban and indirect Soviet involvement in the arming of El Salvador's leftist insurgents." The highlight was his respectful recounting of a "modern-day domino theory" in which Cuba and Nicaragua first "subverted" El Salvador and then overran Honduras and Guatemala, "making Mexico very vulnerable."

Secretary Haig had scored some early successes, but both Jim Baker and Mike Deaver had been leery of the Central America initiative from the start, and once Haig's remarks about going to the source in Cuba triggered the rash of Vietnam stories, they were determined to act.

"Baker and I tried constantly to keep under control the whole Central America thing," recalled Deaver. "Haig wanted to go in there and clean house. I can't even *tell* you what he said; things that were outrageous. And I remember him saying, in his inim-

itable style, 'Mr. President, this is one you can *win!*' Talking about
Nicaragua.'' Shaking his head at the memory, Deaver added during a November 1986 interview, "This was five years ago: this is
one you can win, and you can win it quickly. Baker and I constantly cautioned the President about that. A, you cannot win.
B, the American people will not stand still for a war in Central
America.''

Extinguishing the fire of controversy generated by Haig's initiative was the first real damage-control operation undertaken by
the Reagan White House media apparatus, and thanks largely to
the press itself, it proved a remarkably easy task. The operation
had actually begun the day after the White Paper's release, when
White House officials put out the word that the press had given
the paper higher visibility than it deserved. Later, following a
formal White House decision in early March, word was passed
to the State Department to "low-key" El Salvador. The decision
reportedly irked Haig (who declined to be interviewed for this
book), though Robert McFarlane saw the wisdom in it.

"This is tough for us—Al, myself and all others in the foreign
policy community," McFarlane explained. "You have to realize,
a President in a given term may accomplish *two* important things,
moving the country in basically two new directions. Now, he may
choose to make both of them domestic. And that means you're
just going to have to live with that, if you're a loyal cabinet officer.
. . . Al wanted a major stress [and] the use of Reagan's high
political standing early in his first term to deal with Central America. [The] President didn't want to do that. He wanted to invest
that capital in tax reduction.''

In carrying out their orders to back off, State Department
officials actually had the nerve to blame the *press* for having made
too much of the Salvador issue, a charge that did not sit well with
the accused.

"I was personally as well as professionally incensed when Haig
blamed us for making too much of a story of El Salvador," recalled
Sanford Socolow, *CBS Evening News* executive producer at the
time. "If he'd been sitting across the room from me, I would have
punched him in the mouth! We got interested in El Salvador
basically because General Haig not only got interested but began
to trumpet the dangers of [Communist involvement in] El Salvador and going to the source. Look, television and the nightly

newscasts are still, and I think should be, reflections; they don't take initiatives. We didn't suddenly decide because we were sitting around sucking our thumbs, bored with what was going on elsewhere, that El Salvador was a big story. We were led to El Salvador by General Haig, and the administration."

And now they would be led away. Administration officials simply stopped talking about Central America to reporters and, in a vivid demonstration of the consequences of the media's passive definition of responsible journalism, news coverage, especially on television, immediately dried up. To be more precise, the U.S. press, with some exceptions, returned to the posture of indifference toward El Salvador it had maintained throughout the 1970s and even during the nightmarish year of 1980. El Salvador itself remained as newsworthy as ever. The war continued, as did the political killings—some 10,000 more civilians would perish at the hands of the armed forces during 1981 alone—but now that Washington was silent, news coverage all but stopped.

Three simple numbers—186, 60 and 62—tell the story. To wit: During the first three months of 1981, the three major networks broadcast a total of 186 news stories about El Salvador, an average per network of nearly five stories per week. During the next three months, from April to June, in the aftermath of the White House's decision to low-key the issue, the number of stories dropped to 60. And during the final *six* months of 1981, a mere 62 news stories were broadcast concerning the tiny, wretched country that, not long before, had been touted by U.S. television as so deserving of attention and so vital to the future of freedom in the Americas.

• • •

WHILE the Central America episode did show how easy it was to manipulate the press, from the perspective of the White House political-propaganda apparatus it nonetheless constituted a distinctly unwelcome distraction. Implementing Reagan's economic program was, after all, the principal goal of the first year. Precious time had now been wasted and political momentum lost. The good cheer that had greeted the newly elected President back in January had been squandered, and replaced by suspicions that he might plunge the nation into war after all.

"I was very worried during that time," recalled Gergen. "Peo-

ple forget this, but after January–February 1981 we began slipping. We were measuring this in the media, and as the attention
went off the economy and up on foreign policy and the situation
in El Salvador and Central America, and we saw stories about
going to the source in Cuba, Reagan began to slip in the polls.
He went down several points in February and March."

Ironically, the incident that, in Gergen's words, "gave us a
second life, a second honeymoon," was the President's near loss
of his life. The March 30 assassination attempt not only elicited
a wave of protective sympathy from the American masses; it
induced a tread-lightly attitude within the news media as well
and, among the White House press corps who covered him most
closely, a new respect for Reagan the man. Like the Hollywood
heroes he emulated, Reagan seemed to laugh in the face of death,
joking to the surgeons about to operate on him, "I hope you're
all Republicans." The press, Deaver observed, "saw a side of
him they didn't know about in the first few days after the assassination. It was a real revelation, that sense of humor and grace
under tremendous stress."

"There is a theory out there," noted Gergen, "I don't know
whether you can substantiate it, that the press held back a little
more" after the shooting. While a number of journalists made
the same point during interviews for this book, a comment Sam
Donaldson made in a 1982 interview with *Playboy* magazine put
the issue in broadest context. There were three reasons, said
Donaldson, why the press had not been as tough on Reagan as
it might have been. One (examined in more detail below) was
that during his first year in office he "beat Congress every time."
The other two? The man's "amiable style" and the attempt made
on his life.

Whatever political difficulties Reagan faced beforehand, "the
March shooting," said Gergen, "transformed the whole thing.
We had new capital." Getting shot can hardly be considered a
stroke of luck, but the fluke of Reagan's brush with death did
give the White House a much-needed second chance to assert
control within official Washington. Deaver, Gergen and the rest
of the propaganda apparatus skillfully exploited that opportunity
by encouraging an emphasis on the President as a Great Communicator whose program deserved the benefit of the doubt.
Throughout his April convalescence, the apparatus kept Reagan

favorably in the public eye by releasing to the press carefully staged official White House photos of him in various stages of recovery. While Democrats on Capitol Hill quarreled over details of pending budget resolutions, the White House, as budget director David Stockman later wrote, "was framing the question in far more politically compelling and dramatic terms: *Are you with Ronald Reagan or against him?*"

Less than a week after the assassination attempt, while Reagan was still in the hospital, Mike Deaver convened one of the first of the White House apparatus's Blair House meetings to decide how the "new capital" of which Gergen spoke could best be invested. The Blair House group endorsed a Gergen suggestion that the President's first public appearance be a nationally televised speech before a joint session of Congress to give a fresh boost to the economic program. This would focus official Washington's and therefore the news media's attention back on the economy, the issue the apparatus wanted to stress, and away from Central America.

In a world where nothing works exactly as planned, the Blair House strategy came about as close to perfection as possible. Reagan's April 28 speech was a masterpiece of political theater. Covered live by all the networks, its image of a fallen but now triumphantly recovered President engendered, at least according to press accounts, fresh feelings of patriotism and hope across the land. The network evening newscasts were second to none in leading the cheers. "A boffo performance!" exulted Frank Reynolds in leading off ABC's *World News Tonight* broadcast. NBC's Roger Mudd, quoting a Republican congressman, referred to the speech as "a velvet steamroller."

And the press seemed determined not to get in the way of that steamroller. Instead of critiquing the substance of the speech—what it meant—news coverage focused on the turn-tail-and-run response of Democrats on Capitol Hill; that is, on what it accomplished. Amidst their disarray the best that Democrats could manage was to sputter that the numbers in Reagan's speech had been inaccurate. In accordance with the media's definition of objective journalism requiring a reply from the opposition party, the charge was duly noted in the next day's news coverage. But television reporting in particular did little to settle the dispute, much less go beyond it and explain the ramifications of Reagan's proposals.

The contest, not its content, was what mattered. As Sam Donaldson concluded: "The lift the President's program may have gotten last night has very little to do with the facts and figures. It was the President as national hero returned, selling his plan on a wave of personal admiration and popularity."

Which is exactly how the apparatus would continue to sell the President and his plan. Time and again when the White House faced a close vote on Capitol Hill the claim was made that the American people had given Reagan a mandate for such changes in the November election. And time and again, despite the objective weakness of the case, the claim was uncritically transmitted in news stories.

Donaldson later denied that the press had done any such thing, protesting to me: "Most reporters thought the 1980 vote was to get Jimmy Carter out of there. I don't know of one who suggested in his copy that the vote was a mandate for Reagan's right-wing Republican economic program. Now Reagan shrewdly used the ten million [vote] margin to *claim* it was a mandate for his program, and the Congress went along with it, but it certainly wasn't led by a pack of reporters."

It was true, of course, that reporters did not lead the Reagan mandate chorus by unilaterally inserting statements to that effect in their copy. That, after all, would be editorializing. Rather, in an example of how the press often functioned as a clear windowpane for the White House apparatus, reporters simply gave Reagan officials a platform for making such statements themselves and then did not bother to question or otherwise balance them. In fact, on three separate occasions Donaldson did this himself. On May 4, after showing viewers footage of Vice President Bush attacking Democrats for trying "to thwart the mandate of the people," the ABC White House correspondent concluded his report not by challenging the mandate notion but by noting that it, and not the merits of the program, was now "the administration's main sales pitch." A similar claim by White House spokesman Larry Speakes was allowed to pass unchecked on June 3, as was another by President Reagan himself on June 16. (Donaldson was hardly unique in this regard. His counterparts at CBS, for example, filed similar reports on the May 4 and June 3 statements.)

Awed by Reagan's mastery of television and fearful of his

ability to sway public opinion, the Democrats also seemed more than willing to accept the mandate thesis. Quickly abandoning any pretense of being an opposition party, dozens of them fell into line behind the President while scores more simply refrained from voicing any strong or sustained criticism of his program. Thus on May 8 the House of Representatives gave Reagan his first big victory on economic policy, approving by a 60-vote margin a White House budget that slashed social spending while gorging the Pentagon.

The crumbling of the Democrats was crucial not just because it delivered victories on Capitol Hill but also because it made for decidedly less critical news coverage of the administration in general. As the opposition party, the Democrats were seen by most Washington journalists as virtually the sole responsible alternative voice to the administration. Thus, when Democrats' criticism of Reagan's program was tepid to nonexistent, the criticism included in news stories to balance administration claims was tepid to nonexistent.

True to its origin in the entertainment business, television news in particular was fascinated not by the pros and cons of President Reagan's program but by the spectacle of getting it passed on Capitol Hill. As the White House scored victory after victory, the media increasingly covered the story as if they were reporting a grudge match in the Roman Colosseum. News coverage, especially on television, focused primarily on Ronald Reagan as an unstoppable political phenomenon and all but ignored what it was he was actually winning and what it meant to the country.

If winning on Capitol Hill was central to the White House apparatus's strategy for promoting Reagan, using network television as a sort of national electronic bulletin board was central to winning on Capitol Hill. One of the great strengths of the White House apparatus was its ability to coordinate its political and its propaganda arms, to project through the press exactly the message needed to help shift votes in the Congress. According to Gergen, "one of the times it worked best was the comprehensive budget-cutting bills," voted on in late June 1981. Reagan by then had already won a number of crucial victories in his campaign to slash social spending, but they had, in effect, been preliminary rounds. This was the final vote needed to pass the entire budget package, and it looked as if the Democrats had the votes to defeat it. But in what David Stockman later called "a staggeringly dumb political blunder," a Democratic leadership fearful of Reagan's personal popularity tried to block a direct up-or-down vote on his budget. The Democrats wanted five separate votes, which would put members of Congress on the record on such specifics of the Reagan budget as cutting Social Security, subsidized housing and child nutrition programs. The White House apparatus saw an opportunity to portray the Democrats as parliamentary tricksters trying to defend Big Government business as usual, and it seized it.

"Congress called [the vote] very quickly," recalled Gergen. "We learned about it the next day. Reagan was flying off to Texas [by then], I was back at the White House, and we worked it out by sending statements to the plane for Reagan to make a planeside statement in time to get it on the evening news. [We wanted] to give it hype, to elevate the issue on the evening news so that the nation was getting a message. We were calling the press and doing whatever we could to build the issue. At the same time, the political office went to work, notifying all their allies around the country, bringing the calls and pressure onto Congress as quickly as possible [by telling them] it's really important for Reagan."

Combining immense pressure from monied interests throughout the land with effective propaganda in the national press, the White House focused a virtually irresistible political force onto undecided members of Congress. "Within 24 hours, one congressman had 75 to 100 calls from businessmen in his district," one Reagan aide told *The New York Times*. As thousands of phone calls and telegrams began streaming into Capitol Hill from corporate, right-wing activist and other conservative networks mobilized by the White House political shop, all three network evening news shows were broadcasting images of a smiling Ronald Reagan appearing before a wildly cheering crowd and lambasting the Democrats for sneaky back-room politics. ABC News in particular got into the proper spirit of things (from the White House point of view) when anchor Max Robinson led the news by dramatically announcing, "It's the President of the United States and the House of Representatives this evening in an eyeball-to-eyeball confrontation over the Reagan spending and tax cuts. President Reagan took to the road with his latest drive *to budge a stubborn House*." (Emphasis added.)

The apparent line of the day, crafted, agreed upon and inserted into Reagan's speech before Air Force One touched down in San Antonio, was a brilliantly shameless piece of rhetoric, delivered in just the right more-in-sorrow-than-anger tone by the President: "It's a sad commentary on the state of our opposition when they have to resort to a parliamentary gimmick to thwart the will of the people." Both ABC and CBS did list some of the specific social programs that Reagan's budget would cut. But they spent just as much time airing the equivalent of a White House political commercial in which Reagan spouted fatuous generalizations about all the good things his economic package would do while he ridiculed Speaker of the House Tip O'Neill as a politician out of step with the country. The visual images of Reagan were especially stunning—his triumphant arrival to the tune of "Hail to the Chief," a capacity crowd in full-throated patriotic ardor as he spoke and one particularly flattering closing shot from down in front of the stage which projected an almost majestically commanding image of the President.

Flying on to Los Angeles that night, Reagan was immediately put to work calling members of Congress back in Washington, as the apparatus sought to pry loose enough votes to win the initial procedural test. The combination of Reagan's personal persuasive skills, the political atmosphere created by the apparatus's media and political outreach shops and, according to Stockman, some last-minute old-fashioned vote buying behind closed doors on Capitol Hill resulted in a narrow 217–210 victory for the White House on June 25. The actual budget bill passed the next day, 217–211. The first full step toward making Reaganomics a reality had been taken.

Television images being regarded as a double-edged sword by the White House propaganda apparatus, care was taken that summer both to make Reagan look good on camera and to keep him from looking bad. Although Reagan understood, as Stockman later revealed in his memoirs, next to nothing about the specifics of his own economic package, the apparatus managed to convey a very different image of the President. Meeting after White House meeting was arranged that spring and summer in which Reagan joined with business leaders, state officials, right-wing labor leaders and other friendly parties, ostensibly to discuss his program. Mike Deaver's unsurpassed skill at staging flattering pictures of Reagan resulted in visual images that portrayed the President as relaxed, decisive, in control, and that, judging from the air play, network news producers loved. On June 1, when the script called for projecting the appearance of cooperative flexibility toward Congress, the apparatus staged a media event which yielded photos of Reagan and Speaker O'Neill smiling and chatting like two old friends; it played as the lead story on all three networks. In keeping with Gergen's lightning-rod theory of protecting the President, the apparatus also made sure to shield Reagan from the cameras when bad news broke. For example, when the White House made its one major political goof of the economic sales campaign, proposing cuts in Social Security coverage, it was first Stockman and then Health and Human Services Secretary Richard Schweiker who were cast before the press.

Appreciation of television's magic did not, however, blind the Reaganites to the uses of print. Mastering the tube was necessary to sway the masses and frighten the politicians, but utilizing newspapers was crucial to the more delicate task of controlling the Washington agenda. Of course, the White House had no monopoly on such manipulation. Stockman complained in his memoirs, for example, that the staffs of Senators Howard Baker and Pete Domenici "pretty much dictated the stories of *The Washington Post*'s Capitol Hill reporter, Helen Dewar." But recalling a September 1981 *New York Times* story quoting anonymous White House sources promising no new Social Security cuts, Stockman concluded that it "had to have come from [James] Baker or Gergen. It was a Steve Weisman story, and they tended to keep him well fed." And Stockman himself boasted of repeatedly employing the Evans and Novak syndicated column, which he described as "a kind of supply-side dartboard [that] you could use to stick somebody in the forehead fast, if you had to."

Deaver, Gergen, Baker and Reagan's other key propagandists had a particularly keen understanding of what James Anderson, a State Department correspondent for United Press International, who had first covered Reagan back in California in the late 1960s, described to me as "the Lemming Principle of Washington journalism: that most network news stories began their lives as a story that morning in *The New York Times* or *The Washington Post*. So it became a routine at the White House to leak to [*Post* White House correspondent Lou] Cannon and [*Times* Washington correspondent Hedrick] Smith overnight, which set the agenda for the next day's TV stories. And meanwhile they were feeding Cannon and Smith another story, so it became a cycle."

Deaver confirmed the practice, explaining his preference for using print reporters by noting that "a print guy could get enough space to do the story and be fair and stick in what you gave him, while the television guy has, what, a minute, so he's going to go with the headline. And the television guy is forced to carry the Cannon or Hedrick Smith story anyway. I looked at Lou and Hedrick, but I also looked at [*Newsweek's*] 'Periscope' [column] as a place you could get a story out where it *had* to be picked up. And you could deal with them on the same [background] basis you could with Cannon or Rick."

Another characteristic of the press eagerly exploited by the White House apparatus was the borderline economic illiteracy of many Washington journalists. Most of the reporting on the Reagan economic program in 1981 was contributed by journalists on the White House and Capitol Hill beats, who generally knew politics well enough but had precious little background or expertise in economics. (The Federal Reserve Bank also benefited from journalists' ignorance of economic matters. It was really Fed chairman Paul Volcker more than President Ronald Reagan who was running the economy during this period. Volcker's squeezing of the money supply would soon overwhelm the stimulative effect of Reagan's tax cuts and force the economy into recession, yet the general press paid remarkably little attention to the Fed's machinations.)

"They focused the press on the economy, which is mumbo jumbo to most White House reporters," Lee Lescaze of *The Washington Post* said of the White House apparatus. "They had Stockman to give the rapid-fire intellectual briefings and Reagan the from-my-heart grace notes. Along with the backgrounders by Baker and Darman, it was a devastating combination." Voicing a recollection echoed by other reporters, Lescaze added, "They convinced reporters that they'd thought it through and knew where they were going. And the argument always at the end of each interview was 'At least give the program a chance to work.' "

• • •

BECAUSE the press failed to ask in anything more than a desultory, haphazard fashion the most basic of all political questions about Ronald Reagan's economic policies—who pays and who benefits?—the true nature of the Reagan Revolution was not made clear to the American people. News organizations instead concentrated their attention on less controversial but more entertaining questions: Would Reagan's budget and tax cuts pass or not? What coalitions would be formed and deals made in the process? Who ruled Capitol Hill, Tip O'Neill or Ronald Reagan? The standard approach was to accept at face value the administration's own neutral-sounding interpretation of the Reagan Revolution as a blow against, as the President liked to pronounce it, Big Gu'mint, and then focus on providing play-by-play accounts of the action on Capitol Hill as he sought to implement it.

To cite one among dozens of possible examples: On the night before the crucial April 28 speech that kicked off Take Two of Mr. Reagan's sales campaign, his personal friend and ABC *World News Tonight* anchorman Frank Reynolds led off his newscast by anticipating "an important decision in Congress on the Reagan Revolution—*reducing the role of government in American life by spending less and taxing less.*" (Emphasis added.) That formulation was less than accurate—Reagan's budget did not so much reduce federal spending as redirect it from domestic to military accounts—but, more important, it begged the questions of spending less on what and taxing whom less. Three subsequent reports by correspondents Charles Gibson and Brit Hume on Capitol Hill and Sam Donaldson at the White House boasted the latest on vote counts and legislative maneuvering in Congress, but shed no additional light on these key questions.

"This was a program that by its nature militated against poor people and for rich people," explained Peter Milius, an editor who helped run the national news desk at *The Washington Post* in 1981. "If someone came down from Mars, it'd be the first thing you'd tell him about it. You were cutting taxes and social welfare spending. Taxes tend to be paid disproportionately by rich people and social welfare spending goes disproportionately to poor people."

Early on, the social effects of Reagan's proposed budget cuts did get some attention, if only because they constituted a noticeable shift in federal policy. Three strong stories on the February 5, 1981, *CBS Evening News*, for example, made it clear that working-class and poor people would be hurt by reduced federal spending for food stamps, job training and unemployment benefits. Over the next few days, ABC, NBC and other news organizations offered similar, if usually paler, versions of the same story. For a moment, the human cost of the cutbacks had seemed poised to become a continuing and thus troublesome story for the Reagan administration.

But the White House apparatus, mindful that "Cares about people" had been and remained the highest negative in opinion poll readings on Mr. Reagan, quickly took countermeasures. The President and his aides had repeatedly promised they would spare the "truly needy" in their budget (a lie which no mainstream news organization would challenge until early 1982), and now they went a step further. To Stockman's chagrin, on February 10 they announced that "basic benefits" in seven major social programs would be completely exempted from cuts. The move quieted the controversy long enough for the press to get interested in other things, notably El Salvador. The economics story was pushed down the network news agenda first by Central America, then by the assassination attempt and convalescence, and did not regain the top spot until the week before Reagan's coming-out speech. By then, a split Democratic party had already capitulated on the basic principle of cutting social spending; the debate concerned how much and from which programs. House Speaker O'Neill was occasionally heard to say that taking a "meat-ax" to these programs was "wrong" and would "cut the heart out of the American dream." But when such comments did make the evening news, it was usually in eight-second sound bites wedged into a piece filed by the White House correspondent and replete with White House propaganda both visual and verbal. With only liberal Democrats now criticizing, much less fighting, Reagan's cuts, the press was not inclined to stick its own neck out by continuing to highlight the issue. The human costs of Reaganomics never did resurface more than sporadically in network coverage throughout the rest of the summer.

One reason, according to Lee Lescaze of the *Post*, was that journalists tended to defer to the White House on matters of substance: "Reporters armed with their own opinions and projections [are] very reluctant to go up against the White House's opinions and projections," he explained. "No one had the confidence to speak their doubts about the safety net. You'd see paragraphs that mentioned fears about the safety net eroding, and then quotes from an administration source saying it won't happen."

Intellectual timidity was often compounded by editorial timidity—running too many critical stories could make a news organization appear partisan—thus allowing the White House to prevail through sheer repetition. What defines a public relations crisis for a politician is not so much the intensity of negative coverage as its duration. Were it not reinforced through repetition, even the worst story could be whisked from the public consciousness by the next day's trivia. There is no better indicator of the (by and large unconsciously) shared values and assumptions of the news media than which facts and stories do—and do not—attract the pack and become continuing stories. For a news story graduates to the status of continuing story only when a critical mass within the journalistic community independently judges it worthy of pursuit, extended attention, amplification and incorporation into subsequent reporting and analysis. That this did not happen with the rich-poor angle on Reagan's economic program was clear testimony to how indisposed the media in general were to going after President Reagan that first summer.

Stories pointing out that Reagan's program promised to hurt poor people and help rich people were not unheard of in 1981; if challenged, a journalist at any of the nation's major news organizations could rightfully claim, "We did that story." They did—once or twice, or buried back on page twelve. That angle on the story was not completely excluded from coverage; it was just that it got but a small fraction of the play and prominence that White House propaganda and the Capitol Hill Colosseum match angle did. As Lescaze added: "When you've got a good story, you've got to run it more than once in a while. You can't just say it once . . . because the White House writes its story every day."

And compared with their coverage of the rest of the Reagan economic program, the press was actually relatively outspoken on the budget cuts. With the Democrats marching side by side with, and occasionally even ahead of, Reagan on the tax and military spending issues, the media (1) were even quieter about what an incredible windfall the 1981 tax cuts were for big corporations and the rich and (2) missed reporting altogether an astonishing Pentagon raid on the U.S. Treasury that eventually won the Defense Department untold hundreds of billions of dollars.

Despite the fantastic amount of money involved, the Pentagon raid was not exposed until David Stockman published his memoirs in 1986, and even then the news media failed to pick up on the story. According to Stockman, Defense Secretary Caspar Weinberger and his deputy (and future Reagan national security adviser and Defense Secretary) Frank Carlucci worked a bookkeeping trick on the young budget director shortly after Reagan's inauguration. At a January 30, 1981, meeting, the three men agreed to a compromise seven percent "real" increase in military spending. (As a candidate in 1980, Reagan had urged between five and nine percent growth.) The trick came when Carlucci suggested that the seven percent growth begin with the 1982 budget—which happened to be $80 billion bigger than the 1980 Carter budget Mr. Reagan had criticized. Carlucci's sleight of hand, in other words, won the military *an extra $80 billion per year* in spending authority above and beyond what even conservative hard-liners had said was needed to restore U.S. military prowess. Beginning with the 1982 budget, the Pentagon would receive, year in and year out, $80 billion of pure gravy. No wonder, to quote Stockman, "they were squealing with delight throughout the military-industrial complex."

Why didn't reporters catch Weinberger and Carlucci? No classified documents were required, only the application of probing skepticism toward official pronouncements and a willingness to study the actual budget numbers. But that was not the modus operandi of the typical Washington reporter. Sources were his stock-in-trade, and until they rang a warning bell, additional investigation was unlikely.

"There's a symbiotic relationship in this town between government officials and outside critics and news stories, and until something is recognized within those circles as a problem, the one or two stories that may get done on an issue tend to run inside the paper," explained *Washington Post* military affairs reporter Fred Hiatt. (Hiatt did not cover the Pentagon in 1981, but he did help uncover the spare parts overpricing scandal, featuring $600 coffeepots and toilet seats, that so embarrassed the Pentagon in 1983–84. Important as such overpricing was, the burden it imposed on taxpayers was dwarfed by that of the $80 billion annual cushion that Weinberger and Carlucci inserted into the Pentagon budget under David Stockman's nose.) "Look, over-spending isn't what people were worried about at the time," he said. "People in the administration and who voted the budgets in Congress were worried about our military being in a depressed state and needing to be upgraded after years of neglect."

A similar if less extreme pattern was evident in network news coverage of the enormous tax cuts of 1981. Tax cuts were the centerpiece of President Reagan's economic program. Not only were they far larger in dollar terms than the budget cuts (over five years the 1981 tax cuts would result in federal revenue losses of some $750 billion); they were the magic wand that, it was promised, would revive the stagnant U.S. economy.

Later, Stockman would confess that supply-side was merely old-fashioned "trickle-down" economics under a new name, and that Kemp-Roth, the legislative embodiment of supply-side, had merely been a Trojan horse intended mainly to cut taxes for the top bracket, the wealthy. As those comments hinted, the supply-side theory was in fact little more than the intellectual justification for a policy of transferring huge amounts of money to the already wealthy.

That was not, however, how Reagan's tax cuts were portrayed in network news coverage at the time. Neither the need for nor the likely effect of the tax cuts was exposed to serious critical scrutiny. Rather, to the limited extent that news stories examined the key theory behind Reaganomics at all, a sort of agnostically optimistic view prevailed. For example, CBS News correspondent Bruce Morton concluded a February 6 story on the supply-side theory by quoting supporters to the effect that perhaps it would not work, but then neither had anything else, so it should at least be given a try. That sentiment was echoed on the night of Reagan's April 28 speech when both ABC and NBC featured Senate Majority Leader Howard Baker's comment that Reagan's plan was "a gamble," but one that must be tried "because nothing else has worked."

Although network news stories regularly voiced concern that the tax cuts might enlarge the budget deficit, they rarely even hinted at how lopsidedly they would favor rich over poor. The White House apparatus deserved some of the credit for that. Reagan was outfitted with populist rhetoric with which to sell the tax program, including the wonderfully misleading phrase "across the board" to describe the cuts themselves. That phrase may have made the cuts *sound* fair, but however they sounded, 10 percent across-the-board cuts of course had radically different effects depending on one's income. For a $20,000-a-year auto repairman, for example, it amounted to a $200 subsidy, while for a $2 million tycoon it was $200,000. (When one calculated in the income effects of the Reagan budget cuts and previously mandated increases in Social Security taxes, a citizen had to make some $75,000 a year to rank among those who came out ahead from the 1981 tax and budget changes.)

Although the math was simple enough, the equity angle was virtually ignored on the evening news except for a handful of stories in June, when Tip O'Neill blasted Reagan's plan a couple of times as a "windfall to the rich." And the extent of the *corporate* tax cuts got even less attention, perhaps because the Democrats and the White House alike favored them. Indeed, the two parties got into a bidding war in June over who could propose the most lavish package of benefits for corporate America. The results were astonishing. The effective corporate tax rate dropped from 33 to 16 percent, loopholes proliferated and depreciation schedules were made so generous that scores of big companies ended up paying no income tax, or receiving rebates, in at least one of the four years from 1981 to 1984. It was an episode budget director Stockman would later recall as a time when "the hogs were really feeding. The greed level, the level of opportunism, just got out of control."

Yet when it came time in late July to vote on the tax measures, mainstream news coverage was virtually empty of any suggestion that the Congress was considering passage of one of the greatest giveaways to corporate and wealthy interests in the nation's history. "The tax bill wasn't challenged before passage, by the press or by those who voted no. The redistributive aspects were hardly looked at," recalled Thomas Edsall, a reporter who covered the story first for the Baltimore *Sun* and then, beginning in July, for *The Washington Post*, and later wrote a fine book on the subject, *The New Politics of Inequality*. It was not so much reporters' editors who discouraged such scrutiny, according to Edsall, as "the whole tenor in the country. The terms of debate had shifted and the question of whether this would benefit one small group at the top is just not one that was asked. It had been pushed out of the political debate. It occurred to me to do stories on the redistributive aspects, but I didn't do them either. . . . People were intimidated against challenging the redistributive aspects because it would have been seen as an attack, or whining, from the left."

The Washington Post was the one major news organization that even began to hint in 1981 at the extraordinary money grab then underway in the nation's capital, and it did so largely because the journalists involved reported on the program itself as much as on what official Washington was saying about it. "What it really comes down to is not sources, not all this mystique of getting David Stockman or anyone else to tell you what's happening. What it really boils down to is to have the brains, and the guts, to do your own analysis of what the hell is happening," said William Greider, the assistant managing editor for national news at the time and a major driving force behind the *Post*'s coverage. "[Reporter Robert] Kaiser has those qualities, so did I, I think, Peter Milius on the national desk—we all tried to understand that thing independently of what the White House was saying it was or what even private sources were saying it was. Obviously you don't want to go off winging it on your own analysis if everybody says it's dead wrong, but when your sources tell you you got it right, then you write it. . . . Really, it ain't a lot more complicated than that."

The *Post* hardly made a crusade out of it, but it did run numerous front-page stories that spring and summer outlining the likely economic effects of Reagan's proposals. Denying any hidden, partisan agenda, Peter Milius argued that "it's not being anti-Reagan to be crystal clear about the dimensions of the program."

News stories describing the regressive nature of the Reagan economic proposals were not exactly what the White House wanted to see on the front page of the capital's leading newspaper, but there was surprisingly little backlash as a result. For one thing, the rest of the Washington press corps failed to pick up on the story. As Dean Reynolds of UPI later explained: "It was pretty well known within the press corps what Reagan's plan was, but the *Post* put it in a little sharper focus than the rest of us wanted to." According to Milius, the White House did not even much bother to pressure the *Post* to lay off. Asked why not, he exclaimed, "They didn't *need* us." (That view was later confirmed by a senior White House official: "I do not believe that the *Post* had that as a theme line to a point that it caused a problem. . . . It was not an unmanageable problem, let's put it that way.") Milius said, chuckling, "It's not as though the President was shut out of the paper, for God's sake. His positions were said and said and said. Presidents by definition don't get shortchanged."

ABC's Sam Donaldson later regretted not having featured more economists critical of the Reagan plan in his 1981 White House coverage, but he was hardly the only reporter to make that mistake; characteristically, he was just more honest about admitting it. Apparently intimidated by the so-called dismal science of economics, wary of crossing the White House without lots of support from the ostensible opposition party and anxious to stand back from the presidential hanging rope this time, the press ended up functioning more as accomplice than as adversary in the selling of Reagan's economic program. Its eagerness to transmit Michael Deaver's cleverly choreographed pictures of the President was especially helpful in spreading the Reagan gospel, but jelly-bean journalism was not the only reason for the White House's success. The single greatest political liability of the Reagan program—the fact that it deprived the many while subsidizing the few—escaped serious and sustained scrutiny by the nation's major news organizations. For television in particular, the story in the summer of 1981 was not Rich vs. Poor but Gipper Sweeps Congress. The fixation on the sport of it all was such that an observation David Stockman later made concerning Congress applied equally well to most of the press: "The real issues that the Reagan Revolution posed . . . had never been seriously debated."

7

"AN AMIABLE DUNCE"

Ronald Reagan left for his summer vacation in 1981 as, in David Gergen's phrase, the King of the Hill. To friend and foe alike, it seemed that the rising of his star had just begun. His aides, flushed with victory, now looked to the future with new confidence; remarkably, everything seemed to be going just as they had planned. As Gergen explained: "The whole theory going in was, go for the economic reforms up front, leave social issues to the side that first year, achieve your economic stimulation, and in the midst of good times, Reagan would have the political power to tackle the social issues."

Gergen and his colleagues discovered the flaw in that line of reasoning soon enough. A more immediate problem arose, however, when the deified image of Ronald Reagan they had so carefully constructed over the past few months suddenly came under suspicion. Gergen, recalling his observation that press coverage of the Reagan administration did not begin to get critical until that first August, later philosophized that by the time Reagan signed the tax bill at his ranch in early August, "he was so far up it was inevitable the pendulum would begin to swing the other way." And swing it did.

On August 19, U.S. fighter planes shot down two Libyan jets over the Gulf of Sidra. Originally planned for July but ordered postponed by White House chief of staff Baker so as not to distract attention from Reagan's legislative victories, the Libyan operation was a public relations sensation. Like the invasion of Grenada two years later, it allowed the administration to purge Vietnam-Iran era feelings of national humiliation by picking a fight it knew it could win. The White House media apparatus was well prepared for the event, whisking the President onto the USS *Constellation* in time for a photo opportunity which yielded suitably patriotic pictures of the Commander-in-Chief for the evening newscasts and subliminally conveyed the false impression that Reagan had actually been present for the attack. But a dangerous seed was planted when White House counselor Edwin Meese let it slip to reporters that he had not bothered to awaken the President during the hostilities.

For months the press had been lauding Ronald Reagan as a man whose courage in the face of death had inspired millions and whose take-charge style of leadership had brought real change to Washington. Now, for the first time since he took office, the troublesome issue of competence surfaced as reporters began questioning just how involved Reagan was in the running of the government. "And the White House [had] a wonderful way of explaining it all away that sort of loads the equation," recalled Dean Reynolds of UPI. "They'd say, 'Well, you know Carter kept track of everything, he knew who was playing on the White House tennis courts, he never took vacations, and look what happened to the country.' What a ridiculous thing! The converse of that is, let's have no President and things will be just great; have nobody paying attention to anything and everything will be hunky-dory."

It was after reporters started questioning "how in charge he really is," according to Gergen, that "the press coverage started getting mushy." And as summer turned to fall, Reagan's slide in the press, and in the polls, accelerated. Explaining why coverage grew less positive after August, Mike Deaver noted simply that "a lot of the story was budget cuts"—not a story that played very well for the Reagan administration. Throughout September the story coming out of the White House was that additional domestic spending cuts were necessary to ensure a balanced budget by 1984. But in sharp contrast to earlier that year, the administration encountered heavy flak on its proposed cuts from legislators on both sides of the aisle in Congress and was forced to retreat, leaving Wall Street convinced that runaway federal deficits were inevitable. In an unmistakable vote of no confidence in Reaganomics, the stock market on September 25 dropped to a sixteen-month low.

There was trouble on the foreign policy front as well. From the start, many people in Western Europe had been alarmed by Reagan's lack of sophistication. The President's remark at his first news conference that the Soviet Union reserved unto itself the right to lie, cheat and steal made him seem like a simpleminded ideologue; more seriously, his unprecedented peacetime military buildup reinforced his image as a reckless cowboy. In October, Reagan confirmed his critics' worst fears when, in a White House session with visiting newspaper editors, he allowed that, yes, he could envision a nuclear war between the superpowers being limited to Europe. NATO governments already faced strong popular opposition to the planned 1983 deployment of U.S. Pershing and cruise missiles; Reagan's comment only strengthened the argument of the peace movement that more nuclear weapons meant less security and that Europe was foolish to entrust its safety to either the Soviets or the Americans.

At home, the economic news continued to get worse. On November 6, the government announced that the official unemployment rate had climbed above 8 percent; 8.5 million Americans were out of work, more than at any time since the 1930s. Four days later, CBS White House correspondent Lesley Stahl reported the damning remarks federal budget director David Stockman had made about Reaganomics in the November issue of *The Atlantic Monthly*. With the first round of Reagan's budget cuts having taken effect on October 1, criticisms began to be heard of both the fairness and the workability of his program. The state of the economy was always the basis of any President's popularity, and at the moment the U.S. economy was plunging toward its first depression in fifty years.

"It was late that year that the economy started slipping," recalled Gergen, "and it was really the economic recession, as it cut more and more deeply, that made [press] coverage so much more negative. . . . As the budget cuts came into effect and the economy was going to hell at the same time and the tax cuts seemed to be benefiting the upper-middle income and the rich, that left Reagan exposed to a lot of criticism."

All this marked a new stage in the relationship between the Reagan White House and the press. By the end of 1981, the honeymoon was fading and a time of testing had begun. The slumping economy seemed to awaken new skepticism in the Washington press corps, if only because reporters' sources throughout the rest of the governing elite were suddenly slightly more willing to challenge White House economic pronouncements and performance.

It was the responsibility of Ronald Reagan's media managers to keep such criticism from destroying his presidency. As impressive a job as Gergen, Deaver and their colleagues had done earlier that year in promoting Reagan and his economic program, it would matter little if they now failed to shepherd him safely through the adversity that lay ahead. The challenge of protecting their four-star general (to borrow Gergen's phrase) from lasting harm during this period would press the skills of the Reagan apparatus to the limit. The apparatus never abandoned its basic approach to news management, but there was only so much that even the slickest public relations hocus-pocus could accomplish in the face of 10 percent unemployment and a rash of business failures unlike anything since the Great Depression.

"It is very easy to be involved with communications with any President when you're in an upswing," Gergen later observed. "The tough time comes when you're on a downswing and everybody says, 'Well, our policies are obviously correct; it must be the way we're communicating them.' " Sure enough, the slide in the President's popularity did spark disagreement within the White House over proper countermeasures; in particular, the simmering conflict between administration hard-liners and pragmatists over how combative a stance to take against the press intensified.

Luckily for the White House, the apparent reversal of Mr. Reagan's fortunes left the American news media equally at odds internally. How critical of Reagan and his policies was the press prepared to be? And who decided such matters? As national and world events increasingly forced such questions into the open, tensions flared at a number of major news organizations, with line and field reporters often favoring tougher coverage while management insisted on "being fair" to the President. The struggle between the White House and the press, and the struggles within each institution, would continue throughout 1982 and into 1983. In the end, there would be no doubt about who was truly in command.

• • •

BEHIND HIS BACK, junior colleagues referred to Steve Smith, editor of *Time*'s national news section during Reagan's first term, as Mr. Perfect. His Waspy good looks, cheerfully cordial manner and colorful but correct wardrobe all contributed to his image, but what especially impressed co-workers about Smith was that he always seemed to know the right thing to say to his superiors. Convivial conversation came easily to Smith—"*Hey*, Hugo! How goes it?" was his gregariously casual greeting when *Time*'s veteran White House observer Hugh Sidey happened to telephone during Smith's interview for this book—but the words flowed less smoothly and the tone grew more measured when Smith tried to explain why taking on the question of Ronald Reagan's competence, as *Time* had done in a December 1982 cover story he edited called "How Reagan Decides," made him uneasy.

Smith was obviously proud of the story, calling it "bold, especially for a mainstream publication like us," and claiming it "had a great impact on how Reagan was perceived—the tone of the coverage changed a great deal after that." Still, it had been tricky. "When you do the 'How Reagan Decides' kind of stories, you're very aware of seeming elitist and patronizing," he said. "For the press to say the President of the United States is out to lunch is quite a statement." In truth, the *Time* story had been far more gentle than that (and Smith quickly retreated from that characterization himself, imploring, "Please don't have me saying he's out to lunch, because I don't think he is"), but it is interesting, and typical of journalists in the Reagan era, that he remembered producing a tougher story than had actually been printed. Equally interesting was his reply when asked why making such a plain-spoken judgment about Ronald Reagan was so hard for the press.

"It's just built into you," he said. "I suppose it's a little bit the respect for the office. But you're making some awfully big assumptions about yourself and the other person, you're assuming superiority there, which I'm hesitant to do in my private as well as my journalistic life. . . . It's one thing to say the Emperor has no clothes. It's another to say the Emperor is out to lunch. It would be easier to say the guy has a terrible temper, for instance, or that he's not interested in arms control, so he doesn't attend the discussions. But to say the guy doesn't know anything about anything is much more difficult, because the guy is by most measurements a success."

Offering an unvarnished portrayal of Reagan's intellectual deficiencies was particularly difficult for a "centrist publication" like *Time*, where, in Smith's words, "you're trying to go down the middle." Too many reminders of Reagan's ignorance concerning, say, the basics of nuclear weaponry would strike most readers as "gratuitous if not unfair," Smith warned. "And they pick up on it right away if they think you're out to get him." *Time*'s homing instinct for the middle of the political spectrum evidently derived from the same mysterious source as its caution against saying the President was out to lunch, for when asked whence it came, Smith replied, "It's almost unspoken here. We try to be objective in the sense that we try to be fair. But since we interpret and analyze the news, there is a built-in subjectivity. But we *are* objective in terms of not having a preconceived notion of how we want things to come out." Except, of course, that they not stray too far from the political middle.

Time was hardly the only news organization that found it hard to report on a President who seemed at least as boneheaded as he was popular. Scouring their thesauruses for the gentlest possible euphemisms, striving to suggest the obvious without offending anyone's sensibilities, journalists at all the major news organizations trod extremely softly when it came to describing the new President's mental acuities. *Newsweek*, for example, in one of the first stories on the subject, published shortly after Reagan slept through the Libyan dogfight, chose "disengaged" to describe the President (a usage satirist Calvin Trillin later confessed in *The Nation* to have found "a bit cumbersome—it struck me as the equivalent of saying 'She's really more than a disengaged blonde' or 'It was nothing but disengaged luck'—but apparently it has caught on in the newsmagazine crowd"). Even the name eventually settled on for the President's malady, the gaffe problem, was a triumph of manners over truth, for it implied that statements such as Reagan's March 1981 assertion that the United States was helping the forces supporting human rights in El Salvador were mere slips of the tongue, when in fact they were simply Reagan being Reagan—mangling the truth through either colossal ignorance or willful deception.

The latter interpretation—that Reagan was more liar than fool—was particularly conspicuous by its absence from press coverage and commentary. As Brian Healy, a top producer in the Washington bureau of CBS News, explained in a separate context, "liar" was one of those words that journalists were extremely reluctant to use. And rightly so: as an accusation, it was not only harsh but difficult to prove. For the distinguishing characteristic of the lie (as opposed to the merely false statement) was conscious intent; to be a liar, one had to *know* that what he or she was saying was untrue. Fathoming the inner workings of anyone's mind was risky business, and in Reagan's case it was an especially dubious endeavor. Who could say? Perhaps Reagan really did believe that the Russian language had no word for freedom, just as he later seemed to convince himself that he had not traded arms for hostages with Iran. Reagan was possessed of an extraordinary ability to embrace, and repeat with great conviction, whatever statement was politically expedient at a given moment. It was not so much that he lied as that, for him, truth was a relative concept, something to be finessed while making the salesman's pitch. And there was the added factor of his likability. Who could bring themselves to suggest that a nice guy like Ronald Reagan would lie through that amiable grin?

What therefore became known as the competence question did not surface again until January 1982, a full five months after the Gulf of Sidra incident. It is unclear how much its absence from the news during these months was due to greater prudence on Reagan's part and how much to self-censorship by journalists. That the press probably passed up at least a few opportunities to raise the issue is suggested by its original disregard of Reagan's October 1981 remark that limited nuclear war was possible in Europe. Although Reagan made that statement in a White House question-and-answer session with U.S. newspaper editors, the three major networks apparently did not consider it sufficiently newsworthy to include it in their nightly newscasts that evening. It took three days, and protests throughout Europe, before most Americans were informed of their President's sanguine view of nuclear warfare.

By January, however, the failing economy had left Reagan more vulnerable to criticism of all kinds, and whisperings about the President's limited knowledge of and involvement in the running of his own government again began to be heard. "More disquieting than Reagan's performance or prospects on any specific issue is a growing suspicion that the President has only a passing acquaintance with some of the most important decisions of his administration," wrote Lou Cannon in *The Washington Post*.

After his January 19 press conference, the White House correspondents for all three networks spent nearly as much time correcting the President's statements as they did reporting them; Reagan's false assertion that unemployment had begun climbing *before* he took office received special notice. Appearing before the press again on February 18, Reagan chastised reporters for fastening on his mistakes at the previous press conference and waved at them a sheet of paper which he claimed proved that he had been right on four of five disputed statements—an eerie echo of Senator McCarthy's brandishing of documents supposedly listing the names of Communist spies within the U.S. government three decades earlier. The White House press office refused to release Reagan's supporting data and had to concede under questioning that Reagan had made additional erroneous statements during the February conference, including a tortured rewriting of the history of the Vietnam War.

Although his press conference errors were duly noted in news accounts, Reagan's ignorance did not become a high-profile, continuing story. Nor did the press vigorously pursue the more fundamental question of the President's basic honesty and intelligence. Reagan had a long history of inane statements—who could forget his claim that 80 percent of the nation's air pollution was caused by trees?—yet a viewer of the next day's, or week's, network White House stories would never have guessed that there was any special reason to doubt this President's knowledge or abilities; his subsequent pronouncements and actions were reported with all the courteous respect customarily accorded the leader of the Western world. It was as if after each glimpse of the unteleprompted Reagan reporters simply purged their brains of all memory of the presidential simplemindedness they had just witnessed.

Shortly after the February 18 press conference, liberal *New York Times* columnist Anthony Lewis accused his colleagues of going too easy on Reagan, but to the men in the White House, even the occasional muted references of the previous six weeks represented a grave threat to their carefully crafted image of Ronald Reagan as a decisive, accomplished leader.

"I was deeply worried about the gaffe problem," confirmed David Gergen. And not least because it arose at the very time that Reagan was under increasing criticism for the unfairness of his economic policies. Although Gergen conceded that gaffes were never a big part of the reporting on Reagan, he emphasized that they still concerned him. "The gaffe question went directly to the question of competence," he explained. "If you had [Reagan portrayed as] both unfair and incompetent, you were in trouble.

"The gaffe stories were the worst when we were doing afternoon press conferences," recalled Gergen. "The only story you got out of the conference was how many mistakes he made." But rather than take Reagan off the air, White House strategists took the offensive, and a risk. Reagan's men had always been "afraid" (Gergen's word) of having the President answer reporters' questions live before a national audience, but they now decided to move his press conferences to the evening, when they would be seen on prime-time television, on the assumption that Reagan's personal charm would outweigh any factual errors. "It was a ballsier approach," said Gergen. "Deaver was for it, the President was for it, I was for it, Baker was for it."

Meanwhile, behind the scenes, the apparatus was responding in much the same way Reagan's media handlers had always responded to their man's bouts of foot-in-mouth disease: they sharply restricted reporters' access to him. Reagan had already approved a January 12 executive order requiring administration officials to obtain advance clearance from the White House before talking to reporters about national security issues, and he apparently had wanted to go considerably further than that. Angered by news leaks and reportedly urged on by both his wealthy right-wing California friends, with whom he had spent the Christmas vacation, and such White House hard-liners as Edwin Meese and national security adviser William Clark, Reagan had originally proposed banning *all* background and off-the-record interviews.

Meese told me that the ban was merely one idea among many that were discussed at the time, "but I thought it might be a way of helping to curb the leaking. I think at that time there was a particularly vicious series of leaks which were having a chilling effect on people giving the President their frank views. . . . I was impressed that in Reagan's administration in Sacramento as governor we never had that . . . and I was hoping to translate that same sense of loyalty and professionalism to the Washington scene." (Mr. Meese's stated opposition to anonymous interviews did not deter him from suggesting that my interview with him be "not for attribution.")

Meese did not succeed in banning anonymous interviews. Baker and Deaver saw a disaster in the making—they believed such a maneuver would not only provoke enormous ill will among the press corps but ultimately prove unenforceable—and eventually they talked Reagan out of it. Nevertheless, the mere consideration of such a ban, not to mention possible future use of polygraph tests to catch suspected leakers, intimidated some officials into canceling interviews or otherwise curbing their contacts with reporters.

It was President Reagan himself, however, not middle-level bureaucrats, who most needed to be shielded from reporters. The White House apparatus was not shy about making that happen, for pragmatists and hard-liners alike agreed that reducing reporters' access to Reagan was a good idea. But because the White House needed the press and especially television in order to govern, it could not afford to bar reporters from every presidential event. The challenge, then, was to get the press to cover the events the White House wanted covered, and to cover them on the White House's terms. It was all part of protecting the four-star general at a time when the going was indeed getting hot and heavy.

Reporters did not like having their access to Mr. Reagan squeezed, but there seemed to be little they could do to resist—until the apparatus sought to implement what came to be known as the Deaver rule. Deaver could not in retrospect recall what specific incident had provoked him, but one day that spring he demanded that White House reporters stop asking President Reagan questions during an Oval Office photo opportunity session with a foreign leader. Deaver claimed that he simply found it "insulting to bring in a head of state to the Oval Office and have him surrounded by a hundred shouting reporters," but network White House correspondents viewed the Deaver rule as simply one more attempt to protect Reagan from public scrutiny of his policies and performance. "It was an attempt to stop the President from being subjected to questions at photo opportunities," charged NBC White House correspondent Andrea Mitchell, "questions that were asked because we saw him so rarely in a give-and-take situation that it would have been unprofessional not to ask."

The Deaver rule provoked a major confrontation between the Reagan White House and the networks. The apparatus had tried at least twice before, without success, to prevent questions at photo opportunities; reporters had simply refused to comply. But this time, according to ABC's Sam Donaldson, Deaver said that if reporters did not stop asking questions, they would not be allowed in the Oval Office at all. Seizing upon their single strongest source of leverage, network correspondents countered that if they did not go in, neither did their cameras—a position which threatened the White House with a loss of precious television exposure.

It was a standoff. The White House apparatus responded by going over the reporters' heads to management. All three of the networks' Washington bureau chiefs were summoned to a White House meeting with Deaver and James Baker. The network executives were apparently prepared to stand behind their reporters, but they were surprised by what they found awaiting them.

"We expected there to be something to be discussed," recalled NBC's Robert McFarland about the White House meeting. But instead the bureau chiefs were presented with "a fait accompli. . . . We were handed a sheet of paper stating the new rules, to which we obviously objected. They said they would think about it, and then it came back to us that the matter was not up for discussion."

By sticking with their prohibition on questions at photo opportunities in the face of reporters' threats to boycott such sessions, Deaver and Baker were, in effect, challenging the networks. When asked later whether taking such a gamble had worried him, Deaver replied, "It couldn't last forever. Maybe the photo op was the only story of the day. I think Gergen got very nervous, but my position on their holdout was 'Screw 'em! They're not going to stick with that.' I mean, we got the Horse. They're getting paid $150,000 a year to cover the President of the United States. You mean to tell me they're not going to bring their cameras in a day or two?"

In NBC's case, it did not take even that long. Although CBS and ABC both decided to make good on their boycott threat, NBC management elected to accede to the White House's demands and send its reporters, and cameras, back to the Oval Office. NBC bureau chief McFarland confirmed that ABC and CBS had initially wanted to continue the boycott. One ABC official privately expressed irritation that NBC had folded, arguing that "it would have been easier for us to make a valid point if we'd all stayed out." But once NBC sent its cameras back in, the other networks apparently felt that for competitive reasons they had to follow suit. Within two days of delivery of the White House fait accompli, all three networks had returned to the fold, and on the apparatus's terms.

Likening the photo opportunity confrontation to a staring contest between the White House and the networks, ABC White House producer David Kaplan observed that the networks "not only blinked [first], they closed their eyes and put on sunglasses." The key turning point, in Kaplan's view, was NBC's decision not to boycott. "[I]f they're not going to back down," Kaplan said of the White House, "and if, more important, the other networks aren't going to go along with you, then they don't care if ABC's not going in, because their message is getting out."

When asked to defend his company's action, McFarland replied that although NBC disagreed with Deaver and Baker, it obeyed the new rule because "it's their White House. He is the *President* of the United States. It is our job to report what he does. And it's their house, it's their Rose Garden. They set the rules." When it was suggested that it was not their White House but the White House of some 240 million Americans and that Ronald Reagan was merely elected to live there for four years, McFarland agreed this was "absolutely right," but still maintained that "the tenants do get to establish some ground rules."

The battle over the Deaver rule was less important in terms of actual ground gained or lost than in the tone it set for the continuing struggle between the White House and the networks. For while the White House succeeded in reducing the number of reporters allowed to attend Oval Office photo opportunities—to the wire services, one broadcaster, and one magazine or newspaper writer, meaning that the average White House press corps regular rotated into the pool only once every three weeks—it was not long before the reporters were again asking Reagan questions during such sessions. Still, a clear if unintentional signal had been sent: when push came to shove, the networks were not likely to shove the White House back. And Michael Deaver had been proven right: the networks could be intimidated; they did have to take whatever the White House gave them. Or at least they thought they did, which amounted to the same thing. As ABC's

Washington bureau chief George Watson explained three years later, in 1985: "The situation we've gotten into, I'm afraid, is one of explaining our concerns to the White House, being refused, and then doing it their way anyhow."

• • •

IN WORD AND DEED, Reagan continued through the summer and fall of 1982 to supply abundant evidence that he was, in former Secretary of Defense Clark Clifford's phrase, something of "an amiable dunce." During Mr. Reagan's trip to Europe in June, for example, members of the traveling press corps watched him doze off so many times—during speeches by French President François Mitterrand and Italian President Alessandro Pertini, as well as during a one-on-one audience with the Pope—that they privately christened the trip "The Big Sleep." It was a clever line, but it would have gotten more laughs if reporters had let their readers and viewers in on the joke; the stories most reporters sent home scarcely mentioned the President's fondness for slumber.

Reporters likewise seemed to spend as much time quibbling about Reagan's various errors with White House spokesmen as they did telling the rest of the world about them. Which was great for Reagan, though it was tough on his aides. In May, for example, Deaver had scheduled a presidential visit to a black high school in Chicago to counter the impression that Reagan was racially insensitive. But during a question-and-answer session with students, Reagan showed just how out of touch he was with black America when he allowed that he was "under the impression that the problem of segregated schools had been settled." The Gipper was spared having to explain that statement to reporters later, but deputy press secretary Larry Speakes was not. As the questions kept coming, Speakes grew impatient, finally barking at his inquisitors, "Don't try to pick me apart on these mistakes again."

"I've had my problems with Larry, but it's been my contention all along that Speakes has one of the toughest jobs in government," said Dean Reynolds. "He's told to go out and say things that he knows to be patently ridiculous. So he goes out there, gritting his teeth, angry at what he's expected to tell [us], knowing that we're going to jump all over him and beat him up and try to make him look stupid or embarrass him. After years of that,

I'm not surprised that Larry has a short fuse or can get vindictive or personal. . . . I'd love to see his bosses come out and try to fend us off mouthing the garbage that he's had to in the past." Whenever Reagan made "some ridiculous mistake," recalled Reynolds, "Larry ha[d] to trot right back out, look us right in the eye, and say, 'Well, he meant to say . . .' And everybody goes, 'Laaaarrrrry.' It's a thankless job."

Eventually the White House apparatus figured that the best way to deal with gaffe stories was simply not to rise to the bait. "We finally just decided we wouldn't worry about it," said Speakes. "I guess the initial phase of it was 'We're just not going to talk about it. You fellas write what you want. Go ahead.' And then after another period of time, we said, 'If he made a mistake, I'm sorry, he made a mistake. That's incorrect.' "

It was an astute tactic on the White House's part, for it played upon the media's essentially passive definition of what constituted responsible journalism. Objectivity required that reporters attribute all statements of fact to a recognized expert or authority. When White House officials withheld quotes and declined to react, it made it that much harder for reporters to file stories about Reagan's bloopers. And those stories that still were done were much less likely to be prominently played or to become what the modern news manager most feared, a continuing story.

But the process worked in reverse as well. Indeed, the gaffe-competence issue might well have never resurfaced at all had not various senior White House sources decided after the November 1982 congressional elections that it was time to speak up if they were ever going to force their President to face reality on the federal deficit. One direct consequence of the aides' sudden candor was the "How Reagan Decides" cover story in the December 13 issue of *Time*. Even Steve Smith had to admit it probably would not have been done had the White House sources not come forward.

"The President has a honeymoon with everyone for the first year," Smith said. "His staff is going to be very careful about what they say about him. I remember that story being very well sourced. The motivation for the people [in the administration] who were willing to discuss those kinds of things with us was very high. They were concerned. They weren't trying to dump on Reagan, or knock him out, but they were concerned. For them to be willing to talk about those things with the press takes a while. Most of them are loyalists who've been around Reagan for a decade or more.''

Perhaps because of its overwhelming dependence on White House sources, perhaps because of the magazine's own conservative worldview, the *Time* story was in fact remarkably polite and restrained, considering the subject matter. Its essentially timid tone was foreshadowed in its title: "How Reagan Decides: Intense beliefs, eternal optimism and precious little adaptability." The text of the article continued in the same vein, promoting the notion that the President was not ignorant so much as stubborn, not blind to economic reality so much as fiercely upbeat. Since the deficit and the administration's economic policy were virtually the only issues discussed in the piece, readers were never apprised of their President's novel views on, say, nuclear weapons, or race relations, or any number of other worthy but uncomfortable topics. About as hard-hitting as the story got was to scold Reagan (gently) for a lack of curiosity and flexibility, for not always knowing what his advisers were up to and for failing to realize that "overseas, not every policy is well founded just because it is anti-Soviet; at home, the greatest threat to American prosperity seems to be the stratospheric budget deficits that are aggravated by Reagan's policies."

The importance of any major *Time* story, along with White House aides' continuing background revelations, triggered a brief resurgence of press interest in the question of Reagan's competence, lasting into early 1983. William Greider, who by then had left *The Washington Post* to become national political correspondent for *Rolling Stone*, recalled that "for about six weeks after [the] initial story in *Time* everybody started doing stories about how disengaged Reagan was. . . . I think those stories said what most reporters [had] believed was true for a long time."

These stories not only portrayed the President as less than fully in control, but told of a White House staff that was dispirited, divided and in general disarray. The bad publicity, coming at a time when unemployment had soared to nearly 11 percent, not only irritated Reagan's senior advisers; it gave the hard-line faction the upper hand in devising the communications counterstrategy. "Meese used to go in every morning and talk about leaks," according to Deaver, "and it would just get the President going up the wall: 'Dammit, let's catch these people!' Baker and I were always saying, 'You can't do that, you're always going to have leaks.' " Drawing on his experience with Reagan in California, Deaver proposed a compromise solution: all telephone calls from journalists to White House officials from now on would be channeled through a central point—David Gergen's office.

"We tried to control it by putting in the whole system of who could talk to the press," confirmed Gergen. "That was to shut down a couple of people we knew were being very destructive. They weren't just talking about [the decision-making] process; they were also putting the knife through others." Gergen explained that the new rules decreed that "people not in the press office couldn't take a press call unless cleared by my office. That system we knew would not last very long, but it had a sort of shock effect at the time." More than one of the journalists interviewed for this book agreed with Gergen on that score. In the words of Jack Nelson, Washington bureau chief of the *Los Angeles Times*: "A lot of people who used to return phone calls quit doing it."

Centralization of press calls was not the only reason, but it was not long before negative stories about a White House in disarray and a President out of touch disappeared from the news agenda— as suddenly and mysteriously, it seemed, as they had originally burst forth. Which provoked a question, articulated by Greider: "If all that was true [about Reagan] in December of '82, did it *cease* to be true after that?" Greider argued that it did cease to be true, at least insofar as portrayed in media coverage. "And that gets to Ronald Reagan's popularity," he continued, "which starts going up in the summer of '83, as well as to this quaint view the press has, and I must say I used to have it too, that once you've told people the truth, that's it, they'll remember whatever you wrote back in December, or whenever."

"I think we got past the gaffe question, basically," Gergen affirmed in one interview for this book. It was a success that left his predecessor, Carter White House media boss Jody Powell, beside himself with frustration at a press corps that had been nowhere near as understanding toward *his* President. "It is very obvious that Ronald Reagan is either the most ill-informed President we've ever had, or the most duplicitous, maybe both," Powell fumed. "But nobody wants to say it. It's like [the press] saying, 'We give up. If we get an administration that is reasonably popular and wants to play real hardball and whose core supporters are meaner than cat shit and write nasty letters and organize letter-writing campaigns and really know how to bring pressure, there's nothing we can do about it. We're going to have to go belly-up.' "

Major news stories generally fade from sight so gradually that fixing their exact moment of departure from the public agenda is all but impossible, but if one date had to be chosen for the demise of the Reagan gaffe story, it would be February 15, 1983. For that was the day *The New York Times*, the nation's premier paper of historical record, officially acknowledged the news media's waning interest in the subject. Noting that the President's aides no longer worried about the gaffe problem, a story headlined "Reagan Misstatements Getting Less Attention" went on to explain that Reagan "continues to make debatable assertions of fact but news accounts do not deal with them as extensively as they once did." White House officials claimed the public had gotten tired of the story, and the *Times* report was only too happy to endorse that assertion. But numerous remarks by journalists interviewed for this book suggest that it was at least as much the *press* who got tired of the story—though reporters were doubtless encouraged in their weariness by their own superiors, as well as by organized pressure from the "core supporters" Powell mentioned.

In a comment echoed by numerous other reporters, George Skelton, White House correspondent for the *Los Angeles Times*, explained, "I used to spend a lot of time writing those stories, but I just gave up. You write the stories once, twice, and you get a lot of mail saying, 'You're picking on the guy, you guys in the press make mistakes too.' And editors respond to that, so after a while the stories don't run anymore. We're intimidated."

Merrill Shiels, *Newsweek*'s national news editor during Reagan's first term, said, "I think everybody in the press corps is a little bit astonished at how many times the President can make horrible mistakes in public. I mean, for a long time we were writing practically every week a little box on what he said that wasn't true. We ultimately just couldn't stand doing it week after week after week because it seemed sort of unfair. Maybe unfair isn't the right word; it seemed like persecuting him or something. It came from our readers. You know, 'What is the matter with you people? Who cares if he knows the exact amount of something?' I didn't feel intimidated, but I'd say the reader response fueled my own. . . . It seems like the same story again and again and again, and it seems kind of picky. You get kind of tired of turning that screw."

NBC Nightly News anchor Tom Brokaw denied that the public had been deprived of a full and accurate picture of their President: "I think people buy the philosophy of Ronald Reagan. They do it wide open. . . . I think he's a gravely underinformed President in a lot of ways about the details of some of the big issues, but I also think that people know that. It's been printed, broadcast, talked about, it's been made fun of on the [Johnny] Carson show, it's part of the fabric of American knowledge about this man."

Without articulating it, Brokaw went right to the brink of the standard rationalization (offered by Reagan and news media officials alike) for the press's eventual abandonment of the gaffe story: popular apathy. In the words of *Time*'s chief of correspondents, Richard Duncan: "People don't care. They discount those errors. I think it was [CBS News correspondent Bill] Moyers who put it very well, essentially that reporters go running around saying, 'He's wrong, he's wrong, he's got the wrong number of barrels of oil reserves in Alaska,' and the American public says, 'We didn't elect this guy because he knows how many barrels of oil are in Alaska. We elected him because we want to feel good.' "

Blaming the public let the press off the hook, but it wasn't an adequate explanation. Because news accounts generally failed to make clear the real-world *implications* of Reagan's inability or unwillingness to distinguish fact from fiction, they often ended up trivializing or personalizing it. Thus Americans were told not about a President who harbored an apparently pathological disregard for truth, but about a well-meaning Everyman who at times got his figures wrong. As presidential scholar James David Barber observed: "Ronald Reagan is the first modern President whose contempt for the facts is treated as a charming idiosyncrasy." Reagan was presented not as a dangerously misinformed or deceptive man, but as an occasionally bumbling but essentially harmless grandfather figure who made, in Lou Cannon's phrase, "the kind of mistakes we all do." The rub, of course, was that many of Reagan's mistakes concerned matters of considerably graver importance than exactly how many barrels of oil were in Alaska.

At least part of the problem with the coverage was the American news media's relentless, ahistorical insistence on focusing on what is new rather than what is important. "They do show Reagan making errors," observed one upper-level network news producer. "The problem is, they don't incorporate it into their subsequent coverage of him. They show him the next day at a rally or whatever, and make him appear like he knows what he's talking about."

"It may be accurate that the media doesn't follow up," Sam Donaldson responded to this critique, "but I don't think it's a realistic assessment of what the press does, or ought to do. . . . In most day's ninety seconds, I'm trying to give you the so-called news: what was said, done or thought here that I know about and can present to you that you didn't know until you heard it. . . . At first I thought it was important when Reagan would fudge up figures on the Health and Human Services budget to make it look like he wasn't cutting, but now I don't have time to put it in. I've told my audience before that he doesn't know facts so often, is it news that today he doesn't know facts again? If he got through a press conference flawlessly, I would certainly say so that night. That, to me, would be news. Now, that lets him off the hook, I agree."

And so by the spring of 1983 the nation's most powerful news organizations had not just left the gaffe story behind; they had enthusiastically (if unwittingly) begun cooperating in what turned out to be a spectacularly successful White House effort to portray President Reagan as a decisive and statesmanlike world leader. Months later, *Wall Street Journal* White House reporter Rich Jaroslovsky told readers the inside story:

> Just before the [May 1983] Williamsburg economic summit, presidential aide Michael Deaver invited Hedrick Smith, *The New York Times*'s chief Washington correspondent, in for lunch. A few days later the *Times* ran a page-one story on President Reagan's vigorous preparations for the summit: how hard he was studying, even how he planned to take the official notes.
> But the real payoff was how Mr. Smith's piece set the tone for the television networks' coverage of the summit. All of the TV broadcasts conveyed the image of a President firmly in charge. ABC News featured Mr. Reagan's note-taking on two successive evenings.
> Actually, this all involved a little hype. Mr. Reagan's diligent

preparations didn't prevent him from watching *The Sound of Music* on TV. His note-taking was hardly unusual, since every host has been the official note-taker for these economic summits.

As subtle media manipulation, however, it was remarkably successful. To people viewing the event, the image conveyed "really answered the question of whether Ronald Reagan could be a world leader," contends Michael McManus, an aide to Mr. Deaver.

If by the spring of 1983 the media as a whole were eagerly singing the praises of the new Reagan, there were at least some individual journalists who recognized how absurd it all was—not only the recast presidential image itself but the press's witless complicity in selling it to the American public. Sam Donaldson, for example, recalled (after the fact) an opinion article written shortly after the Williamsburg summit by one of his favorite columnists, Richard Cohen of *The Washington Post* (no relation to CBS News producer Richard Cohen). Noting that everyone had pronounced Reagan's performance at the summit "such a triumph on his part," Donaldson went on to paraphrase Cohen's column: "They [in the White House] have now got us, because they have got us to judge [Reagan] by a standard of just bare mediocrity. If he stays awake, we're to applaud. If it can be said that he actually could discuss for twenty minutes microeconomics, and know some of the terms, we are to say, 'Hooray!' When in fact that should be just a minimum threshold. Cohen had him dead to rights," concluded Donaldson. "And he had us."

8

CENSORSHIP AT CBS

BOTHERSOME as the competence question was, it was not the primary danger facing the Reagan public relations apparatus in the troubled year of 1982. "The most important thing to remember," Gergen emphasized, "is that it was the economy plus the fairness issue that was bringing us down, not gaffes." As in the case of other modern Presidents, Reagan's popularity was directly related to the state of the economy; traditionally, there was a strong inverse correlation between the unemployment rate and a President's approval ratings. Thus as the jobless rate climbed into double digits in 1982, Ronald Reagan's job approval numbers plummeted, eventually bottoming out at a meager 35 percent by January 1983. But with the help of a cowardly opposition party and a gullible press, the Reagan apparatus managed to explain away even this piece of bad news.

"Baker, Deaver and Wirthlin really orchestrated this brilliantly," marveled Patrick Caddell, the pollster for every Democratic presidential candidate from 1972 to 1980. "Ronald Reagan had the lowest approval rating numbers of any first-year President in history, but these guys said, 'Oh, but he's still popular personally.' "

As with all good propaganda, there was a kernel of truth to the claim. Reagan's personal appeal ratings *were* consistently higher than his job approval ratings. It was this differential that gave rise to the view, widely advanced for the balance of Reagan's first term, that he was a spectacularly popular President, so much so that even Americans who disagreed with his policies still liked him.

The fallacy in all this, as political scientists Thomas Ferguson and Joel Rogers explained in their book *Right Turn*, was "that significant differentials between performance and personal approval ratings of Presidents are utterly routine, that they always show greater personal approval than performance approval (since Americans, for whatever reason, want to believe their Presidents are nice guys), and that in fact the differential Reagan enjoyed was proportionately smaller than those of most of his predecessors, not larger." Even Jimmy Carter at the height of the Iranian hostage crisis, the authors noted, benefited from a stronger "nice-guy effect" than Reagan did during his first two years in office.

Despite the objective weakness of its argument, the Reagan apparatus found a receptive audience for it among the press. "A look at press coverage in *Time, Newsweek,* and three leading newspapers—*The New York Times,* the *Los Angeles Times,* and *The Washington Post*—during the first two years of the Reagan administration shows that the press consistently assumed a degree of popularity that was not reflected in the polls," Elliot King and Michael Schudson later reported in the *Columbia Journalism Review.* "At a time when President Reagan's poll ratings were significantly lower than those of other Presidents, the press reported that Reagan was unusually magnetic and popular."

Capitol Hill Democrats, still mindful of the avalanche of political pressure exerted on Reagan's behalf during the summer of 1981 tax and budget bill battles, also swallowed the White House's self-serving claims. "I remember going to meetings in '81 and '82 with [House Speaker Tip] O'Neill and other Democratic congressional leaders and arguing that you've got to engage this guy," said Caddell, "but they wouldn't hear of it—too risky. It became a self-reinforcing circle: the White House had convinced the press that Reagan was fantastically popular, the press convinced the Democrats, who were afraid of their own shadows to begin with, and then the Democrats became the source and confirmation of news stories saying that Reagan was so popular! I used to argue the historical data with various journalists, and point out that he really wasn't that popular historically, but their attitude was 'Yes, he is. The White House says so, and the Democrats do too.' "

Despite their success at launching one of the great sustaining myths of the Reagan presidency, the President's PR advisers remained deeply concerned about the fairness issue. In public, Reagan officials always had a ready answer when asked whether their economic policies would not hurt the poor: No, the truly needy would not suffer, because the administration was keeping the social safety net intact. But in private, the Reagan men apparently knew better. According to Michael Deaver, he and other top White House media strategists were worried about what came to be known as the fairness issue "from the very first. Well, from the time the new budget was approved *and we knew it was going to hurt a lot of people.*" (Emphasis added.)

The Reagan administration's public protestations of innocence on the fairness issue were masterpieces of sophistry, built around two of the slipperiest buzzwords of the Reagan era. Who defined "the social safety net"? How exactly were needy people distinguished from "truly needy" people? Still, that was the official line, and it succeeded in holding the press at bay for quite a while. For it was often the case that Washington journalists reported not reality so much as what government officials said about reality. In matters of official policy, they tended to take the government at its word unless and until events unequivocally proved otherwise. Thus as long as the administration resolutely denied that its budget cuts would cause undue hardship, most journalists, whatever their private doubts, shrank from strongly challenging the deception in their reporting.

All of which helps explain why David Stockman's revelations in the November 1981 issue of *The Atlantic Monthly* constituted such a public relations disaster for the Reagan apparatus. As Stockman later admitted in his memoirs, evidence was available very early on in 1981 to demonstrate what common sense should have suggested—that the numbers simply didn't add up: huge tax cuts plus an unprecedented military spending spree would clearly result in a massive budget deficit. One would never have guessed that, however, from the vast majority of mainstream news reports of that spring and summer. Now, with Stockman disclosing that beneath all the previous assurances of prosperity for all and a balanced budget by 1984, the truth was that he had fudged the numbers and that Reaganomics was really just old-fashioned trickle-down economics repackaged for the 1980s, it became impossible for the press to avoid or for the administration to finesse the fairness issue any longer.

Even so, fairness was by no means the overriding theme in initial network coverage of Stockman's remarks. "The process of the presidency far outweighs the policy of the presidency as a point of coverage and story development" for the networks, explained former ABC *World News Tonight* executive producer Robert Frye. In Stockman's case, "everyone covered his going to the woodshed and no one bothered to read the goddamn article!" Mr. Frye exaggerated somewhat, but it was true that the network evening news shows seemed at least as intrigued by the scandal of it all as by what Stockman actually said. Treatment of the story was substantially the same on all three networks: a brisk listing of four or five of Stockman's juiciest quotes, followed by companion pieces of equal or greater length reporting what legislators on Capitol Hill thought about Stockman now. That the administration had previously misrepresented its economic program was made clear, as was the program's bias in favor of the wealthy, but that was as far as the networks went in analyzing the substance and implications of Stockman's remarks.

Apparently more interesting to the media was the question of Stockman's loyalty to his President. (That was also the primary concern of Michael Deaver, who, alone among the President's top aides, argued strenuously that Stockman should be fired. "No, it wasn't damage control," Deaver later explained. "I was just outraged that the guy would say those kinds of things about the President when he's working for him and, in fact, recommended all that crap, er, all that policy.") Network news reports portrayed the young budget director not as a contemporary Robin Hood in reverse but rather, in *NBC Nightly News* co-anchor Roger Mudd's phrase, as a man guilty of "one of Washington's oldest sins . . . a loose tongue." William Greider of *The Washington Post*, who wrote the Stockman article for *The Atlantic Monthly*, later marveled at his colleagues' reaction: "One would think that if first principles of journalism really guided the press they would celebrate [Stockman] for his truth telling. But the whole tone of their coverage was: How could he do this? This is irresponsible for a member of the President's Cabinet to say these things in print, and how could he possibly survive in government?" In fact, Stockman survived by appearing at a press conference two days after the story broke and offering up the (false) metaphor of Reagan taking him for an after-supper visit to the woodshed, thus encouraging the focus on his own fate rather than that of the American economy, and satisfying network news producers that the story had run its course.

(The Washington press corps again revealed its palace court

character when Stockman's memoirs appeared in the spring of 1986. *The Triumph of Politics* may well come to be regarded as one of the most important economic documents of the Reagan era, but that was not how it was received by the political-journalistic establishment in the nation's capital. David Broder of *The Washington Post*, widely regarded as the nation's premier political commentator, archly denounced Stockman in his nationally syndicated column for saying such terrible things about his former colleagues. Most subsequent news stories and commentary depicted the former budget director as a traitorous brat and entirely shirked the more important task of exploring his extraordinary revelations. The coverage reflected the scolding tone of columnist George Will's comment that one requirement of Washington politics "is a kind of loyalty [which] includes a certain reticence when you leave office.")

The long-term effect of Stockman's confessions was to legitimize more aggressive and skeptical press coverage of Reaganomics, to edge the fairness issue into what Professor Hallin calls the Sphere of Legitimate Controversy. Out in the real world, of course, the consequences of Reagan's policies were no different than before. But now that a top government official had, as it were, admitted that the sky was blue, the press was much more comfortable in repeating the charge. In that sense, the Stockman episode was reminiscent of the Pentagon Papers story of ten years earlier, in that it illustrated how very reluctant the press was to point accusatory fingers until the government itself admitted guilt.

If publication of Stockman's comments effectively gave the Washington press corps permission to go after a story they should have been pursuing all along, other forces had by late 1981 also begun encouraging a more critical stance. As evidence mounted that the economy was shuddering to a halt, the Democrats grew slightly less timid in their criticism of Reagan. Nor were Capitol Hill Republicans completely steadfast in their support for the President, as the dismal failure of the White House's so-called Fall Offensive to achieve new budget cuts had shown. Few Washington politicians were willing to criticize Reagan openly, but the political winds that had swirled so powerfully through the capital earlier in the year had now died down, at least for the moment, with the result that the Reagan administration could no longer count on getting its way on every issue. And the farther the economy sank, the more challenging the questions directed at the White House became.

"The fairness issue was exacerbated by the recession," said Gergen. "Only in the middle of recession could you understand how powerful the fairness issue could be politically. . . . [The recession] left a lot of people in trouble, and the people in trouble needed government help." But because other economic objectives took priority within the Reagan administration, no such help was forthcoming. The White House, it will be recalled, had expected to divert attention from the inequity of its tax and budget cuts by sparking an economic expansion. At the same time, it was also determined to wring inflation from the U.S. economy once and for all. Purging inflation, however, required the encouragement of Federal Reserve Bank chairman Paul Volcker as he enforced a monetary policy so restrictive as to make growth impossible. Meanwhile, President Reagan was also unwilling to scale back either the gargantuan military spending increases demanded by the Pentagon or the tax reductions enacted the previous summer. As a result, for the White House to make any progress toward reducing the suddenly enormous deficit, Gergen explained, "inevitably we had to go ahead with budget cuts and proposals in late '81 and early '82 in the teeth of the recession that sounded like they were really heartless."

In sharp contrast to the year before, television coverage of the budget Reagan released in February 1982 did hit the fairness issue hard, making frequent explicit references to its differing effects on rich and poor. All three networks made a point of juxtaposing the administration's call for $26 billion in cuts in social programs with its proposal for a $44 billion increase for the military. The toughest and most informative report came from NBC, whose co-anchor John Chancellor noted in his lead sentence the criticism that Reagan's was "a budget for the rich," an observation that a year earlier would have been unthinkable. Chancellor went on to point out that "the losers in the President's budget plan are people who get help from what are called social programs—Medicare, Medicaid, school lunches, welfare, food stamps. . . . The winners in the President's proposed budget are the armed forces." Mr. Reagan was given ample time and space to defend his budget, but defend is the key word. The presidential quotes chosen by network journalists for inclusion in their newscasts were not those where Reagan promised eventual economic recovery but those where he denied that the budget was "balanced on the backs of the needy." Such claims were then implicitly undercut by companion stories featuring budget cut victims whose plights made the Reagan proposals seem just as heartless as Gergen later admitted they sounded.

With the help of longtime Reagan adviser Richard Wirthlin's opinion polls, however, the White House apparatus not only had already detected rising public resentment against Reagan's class-biased policies but had taken steps to contain the problem. On February 5, many of the White House's top political and public relations advisers had gathered for a daylong retreat at Camp David to discuss long-term strategy and direction for the President's second year. Although the agenda included a wide range of issues, Michael Deaver later confirmed there was special concern among Reagan's image enhancers about the growing popular perception of the President as "a friend of the rich," a view fueled by increasing news coverage of First Lady Nancy Reagan's lavish lifestyle in the midst of hard times. "We had all those negative stories on Nancy at that time," remembered Deaver. "You take the budget cuts stories and pair them with the stories about the [new White House] china and the refurbishing of the dresses and all that, and it was beginning to hurt. We could see it in our polls. Camp David was just a strategy session to think of positive things we could do, things we could emphasize that the press would have to cover."

This proved a fairly easy task. In a move cleverly designed to enlist the sympathies of the capital's press establishment, Mrs. Reagan's advisers arranged for her to appear in March at the Gridiron dinner, the establishment's annual social gathering and the ultimate expression of the palace court nature of Washington journalism. As cartoonist Tony Auth of *The Philadelphia Inquirer* once remarked, Gridiron dinners were "a structured way for people to say, 'We're all in the same boat here.' " In the weeks preceding them, news organizations competed fiercely to see who could attract the most high-powered collection of government officials to their tables as honored guests, and the evenings themselves were spent laughing together at a series of musical skits staged by the journalists, skits which poked extremely gentle fun at the governing authorities but which the journalists themselves apparently regarded as quite daring satires. Mrs. Reagan charmed the 1982 dinner audience when, following a separate skit spoofing her expensive tastes, she strode on-stage unannounced, dressed as a bag lady, and sang, to the tune of "Second Hand Rose," a ditty about wearing second-hand clothes.

No First Lady's image since Eleanor Roosevelt has been complete without an appropriately compassionate volunteer project, however. Deaver & Co. hit upon the topic of drug abuse, and before long Mrs. Reagan was seen visiting counseling centers and tenderly lecturing schoolchildren on the evils of drugs. Although her advisers had actually gone so far as to enlist a White House speechwriter to draft humorous rejoinders to any further criticisms of her lifestyle by reporters, the need for such quips soon diminished as word was passed down through the ranks of the press, both subtly and not so subtly, that Mrs. Reagan was not, after all, the President and should not be badgered.

When the First Lady made a photo opportunity visit to Phoenix House, a drug rehabilitation center in New York City, for example, one *New York Times* reporter had the temerity to write a story lead noting the irony of Mrs. Reagan posing with impoverished junkies while wearing a designer dress worth thousands of dollars. The lead enraged one of the paper's senior editors. He stormed into the middle of the newsroom and, in front of numerous other reporters, loudly berated the reporter, warning that the reference to Mrs. Reagan's dress was injurious both to the *Times* and to the reporter's career and ordering the lead changed immediately. Likewise Lee Lescaze, who was transferred from the White House beat to *The Washington Post*'s "Style" section in 1982, remembered how "it suddenly became clear we were not to take swipes at Nancy Reagan. I was never told specifically to do or not to do stories. [*Post* executive editor Benjamin] Bradlee was very good at shielding us, but there was a kind of atmosphere of: enough is enough; she's not running the country."

Protecting the image of Mrs. Reagan's husband proved rather more of a challenge. Even before the Camp David retreat, Deaver had felt it necessary to switch Blair House meetings (the Friday planning meetings where he, Gergen, Richard Darman and others set long-term communications strategy) from occasional into regular weekly events. Now, mindful of Wirthlin polls that cited "Cares about people" as the President's highest negative, he sought to arrange public appearances that would cast Reagan in a more compassionate light. Gergen's lightning-rod theory of distancing the President from bad news about his administration would seem to have suggested caution about sending Reagan out to talk about the economy in 1982, but Deaver was determined to keep his man before the cameras, even though the President's job approval rating was plummeting. "His personal popularity was staying up," explained Deaver. "That always stayed in good shape, so we could continue to use him as often as we could. He was the best spokesman we had, regardless of what was happening."

Putting the President on the road may have made the slide less steep, but by the spring of 1982, with the U.S. economy continuing to contract, it was impossible to prevent Reagan's approval ratings from deteriorating. Within the White House, recalled Gergen, "there was a sense we were spinning out of control. . . . You wondered if things could collapse on him." The external difficulties were compounded by internal bickering and recriminations. The President's right-wing supporters apparently saw an opportunity to discredit the so-called moderates in the White House by blaming them for Reagan's misfortunes. Gergen later remembered how the conservatives would argue that "the Baker group, the pragmatists, can't handle this. If they would just go out there and preach the conservative ideology more forcefully, everything would magically turn around because obviously the whole country's now conservative, considering the election of 1980. Well," he added, "that was hogwash. We didn't believe it, Wirthlin didn't believe it. Wirthlin's conservative credentials are well established. Everybody who knew anything about politics knew that Reagan at that point was being dragged down by the recession."

Reagan's tumbling popularity would continue to bedevil the White House apparatus throughout 1982. David Gergen had never intended to stay in the White House for Reagan's entire first term, but now he found himself driven to extend his tour of duty by the President's predicament. "I would say '82 was the toughest year of the first term," he said. "One of the reasons I stayed—I knew I wanted to leave before the '84 election—but I didn't want to leave then, because I would have left defeated, in effect. I had to stay long enough to be back on top again."

• • •

DAVID GERGEN liked to present himself as a man who favored the carrot over the stick in dealing with the press, but now that he felt he was fighting for the President's survival, not to mention his own professional reputation, he seemed infused with a spirit of combativeness. His immediate concern was the fairness issue, which continued to attract dangerous amounts of press attention. "Reagan's America: The Poor Get Poorer" read the cover of one *Newsweek* issue. The April 9 edition of ABC's *World News Tonight* concluded with a special report by correspondent Richard Threlkeld that pointed out that while Reagan had kept the social safety net intact for such middle-class programs as Social Security and Medicare, "the safety net for the poor . . . has been slashed." The same point was made more powerfully on April 21 when CBS News broadcast a prime-time documentary entitled "People Like Us." Hosted by correspondent Bill Moyers, the CBS report profiled a handful of indigent Americans and conveyed in graphic terms the severe extra hardship they had encountered after the first round of President Reagan's budget cuts went into effect the previous October. A cerebral palsy victim deprived of Social Security benefits, a former welfare mother quitting work and going back on welfare in order to qualify for Medicaid coverage of a vital operation for her son—it was undeniably moving television, and few who watched it were likely to quarrel with its conclusion that "some of the truly needy are truly hurting."

With "punishing the poor" threatening to become a major and continuing theme in media coverage of the Reagan administration, Gergen decided it was time to fight back. The day after "People Like Us" was broadcast, he launched a highly visible counteroffensive, appearing on television and granting extra newspaper interviews to denounce the CBS documentary as unfair and "below the belt." After having received an advance copy of the script from a White House sympathizer within CBS, Gergen had requested, unsuccessfully, that he be allowed to view the documentary before it was aired. Now he pressed CBS to grant the White House thirty minutes of free airtime in which to defend its record. "Frankly," he explained in retrospect, "we thought if we asked and they refused us it would improve our standing to go to the public and say, 'We were wronged—the unfairness of the show extends to where they wouldn't even let us have anybody dispute them on the air.' " (The producer of "People Like Us," Judy Reemstma, later said that no Reagan spokesperson had appeared on the show because "we made a decision that the administration's point of view had already been put to the public in lots of other ways.")

Although his new aggressiveness did not sit well with all of his White House colleagues, Gergen never doubted he had done the right thing. "I know Darman thought it was a mistake to attack the Moyers program," Gergen recalled. "In fact, he attacked me in the press. He didn't use his name, but I was aware of what was happening. I frequently felt that Dick didn't appreciate the full power of television. The Moyers piece was seen by a lot of people. And unless one responded to it, silence was acquiescence. And that [was] the best way to chase people off; it was important to show the networks on some occasions that you were just not going to let them beat you up—you were going to fight back. I think that's part of what a guy ought to be out there doing. I know [Darman] disagreed with that, felt it kept it in the news for a few days. I felt the long-range effects were better."

Around the time of Gergen's attack, CBS News management began pressuring journalists on its *Evening News* staff, and especially White House correspondent Lesley Stahl, to tone down criticism of President Reagan and stop being what management considered overly negative in their coverage of public affairs and especially the economy. According to various CBS sources in both the Washington bureau and New York headquarters, the campaign to soften coverage of Reagan began in 1982 and continued well into the 1984 election year. It took many forms, ranging from the fostering of a newsroom atmosphere where, in one source's words, "there was a sense in the air that we don't want any more of the predictably liberal stories" to, in Stahl's case, outright rewriting of scripts. How much difference all this made in CBS's actual news coverage cannot be measured exactly—the original scripts are unavailable for scrutiny, and one can only guess at what kind of stories might have been broadcast had a different climate existed in the newsroom—but it is significant that both CBS journalists and White House officials felt the coverage was gentler than it otherwise would have been. Gergen, for example, confirmed he did "sometimes" detect a backing off in Stahl's coverage of the President (though he still considered her "the toughest" of the television correspondents on the White House beat).

Many of those who served as top officials of CBS during this period refused to be interviewed for this book. Lesley Stahl, by all accounts a central figure in the controversy, refused to talk as well, but only after confirming the essence of the story. When asked to grant an interview to discuss colleagues' claims that her scripts had frequently been altered and her story proposals rejected by superiors in New York in order to make her coverage less critical of Reagan, Stahl quickly replied, "Well, all that happened, I can't deny it." Some CBS staffers were willing to speak on the record about the controversy, but others, fearing for their jobs, agreed to tell what they knew only on a not-for-attribution basis. The stories told by these two groups of sources were, however, by and large free of serious contradiction.

"The managers of CBS News seemed acutely conscious that the public image of us was [that] we're negative, especially with a President as popular as Ronald Reagan," recalled *Evening News* producer Richard Cohen. "Everyone in the field wanted to be tough on Reagan; the caution was much more in the fishbowl and the front office." (The fishbowl was the nerve center and command post of the *Evening News*, a glass-encased room where the executive producer and the program's four other top producers planned out the broadcast.) Noting that CBS News came under new management in early 1982, Cohen said that the new bosses "had a view of what kind of news made for good ratings: more features, make it light and bright, soften it up. Don't be negative about the President, people don't want to hear that." In a later interview, speaking about management's concern that CBS News was being too critical and downbeat in its reporting, Cohen added, "There was never a meeting where that was said, but it was said to me directly, by [*Evening News* executive producer] Howard Stringer, and to many others all the time. They made no secret about it."

White House coverage in particular apparently was regarded as overly negative. Brian Healy, an *Evening News* producer in the Washington bureau, paraphrased a mid-1982 conversation with Stringer as follows: "He said, you know, 'How many times are we going to kick this guy in the ass? Every time he does something, we kick him in the ass. The guy just passed his budget, just passed his tax cut, he's got a 95 percent approval rating in this country [sic], maybe we should tuck in our desire to kick the guy in the balls every time and try to be a little bit more objective.' That assumed we hadn't been objective before, but the point was very simple: we're not going to play the advocate that the guy's an asshole anymore."

"There was real tension between our White House reporters and the fishbowl," said *Evening News* producer Richard Cohen. White House reporters felt the fishbowl "was emasculating their coverage [of Reagan] on a daily basis throughout 1983 and 1984, before which it showed itself in smaller ways," added Cohen. "There is no question it was a commonly held view in CBS's White House office that they were being sat on by *Evening News* headquarters in New York."

Van Gordon Sauter and Edward Joyce were the executives in charge of CBS News during this time. Each man adamantly denied that he had ordered CBS journalists to be less critical of the President.

"Tension between some in the Washington bureau and the 'fishbowl' in New York did exist," confirmed Joyce, who was then CBS News executive vice president, but not, he emphasized, because they were being sat on. While Joyce refused to be interviewed for this book, in a letter to the author he suggested that the Washington staff's anger had more to do with ego than politics. The tension, he wrote, "existed because other bureaus in the United States and around the world had been improved and were competing vigorously with the Washington bureau with story offerings. It also existed because the editorial staff of the fishbowl . . . were demanding better work from some in Washington."

Sauter, who initially twice declined written requests for interviews, told me in October 1987 that "I don't know of any journalist being told to soften their coverage or to do anything other than report the news as well as they could." Sauter was also at a loss concerning the charges that he had fostered a newsroom atmosphere in which predictably knee-jerk liberal stories were unwelcome: "Again, I just don't know how to respond to that. We were committed to producing the best broadcast we could.

If we fell short of that occasionally, it was not out of any reluctance to tell people the reality of what was going on in the country, or to impose any sort of political slant on the coverage, or to go easy on a popular President."

On a day-to-day basis, it was executive producer Stringer who enforced the Sauter-Joyce approach to news at CBS. A documentary producer for *CBS Reports* for twelve years, Stringer had zero hard-news experience. His British accent, remarked one colleague, "made him sound about four thousand times smarter than he really is," and he had a knack for impressing and socializing with his superiors. He had a reputation as a gifted filmmaker, an accomplished leader and a witty and sensitive man, but in his new job he quickly proved he would not let sentiment stand in the way of carrying out the boss's orders. Recalling how the New York office had communicated its desire for a change in coverage from Washington, *Evening News* producer Healy said, "It was very direct. We're talking here about people who don't deal with obfuscation. 'You may wonder why your piece didn't get on the air last night,' Howard might tell you the next morning. 'It didn't get on because it was boring, it was dull, it was done in a way that no one could care about it.' " (Mr. Stringer refused repeated requests for an interview.)

Sauter, Joyce and Stringer were, if anything, even less sparing toward the New York staff. In the old days it had been virtually unheard of for the president of the news division to appear in the newsroom during the workday, but Sauter soon became a common sight there. However, it was after the broadcast that Sauter really laid down the law, in nightly postmortem sessions held in the fishbowl. Regular participants included the broadcast's four senior producers plus executive producer Stringer (who were themselves collectively known as "the fishbowl"), Dan Rather, Joyce and Sauter, who chaired the meeting. The word most commonly used to describe these gatherings was "bloody."

"They'd troop in, and the door would close," said Richard Cohen. "We didn't hear much, but you could see the strain on people's faces. It was very uneasy, very tense. They were flogging the fishbowl about the broadcast every night."

"Van started a marking system," recalled another producer, "a scale of ten. If the broadcast had been a six or higher, things were okay; anything below a six, yeah, it got bloody. . . . The problem was the show had no executive producer then; Van Gordon Sauter was the executive producer. These were collegial gang bangs, and there were nights when the blood flowed freely. The tension used to be tremendous. . . . The work atmosphere of course was terrible, because you realize you don't really have a boss, he was just doing the bidding of *his* boss."

"We had discussions, and often they got heated," conceded Sauter. "But I see nothing wrong with colleagues arguing forcefully and candidly about one another's work. And in the end we reached consensus on what the broadcast should be and on what quality of work it demanded."

"When you're talking about changing pieces during that period—they would say to be more objective, [Lesley] would say to curry more favor with the President—Lesley is the center of that more than anyone else," remarked Brian Healy. Healy, who described himself as "more conservative on things than most of my colleagues," added, "I thought for a time it went a little too far; Lesley thought they gutted all her pieces. . . . [Reagan] was proposing all these changes, and we had a right and obligation to say, 'Look at what this is going to do, look at the effect on this program and this program.' The question is, how long can you do that? There's a difference between giving both sides and being perceived as an opponent. Some people in the company were saying, 'Well, why are we doing this? Maybe the man has an occasional bright thought, an occasional good idea.' "

Susan Zirinsky of the Washington bureau, who produced most of the White House stories broadcast on the *Evening News* during this period, including many by Lesley Stahl, said that the pressure from upstairs to be less critical was never communicated to her directly. "No one said to me, 'We're being more positive, we're out to be less shrill,' if you will. When occasionally a piece would have a sharply critical close, I found it coming back changed, with editorial suggestions that took the hard edge off the piece. New York, as it had on occasion during the Carter years, said they felt we couldn't substantiate some of the critical conclusions we reached. And I'm on deadline, I'm racing the clock, and they're your boss, they're your editors, so you say yes. How many times has a print reporter opened up his paper in the morning and found his lead changed and wanted to pull his or her hair out?"

"There was a particular feeling on the part of some folks in the fishbowl that Lesley's pieces, while they'd be objective, at the end there was always [a] 'the President is an asshole' close," added Brian Healy. "So they would start working on her very, very heavily. The other problem is, Lesley's a terrible writer. . . . So there were times they were [merely] trying to fix the language that she interpreted, in her words, as ripping the guts out of her stories. And there were other times they were trying to tone it down. Absolutely. . . . Lesley had some fairly contentious phone calls with the folks who run the show. [Then senior Washington producer] Joe Peyronnin was the point man with Washington and the mediator. He'd take her copy and clean it up for style and editorial and send it to New York, and they'd send it back to him—it'd be the executive producer, Howard Stringer or [his successor] Lane Venardos. Lesley would scream and holler and yell at Joe, and most often comply to a degree; Joe would yell at them. It was very contentious in that way. But it was also like running a nuclear power plant—everything was done by remote control. [Although] sometimes Lesley would call them up at the end of the broadcast and go crazy."

Dan Rather was not just the anchor but the managing editor of the broadcast during this period. Because he too refused to be interviewed, it is difficult to say how vigorously he may have used his influence to resist internal pressures to tone down CBS coverage. If he did resist, his efforts seem to have met with little success. And in fact, while Rather was known to the outside world as the ultimate journalistic tough guy, that image actually clashed with the content of most of his work. Except for a few well-publicized scraps with already vulnerable politicians, most notably President Nixon in 1973 and Vice President Bush in 1988, Rather tended, especially after becoming the CBS anchorman in 1981, not to make many waves. As illustrated by incidents recounted elsewhere in this book, he more often than not reported the pronouncements of public officials with considerable respect, conferring upon them an authority that was often unwarranted. Contrary to his liberal reputation, he came across on the air as a stern anti-Communist. Indeed, he could be downright fawning in his embrace of right-wing ideology, as when he asked President Reagan before the 1987 summit meeting with General Secretary Gorbachev how he planned not to let "this young, energetic, intelligent Marxist-Leninist eat you and us up." Leaving aside his breathy delivery and his obviously forced sincerity on camera, it was on this substantive level that Rather most clearly fell short of the example set by the original CBS broadcasting hero, Edward R. Murrow.

CBS management apparently worried about seeming too negative not only about President Reagan but also about the economy. It was a hard subject to be upbeat about when so many Americans were out of work, and CBS by and large was not during 1982; but once the official unemployment rate was seen to have peaked at 10.8 percent in December 1982, there was increasing pressure around the newsroom to knock off the gloom and doom and cheer on the recovery.

"There came a point where there was concern we were out of step with the country," recalled Healy. "Especially once the economy began to turn around a little bit, that with all our stories about long unemployment lines and budget cutbacks and no hope for people, the liberal elite network was out of step; it was apparent that many people around the country thought we were, and some people in New York as well. I think Howard Stringer, whom I really respect as someone who thinks a lot and worries a lot and intellectualizes about things, came to believe we had crossed a line into a political line. And he tried to bring it back."

Stringer's concern about negativity, according to Richard Cohen, who produced some of the evening broadcast's economics stories in 1983, "manifested itself in the editing process. I'd walk into the fishbowl with an economics script, take a deep breath and wait to fight it out. . . . Howard and I invariably clashed over them because I wanted to be more critical. I can't say I won many times. It was more that he toned down my stuff, though not as far as he would have liked; I still managed to get in more critical stuff than he would have liked." (Cohen eventually paid for the independence of mind he exhibited at CBS. In March 1988, he was fired from his post as the senior producer in charge of political coverage for CBS News.)

"Howard felt we had a knee-jerk need to say 'Yes, but . . .' to any good piece of economics news," Cohen explained in a second interview. "But that was part of the story. Reaganomics was seen as a success when [the administration's policies] had nothing to do with the recovery. I thought if we gave [Reagan] any credit for it, it was too much. Inflation came down, but on the backs of the poor. He got lucky with an oil glut and good crops [which helped reduce inflation], and the growth came from old-time Republican medicine, a policy of recession."

One day, recalled Cohen, Stringer reinforced his argument by good-naturedly tossing onto Cohen's desk a copy of a *Washington Journalism Review* article castigating CBS News for the very "Yes, but . . ." attitude that Stringer himself had previously criticized. The piece was written by pro-Reagan columnist Fred Barnes (provoking Cohen to reply, "Come on! Do you know who he is?"), and was typical of the criticism CBS and to a lesser extent the other networks would receive in the months to come from corporate and right-wing forces. *The Wall Street Journal* on March 6, 1984, for example, published an opinion article by Holmes M. Brown, president of the Institute for Applied Economics, a New York group sponsored by three dozen U.S. corporations, that accused the networks of "turn[ing] the good news into bad news" during the second half of 1983 by "concentrating on the pockets of recession within the overall recovery, thereby implying that behind the good news of falling inflation and rising employment there were black clouds of economic misery."

The complaint was that the networks did not cheer loudly or soon enough about the supposedly splendid recovery visited upon the American economy in 1983. In fact, however, all three networks began using the word "recovery" to describe the state of the U.S. economy as soon as the government announced early in February that unemployment had fallen for the first time in eighteen months. ABC economics correspondent Dan Cordtz, for example, on February 4 said the drop in unemployment to 10.4 percent in January suggested that "a recovery . . . may be underway." By April and May, the recovery was portrayed as not just a reality but a cause for celebration. Dan Rather led the April 15 *CBS Evening News* by exulting over that day's record stockmarket performance, while correspondent Wyatt Andrews later affirmed that the nation was enjoying a "true recovery." Tom Brokaw led the May 13 *NBC Nightly News* by announcing that "the economic recovery is looking even brighter tonight" before introducing economics correspondent Mike Jensen, who offered no dissent from Reagan administration chief economist Martin Feldstein's remark that the recovery was "shifting into high gear" and closed his piece by asserting, at a time when nearly ten million

Americans remained officially unemployed and poverty was rising sharply, that the only dark cloud on the horizon was "the enormous federal deficit."

• • •

IN THE specific case of CBS News, the obvious question is: What motivated management to urge its journalists to go easy on Reagan? Was it White House pressure? Tom Bettag, at the time one of the fishbowl producers and later appointed the executive producer of the *CBS Evening News*, confirmed that the broadcast altered its coverage of Reagan and Reaganomics in 1982–83 and that this sparked tension with the Washington bureau, but he denied that the White House had anything to do with it; the decision, he said, was CBS's alone. "We were trying in our coverage not to be knee-jerk," Bettag explained. "Every time Reagan proposed a program cut, we went out and did a story on who would be hurt by that cut; we sought out those stories. We later came to feel that in a presidency that was proposing budget reductions as a matter of policy, that story was becoming formula. We knew it made for sympathetic, dramatic television, but we worried that it would overwhelm the corresponding stories about how budget cuts would reduce the deficit, which weren't so visual and weren't being covered so well."*

Mr. Bettag conceded under questioning that there was another reason as well for the shift in coverage: a belief that upbeat, positive, "patriotic" reporting about the President would make people feel good and thus produce higher ratings. "There is that line of argument," said Bettag, "and that generally comes from corporate people. But serious news people can argue separately that there was knee-jerk coverage of the deficit and program cuts. I reject the first argument, and regret the two were being argued at the same time. I'd [make the second argument] to people in the Washington bureau and I knew they were figuring I was just

---

* Perhaps it was mere coincidence, but there was an eerie resemblance between that line of reasoning and one of the criticisms of CBS economics coverage that Fred Barnes had offered in a June 1982 *Washington Journalism Review* article. "CBS flirts with unbalanced coverage when its emphasis is so heavily devoted to the negative," wrote Barnes. "And the more emotional its spots get, the less thoughtful they tend to be. There is no perspective, no sense of the trade-offs in modern economic life, no inkling that cuts in, say, funds for day-care centers might have some beneficial economic effects."

a pawn in the corporate argument, which I sort of resented, because I do think our coverage was knee-jerk."

For their part, White House officials denied launching any effort to intimidate CBS journalists by going over their heads to corporate superiors in New York. White House chief of staff James Baker was known to be friendly with Thomas Wyman, then the chief executive officer of CBS, Inc., but in an interview Baker denied ever discussing the network's news coverage with him. David Gergen, when asked whether he knew about any pressure on correspondent Stahl mounted by CBS corporate headquarters, said, "I wasn't aware that much of pressure from the top. I'm not surprised by it, but we weren't that much aware of it. . . . We were pressing more at the producer and [Washington bureau chief] level here, rather than going up the road to New York."

Gergen did not dispute that his public attack on the "People Like Us" documentary might have been what led CBS management to question whether the network was being fair enough to the White House, but he suggested that the networks had their own reasons for going easy on Reagan as well: "I have friends in the press, both in print and the networks, who felt that management was cowed too often by a sense that we've got to be fair to Reagan, maybe they've got a point, and we're beating up on the guy too much," Gergen affirmed. ". . . The press in general was worried as Reagan came into office that they had been an unwitting participant in the destruction or downfall of at least two Presidents, and they felt that the public was not sympathetic to their role. They were worried about losing viewers, losing audience, losing public support and being regulated. All of those were legitimate fears. Of course, the networks by that time *were* losing viewers, to cable and elsewhere. That was working in Reagan's favor coming in, and it wasn't hard to fan those flames from within the White House."

That was especially true in the case of CBS News. Ratings for its flagship program, the *CBS Evening News*, had fallen precipitously during 1981. Triggered by the March departure of Walter Cronkite, the descent cost the network its traditional commanding lead in the evening news ratings race and raised questions about the wisdom of having signed Dan Rather to a ten-year, $25 million contract to serve as Cronkite's replacement. By October, the broadcast had begun dropping into third place, and it was clear something had to be done; the decline had forced CBS to lower the average price of a thirty-second commercial on the program from the $40,000 of Cronkite's day to the industry standard of $30,000.

Nothing raised eyebrows at Black Rock, the New York headquarters of CBS, Inc., quicker than falling revenues, and in November, Gene Jankowski, vice president of the CBS Broadcast Group and the news division's immediate corporate superior, took action. He turned the news division over to the man who then ran CBS Sports, Van Gordon Sauter,* who had a history of reversing ratings slides for CBS. Mr. Sauter had first earned Black Rock's appreciation by turning the trick at WBBM, CBS's owned-and-operated affiliate station in Chicago, where he served as news director from 1973 to 1975. In 1977, Sauter repeated the feat at KNXT, the network's o-and-o in Los Angeles. In between, he sandwiched in time as CBS News Paris bureau chief and, in 1976, a stint as the network's censor, a portentous fact generally mentioned in passing, if at all, in subsequent press profiles.

For all his obvious ambition to climb the corporate ladder, Van Sauter's personal style and appearance—invariably lauded as "colorful" in those same profiles—suggested not that he was management's boy but rather that he was one of the boys. A pipe-smoking, full-bearded, owlish-faced man of forty-six at the time he took over CBS News, he was fond of wearing funny hats around the office, or no socks, anything to appear offbeat. He harbored a passion for fishing that approached the fanatical. Although he had ascended out of the affiliate ranks himself, Sauter apparently dreaded attending affiliate meetings once he became division president. So he had senior CBS News executive Peter Herford arrange coincident fishing trips, to which he would routinely skip out during said meetings—though he first made sure, Herford recalled, "to go to one cocktail party [and] charm the bejesus out of everybody." Flamboyant, energetic, and extremely adept at bureaucratic politics, he brought a very hands-on management style to the task of transforming CBS News.

He also brought in Ed Joyce, whom he had met years before

---

* Sauter did not formally become News president until William Leonard's February 1982 retirement.

while each was directing all-news radio stations, to serve as his deputy. On the face of it, a more unlikely twosome was hard to imagine; within the CBS affiliate community, the two men were reportedly known as Santa Claus and Mack the Knife. With his correct tailoring, aloof manner and relentless focus on the bottom line, Joyce, then forty-nine, was the quintessential organization man. Stories told by CBS subordinates portrayed him as a corporate hatchet man who relished his ruthless reputation. During a speech delivered back at WBBM, according to one such tale, Joyce acknowledged the aptness of another of his nicknames, "the Velvet Shiv," then slyly added the punch line, "I just don't know where the *velvet* came from!" He was just the sort of lieutenant Sauter needed as he set about reconstructing CBS News, a man who could eliminate bureaucratic enemies, slash budgets and generally play the heavy while Sauter stayed clean and jollied the troops on to victory. According to Herford, who worked closely with both men, and watched helplessly as they gradually moved against the entire Old Guard of CBS News (including Herford himself, eventually), disposing of distinguished veteran producers and executives with the phrase "He's yesterday," Sauter and Joyce functioned as the classic good cop–bad cop team, inspiring fear, respect, admiration and finally obedience among their work force through a practiced mixture of reward and intimidation.

Like many of their peers at the top of other major U.S. news organizations, Sauter and Joyce were decidedly right-of-center politically. Yet while it is of course possible that personal political preferences influenced their news judgments, Sauter and Joyce seem to have been motivated above all else by economic considerations—in particular, the desire to please the crowd and thus rebuild the CBS audience. "Van is essentially an amoral person," remarked Peter Herford. "When he sets a goal, he'll do whatever he has to do to reach it. If he thinks taking it easy on a President will help him achieve that goal, he wouldn't hesitate. Now, that doesn't mean that the next day he wouldn't turn 180 degrees and go after him hammer and tongs if he thought *that* would serve his purposes."

Sauter's top priority when he arrived on the scene in November was rescuing the *CBS Evening News* from the ratings basement, a challenge which in his view required a complete revamping of the broadcast. Look, tone, pace, content—everything was up for grabs. Except for White House coverage, Washington stories in particular would be scaled back considerably, on the assumption that the average viewer did not much care what the average congressional committee or federal agency had done that day. Finally, there would be a marked increase in so-called human-interest stories. The new *CBS Evening News* would boast feature after feature on wild animals, celebrities, natural disasters, medical breakthroughs, individual hard luck or good fortune stories, violent crime, the weather and various other topics that had traditionally been dismissed as too trivial to warrant coverage.

What Sauter was demanding was nothing less than a radical redefinition of what constituted news at CBS. The changes he wrought provoked howls of protest from both outside critics and the CBS Old Guard, who charged that he was cheapening the news. The controversy between the traditionalists and the innovators at CBS soon became common knowledge within the broader television news community. Yet for all the earnest appeals to journalism's public trust voiced during this period, and all the invocations of the spirit of Murrow, the practical *political* effects of Sauter's news philosophy—a softening of CBS coverage of the President—went strangely unremarked.

It was Van Gordon Sauter's view that the three network evening newscasts inevitably ended up setting "a national agenda of aspirations, of apprehension, of joy and purpose." That conception of journalism was all but incompatible with adversarial coverage of the status quo; after all, challenging the President, the one figure the whole country shared in common, was hardly the best way to lift Americans' spirits and unite the country. One disgusted *Evening News* staffer accused Sauter of "social bio-engineering through the media," but there was commercial method to the madness. As illustrated by the box-office success of the escapist Hollywood films of the 1930s, there is a ready market in economic hard times for cultural impresarios who help people forget their troubles by offering them an idealized, utopian vision of life. Tabloids loved royalty for that very reason: their wealth and majesty fascinated the commoners, and their status as human symbols of the national identity made it possible to appeal—that is, to sell—to the entire population at once. CBS rarely refrained from poaching on the traditional source of such stories during the Sauter era—"There were periods when I thought the British royal family had signed on as correspondents, so frequent were their appearances," special correspondent Bill Moyers later smirked to *Newsweek*—and the mind-set carried over into the coverage of the Citizen-King on this side of the Atlantic as well. A protective, celebratory, often almost reverential attitude toward Mr. Reagan was all part of making Americans feel good about themselves again—by helping them feel good about their President.

Whatever softening there was in CBS's coverage of President Reagan seems to have flowed first and foremost from this market-driven tabloid approach to journalism. Which is not to say that Sauter and Joyce went around the newsroom ordering their charges to go easier on Reagan in order to get the ratings up. To be sure, CBS journalists were often reminded during this period that they were in a ratings race. "Ratings became part of our daily relationship with [the New York office]," said one Washington bureau hand. "They came out every Tuesday morning, and we'd be called about them, even on the road." Still, for management to demand kinder coverage of the President explicitly for the purpose of attracting higher ratings would have been too crass a violation of the journalistic ethic; such matters were best left implied, unsaid. Just as the Washington press corps's return to deference as Ronald Reagan came to power was, as Ben Bradlee explained, "totally subconscious," so apparently was the softening of CBS's coverage. As one *Evening News* producer said of his superiors: "They don't have to go to a meeting to decide those kinds of things. They all belong to the same church."

The media mogul Van Gordon Sauter most closely resembled—indeed, was the television equivalent of—was Rupert Murdoch, the Australian reactionary who had made millions by publishing abominably low-minded newspapers on three continents. The effect Sauter had on network news in the 1980s was remarkably similar to that Murdoch had on New York City journalism, and especially the once sensible *Daily News*, after he bought the *New York Post* in 1977—an all-out circulation war that resulted in a drastic lowering of journalistic standards and a debasement of the public discourse. It was not the pursuit of circulation per se that distinguished Sauter and Murdoch from their peers, for that was the name of the game in American journalism. But because audience was their first, last and overriding concern, flaws common to most conventional American journalism—a preference for the superficial over the comprehensive, a mindless and often bellicose nationalism masquerading as patriotism, a reinforcement rather than a challenging of conventional wisdom and common prejudice, a relentless focus on today and history be damned—were magnified to grotesque proportions in their news product.*

However much critics inside and outside of CBS castigated the cheapening of the news under Van Gordon Sauter, it did seem to pay off. Ratings of the *CBS Evening News* began climbing in the summer of 1982, and by the fall the broadcast had reclaimed the number one spot. It would remain there (except for a brief two-week drop into second place during the 1984 Olympics) for some 150 weeks. NBC and ABC quickly responded in predictable fashion, mimicking the very lowering of journalistic standards that seemed to have worked so well for CBS. As the ratings chase intensified and the competition increasingly sought to refashion itself in the image of CBS, the intelligence quotient of network news, never terribly high to begin with, inevitably deteriorated. "The values transformation is pervasive," mourned one journalist at CBS. "The irony is that CBS *led* it."

"All the things that happened to local first are now happening to network news," then NBC News president Rueven Frank later observed. "The editorial judgments are kind of drifting over. Responsibility and professionalism are luxuries which you cannot afford." Frank was of the old school in network news—he had joined NBC in 1950, been the original executive producer of *The Huntley-Brinkley Report* and served as NBC News president from 1968 to 1973—and he recalled feeling distinctly out of place when he was talked into returning as president in 1982 to restore staff morale after the reign of William Small. "Everyone was worried about ratings," he recalled. "We never used to talk about ratings. People knew about them, the sales department knew about them, but this ratings-driven approach was new. Now everybody knows

---

* Beyond their philosophical congruence, Sauter and Murdoch were also known to see each other socially in New York in these years. And ironically enough, Sauter went on to work for Murdoch, albeit indirectly and very briefly, after being fired as news division president during the 1986 corporate takeover battle for CBS, Inc. Sauter delivered on-air commentaries on the ten o'clock evening news show of KTTV, the Los Angeles affiliate of Murdoch's Fox television network, for a few weeks early in 1987, until another management shake-up sent him packing.

what the ratings are at all times, to the slightest fraction of the hour and the slightest fraction of a share point. You talk to affiliates, that's all they talk about, that and [*Today* show co-host] Jane Pauley's hair." It apparently was also all that Frank's corporate superiors talked about: "I once accused [Robert] Mulholland [the NBC corporate official responsible for the news division], 'You never talk English to me, you only talk numbers—either ratings or budgets.' " And as for the network's top man: "[NBC chairman Grant] Tinker didn't know me and didn't care a damn about the integrity of the news or how we used to do it in the fifties, so I had no effective support."

In a vivid demonstration of the new values and realities of the network news business, Tinker removed Frank as NBC News president in 1984. Installed in his place was Lawrence Grossman, a career advertising man, whose old firm's best-known slogan, penned for the United Negro College Fund, now struck a note of irony: "A mind is a terrible thing to waste." Grossman had run NBC's advertising department in the 1960s and served as president of the Public Broadcasting System from 1976 to 1984, but had had no real journalistic experience since his days as managing editor of a student newspaper, the *Spectator*, back at Columbia University. (Grossman was not the only member of the class of '52 to achieve news media stardom. His roommate, and editor of the *Spectator*, was Max Frankel, who became editor of *The New York Times* in 1987. The school paper's news editor, Richard Wald, edited the *New York Herald Tribune* in the 1960s and later became ABC News senior vice president. The school yearbook was edited in 1952 by the man Grossman would now compete against, ABC News and Sports president Roone Arledge.) By his own admission, Tinker discussed the idea of hiring Grossman with no one in the NBC news shop, and a number of those quaintly referred to as traditionalists were frankly leery of a PR man taking over their operation.

The new president's actions did not reassure. It was Larry Grossman who conceived of putting the *Today* show on highly publicized road trips to the Soviet Union and Rome, for example; Grossman who began heavy promotion of *NBC Nightly News* anchor Tom Brokaw (in the form of embarrassingly cloying full-page ads in major newspapers, featuring pictures and simulated interview quotes on the theme "A Day in the Life of the An-

chorman"); Grossman who in another blizzard of print adver-
tisements touted NBC as the network that broke the story (years
after the fact, unfortunately) of the horrific Ethiopian famine.
"There was a significant change in news policy at NBC after
Rueven Frank left," charged one network veteran. "Instead of
pursuing a story because it's newsworthy, it's now pursued only
if it's got promotional value." But as with Sauter at CBS, Grossman had the numbers on his side: by the end of 1986, both *Today*
and the *NBC Nightly News* would be rated number one.

• • •

MANAGEMENT pressure on CBS journalists to curtail their critical
instincts eventually became so pervasive and intense that it caused
speculation that, in the words of one journalist, "there was a
bigger fix in between CBS and the Reagan administration . . .
[and] that word had come all the way down from Black Rock"
to go easy on Reagan. In theory, of course, this was impossible;
news judgments were supposed to be the business of the news
division alone; interference by corporate headquarters was ver-
boten. It is doubtful that journalists at CBS or anywhere else in
the U.S. news media were ever as independent as they liked to
believe, but during the 1980s network news divisions became
noticeably less insulated from corporate influence and from the
marketplace's invisible but ubiquitous hand.

"Under the . . . [1966–78 CBS News president Richard] Salant
administration, there was a shield that existed," explained CBS
veteran Joe Peyronnin. "Salant would deal with the guys in corporate . . . get the views of the corporation, the attorneys, of
[then CBS, Inc., chairman William] Paley, and he would do with
it what he wished. Today I think this organization is more open,
it's grown, it's managed differently, and opinions that occur
among the lawyers and other corporate people are filtering down
past the level of Ed Joyce and Howard Stringer to the executive
producers, whether to the detriment or not of the broadcast. I
firmly believe and know that it does get down, where it didn't
before." Peyronnin, who, it should be noted, firmly denied that
CBS coverage of Reagan had been toned down, nevertheless said
he was also "convinced" that "the Reagan administration has
probably worked very hard to try to convince the likes of Tom
Wyman, Van Sauter, Ed Joyce, Gene Jankowski, that our coverage is not fair."

White House officials denied that charge, as did Van Sauter. But whether such conversations actually took place may be less important than the general relationship that existed between CBS, Inc., and the Reagan White House. Like the parent corporations of the other two major networks, CBS, Inc., had been given ample reason to look favorably on Reagan's administration, not only by its unabashedly pro-corporate economic policies but by particular favors Reagan's Federal Communications Commission had done for the networks.

In the name of free enterprise, Reagan's FCC relaxed or eliminated numerous regulations intended to ensure that public as well as private interests were taken into account in the utilization of the nation's airwaves. Owners of television and radio stations were allowed to broadcast more commercials. License renewals became virtually automatic; no longer would owners even in theory have to earn their access to the publicly owned airwaves by operating their stations according to recognized standards of the public interest. Most important and lucrative of all from the standpoint of the television networks and other major media corporations, the FCC also increased the total number of radio and TV stations any one company was permitted to own.

Television networks became increasingly attractive takeover targets in the deregulated marketplace fostered by the Reagan administration. Indeed, ownership of all three major networks changed hands during Reagan's second term. Capital Cities, Inc., a media conglomerate, swallowed ABC in 1985. NBC was sold from one of the nation's biggest military contractors—RCA—to a still bigger one—General Electric—in 1986. Also in 1986, CBS barely fought off the pursuit of Cable News Network founder Ted Turner before succumbing to New York financier Laurence Tisch.

By contrast, when Reagan came to power in 1981, the networks had faced a crisis situation. According to the A. C. Nielsen Company, ABC, CBS and NBC combined had attracted 87 percent of the national television audience during the 1980–81 season. That was a hefty amount, but it was down from historic levels, and with the increasing reach and popularity of cable television, it was clearly bound to fall further. (And it did; by the time of the 1986–87 season, the networks' market share had dropped to 75.6 percent.) Smaller audiences naturally meant less advertising revenue and, all other things being equal, less profit. It also meant sharper competition. Not only were the networks striving to limit cable's market penetration, but, as that increasingly looked like a losing battle, they were also fighting among themselves for bigger pieces of a shrinking market.

President Reagan's 1981 appointment of Mark Fowler as chairman of the FCC ushered in an era within the broadcasting industry where, in the words of then CBS News president William Leonard, "there was a sense that you could do whatever the hell you wanted." A former disc jockey-turned-radio industry lawyer, Fowler quickly distinguished himself with the observation that television "is just another appliance—it's a toaster with pictures," and with his philosophy that the marketplace alone, not the government, should govern the broadcasting industry's conduct. The networks, under pressure to maintain and increase profits in the face of declining audience share, were anxious both to find new revenue sources and to pare current operating costs; Fowler's FCC would prove extremely helpful on both counts.

When it came to cutting costs at the networks, the news divisions were obvious targets, for news was traditionally a money loser. From the corporate standpoint, news was "a philanthropy," explained Rueven Frank of NBC. "Even when the news does well—with the exception of *60 Minutes*, and calling that news is really a lexicographer's problem—but even when the news makes a profit, it could be argued that what would replace it would make a greater profit." Historically, losses from news had been tolerated, if not encouraged, for political reasons: they made it easier to justify to the Federal Communications Commission the outrageously fat profits made on sports and entertainment programming. A strong commitment to news and public affairs programming was, in effect, the price the networks had to pay in order to enjoy monopoly use of the nation's airwaves, which were, after all, public property.

All that changed during the Reagan years. Mark Fowler and his fellow commissioners made it clear very early on that they did not plan to tell broadcasters what they could and could not broadcast; if viewers didn't like what they saw, Fowler reasoned, they could simply "pull the plug." The FCC requirement that television stations broadcast a minimum quota of public affairs programs each year was not formally abolished until 1983, but long before that it was evident to industry leaders that de-emphasizing news would not jeopardize renewal of their broadcast licenses. "News isn't the main business of the networks; entertainment is," observed one NBC News official. "So when the licensing requirement is removed, network corporate officials ask, 'Why should we spend money on something that is losing us money?' "

In the past, corporate headquarters had merely sought to contain news division losses—"I can remember a president of CBS [Inc.] saying to me, 'We may have to limit how many dollars we can afford to lose per year in the news division,' " recalled William Leonard—but in the Reagan-Fowler era they felt free to go further, ordering extensive budget cuts and demanding more news programming that, like *60 Minutes*, actually made a profit. Thus did documentaries rapidly vanish from national television, replaced by such so-called news magazine shows as CBS's *West 57th* and ABC's *20/20*. In the 1960s, goaded by then FCC chairman Newton Minow's famous "TV as Wasteland" speech, in which he warned broadcasters they had an obligation to help create an informed public opinion, each network had broadcast some twenty documentary programs per year. By 1985, the three networks together were broadcasting a mere fourteen *hours* worth of documentaries.

Far more valuable in dollar terms than the permission to cut news budgets, however, was the Reagan FCC's expansion of how many television and radio stations the networks (or, in theory, anyone else) could own. When Congress created the FCC with the Communications Act of 1934, it charged the new Commission with conducting its regulating activities in accord with "the public interest," a concept which early court and Commission decisions defined as requiring that the public receive its information and ideas from "diverse and antagonistic sources." Nevertheless, over the years pressures from business interests had led the Commission to allow an individual owner to control first five and, by the time Reagan came to power, up to seven television stations around the country at one time. Known as the 7-7-7 rule because the same individual could own seven FM and seven AM radio stations as well, this relative restraint against oligopoly control of the public airwaves had long been anathema to Fowler. According to William Russell, Fowler's chief press spokesman in 1981, Fowler began discussions with policy advisers about repealing the 7-7-7 rule even before he had been confirmed as FCC chairman. Resistance from Congress forced Fowler to retreat somewhat, but a compromise reached in 1984 still allowed for an increase in ownership to twelve television, twelve AM radio and twelve FM radio stations. In short, the 7-7-7 rule became the 12-12-12 rule.

What made this shift such a windfall for the networks was that owned-and-operated stations were the chief source of their vast wealth. While non-owned affiliate stations shared only a portion of their profits with their respective networks, and even had to be paid a fee for broadcasting network programming, the networks received *all* of the profits generated by affiliates they owned themselves. At a time when the networks' overall revenue base was shrinking because of declining national audience, for the Reagan administration to allow them nearly to double, from seven to twelve, one of their most lucrative areas of operation was a favor of colossal proportions.

It also pointed out yet another stark difference in how the Reagan and Nixon administrations went about taming the press. Just as the Nixon men had chosen to withhold information from reporters and go over the press's head via direct television addresses to the nation—while Reagan's men employed a "manipulation by inundation" strategy to go right through the press—so too did the Nixon administration prefer the combative to the seductive in dealing with the news media as a commercial entity. Probably the single roughest tactic used by the Nixon White House in its bare-knuckled battle against the press was its threat, during the Watergate scandal, to revoke the broadcasting licenses of local television stations owned by such major media corporations as CBS and *The Washington Post*, thus depriving them of untold millions of dollars. Consciously or not, the Reagan administration took exactly the opposite tack: rather than create bad blood by threatening to strip the networks of their affiliate cash machines, it in effect bribed them by permitting ownership of five more. One approach inspired fear and resentment, the other gratitude and goodwill. One administration went down in flames, the other benefited from extraordinarily gentle treatment at the hands of the press.

Which is not to assert that the Reagan administration's generous FCC policies led directly to CBS, Inc., ordering its news division to go easy on the White House. Few, if any, direct orders seem to have passed between Black Rock and the news division demanding a more sympathetic portrayal of the Reagan administration. While officials of CBS, Inc., must have been pleased by the regulatory changes being proposed by Reagan's Federal Communications Commission, the available evidence still suggests that the Sauter-Joyce regime's fixation on the ratings chase was probably the more immediate cause of any pulling of journalistic punches on CBS's part. (Although Sauter and Joyce's ardor about boosting ratings was, of course, a separate form of obedience to corporate superiors.)

The pressure for upbeat, patriotic, non-liberal news coverage reduced, but did not eliminate, critical sentiment from CBS coverage of the Reagan administration. For the network chain of command was not airtight, especially near the bottom. By virtue of their primacy in the news production process, the journalists who actually gathered, prepared and broadcast the news at CBS had limited but definite power to resist the preferences of management. Bill Moyers's work, for example, which was cited in Ed Joyce's letter to the author as evidence that no ban on "sharp-edged" coverage was imposed on CBS journalists, was indeed more often than not critical of Reagan policies. To be sure, not all of Moyers's colleagues had the inclination or star power that Moyers did to buck the happy-news atmosphere Van Gordon Sauter fostered around CBS, but enough of them did to cause David Gergen to identify CBS as the toughest of all three networks in its coverage of the Reagan administration. It is a truism of journalism that often what matters most about a news story is not so much what it reports as what it does not. Unfortunately, the truly intriguing question about CBS News coverage of the Reagan administration during the first term—how much tougher would CBS have been on Ronald Reagan had management not intervened on the President's behalf?—will probably never be answered.

9

DEFUSING THE COWBOY IMAGE

FROM THE TIME they first entered the White House, Ronald Reagan's advisers knew that foreign policy was politically treacherous territory for their boss. Years of rash statements, culminating in his 1980 campaign statements that the Vietnam War had been "a noble cause" and that the United States should challenge the Soviet Union to an arms race, had earned Reagan a reputation as a trigger-happy extremist, and that reputation did not disappear just because he was now President. In fact, according to Richard Wirthlin's polling data, many Americans feared throughout Reagan's first term that he would get the country into a war.

Defusing the President's cowboy image thus became a top and enduring priority for Reagan's men. Toward that end, they sought to keep foreign affairs out of the news as much as possible; witness their hasty retreat on the El Salvador issue in early 1981.* Their task of moderating Reagan's image was complicated by the fact that his foreign and military policies struck many citizens as quite radical. While Americans certainly did not want to "lose" the nuclear arms race to the Soviets, for example, they were increasingly skeptical that it could be won at all, by either side. As Reagan's unprecedented peacetime military buildup accelerated, as Reagan officials, including the President himself, publicly spec-

---

* The one time during his White House service that Michael Deaver threatened to resign was during the Israeli invasion of Lebanon, an event that dominated U.S. television newscasts throughout the summer of 1982. To hear Deaver tell it, it was compassion for the women and children of Lebanon that moved him to urge Reagan to pressure Prime Minister Begin for an Israeli withdrawal; he even went so far as to say that he felt Providence had chosen him as its vehicle for ending the slaughter. However strong his humanitarian impulse, however, Deaver's public relations sense must also have told him that it simply would not do for Reagan to be associated in the public mind with such grim images as the armless children of Lebanon.

ulated in the fall of 1981 about the possibility of limited nuclear war and as negotiations with the Soviets yielded little apparent progress, Americans grew increasingly anxious that the drill for death called the arms race be brought to a halt.

Likewise, while the public opposed Communism, in the wake of Vietnam it opposed even more strongly the use of U.S. force abroad, especially the dispatch of U.S. troops. No matter how insistently Reagan officials raised the specter of a Communist takeover of Central America, they would not be able to overcome this sentiment. Yet the administration was determined to continue and even expand its use of military force to secure its objectives in the region.

If Vietnam had shown the American press that the government was perfectly willing to lie to achieve its goals, it had taught government officials that, next time, they had to do a better job of managing public opinion back home. Robert McFarlane, who began his service to Reagan as the number three official in the State Department and later became national security adviser, told me that he had first come to appreciate the supreme importance of public opinion management while working at the National Security Council in the mid-1970s for Henry Kissinger (who was himself a master of media manipulation). For McFarlane, the lesson of Vietnam was not that U.S. policy was ill conceived but that it simply had not been properly explained to the American people. Vietnam was a PR, not a policy, failure.

"I spent a couple of years in Vietnam, as did millions of others," McFarlane recalled in his ponderous, lifeless monotone. "Time that was wasted, basically. Among the several reasons for failure, I cite foremost the inability of the political leadership to define the problem for the American people, define the solution and evoke popular support, and then of course to carry it through to a solution. It was this incompetence at communications basically which has led today to a climate in which no administration can expect to sustain a policy unless it can evoke popular support for it."

Ironically enough, McFarlane delivered this pronouncement on November 5, 1986—the day after the news that the Reagan administration had sold weapons to Iran was first reported in the United States. Judging from his role in the Iran-contra affair, Mr. McFarlane found it harder to practice than to preach his gospel of pursuing only those foreign policies likely to evoke popular support. But the uproar triggered by the news of Reagan's Iran dealings only confirmed the truth of McFarlane's dictum; unless permanently kept secret, a policy that could not be compellingly articulated to the American people could not long be sustained.

Thus the need to hide the realities of the war being waged in Central America from the people of the United States. One of the conclusions U.S. war planners had drawn from the Vietnam experience was that it paid to hire someone other than American troops to do the dying and other dirty work required to project U.S. power abroad. In Nicaragua, the solution was to fund a mercenary army, the contras, to fight a U.S. war that the Reagan administration could deny was a U.S. war. In March 1981, the very month when the White House was publicly backpedaling on sending U.S. troops to El Salvador, President Reagan was secretly approving CIA director William Casey's plan to create and train the contras to overthrow the government of Nicaragua. Yet another lesson of Vietnam was that sustained media attention could be avoided if military hostilities were kept at a relatively low, constant level. This waging of a "low-intensity conflict" was the approach applied to counter the insurgency in El Salvador.

Because of their position as middleman between the public and the government, the news media were, of course, critical to the success of Reagan policy in Central America. While the administration did encounter aggressive or otherwise troublesome reporting from some journalists, most notably Raymond Bonner of *The New York Times*, such behavior was the exception rather than the rule. Moreover, just as it had with CBS on the domestic front, the administration benefited from media management's willingness to restrain those journalists who consistently contradicted the officially sanctioned version of reality. Such restraints proved to be of enormous value as the men of the Reagan apparatus worked to defuse the President's cowboy image. In Reagan's America, it turned out that black could sometimes be white after all.

• • •

WHEN Ray Bonner passed up a chance at a high-powered government job in 1979 and, at age thirty-seven, took off to travel through Latin America, he had no journalistic training. Still, the idea of free-lance reporting appealed to him, so before he left he sent some fifty letters to editors and producers at major news organizations, trolling for signs of interest in his plan to send home occasional news stories during his travels. He got nibbles from ABC and *Newsweek* and set off. Later he would laugh at how green he had been in those early days. Happening upon a tin miners' strike in Bolivia, "I wrote about it like it was the biggest thing that ever happened," he said, chuckling. "Of course, it didn't get a single inch of space in any of the newspapers back here."

Bonner first visited El Salvador in February 1980, at the height of the military's war against the civilian population. He did not settle there until December, when the roadside killing of four U.S. churchwomen sparked a sudden surge of interest in the story back in the United States. By this time he had sold enough stories—both *The Washington Post* and *Newsweek* had published his dispatches on the brutal right-wing coup in Bolivia in the summer of 1979—to establish a reputation and attract interest from other news organizations. *The New York Times*, at the time casting about for a correspondent in El Salvador, gave him a two-week tryout that December during which he reported on the murder of the churchwomen, as well as on the earlier kidnapping and murder of five leading Salvadoran political opposition leaders. Apparently satisfied with his performance, the *Times* hired Bonner as a full-time correspondent in February 1981.

Bonner joined the *Times* a month after the Salvadoran rebels' supposed Final Offensive, a nationwide military push intended to present the incoming Reagan administration with a choice between watching its client government fall or sending U.S. combat troops to save it. The offensive was a dismal failure, and most of the U.S. press went back to ignoring the Salvador story until Secretary Haig began making his noises about "going to the source" in Cuba. As the Washington policy debate intensified, reporters were occasionally dispatched southward to produce companion stories about the situation "on the ground." But once White House officials, in Gergen's words, "pulled the string" on Haig's Central America initiative in March, such stories from the field dwindled down almost to nothing as the press again lost interest in the Salvador story.

Bob Rivard, who that spring set up a Central America bureau

for the *Dallas Times Herald* (and later went on to become chief of correspondents at *Newsweek*), recalled that there were so few U.S. reporters in the region once the Washington angle went cold that "there was no competition on stories. Bonner, [*Washington Post* reporter] Alma [Guillermoprieto] and I were the only ones there." (And Bonner, it must be noted, was frequently back in New York, where he was formally assigned to the *Times*'s metropolitan desk.) But because that threesome included representatives of the nation's two most influential daily newspapers, the continuing violence and misery racking El Salvador were not completely blacked out back in the United States.

In December 1981, over strenuous administration objections, the Congress took a feeble step toward discouraging human rights abuses in El Salvador. Additional military aid to the U.S.-backed junta would henceforth be contingent on improvement in the junta's human rights record; every six months, the President would have to certify to Congress that such improvement was being made or no money would be released.

The Salvadoran military provided gruesome new evidence of its bloodthirsty nature just days after passage of the certification law. The elite Atlacatl Battalion, the first military unit to be trained by the U.S. advisers President Reagan had sent to El Salvador nine months earlier, swept through Morazán province right before Christmas, massacring hundreds of peasants, mainly women, children and old people. Subsequent reports by Bonner in the *Times* and Guillermoprieto in the *Post* numbered the victims at 733 and 926, respectively. Morazán at the time was a rebel stronghold, and the two reporters had visited the massacre sites while traveling, separately, with guerrillas and their peasant supporters in January 1982. Observing the physical evidence of the massacre for themselves—corpses, charred skulls and partial skeletons were discovered in hut after hut—the reporters relied on interviews with survivors to describe the cold-blooded manner in which the dead had been killed.

The stories by Bonner and Guillermoprieto were published on the front pages of the *Times* and the *Post* on January 27, 1982—one day before President Reagan formally certified to Congress that the U.S. client regime in El Salvador was making "a concerted and significant effort to comply with internationally recognized human rights" and was "achieving substantial control over all elements of its own armed forces, so as to bring an end to the indiscriminate torture and murder of Salvadoran citizens." Thus did two main organs of the American press directly contradict a government effort to portray black as white. There were at least two adverse consequences for the Reagan administration. First, the Bonner and Guillermoprieto stories complicated administration efforts to secure congressional approval of an additional $100 million in military aid to the Salvadoran junta. Equally important, they opened up enough new political space so that the rest of the press could feel free to report information at odds with the official version of Central American reality as well.

This space, alas, often went unfilled. The day after the massacre reports, for example, Dan Rather spent a mere thirty seconds of the *CBS Evening News* reporting President Reagan's certification of human rights progress in El Salvador. Rather uttered not a single contradicting word about the horrors so recently perpetrated there by U.S.-trained troops. Likewise, Guillermoprieto's colleagues on the editorial page of *The Washington Post* averred the following morning that Reagan's certification was "the right and necessary thing" to do. And when Assistant Secretary of State Thomas Enders appeared before Congress on February 1 to defend additional military aid on the grounds that "losing" El Salvador to the rebels would mean the "loss" of all of Central America, ABC's Barrie Dunsmore hastened to endorse the domino theory (just as he had a year earlier during Haig's propaganda push on Central America), terming a rebel victory in El Salvador "unacceptable." Continued U.S. support for "a regime with a bad human rights record," on the other hand, Dunsmore deemed merely "undesirable."

Others in the press, however, displayed more critical distance from the administration perspective. Dunsmore's friendly report on *World News Tonight*, for example, was followed by ABC correspondent Timothy Ross's exposé of yet another massacre by Salvadoran armed forces. And in an even more striking departure from routine, NBC *led* its evening newscast with the story of the second massacre (conducted at San Antonio Abad, it claimed the lives of twenty civilians) before shifting to the Enders testimony on Capitol Hill.

Journalistic dissent from the administration line remained, for the moment, the exception rather than the rule. But such stories were like trickles of water leaking through a previously secure dike: left unattended, they could easily grow in strength and destructive capacity and eventually overwhelm all before them. At a time when President Reagan and his administration were coming under increasingly heavy fire about the deepening economic recession gripping the United States, additional trouble on the foreign policy front was especially unwelcome.

What made the Morazán massacre stories so threatening was that they repudiated the fundamental moral claim that undergirded U.S. policy. They suggested that what the United States was supporting in Central America was not democracy but repression. They therefore threatened to shift the political debate from means to ends, from how best to combat the supposed Communist threat—send U.S. troops or merely U.S. aid?—to why the United States was backing state terrorism in the first place.

In so doing, they quickly called forth a powerful backlash from right-wing forces both in and outside the government. The basic plan of attack was to deny that any massacres occurred and to smear the reputations of any who suggested otherwise. Assistant Secretary Enders lambasted press accounts of the Morazán massacres in his congressional testimony, arguing—falsely, according to cable traffic later obtained by Bonner himself under the Freedom of Information Act—that U.S. embassy officials in El Salvador had found "no evidence" of a massacre. *The Wall Street Journal*'s editorialists soon joined the attack. Ray Bonner and Alma Guillermoprieto, they charged on February 10, had been "overly credulous" of peasants' accounts of the massacre, suckered by what had obviously been a calculated "propaganda exercise." Noting that the reporters had come upon the story while traveling with the Salvadoran rebels, the editorial likened them to a modern-day Herbert Matthews—a disparaging reference to the *New York Times* correspondent who had traveled with and reported on Fidel Castro and his Cuban revolutionaries before their overthrow of the U.S.-supported Batista regime in 1959. Matthews's dispatches had been criticized at the time for being overly sympathetic toward a leader and popular movement that, after all, turned out to be Marxist. Shortly after Castro came to power, Matthews was removed from the Cuba story, and he subsequently left the *Times*. The right-wing pressure group Accuracy in Media also blasted the reporting of Bonner and Guillermoprieto that spring, while President Reagan himself, in a March 20 interview with *TV Guide*, complained about allegedly unfair press coverage of Central America as well.

In part because of the political attacks against him, Bonner's editors back in New York felt that, as Bonner recalled one of them telling him, "we've got to take extra care when your name's on the story." One story in particular had given his critics the proverbial sword with which to skewer him—an account of torture sessions in El Salvador allegedly overseen by a U.S. military adviser. Reflecting his inexperience, Bonner based his story on a single source, a risky practice under any circumstance but particularly ill advised on a story with such explosive political overtones. Although an embassy official later told him that U.S. advisers had indeed occasionally observed torture sessions, Bonner subsequently expressed regret at not having sought a second source for his story.

Speaking three years after the fact, Ray Bonner remained highly critical of what he perceived as the journalistic double standard employed in attacking him and other journalists who strayed from the official U.S. line on El Salvador. "There was more latitude to write critical stuff before Central America became such a big issue back in Washington and all the indirect political pressure began to be exerted," he said. "Nobody [in the press corps] wants to go down as soft on Communism, because the name of Herbert Matthews gets dragged out. But name me one reporter who's been called too soft on [U.S.-backed Chilean dictator Augusto] Pinochet, or [U.S.-backed Philippines dictator Ferdinand] Marcos! It doesn't happen. Who'll criticize them? *The Nation, The Progressive*—the liberals, who've never had power in this country and don't now. But reporters do care about criticism from those who are in power." The moral of the story, according to Bonner, was: "It's hard to write against the prevailing wisdom in Washington, no matter who is in power."

• • •

CONDUCTED a mere two months after the Morazán massacre, the 1982 national elections in El Salvador were one of the biggest foreign policy stories of Reagan's entire first term, for they were essential to the U.S. campaign to portray that nation as a working, if struggling, democracy. The administration scored a propaganda victory of the first magnitude when the American press, echoing the sentiments of election observers from both sides of the aisle in Congress, hailed the March 28 voting as welcome evidence that democracy was finally taking hold in that beleaguered land. On a CBS election special, for example, Dan Rather pronounced the election "a triumph." Frank Reynolds of ABC called it a "gratifying, even inspiring . . . exercise in democracy." Similarly effusive comments were heard throughout the mainstream media as the press issued a virtually unanimous declaration of confidence that an important corner had been turned in El Salvador.

"It was the biggest and best election El Salvador has ever had, and apparently the most honest," enthused ABC correspondent Richard Threlkeld, who, like most of the approximately seven hundred journalists who suddenly descended on the country to cover the election, was seeing Salvadoran politics up close for the first time. The dominant visual image in Threlkeld's highly typical March 29 report was of long lines of peasants who "walked for miles . . . stood for hours in the hot sun [and] braved the bombs and bullets just to vote." Congratulating them for doing "the right thing," Threlkeld went on to note that Salvadoran voters had given President José Napoleón Duarte [a member of the ruling junta during the last two years of extreme repression and winner of 35 percent of the vote] "a mandate for his middle way." Threlkeld further speculated that Roberto d'Aubisson [the alleged boss of the country's notorious death squads and winner of 26 percent of the vote] could now "start to make people forget he was ever a right-wing roughneck." As for the rebels, all three networks agreed that the unexpectedly large turnout was, in CBS correspondent Gary Sheppard's words, "a clear repudiation of the extreme left, the insurgents who had called on Salvadorans to support their side by boycotting the ballot box." Indeed, according to the networks, the real threat of violence in El Salvador came from the rebels, whose tactic, ABC's Hillary Brown reported, "was to so terrify the people that they would stay away from the polls."

Having delivered their judgments, most U.S. journalists left for home or their next assignment blithely unaware, one must assume, of how utterly misleading a picture they had left behind. Ironically, they had committed the very sin *The Wall Street Journal* had attributed to Bonner and Guillermoprieto: being "overly credulous" of what was first and foremost a "propaganda exercise."

The bulk of the coverage reflected the official U.S. view of the elections, illustrating a point made by *Wall Street Journal* investigative reporter and author Jonathan Kwitney: "To get the stories that a lot of foreign reporters file, editors could just as well save a lot of travel money and send them straight to the State Department in Washington. They end up going to the U.S. embassy for most of their information anyway."

One basic problem with the 1982 election coverage was that, in the mind of the average U.S. journalist, elections equaled democracy. But this formulation did not necessarily hold in El Salvador. As the country's National Federation of Lawyers pointed out while declining to help draft a law governing the 1982 elections, meaningful elections were impossible when the country was literally under a state of siege, with freedom of speech and of the press nonexistent.

And how could the elections be considered free and fair when the politicians of the FDR-FMLN rebel movement were unable to participate? Echoing their U.S. embassy sources, most American journalists ascribed the rebels' boycott of the election either to a fear of defeat or to an anti-democratic preference for shooting their way into power. In fact, it was simple self-preservation. Had any rebel political leaders returned from exile to campaign in 1982, they surely would have been murdered, just as five of their comrades had been murdered in November 1980. Even U.S. ambassador Deane Hinton recognized the suicidal risks leftist candidates would run. (His suggested solution reportedly was that they campaign with videotapes.) Although references to the dangers facing rebel politicians were not entirely absent from mainstream U.S. news reports—CBS raised the issue in a March 26 broadcast—the dominant message was that the anti-government guerrillas were typical Communists, interested only in disrupting the elections through violence.

This analysis was heavily promoted by the U.S. embassy, as was the related and equally misleading view that the election results represented a decisive repudiation of the left. In all their excitement over the large turnout, U.S. reporters failed to point out that voting was, for all intents and purposes, not a voluntary act in El Salvador. A Salvadoran had to vote on election day or he would not get a stamp on his *cédula*, the identity card he was required to carry at all times. Any peasant found without a stamped *cédula* would probably be suspected as a rebel sympathizer, and would likely be arrested, or worse. Under the circumstances, was it any wonder that so many peasants waited hours in the hot sun to cast ballots?

The coercive political climate in which the 1982 elections took place made them approximately as legitimate and meaningful as elections in Bulgaria. Indeed, they served much the same purpose as Eastern bloc elections: to legitimize the status quo and confer upon an authoritarian political system the illusory façade of free and democratic government. The primary targets of the charade were the U.S. press and Congress, and most willing targets they were. In the two months between the Bonner-Guillermoprieto reports of the Morazán massacres and the March 28 elections, U.S. policy toward Central America had seemed newly vulnerable to criticism if not outright revision. An apparently emboldened press had drawn further public attention to the grisly doings of U.S. client states in the region, and had even revealed that the Reagan administration had secretly begun conducting covert operations against the government of Nicaragua.

The seemingly successful elections in El Salvador changed all that. By convincing most of Congress and the press that democracy was taking root there, the elections effectively silenced mainstream domestic criticism of Reagan policy. Terror remained the basis of government rule in El Salvador, but the media no longer seemed to care. The *NBC Nightly News*, for example, devoted a paltry twenty seconds on April 19 to the news that forty-eight civilians had been massacred "by unidentified killers" just days before the newly elected legislature was to convene, while its counterparts at ABC and CBS ignored the story entirely. Journalists were by then busy providing saturation coverage of the Falklands-Malvinas war between Great Britain and Argentina, which erupted just five days after the Salvador elections and occupied the attention of television in particular until it was supplanted by the Israeli invasion of Lebanon in June. Since it was a rule of thumb within the U.S. news business that Americans will follow only one major foreign story at a time, El Salvador was out of luck—banished, for all practical purposes, from the U.S. news agenda.

U.S. law, however, still required the administration to certify to Congress every six months that El Salvador was making progress in curbing the torture and murder of its citizens. This the administration gamely did, with the media by and large acquiescing in the sham. The networks, as usual, were the worst. During the three certifications between July 1982 and December 1983 (after which Reagan vetoed a bill requiring further such certifications), the common practice of all three network evening news shows was to devote twenty to thirty seconds to the story, announcing the administration's action but offering only the slightest, if any, hint that the truth might be otherwise. Defending the coverage, Jeff Gralnick, then executive producer of ABC's *World News Tonight*, affirmed that he did "feel clean about our handling of Central America." Paraphrasing ABC's reports, Gralnick added, " 'The administration today said X.' That's a news story. We reported it. Clearly there was subsequent reporting on human rights violations in Central America."

But not very much. If Washington expressed no interest in a given foreign story, neither did the press. Guatemala, El Salvador's neighbor to the north, offered an even more striking example of this phenomenon. Social conditions in Guatemala were distressingly similar to those in El Salvador—a poor peasant majority being economically exploited by a small landed elite and militarily repressed by the armed forces, with an estimated 50,000 Guatemalans perishing at the hands of the security apparatus during the early 1980s—yet in the United States the tragedy of Guatemala received not even the truncated press attention that El Salvador did. But then Guatemala was, in the official U.S. view, "stable." U.S.-backed dictator Efraín Ríos Montt seemed firmly in control; left-wing guerrillas had yet to coalesce into a threatening fighting force. Indeed, Guatemala was commonly regarded in U.S. journalistic circles as a democracy, especially after the demonstration election staged there in 1982.

The air war the Salvadoran military launched with U.S. help in 1983 also escaped mainstream press attention in the United States. Justified as necessary to flush the guerrillas out into the open where they could be engaged by the army's numerically superior ground forces, the aerial attacks actually punished defenseless peasants the most, destroying their houses and claiming untold lives. The shift in tactics—from urban death-squad assassinations to countryside air strikes aided by U.S. reconnaissance flights—highlighted what arguably was the single most important fact about the civil war in El Salvador: that it was primarily a war waged by the government against unarmed civilians. Yet the air war, which intensified in 1984 and 1985, received scant mention in the U.S. news media. "We didn't do well on that story," conceded *Washington Post* foreign editor Karen DeYoung. "It was something the reporters and I talked about a lot and always meant to get around to doing, but it's a difficult, time-consuming story to report and the daily routine stuff always seemed to take first priority."

• • •

FOLLOWING the March 1982 elections, Ray Bonner continued to author stories unlikely to curry favor with the U.S. embassy, including reports of massive fraud in the elections and of suspension of the already stalled land-reform program. But the end of his tour was rapidly approaching. The newspaper for which he had risked his life on numerous occasions in Central America was preparing to withdraw him from the beat. The phone call came in August. An editor on the foreign desk informed Bonner that he was being reassigned and that he should return home as soon as possible.*

Bonner's sudden departure unnerved his remaining colleagues and had a predictable effect on news coverage of El Salvador. "I've had other Central America reporters tell me that after I left they found it harder to get some of *their* stuff in," Bonner later remarked. "With *The New York Times* reporting this much," he said, spreading his arms wide and tapping the table in front of him, "there was that much space for others to file similar stories. Several reporters told me that after I left, it left them with that much *less* space, since their stories weren't being legitimized by [their editors] seeing the same angle being reported in *The New York Times*."

It was widely assumed among U.S. reporters in El Salvador

---

* Bonner was dispatched to the financial desk, where he labored for a year before taking a leave of absence in July 1983 to write a book about El Salvador. *Weakness and Deceit* was published by Times Books in 1984. Upon returning to the paper, he was first sent back to the financial desk, and later to the metropolitan desk, a clear demotion. Bonner resigned from *The New York Times* on July 3, 1984.

that the embassy had forced Bonner out, according to a *Columbia Journalism Review* article by Michael Massing, who quoted one reporter as saying that Bonner's transfer "left us all aware that the embassy is quite capable of playing hardball. . . . If they can kick out the *Times* correspondent, you've got to be careful." After all, the embassy had long since barred Bonner from official briefings, and staff members made a habit of denigrating him to other reporters. At the traditional Fourth of July reception at the ambassador's residence in San Salvador, Colonel John Waghelstein, commander of the U.S. military advisers stationed in El Salvador, reportedly told one U.S. reporter, "I'd like to get [*Washington Post* reporter John] Dinges and Bonner up in a plane."

A. M. Rosenthal, executive editor of *The New York Times* at the time, emphatically denied that political motivations played any part whatsoever in his decision to recall Bonner from El Salvador. "He was not brought back, as this Columbia Journalism School article implied, because we bowed to State Department pressure. . . . That's bullshit. There's no other way to put it. It's plain, old-fashioned bullshit. The State Department never pressured me about Bonner. I don't believe his name ever came up in any conversation. I don't discuss our correspondents with the State Department or anybody else. That's all this conspiratorial bullshit that just doesn't happen."

Still, other reporters' *perceptions* of what happened—which were at least as important an influence on subsequent coverage as what actually did happen—were that politics had indeed played a large role in Bonner's ouster. Although Craig Whitney, then foreign editor of the *Times*, seconded Rosenthal's denial, saying Bonner "wasn't yanked back and punished," he did concede that "that myth grew up. . . . Unfortunately, the times were such that this was seized on as an example of *The New York Times* caving in to right-wing pressure. I don't think it was."

The Bonner affair became an important episode in the history of the *Times*, raising as it did disturbing questions about the newspaper's political independence and loyalties. It was an especially sensitive topic for Abe Rosenthal. During his interview for this book, it was Rosenthal himself who raised the Bonner issue. Veteran *Times*man Harrison Salisbury had reported in *Without Fear or Favor*, his masterful portrait of the modern *New York Times*, that Rosenthal, shortly after taking over the paper as managing editor in 1971, had been concerned that the paper was drifting to the left. When I asked Mr. Rosenthal about his alleged efforts as editor to nudge the paper back to the right in order to return the *Times* to a politically centrist orientation, he interrupted the question with a smile: "Bonner, right?" It was less than a year after the *Times*'s mandatory sixty-five-year-old age limit had forced Rosenthal to retire as executive editor. Now, seated on a couch in his office in the paper's "Editorial" section (where he wrote a regular column called "On My Mind" for the *Times*), and occasionally pacing the floor to stretch his chronically stiff legs, the legendary editor explained the journalistic philosophy by which he had guided the world's most powerful newspaper for some sixteen years.

"What I believed was that it was my job to keep the news columns of the paper straight, non-discernible politically," Rosenthal began. He elaborated by means of a hypothetical example: "If I were the editor of a paper with the traditions, background and ideals of *The New York Times* that was published in Tulsa, Oklahoma—a city I don't know, but I assume is a conservative city—I would constantly have to look for a drift on the part of the *Times* toward the right, because that is the neighborhood and intellectual ambience in which we [would be] printed. . . . Now, in New York, we publish in a certain environment, an environment that to a large extent may reflect what I believe, and it is a liberal environment. . . . So as the editor of a paper of national importance, published in New York and not in Tulsa, I had to watch out for drifts left of the center, very rarely right. So to the extent that I saw a drift to the left, which was very slight—you know, we're talking about minor [drifts], but they're only minor because you watch them—I had to pull it back. . . . And that's the *whole* story."

As for his own politics, Rosenthal happily confirmed that he considered himself a "bleeding-heart conservative." He held to traditional liberal positions on social issues—supporting civil rights and the ERA, for example—while taking a harder line on foreign affairs. Although he had a reputation as a fierce anti-Communist, Rosenthal himself claimed he was actually "anti-authoritarian. I'm anti-Communist, I'm anti-fascist. I'm anti-Korean dictator, I'm anti-Chilean dictator. . . . I don't pick my dictators. Certainly on foreign affairs I'd be considered conservative. I'm suspicious of the Soviet Union, I believe Eastern Europe is a captive nation, [and] that until recently the Soviet Union was *indeed* an evil empire. . . . But from that, *The Village Voice* and Columbia School of Journalism publications have built a theory of conspiracy about me."

Rosenthal was particularly irritated by the aforementioned *Columbia Journalism Review* article about the Bonner affair, which he denounced in harsh, frank, sexual terms. Of the article's author, Michael Massing, he said, "He wrote a perverted piece. That was a classic example of the conspiracy theory of journalism. I remember what Churchill said about somebody: he gave buggery a bad name." After an additional slap at the article as "assassination journalism," Rosenthal offered his own version of what had happened with Ray Bonner.

Like Craig Whitney, Rosenthal said he was satisfied with the job Bonner had done for the *Times* in El Salvador. "I had no problem with his reporting. . . . [If I had] I would have called him in and told him that, which I've done with other reporters." It was simply that Bonner needed more training if he was to become the sort of well-rounded foreign correspondent desired by the *Times*.

"What happened was, in a sense we exploited Bonner," Rosenthal explained. "We kept sending him back [to Central America]. He wanted to go, we didn't have that many Spanish-speaking people, and we were always sending him back. The general impression among me and some others was that Bonner was first-rate, but we were really screwing this guy, because he wasn't getting what you *really* need to be a reporter. You don't have to get it necessarily at the *Times*, but you have to have some background in reporting non-foreign affairs in order to be a foreign affairs reporter. You have to know how a paper runs, what a paper considers its standards, and so on."

Returning to the Bonner question later in the interview, Rosenthal declared, "What interests me is mind-set. It never occurs to critics to say, 'How is it that Abe Rosenthal, who *was* involved with [publishing the] Pentagon Papers, who *was* involved in exposés of the CIA, including assigning a man to examine *The New York Times*'s connections to the CIA, who's written exactly what he believes all his life, how is it possible a guy like that will suddenly turn into a real son of a bitch and bow to State Department pressure and pull in a guy like Bonner?' "

Accompanied by *Times* deputy foreign editor Warren Hoge,

Rosenthal had visited Central America in April 1982, shortly after the campaign against Bonner had begun, to see things for himself. During his visit to El Salvador, Rosenthal met with Bonner. He also had lunch with U.S. ambassador Hinton, a vehement critic of Bonner, who reportedly took the opportunity to complain about Bonner's reporting. Rosenthal later denied to the *Columbia Journalism Review*'s Massing that Bonner's name was ever mentioned at the lunch: "At no time, in no way, did any official of the U.S. embassy or government suggest to me, directly or indirectly, that we ought to reassign Bonner. They're too sophisticated for that."

The same could be said of *The New York Times*. It was extremely rare for a reporter to be sacked in full public view as Ray Bonner was; the internal procedures of the *Times* tended to prevent potentially troubling and embarrassing situations from ever reaching such a crisis point. "The way the top really communicates its views to the rest of the paper," veteran *Times* correspondent R. W. Apple explained in a separate context, "is through the subordinate editors, and even more important than that through longtime discussions with and shaping of people who are going to be senior correspondents. You can't do a lot as an editor in New York to set the tone of a Moscow correspondent's dispatches; it's just too far away. So you send somebody to Moscow who is in tune with what you want the paper to be. You use your system of promotion and personnel assignment to see that that happens."

In Bonner's case, this system had not so much broken down as been circumvented by events. When the El Salvador story suddenly flared in December 1980, the *Times* needed to hire a correspondent quickly. Since none of its traditional Latin American reporters were available, the job fell almost by default to Bonner, and the *Times* suddenly found itself employing an unknown newcomer on a very politically sensitive story. By the time a representative of the "top" of the paper, in the person of Rosenthal, finally arrived for a "shaping" discussion, the correspondent's reporting had already brought the *Times* nothing but grief from those in high places.

Jettisoning Ray Bonner was only part of the rightward course steered by the men in charge of *The New York Times* during the Reagan years. Around the time of Bonner's departure, for example, the *Times* began printing bylined stories by Claire Sterling.

Ms. Sterling was the author of the Bulgarian Connection conspiracy theory, which accused the KGB and the Bulgarian intelligence service of hiring admitted assassin and apparent madman Ali ("I am Jesus Christ") Agca to shoot the Pope. With the help of the *Times* and NBC's Marvin Kalb, she saw her theory come to be embraced as conventional wisdom by the rest of the American press, despite holes in her argument the size of bulldozers. Although not on the staff of the *Times*, Sterling was repeatedly awarded precious page-one space to propound her subsequently discredited theories, even after the *Times* itself wrote in an August 15, 1985, editorial that Agca, whose testimony was critical to proving the Bulgarian Connection, "lacked credibility."

In 1985, Rosenthal hired Shirley Christian, a *Miami Herald* Pulitzer Prize-winning reporter. Christian's journalism was at least as politically charged as Ray Bonner's was, though, by contrast, hers was congruent with official U.S. policy. Described by Pete Hamill in *The Village Voice* as "the best friend the Nicaraguan contras had in American journalism" (an honor which ABC News correspondent Peter Collins actually deserved to share with Christian), she was highly critical of the Sandinista government in Nicaragua and of U.S. press coverage of it. In a widely cited 1982 article in the *Washington Journalism Review*, she had accused mainstream journalists, including some at the *Times*, of romanticizing the Sandinista revolution in Nicaragua.

Also in 1985, veteran *Times*man Sydney Schanberg was forced out, resigning after his regular column on New York City was summarily canceled. Schanberg had made his reputation, and risked his life, covering the 1975 Khmer Rouge conquest of Phnom Penh for the *Times*, an experience later dramatized in the motion picture *The Killing Fields*. His urban affairs column, initiated in 1980, had, however, frequently skewered the rich and powerful of New York and championed the downtrodden—toward the end, Rosenthal had reportedly taken to addressing Schanberg as "St. Francis"—and that was not a perspective welcome in the new, neoconservative *New York Times*.

Ray Bonner and Abe Rosenthal did agree on one thing: it was not the State Department that got Bonner recalled from Central America. During public talks on El Salvador that Bonner gave after leaving the *Times*, audience members would ask the former reporter if he thought the Reagan administration had ordered his removal. "I always say, very lawyerlike, 'I don't think I got transferred from El Salvador because of administration pressure,' " Bonner recalled. What Bonner did not say in public was that "the administration didn't like it, but I think the real problem was that my reporting didn't fit the tenor of the times, or of the *Times* under Abe Rosenthal."

Bonner was not alone in this conclusion; numerous *Times* reporters and editors, some quite senior at the paper, privately expressed the same opinion to me. When I asked Mr. Rosenthal about these suspicions—that Bonner had been recalled because his reporting did not comport with Rosenthal's alleged anti-Communism—the former executive editor seemed impatient. "Let's go on to something else. This is ridiculous. The answer is no. Nonsense. . . . What do you think, I'm some kind of a nut? That if somebody reports the right-wing death squads are shooting people in El Salvador I'm going to pull the guy out because I'm against the Communists? I'm not an anti-Communist, I'm an anti-everything. It is the people who can't understand this who say these things."

At the same time, the coincidence of events is striking. An inexperienced but undeniably gifted reporter was filing stories that put the *Times* well ahead of the competition on the hottest foreign policy story of the moment. Because those stories contradicted the official truths proclaimed back in Washington, the Reagan administration and its political allies responded by attacking the reporting as biased and the reporter as a Communist sympathizer. Although the reporter's superiors had confidence in his work, he was transferred off the beat within six months. In his place were installed a succession of reporters experienced in the ways of *The New York Times* but largely ignorant of the realities of El Salvador. These replacements proved themselves far more willing to convey the official U.S. view of the war. From a journalistic standpoint, the reporting suffered, as even foreign editor Whitney, who supervised it, later conceded: "It did," he said. "Not intentionally. It's unfortunate. Ray did a fine job and I think the paper has nothing to be ashamed of for what he did in that period. If the successors didn't do as well, it isn't because we weren't trying to."

Whatever the intent, the effects of Ray Bonner's removal were clear. El Salvador was whisked from the U.S. news agenda; a nasty thorn was removed from the paw of the administration; other journalists were warned against reporting too frankly about U.S. policy in Central America; and the American public was deprived of a full and accurate accounting of exactly what was being done in its name in the troubled lands south of the border— all of which proved most helpful to a White House anxious to defuse President Reagan's cowboy image.

• • •

RONALD REAGAN was known as the Teflon President because blame never seemed to stick to him. Pundits and politicians alike usually ascribed the Teflon phenomenon to Mr. Reagan's personality, or his extraordinary luck, or the public's special love for the man. Rarely if ever did anyone suggest that the press may have had something to do with it. Yet, as noted earlier in this book, two of Reagan's most senior aides, David Gergen and Richard Darman, independently and without prompting offered the opinion that the press had indeed helped to apply the Teflon coating that proved so valuable to the President. "I think a lot of the Teflon came because the press was holding back," said Gergen. "I don't think they wanted to go after him that toughly."

It is important to specify exactly who "they" are. The evidence presented above supports Gergen's view that the press held back on Reagan. But it also suggests that it was as much (if not more so) the managers and executive overseers of the press who didn't "want to go after him that toughly" as the journalists themselves. For when journalists did take aggressive positions—whether against White House policies to control the news, as in the Deaver rule, or with critical coverage of the administration's economic policies, as at CBS, or by highlighting the brutality of the U.S. client regime in El Salvador—those positions were invariably tempered by their superiors. In effect, the nation's press bosses reined in their troops. The power struggle between the Reagan public relations apparatus and the establishment news media turned out to be not much of a contest.

Gergen had vowed during the dark days of early 1982 that he would not leave the White House defeated; he would stay long enough to be back on top. He got his wish in 1983. Indeed, by that fall, the major public relations problems facing the Reagan apparatus had all but disappeared; the national political debate was once again proceeding on terms very favorable to the administration. Despite sharply rising levels of poverty and hardship, the economy was said to be in the midst of an increasingly impressive recovery because of President Reagan's policies. Despite dozens of displays of either crass lying or staggering ignorance, Reagan himself was regarded not as a dangerous simpleton but as a principled and inspiring leader. El Salvador was regarded not as a brutal military dictatorship but as a fledgling democracy, Nicaragua not as the target of an illegal U.S. war but as the totalitarian source of all trouble in the region. True, doubts remained about Mr. Reagan's commitment to nuclear arms negotiations, but the Soviet Union's downing of the KAL 007 passenger plane on September 1 had nulled that problem, at least for the time being.

Time had begun offering the opinion back in July that Ronald Reagan would be a hard man to beat if he chose to run for reelection in 1984, and as the months went by, more and more of the rest of the press came to share this view. David Gergen knew he did not want to work through another presidential campaign, and feeling secure in his accomplishments and the President's standing, he went to Jim Baker early in the fall and told him that he planned to leave the White House. Gergen had the highest regard for his boss and was grateful to receive his blessing. But before he could tear himself away from the White House whirl, Gergen would find himself caught up in unforeseen events, events that not only would bring him into conflict with Jim Baker but would forever tarnish his memories of serving in the Reagan White House.

10

THE GRENADA HIGH

It was late in the afternoon and the other reporters staking out the Grantley Adams International Airport in Barbados had already given up and gone home. Producer Sharon Sakson of ABC News wanted to leave too, but her partner, correspondent Mark Potter, was determined to stay. Five days had passed since the coup which overthrew the government of Prime Minister Maurice Bishop on the neighboring island of Grenada, and rumors were rife throughout the region that a U.S. invasion was now imminent. U.S. embassy officials had returned from Grenada the day before and declared that the roughly one thousand medical students and other U.S. citizens on the island were in no danger, but the invasion rumors had only intensified, and today, Monday, October 24, 1983, the airport had been unusually busy as the government of Canada, for one, sought to evacuate its people from Grenada.

Perched on an open-air balcony above the airport's main terminal, Potter and Sakson, along with cameraman Bobby Freeman and soundman Joe Lamonica, were scanning the skies when suddenly, as if in reward for their perseverance, a U.S. Navy jet swooped into sight well off to their right, landed and pulled up behind a smaller, outlying terminal a couple of hundred yards across the airfield. The dull buzz of whirring rotor blades could be heard as three U.S. Marine helicopters quickly followed and settled down near the jet.

Grabbing their equipment, the ABC crew ran to the car and sped across the airfield, approaching the terminal from the back. The building looked to be abandoned, but, recalled Potter, "we went up a couple floors and lo and behold there was a window looking out over the whole scene. Bobby set up his camera right in front of the window and got some great pictures. Soldiers were carrying equipment from the jet to the helicopters. Civilians wearing business suits and carrying briefcases were transferring onto the copters too. It took about half an hour. We weren't trying to hide ourselves, but I don't think they ever saw us."

While Potter supervised the shot, Sakson ran downstairs to call a trusted source in the U.S. embassy, who read her a prepared statement saying that the United States had always maintained the right to evacuate its citizens from Grenada and it was now exercising that right. The source declined to answer further questions.

Sakson rejoined her colleagues, and all piled back into the car and drove to the satellite station in Bridgetown, from which they could "feed" their pictures to New York. As producer, it was Sakson's job to alert the home office to what was coming. Telephoning from the feed station, she spoke directly with Robert Frye. The two were friends from their days working together in ABC's London bureau in the late 1970s. Now Frye, as the show's executive producer, exercised final control over what appeared on the *World News Tonight* broadcast.

Sakson was very careful of her diction when she related what she had just seen at the airport. "I remember Frye kept asking if it was an invasion. He wanted to be very clear on that, and I kept saying, 'The guy at the embassy said this was an evacuation.' " Sakson later explained her choice of words, saying, "I didn't want to take liberties with the truth, but I didn't understand Bob's thinking on it, that calling it an evacuation somehow made it less important. I thought I was just clarifying what the news copy would be so ABC wouldn't get in trouble."

But to Bob Frye, thousands of miles away in the midst of a network newsroom pulsing with deadline urgency, Sakson's caution sounded like uncertainty. "We had pictures, but we didn't know what they represented," he later recalled, adding, "Our producer and correspondent didn't know it was an invasion."

When Frye hung up the phone with Sakson, approximately half an hour remained before his broadcast went on the air at 6:30 p.m. He ordered the Washington bureau to seek confirmation of the Grenada story, and had a script prepared for it. The White House, in Frye's words, "made itself unavailable for comment," but ABC Pentagon correspondent John McWethy did manage to reach a trusted Defense Department source.

"The desk called me as we were getting ready to go to air about unusual helicopter activity on Barbados, and I checked it out," said McWethy. "I went down to an extremely reliable guy and talked to him and he said, very cleverly, 'Well, you know, when a carrier is operating in an area [this was a reference to the USS *Guam*, which officially was said to be headed for Lebanon but which in fact would support the Grenada invasion the following morning], frequently people get left behind and they have to catch up by being hopped aboard.' He didn't say that's what they were doing, he just offered that. And I bought it, so back I trotted and waved them off."

Barely a minute before airtime, McWethy relayed his information to Robert Frye, thus confronting the executive producer with a dilemma. Would he air the story despite the Pentagon wave-off and risk being wrong on a global scale? ABC had done that before, by breaking into regular programming to announce in 1975 that Spain's Generalissimo Francisco Franco had died, and again in 1981 by incorrectly announcing that White House press secretary James Brady had died following the Reagan assassination attempt. Or would Frye *not* broadcast the story, passing up a chance for a fantastically newsworthy scoop and leaving his viewers uninformed as well?

There was, of course, a third option: simply report everything ABC knew, including the Pentagon denial. Broadcast the pictures of the jet and helicopters in Barbados, mention that rumors of a U.S. invasion of Grenada had been intensifying since the overthrow of the Bishop government the previous Tuesday, add that U.S. warships had been diverted toward the region, report that the U.S. embassy in Barbados had said that afternoon that the troops and aircraft were indeed on their way to Grenada to evacuate U.S. citizens there, point out that this statement clashed with a Defense Department claim that the troops were joining a carrier headed for Lebanon, and note finally that the White House made itself unavailable for comment.

ABC ended up saying not a thing about Grenada during its *World News Tonight* broadcast. In a telephone conversation after the show, Frye explained his decision to Sakson.

"He was very concerned," Sakson recalled, "and explained they didn't go with it because McWethy checked and it wasn't true. . . . When I told Bob we'd seen it with our own eyes, he said, 'McWethy's our man in the Pentagon and they waved us off this.' That was the phrase he used, waved us off. Meaning, we're about to commit a major mistake on the air and they prevented it, which is what he honestly thought."

Distraught, Sakson and Potter checked the Pentagon explanation with their embassy sources. "They said that was wrong," remembered Potter. "In fact, the guy I talked to laughed." Armed with reconfirmation of their original information, Sakson got back on the phone to New York in hopes of persuading *Nightline* to run the story. But producers there had already been waved off by colleagues at *World News Tonight* and were unmoved by Sakson's entreaties. By this time, the two ABC reporters in Barbados were beside themselves. "In hindsight, I'm furious about it," said Sakson. "I'm there on this island a thousand miles off the coast of the United States saying, 'I can't believe this. There's going to be a military operation on Grenada tomorrow, and nobody in the United States believes me!' "

Mark Potter eventually did manage to file reports for ABC Radio and for the next day's edition of *Good Morning America*, but nevertheless felt defeated when he went to bed that night. "Sharon and I both did," he said. "We were devastated that the material hadn't made the air. . . . I could have accepted it if someone had called me back and said, 'We're not going to run it because we're afraid someone will get hurt if we broadcast this information.' But nobody ever said anything about its being a security concern. It never got to that stage, because the information wasn't fully accepted in the first place."

What about the possibility that ABC News officials, in response to actual or anticipated government pressure, ordered the story spiked? Certainly there were precedents for such actions, perhaps the best known being *The New York Times*'s agreement to a Kennedy administration request to withhold news stories revealing the planned Bay of Pigs invasion of Cuba in 1961. For such a scenario to be true in this case, however, Robert Frye would have had to contact superiors in the half hour between his second phone conversation with Sharon Sakson and airtime, and they would have had to consult with government officials, be urged to withhold the story and agree to do so. Not only does Frye explicitly deny having done this, he had little reason to do it, since by all accounts he was far from convinced the invasion story was real in the first place.

Moreover, David Burke, ABC News executive vice president and one of Roone Arledge's two top deputies, could barely recall the incident at all when questioned about it two and a half years later, much less the reason the Potter-Sakson story was not broadcast. "If McWethy gets a wave-off, if it makes sense to McWethy, it makes sense to us. . . . It never hung in my mind that 'oh boy, we really blew this one.' " Skeptics might suggest that Mr. Burke's memory lapse is conveniently self-serving, but there is yet another reason to doubt that a corporate order from upstairs squelched the story. As Mark Potter pointed out, any such edict would have pertained throughout the news division and thus would have precluded producers at ABC Radio and the morning news show from accepting the pieces Potter later submitted there.

So why didn't ABC run the story? Anticlimactic as it may sound, the reasons were apparently more banal than sinister. To search for a hidden smoking gun in the affair is to miss the fact that no extraordinary measures were required to keep the Grenada story off the air. It was aborted in the normal course of business, a casualty of the underlying values and assumptions that in practice constituted the daily routine of mainstream American journalism.

For all its world-weary cynicism about politics, the U.S. press displayed more often than it cared to admit a remarkable tendency to accept the basic truth of what its government told it. In the present case, that mind-set manifested itself first in Sharon Sakson's acceptance that the United States planned an evacuation rather than a full-scale invasion of Grenada; second in John McWethy's confidence that the helicopters sighted in Barbados were ferrying stragglers to a Mediterranean-bound aircraft carrier rather than preparing for an invasion of Grenada; and finally in Robert Frye's unwillingness to report information gathered by his own reporters in the field because the government in Washington would not confirm that information. "I took the line on Grenada," Frye later acknowledged. "I played the national interest, albeit unwittingly."

A report on *World News Tonight* would probably not have stopped the U.S. invasion of Grenada. But how many other stories have never been shared with the public because of news organizations' tendency to take the government at its word and to hesitate before challenging its version of reality? In the days to come, the Reagan White House and the Pentagon would do their best to prevent free and independent reporting of the United States invasion of Grenada. But let the record show that the first act of censorship was of a more insidious and common sort than the heavy-handed official suppression about to be imposed by the Reagan administration; it was not government censorship *of* the press but self-censorship *by* the press. Silence about Grenada was first imposed not by the state but by journalists themselves.

• • •

As JOURNALISTS who covered it later emphasized, the invasion of Grenada cannot be understood without recalling what was happening in Lebanon at the same time. Correspondent John McWethy, for example, in conceding that he had been "clearly snookered" by the Pentagon source who waved him off the invasion story, nonetheless noted that he had been completely exhausted by the time the two men spoke. Just the day before, Sunday, a suicide bombing had destroyed a housing compound for U.S. marines in Beirut. As the death toll quickly soared over two hundred, with bodies still being recovered from the wreckage, the Beirut bombing began to take shape as one of the biggest stories of 1983. Like most Washington-based foreign affairs reporters, McWethy had been covering the story virtually nonstop since Sunday morning, and was understandably distracted when ordered to check out the Grenada angle on Monday evening.

The Beirut bombing had all the makings of a major political disaster for President Reagan, and on the eve of the 1984 presidential campaign no less. Deaths of U.S. servicemen in overseas combat were always politically dangerous for sitting Presidents, but Reagan had more reason to worry than most. In September the White House apparatus had busily promoted his non-military response to the KAL 007 incident as evidence that he wasn't trigger-happy, but Richard Wirthlin's polls privately showed that many Americans still feared that Reagan might lead the country into war. Now, hundreds of young Americans had been slaughtered in their sleep, and for what purpose?

Later there were those who suspected that the Reagan administration launched its invasion of Grenada precisely in order to divert public attention from the tragedy of Beirut. The evidence, however, suggests otherwise; the go-ahead from Washington to invade Grenada was given at least three days before the surprise bombing took place in Beirut. Moreover, U.S. representatives had secured from the Organization of Eastern Caribbean States their formal invitation to intervene militarily in Grenada on Saturday, October 22, the day before the Beirut bombing. Nevertheless, from Reagan's standpoint, the timing of the Grenada invasion could hardly have been more fortuitous. The invasion yielded precisely the kind of public relations dividends that skeptics charged the administration had been seeking. The news media immediately made the invasion the nation's top story while relegating Lebanon to secondary status. And the invasion itself not only encouraged people to forget about the Beirut tragedy; it provided a release for the emotions of anger and grief it had triggered, emotions that might otherwise have been vented on Reagan.

The propaganda windfall was such that some Washington reporters later speculated privately that it had been Michael Deaver who dreamed up the Grenada operation after observing how the 1982 Falklands-Malvinas war had boosted British Prime Minister Margaret Thatcher's sagging popularity. One Reagan press aide later confirmed in an interview for this book that "there were a lot of discussions by some White House people about what the British had done in the Falklands." Deaver himself denied having engineered the invasion of Grenada, but volunteered that he had wholeheartedly supported it, partly because, in his words, "it was obvious to me it had a very good chance of being successful and would be a good story." Asked whether he did not fear that attacking such a weak and tiny country would in fact expose the President to ridicule, Deaver replied, "No, because I think this country was so hungry for a victory, I don't care what the size of it was, we were going to beat the shit out of it. You know"—he chuckled—"two little natives someplace, if we'd have staked the American flag down and said, 'It's ours, by God,' it would have been a success."

But to *ensure* that the public applauded the invasion, Deaver believed the government had to control to the maximum extent what Americans were told and especially what they were shown about it. (This lesson of Vietnam and the Falklands would later be applied to great effect by the South African government as well; its 1987 press ban led to substantially less TV coverage abroad, thus reducing foreign protest against apartheid.) The reason the public supported the Grenada action, explained Deaver in retrospect, was that "they didn't have to watch American guys getting shot and killed. They can't stand that every night. They'll accept strafing a Libyan ship or going down and having a forty-eight-hour action in Grenada, but they couldn't stand day after day of armless children in Lebanon. We could stand all that when [World War II newspaperman] Ernie Pyle was writing it and once a week you go down and see the newsreels, but that's a lot different than nightly on your television set. I firmly believe this country, because of television, will be prevented from ever fighting a ground war again."

ABC's John McWethy disagreed that television made future ground wars impossible, but conceded that the press had "a profound impact on the way they are able and not able to fight wars. We stopped the Israelis short of demolishing Beirut [in 1982] with our pictures. The tanks drew up and stood there for a while, and day after day we broadcast pictures of what they were doing to what was a civilized city, and the world went nuts."

The Reagan administration nulled that problem by first barring the press from Grenada and then releasing its own sanitized videotapes of the operation (which each of the three major networks broadcast). "Their pictures weren't lying, but because they weren't *all* the pictures, they ended up being distorting," commented McWethy. "Because there was not a single piece of combat footage, it was not an accurate reflection of what was going on down there. The administration's argument is, if you had one frame of that stuff, that's the only thing you'd show. Well, that's probably true. The lead picture in our broadcast would not be students getting off the airplane and kissing the ground, it would have been a soldier with his guts blown away. And that would have turned public opinion around in a big hurry."

And public opinion, as much as anything else, was what Grenada was all about. The invasion of Grenada came to be remembered in the United States as a reaffirmation of American power and resolve after the humiliations of Vietnam and Iran. Less often remembered were the handsome political dividends it paid to President Reagan a year before he faced re-election. Reagan's overall popularity rating jumped sharply after the invasion, and public sentiment on his handling of foreign policy flip-flopped, moving from 50 to 42 percent disapproval in September to 55 to

38 percent approval in November. Part of the shift is attributable to the Beirut disaster and Americans' tendency to rally behind any President in a moment of crisis. But there is no denying the role Grenada played in rekindling among the American people the spirit of old-fashioned nationalism which the Reagan campaign would so skillfully encourage and exploit during the 1984 presidential contest. Within eight weeks of the invasion, the President was assuring the nation in his State of the Union address: "Our days of weakness are over. Our military forces are back on their feet and standing tall."

The rest of the world, it must be added, was considerably less impressed by Grenada. Allies and adversaries alike condemned the United States and, behind its back, smirked when it crowed about overpowering such a postage stamp of a nation. Self-absorbed isolationists by temperament and tradition, most Americans never realized that it was only in the United States (and its eastern Caribbean client states) that the invasion of Grenada was applauded as a wonderful thing, but no matter. The primary target of the operation was not in Grenada or Nicaragua, or even in Cuba or the Soviet Union, for that matter; it was among the electorate of the United States.

• • •

THE Reagan administration found itself entangled in deception before the shooting ever started on Grenada. In order to control American mass opinion about Grenada, the administration had to control the press, but in order to control the press it first had to mislead its own press office. Word of the impending invasion was leaking in Washington the day before to key members of the capital's press corps. The only way for the White House to keep the story from breaking, and thus unleashing a flood of reporters onto Grenada, was to lie.

"I was personally told by someone I've known for many years that the United States was going to invade Grenada," recalled CBS White House correspondent Bill Plante. "I said, 'Well, maybe they'll evacuate the students, but surely you don't mean an invasion.' And he said, 'Yes, an invasion.' "

Plante immediately put the question to White House deputy press secretary Larry Speakes, who promised to get back to him. Les Janka, Speakes's deputy for foreign affairs, also recalled getting calls about Grenada from reporters beginning right after lunch. Robert Sims, another deputy press secretary specializing in foreign affairs, called Rear Admiral John Poindexter, then deputy national security adviser, to check out the story.

"He said that report was preposterous," Sims recalled. "I was concerned the operation could be compromised by false early reports about it, so I called Speakes and Les to say [the story] was inaccurate."

"I had [Associated Press White House correspondent] Mike Putzel there with me because I wanted a witness," said Bill Plante, "and Speakes, in typical Speakes fashion, said, 'Plante: Grenada. Preposterous. Knock it down hard.' " Plante relayed this response to his colleagues in Washington and New York and it was agreed not to pursue the story.

"There wasn't much of a debate about it," said Plante. "There are unwritten rules concerning the qualifiers and statements made by White House spokesmen. And with that much of a knockdown, there wasn't much choice. Given the normal rules of the game, you have to assume they're not lying."

White House chief of staff Baker later defended the blackout decision (which he said had been thrust upon the White House by the military) and said he would make it again if faced with similar circumstances.

"I never, ever ordered anyone to lie to the press," Baker exclaimed. "I might have told [Poindexter] not to tell the press office about it. That's different. That White House had been leaking like a sieve, and there were American lives at stake. . . . It was my view that because the military operation depended on surprise, and lives therefore depended on surprise, we should make certain there was no risk of premature disclosure."

As it happened, however, the invasion of Grenada was, in the words of David Gergen, a self-described big fan of Baker, "not that big a surprise to the Grenadans." Political observers throughout the Caribbean had been speculating about a U.S. invasion for days, especially since the Saturday meeting in Bridgetown of the Organization of Eastern Caribbean States. Cuban leader Fidel Castro was informed sufficiently in advance that he sent urgent diplomatic messages to Washington urging negotiation and pledging that the Cubans on the island would stay clear of any fighting between U.S. and local forces. In fact, as Gergen ruefully noted, the invasion of Grenada "was only a surprise to the American press and the American people."

The first official notification Gergen, Janka, Sims and Speakes received about their government going to war in Grenada came at a six o'clock breakfast briefing conducted by Baker and Deaver on the morning of the invasion. U.S. warships and planes had been bombarding Grenada for a full hour by the time the four spokesmen gathered in the White House basement dining room and heard Baker describe the size, timetable and goals of the operation, then outline how the press was to be handled. The President would deliver a formal statement before cameras later that morning justifying the military action as necessary to rescue U.S. citizens and restore order on the turbulent island. At Deaver's suggestion, he would be accompanied by Mrs. Eugenia Charles, Prime Minister of Dominica, a neighboring island nearly as tiny as Grenada, who would applaud the invasion on behalf of the Organization of Eastern Caribbean States. Secretary of State George Shultz would make similar arguments during an early-morning appearance on NBC's *Today* show. Questioned about whether the press would be allowed in to cover the fighting, Baker responded that military planners had not wanted to bring reporters along and that the White House was not going to overrule them, a stance that alarmed a number of the spokesmen.

"I said to Gergen after breakfast, 'Dave, we can't do this,' " recalled Les Janka. " 'We've got to get the press in there, and it is clear there is no plan to do it.' Of course, it was all supposed to be over in one day. Tomorrow's story was supposed to be 'Students Rescued.' "

When journalists and news executives learned that the military not only had failed to invite them but was actively preventing them from tagging along on the invasion (the United States had closed off the air and sea space around the island to all but its own vessels and aircraft), indignant cries of protest erupted. Robert McFarland of NBC was chairman of the White House television "pool" that month (the position rotated quarterly among each of the four major networks' Washington bureau chiefs), so it was he who telephoned the official protest to Gergen on Tuesday morning. "If you've got an invasion going, we've got to get some television crews in there and we've got to get them in there right now," McFarland recalled saying. "And Gergen's phrase was: 'I hear you.' "

Gergen had heard the same argument from other journalists, and had already failed to budge Baker on the matter twice, but he did not give up. "Later that morning I was with Larry [Speakes], and Jim happened in and this was the third time I did it," said Gergen. "He flared that time—it's one of the [few] times Jim's flared—and said, 'Goddammit, don't keep bringing this up. This is what we're doing.' This was at eleven o'clock and I remember it very clearly, because he rarely does that. I think he felt we were beating up on him."

Which is a fair description of what reporters did to Baker's press lieutenants an hour later at that day's regular noon press briefing. Repeatedly, the spokesmen's "Preposterous!" reply of the day before was sarcastically hurled back in their faces by angry reporters grown freshly skeptical of the answers they were being given. After the briefing, Janka retired to his office, drafted a letter of resignation, then retrieved his telephone call sheet from the day before and called back each of the reporters he had unwittingly misled about the impending invasion and apologized. He later explained his decision to resign: "I worked through Watergate, and this time when the finger pointed at me to lie, I said, 'No way.' "

Journalists and news executives were reassured, if not becalmed, by off-the-record assurances from Gergen that he and other White House officials were doing all they could to arrange for speedy access to Grenada. (It was not until that evening that Baker finally relented and began working to overturn the military's order.) Such efforts notwithstanding, it would still be four days before camera crews not belonging to the Department of Defense were allowed on the island, and then only under severely restricted conditions.

In the meantime, news organizations had to cover the story as best they could. And what was the story? Surely the invasion itself was big news, but so, one would think, was the press blackout. Yet both in their initial deliberations and, more importantly, in their subsequent reporting to the American public, major news organizations treated the censorship imposition as a separate and decidedly lesser story.

The simple fact that the government was now censoring the

news was barely reported at all, for example. It was almost as if the very fact that censorship had been imposed had itself been censored. None of the five leading national news organizations pointed out in its Day One coverage* of Grenada that the Reagan administration was pre-emptively censoring news about the invasion and that everything it said should be evaluated with that fact foremost in mind. *CBS Evening News* anchor Dan Rather, for example, in his introduction to the Tuesday-evening, October 25, broadcast, reported President Reagan's rationale with all due respect—"he had no choice, the invasion was necessary to protect Americans on Grenada from a Cuban-connected military junta"—then passed over the press ban, noting merely that "the American military has allowed no journalists on the island; we therefore begin our coverage in Barbados." Three subsequent reports expanded on the official reasons for invading; there was no mention of the press ban. Neither ABC nor NBC so much as hinted that reporters were being kept off the island; nor did *The Washington Post* the next morning. *The New York Times* did publish a story on page A23 headlined "Reporting the News in a Communiqué War," whose third paragraph calmly noted that since "no reporters were allowed to accompany the invasion force . . . the major stories were written by reporters in Washington, based on information given to them by State Department and other Government sources."

By Day Two, when it had become clear to even the most trusting of journalists that leaving the press behind had not been an oversight, references to the restrictions began to appear in news coverage. The sharpest remarks came from *NBC Nightly News* commentator John Chancellor, who, alone among his professional colleagues discussing the issue on Day Two, dared to speak the word "censorship" (albeit not about Grenada per se). Noting that the Secretary of Defense had explained casualties in Grenada by saying the price of freedom is high, Chancellor asked, "What freedom? The freedom of the American people to know what their government is doing? This administration clearly doesn't believe in that." Yet, incongruously, Chancellor's excor-

---

* "Day One coverage" refers to the first evening of television newscasts about the invasion, on Tuesday, October 25, as well as to the first morning of newspaper coverage, on Wednesday, October 26. "Day Two coverage" includes Wednesday-night broadcasts and Thursday-morning newspapers, and so forth.

iation, which appeared over twenty-one minutes into the October 26 broadcast, did not prevent NBC from leading the news with a report by Pentagon correspondent Jack Reynolds which uncritically transmitted self-serving statements made at a morning press conference by the government's two top censors: Joint Chiefs of Staff chairman General John Vessey and the very man Chancellor would ridicule in closing, Defense Secretary Weinberger. Viewers were not once warned that there was no independent confirmation of Weinberger's claims that the invasion was going well and that "a major Cuban installation" containing "command and control equipment, as well as a quantity of secret documents," had been captured.

It was not until Friday night, October 28—by which time the censorship had accomplished its purposes and been relaxed slightly—that *CBS Evening News* viewers saw or heard much about "censored" news. Three times that night CBS flashed the words "Cleared by Defense Department Censors" over pictures of the invasion released by the Pentagon. A follow-up piece by correspondent Bernard Goldberg featured CBS icon Walter Cronkite explaining the connection between a free press and democratic politics, but by then such edifications were, as Goldberg said of the administration's decision the day before finally to allow reporters onto Grenada, "a day late and a dollar short."

ABC News was even more circumspect. It was not until Thursday, the 27th, the third night of Grenada coverage, that viewers of *World News Tonight* were even told that reporters had been barred from witnessing the invasion for themselves. And even on the 27th, news of the press ban was mentioned only parenthetically and, even more astonishingly, in the context of an official rationalization for it. In the midst of a report detailing the Pentagon's version of events in Grenada, John McWethy announced that "Pentagon sources say one of the reasons the press was kept off the island during the early stages of the operation had to do with the presence of the super-secret Delta Group."

ABC News officials, including vice presidents George Watson and David Burke, later expressed astonishment at the long initial delay in *World News Tonight*'s reporting of the press ban (and in fairness it must be noted that ABC's *Nightline* did explore the topic on Wednesday night, October 26), but in fact the delay was only a more extreme manifestation of a general neglect of the story throughout the news media. A greater emphasis on the censorship angle may well have made it more difficult for the government to pass off as true so much information which later was discovered to be false. But for a variety of reasons, U.S. journalists were not disposed toward such an approach.

"We were focused on getting our arms around the story," explained Burke. "We can't get in; that you bitch about later. Our whole energy at that point was not going toward banging our cup on the high chair but toward getting the story to the extent you could under the existing conditions. Those conditions may be intolerable, but bitching and moaning about that is not the first priority of a news organization."

As Burke's likening of the press to a cranky infant in a high chair suggested, it was considered bad form for journalists to complain about how difficult it was to report a news story. It distracted from the story itself, and could make the journalist appear self-righteous. Official channels and procedures existed through which appropriate representations could be made when necessary, and in the case of Grenada these were amply utilized. But the messages sent by top executives of the major news organizations were rather more genteel and subdued than those communicated by their reporters at the White House's noon briefing. The telegram ABC News Washington bureau chief Ed Fouhy sent over ABC News president Roone Arledge's signature to Defense Secretary Caspar Weinberger that afternoon, for example, was more plea than protest, and seemed to assume that the Pentagon had left the press behind during a spasm of absentmindedness. "I am seeking your assistance and approval in allowing ABC News correspondents, camerapersons and producers to cover the military operation [in] Grenada," began the message. "The problems we are encountering are largely logistical," it continued, before assuring Weinberger that ABC would assign "only our most experienced broadcast journalists to the story, pay their way to Grenada, and accept responsibility for their safety."

In the days to come, the editorial pages of many of the nation's leading daily newspapers would feature somewhat more eloquently stated criticisms of the Reagan administration's news blackout. One week after the invasion, ABC's David Brinkley, NBC's Chancellor and CBS News president Edward Joyce appeared before a congressional subcommittee to enter formal protests of the press ban. And eventually, even the American Newspaper Publishers Association, as conservative a grouping as existed within the journalism business, declared itself against the administration's action, condemning it as "unprecedented and intolerable."

All in all, it was a response that leading news media officials later recalled with pride. Asked whether he believed the press had responded strongly enough to the Reagan administration's press ban, NBC News Washington bureau chief Robert McFarland replied, "Oh yeah. We raised unmitigated hell. We screamed to high heaven."

Los Angeles Times Washington bureau chief Jack Nelson was one of the few journalists who believed the press did not do enough to sound the alarm. "We should have done more on it, there's no question about that," said Nelson. "I don't think it was timidity. It was a matter of people just not thinking about it. We had invaded; that's the story."

Robert McFarland, however, argued that the press "got an interesting response from the American public" when it raised "unmitigated hell" about being barred from the invasion: "They were right and you were wrong. Shut up."

Contrary to what became the conventional wisdom within the journalistic community, that was not exactly the public's response. The view that Americans had sided with the government and against the press was not without foundation, of course, and in a perverse sort of way it was comforting for journalists to believe it; their protestations took on a certain extra nobility if one assumed public hostility to them. But other evidence suggested that the public was not so simpleminded. The *Los Angeles Times*, for example, conducted an opinion poll three weeks after the invasion which found that while Americans supported by the relatively narrow margin of 52 to 41 percent the Reagan policy of "denying unrestricted press access" during the Grenada invasion, they opposed by a two-to-one margin the administration's announced intention of making the blackout a precedent for future combat operations. And the further the post-invasion rush of nationalistic adrenaline receded, the more dubious Americans became about the press ban. A Harris poll conducted at year's end found Americans opposed to the government's Grenada press restriction by a solid 65 to 32 percent.

Precisely how much is impossible to say, but the press itself bore a certain amount of responsibility for the public's intitial acceptance of the Grenada press ban. Without turning partisan or unprofessional, U.S. news organizations could have done far more than they did to warn of the dangers the ban posed. But news coverage neither encouraged public concern about the imposition of censorship nor highlighted the opportunity it gave the government to manipulate mass opinion for its own ends. Emphasizing how reporters had been left out of the action, rather than the deeper point that the public was therefore receiving mainly one-sided information, did make the press sound whiny. Worse, it suggested that its protests were motivated more by self-interest than by principle. By the time the press worked up the courage to do more than clear its throat publicly about the censorship, three or four days after the invasion began, it was too late. The press had relayed enough government propaganda, sufficiently uncritically, so that the administration had successfully and irrevocably sold its version of the story to the public; the game of shaping public opinion was over and won for Reagan. In the process, the press had become, without knowing it, a passive accomplice in its own censorship.

• • •

EGREGIOUS as it was, the Grenada media blackout was hardly the sole instance of government suppression of freedom of the press and information during the Reagan years. In fact, barring the press from covering the invasion of Grenada was only the most blatant assertion of state secrecy by an administration that had waged, in the words of author Walter Karp, "a concerted assault on the habits of freedom" since first coming to power some thirty-three months before. In the November 1985 issue of *Harper's*, Karp listed dozens of examples large and small of the steps the Reagan administration had taken to expand government secrecy.

In 1981, the administration sought to gut the Freedom of Information Act (FOIA) while exempting the CIA and FBI from it entirely, declared a moratorium on the publication of government information documents, deprived citizens of due process by excluding the public from oversight of federal rule-making proceedings, invoked the President's personal executive privilege to justify withholding Interior Department documents from Congress and authorized the CIA to monitor the private conversations of American citizens.

In 1982, the administration went after the FOIA again. (Executive Order 12356 drastically slowed, and in some cases indefinitely postponed, declassification of government documents. It also reversed Carter era provisions that forbade classification of a document after a request had been made for it and that mandated that, when in doubt, government officials should decide in *favor* of declassification.) The administration also attempted to control the public dissemination of private scientific research, ordered the reclassification of millions of previously declassified government documents and mocked the constitutional doctrine of separation of powers, first by claiming for the federal budget office the power to decide which acts of Congress it could afford to enforce and later by defying congressional subpoenas for Environmental Protection Agency documents on toxic waste.

The FBI was awarded the right to infiltrate political organizations in the name of "domestic security" in 1983, the same year that government officials with access to "intelligence" information were told they would have to submit to an extraordinary system of official, lifetime censorship: for the rest of their lives, as many as 128,000 former and present officials would have to submit any articles, books, speeches or other public statements related to national security to government censors for pre-clearance before delivery.

The Reagan administration's campaign to expand the federal government's power to conduct its business in secret, safe from inconvenient public scrutiny, was itself conducted quietly. "The steps taken by Mr. Reagan to promote government secrecy have been taken one at a time in a non-combative manner, a strategy designed to minimize public opposition," charged Jack Nelson of the *Los Angeles Times* in a speech shortly after Grenada. "But they have had a profound cumulative impact and have set a policy and tone for secrecy in government that exceeds anything since Watergate. In fact, not even during the Nixon years were so many steps taken to establish secrecy as government policy." (The Reporters Committee for Freedom of the Press, in a March 1987 report, listed some 135 Reagan administration actions "aimed at restricting public and media access to government information and intruding on editorial freedom.")

If anyone should have recognized the danger posed by the measures undertaken by the Reagan administration, it was journalists. After all, in the American system, it was their responsibility to extract essential information from the government and present it to the people for their consideration. *The Washington Post* and some other major newspapers did cover, in some cases quite diligently, various individual steps in the Reagan secrecy campaign, but the campaign itself never became a major story or focus of press attention. The three major television networks proved themselves particularly uninterested in the story, perhaps because if offered few enticing visuals. The result was a pattern of neglect that made the Reagan drive to increase official secrecy, exalt the power of the executive branch and limit the liberties of individual citizens one of the most underreported stories of the Reagan presidency.

The administration's antipathy to the Freedom of Information Act first clearly surfaced on May 3, 1981, when Attorney General William French Smith introduced new regulations limiting public access to government documents under the act. Of the three networks only ABC found time to report this move at all, lavishing a full twenty seconds on it. On October 15, the White House sent legislation to Congress to "reform" the act. Its major provisions would have, in Mr. Karp's words, "put out of the public's reach precisely those documents that give the governed their 'check on government snooping' as well as made it vastly more difficult for citizens to monitor how well federal bureaucrats were enforcing environmental, consumer and various health and safety regulations." Another "improvement" would have made the FOIA prohibitively expensive for all but the wealthiest of Americans to use. Viewers of the *CBS Evening News* heard not a word about these proposals. ABC's *World News Tonight* spent twenty seconds on the story, while NBC found two and a half minutes on two consecutive evenings to explain the proposals and even offer a brief rebuttal to the government's arguments.

The arrest on October 1, 1984, of civilian naval official Samuel Loring Morison on charges of espionage raised the most serious questions about government secrecy as well as freedom of the press. Morison was detained after having sold three classified satellite photographs of a Soviet aircraft carrier to the British military magazine *Jane's Fighting Ships*, for which he worked as a part-time editor. Not even the government claimed that the photos damaged the national security; the Soviets had seen such photos before and were well acquainted with the capabilities of the satellite. Instead, the Reagan administration apparently hoped that a successful and well-publicized prosecution of Morison would deter other government officials from leaking information to the press.

What made the Morison case so significant was the government's implicit argument that passing harmless information to the press was as bad as sharing state secrets with the enemy, and should be penalized just as severely. Morison was charged under the Espionage Act, a law passed in 1917 to punish those who transferred military secrets to a foreign power. (The law had been employed to prosecute civilian officials only once in the intervening sixty-seven years, in the Pentagon Papers case of 1971, which was eventually dropped on the grounds of government misconduct.) The dangerous precedent a successful prosecution of Morison would establish was explained in an opinion column by Tom Wicker of *The New York Times*, published *after* Morison had been sentenced to a two-year prison term:

> If it is a crime to make classified information available to the public, as the Morison precedent suggests, the Government's ability to conceal *any* information is greatly increased. Just classify it, whether secrecy is warranted or not, and the threat of criminal prosecution will become a far stronger deterrent to potential whistle-blowers than any now in existence.

And not just to whistle-blowers. Journalists who broadcast or published classified information would also be subject to prosecution, with potential penalties of ten years in prison and $10,000 in fines for any conviction.

Simple self-interest should have spurred America's major news corporations to pay close attention to the Morison case, but for a long time it did not. Morison's October 1984 arrest was mentioned only briefly in network evening newscasts, and in the context of the case of an East German woman picked up in New York on spy charges the same day. Network producers facing daily deadlines could perhaps be excused for not immediately recognizing the deeper significance of the arrest; the issues were complex, and journalists were soon overtaken by a second and more sensational spy case when FBI agent Richard Miller was arrested the next day for allegedly spying for the Soviet Union. Yet by the time a judge in Baltimore issued his stunning ruling in March 1985 that the Espionage Act did indeed apply to Morison's case, there had been plenty of opportunity to become educated on the issue. Columnist Anthony Lewis, for one, had written a number of articles for *The New York Times* Op-Ed page illuminating the potential threats to freedom of the press and public debate. Yet not one of the networks made the slightest mention of the judge's ruling. ABC and NBC continued their silence when Morison was convicted on October 17; CBS aired a forty-second tell. ABC and NBC were apparently holding their fire until Morison's sentencing, when they devoted twenty and sixty seconds, respectively, to the story, while CBS ignored it. The single substantive network evening news story on the Morison case was a three-minute-and-ten-second piece aired at the end of NBC's November 29 broadcast which focused largely on the failure of Morison's disclosures to damage national security and barely mentioned the constitutional issues the case raised.

"There wasn't even lip service paid to the Morison case as a story," complained one producer at ABC News. "People at the top of this news division were incredibly ignorant about it. And they don't, frankly, want to stand up to this administration."

ABC was hardly alone in that regard. Capitulation to the administration's passion for secrecy became the norm for major news organizations in the post-Grenada years. Some examples:

- In December 1984, both NBC and the Associated Press obeyed a request from Defense Secretary Caspar Weinberger that they suppress news stories about an approaching space shuttle flight on grounds of "national security." Once again, there seemed little genuine rationale for the secrecy order; the military purpose of the flight had been public knowledge for months. (When *The Washington Post* eventually did publish a story based on publicly available information, Weinberger said such disobedience "can only give aid and comfort to the enemy," the exact wording of the constitutional definition of treason.)

- In July 1985, ABC, CBS, NBC, and the Cable News Network all obeyed government subpoenas requesting "outtakes" (unbroadcast videotapes) of their coverage of the TWA flight 847 hijacking, which resulted in thirty-nine U.S. citizens being held hostage in Beirut for seventeen days that June. Justice Department investigators said the tapes were needed to determine the identity of the hijackers, but critics feared the implications for a free press. "It doesn't take much imagination to see that if this becomes a general practice, anybody with a television camera or a notebook will be regarded as an arm of the police or government," said Ben Bagdikian, former *Washington Post* reporter and editor and noted press critic.

• In March 1986, ABC News apologized to the White House for allowing Radio Moscow correspondent Vladimir Posner a full seven minutes to respond to anti-Soviet contentions made in a nationally televised speech by President Reagan. The White House position was publicly endorsed by *Washingon Post* executive editor Benjamin Bradlee, foreshadowing the next episode in the media's subservience to state authority.

• In May 1986, after withholding the story for nearly six months at government request, the *Post* finally published a highly sanitized version of a story describing information given to the Soviet Union by accused spy Ronald Pelton. The paper also deleted 150 words, apparently the main substance of the report, from one of its stories on the Pelton trial itself.

Perhaps emboldened by the servile responses to their previous efforts, Reagan officials continued their campaign to transform journalists from independent professionals into obedient functionaries of the national security bureaucracy throughout Reagan's second term. On May 28, 1986, CIA director Casey and National Security Agency director Lieutenant General William Odom warned journalists against "speculation and reporting details beyond the information actually released at the trial" of Ronald Pelton. The totalitarian designs toward the press revealed by the Casey-Odom decree were hinted at by author and journalist Ronnie Dugger:

> The chiefs of the CIA and the NSA, who within the government are czars of information, were here cautioning American journalists not to speculate about . . . and thus implicitly not to dispute the information from the government. Suppose that, however superfluously, the head of the KGB had made exactly this statement to Soviet journalists concerning a trial, and the statement had somehow leaked to the Western press. Would we not have pounced upon this as yet another confirmation of the nature of Soviet journalism as an agency of the state?

• • •

REMINISCING more than two years after the fact, Michael Deaver suggested that he knew all along that the press would submit to censorship of Grenada without too great a fuss. Asked directly whether he ever worried that barring the press would provoke a backlash of negative coverage, he replied, "I didn't. If the invasion had not been successful, keeping the press out would have been a serious problem. But it was such a positive story, Americans totally supported it, that the press really couldn't take us on."

True, the press did complain about the news blackout, but it did so mainly behind the scenes. For his part, Deaver said he "didn't worry about the flak. It didn't bother me." In his view, politely critical commentary that few people would read and indignant telegrams that the administration could ignore were a small price to pay for control over the hard-news stories about Grenada. After all, all the while that they were huffing and puffing in private about the press ban, the nation's leading news organizations were running essentially the very story Deaver and his White House colleagues wanted to see on the front page and on its modern electronic equivalent, the national evening news broadcast.

It was not that critical sentiments were totally absent from news coverage. By reading carefully beyond the front pages of *The New York Times* or *The Washington Post*, the diligent news consumer could learn, for example, that not just the Soviet Union but U.S. ally Great Britain had criticized the invasion. The press also raised questions about whether the invasion was legal and whether the Congress should not have been consulted in advance. These procedural matters were ventilated ably enough, but always within the broader context of the Good Guys versus Bad Guys morality play scripted by the White House.

One of the most important moments in that play came when a number of the medical students evacuated from Grenada kissed the ground upon returning to the United States. White House press strategists had hoped "Students Rescued" stories would lead Day Two news coverage, but this was a special bonus. Images of American students exiting a U.S. military plane, kneeling and kissing the tarmac dominated Day Two coverage of newspapers as well as television, thus giving a tremendous boost to the Reagan administration's efforts to portray the intervention as a successful humanitarian act.

In all the commotion surrounding the return of the rescued students, many journalists apparently forgot to ask a key question: rescued from what? The clutches of Cuban-trained Marxists, or the combat ignited by U.S. invaders? There was no disputing that some students had been frightened. But that they had been in danger *before* the U.S. invasion began remained an unproven assertion, to say the least. Considerable evidence suggesting that Americans on Grenada could have departed peacefully was already available by the time the kissing-the-ground photos were flashed across the nation on Wednesday night, and more would accumulate in the days to come. Some of this evidence, such as the formal efforts the governments of Grenada and Cuba had made over the weekend to arrange departures for any Americans who wished to leave Grenada, even got reported in Day Two news stories. But all the news copy in the world could not match the power of those visual images.

Pictures of returning students kissing the ground were the kind of dramatic, human-interest shots that photo editors and television producers found irresistible, but they distorted the reality they purported to convey. Only a handful of the students had actually kissed the ground upon returning home, and subsequent reporting revealed that as a group the students were in fact divided on whether they had truly been in danger before the invasion. The disproportionate emphasis news accounts placed on students who did feel endangered, however, suggested that a virtual unanimity of opinion existed among the students, and moreover that it supported Reagan's justifications for invading. Inadvertently or not, press coverage of the students' homecoming implied that the administration had been right all along about Grenada.

Journalists were so eager to embrace the administration's second justification for invading—that Grenada was being turned into a Cuban-Soviet military base intended to subvert the entire Caribbean and Central American region—that they did not even wait to see the evidence for themselves before beginning to spread the news. Indeed, two of the three major networks began to trumpet the Cuban connection before the White House even argued the case itself. "The Cubans Are Coming" was the dominant theme of both the ABC and the CBS evening newscasts the night of the invasion, despite the fact that neither President Reagan at his morning press conference nor Secretary of State George Shultz at an afternoon press conference had cited Cuban actions as a rationale for the U.S. mission.

Anchor Peter Jennings opened ABC's *World News Tonight* broadcast that Tuesday night, October 25, by asking, in an ironic tone of voice, what would make a nation of 200 million people invade an island of 100,000, a fair and evenhanded question. The answer delivered by State Department correspondent Jack Smith's lead story could scarcely have been improved upon by President Reagan's own speechwriters. Grenada, ABC viewers were told, was a country where Cuba was building a large modern airstrip and the Soviet Union hoped to install a deep-sea port facility, and where Maurice Bishop, the leftist former Prime Minister, had been killed in a bloody coup and replaced by "a committed ideological Marxist." A picture of Cuban President Fidel Castro flanked by Nicaraguan leaders Daniel and Humberto Ortega flashed on the screen as Smith then spun out an anti-Communist, domino-theory rationale for the U.S. invasion:

> With Fidel Castro now firmly established as an ally of Nicaragua's leftist regime and with the guerrilla war now being fought in El Salvador, the last thing the U.S. or its Caribbean allies wanted was another Soviet or Cuban base, especially since Grenada sits astride the Trinidad Channel, which is the preferred route for half of the U.S.'s imports en route to Gulf Coast refineries.

Smith closed by harking back to the 1965 U.S. invasion of the Dominican Republic, an intervention, he said, taken against "leftist rebels" which eventually restored "democracy. It remains to be seen if today's action will turn out as well."

CBS viewers were also advised that the invasion had been a good thing, and the endorsement came from a perhaps unexpected source. Bill Moyers, the most liberal commentator in network news and thus a man often critical of Reagan's domestic policy, defended the invasion with language and reasoning strikingly similar to Smith's. "That huge airstrip . . . built with Soviet and Cuban help" and "harder-line Marxists trained in Cuba" bothered Moyers too. Likewise, the Grenada action reminded him of the Dominican Republic intervention of eighteen years previous, an action he said was undertaken to "prevent a Com-

munist takeover." The "strategic consequences of yet another
Soviet base in the Caribbean" were unacceptable; it was no wonder that President Reagan, like his predecessors Kennedy and
Johnson (the latter of whom Moyers served as press secretary
during the Dominican crisis), would "consider the use of force
legitimate in the Caribbean."

In a straight news piece, Moyers's colleague Bob Simon was
good enough at least to mention two of Grenada's counterclaims
before dismissing them:

> The Grenadians said their new all-weather night-and-day airport,
> with its 10,000-foot runway built by Cubans, was for jumbo jets
> carrying tourists. Washington said, "Nonsense." The Grenadians
> said the new port facilities under construction were for banana
> boats. Washington said, "No way." Washington believed this tin-
> iest Caribbean country was being redesigned from a tourist haven
> to a Communist air base and way station.

John Chancellor at NBC made it unanimous. Like Moyers a
former professional spokesman for the United States government
(Chancellor directed the Voice of America from 1965 to 1967),
he found it easy to empathize with Washington's concerns. He
drew the same parallel to the Dominican invasion that Moyers
and Smith did, and saw no reason to object to "the downfall of
the pro-Cuban regime in Grenada" and its presumed replacement
with "a pro-American democracy."

The rush to convict Cuba (in which *The New York Times* and
The Washington Post also joined, offering more nuanced charges
in respective front-page articles) made a mockery of journalistic
standards of fairness and balance. ABC especially and Jack Smith
in particular had reason to know better than to regard Grenada's
unfinished airport as unequivocal evidence of an impending Cuban takeover of the island. Back in March 1983, when President
Reagan had first sounded the alarm about the airport in a nationally televised speech, ABC had been the only major news
organization to dispatch a team of reporters to Grenada to investigate, and their findings had contrasted sharply with the President's contentions. Among those findings was the news that,
contrary to Reagan's assertions, the Soviets had made "absolutely
no contribution" to airport construction. And while Cuba was
indeed providing some labor and materials, U.S. companies were
also participating in the project, and Venezuela, Mexico and the
European Common Market were providing financing.

It was not until Days Three and Four of the Grenada story that the campaign to pin the blame on the Cubans reached full intensity. That the United States had got to Grenada "just in time" to forestall a major Cuban military buildup became the central assertion in the administration's propaganda campaign, and the press proved a willing and none too skeptical conveyor of it. Preparing their viewers for President Reagan's national television address on Thursday, the 27th, all three networks led their evening broadcasts with reports which uncritically relayed Defense Department claims that the number of Cubans on Grenada was nearly twice as large as originally thought. The new estimate of over one thousand Cubans, "virtually all of them soldiers," was based, ABC's John McWethy reported, on "secret documents" that U.S. intelligence officers had taken from a Cuban facility captured the day before. Moreover, U.S. forces had also discovered, in the words of NBC's Jack Reynolds, "a staggering amount of weapons . . . three warehouses full," supplied by Cuba and the Soviet Union.

Subliminally reinforcing the government's claims with colorful electronic graphics, ABC's companion piece by Sam Donaldson featured a map with the face of Ronald Reagan rising up out of the sea north of Grenada like Poseidon in full glory, and the words: "INVASION THWARTED SOVIET-CUBAN PLANS TO MAKE GRENADA A BASE FOR HEMISPHERIC AGGRESSION." Television is a visual medium, where the eye, in Donaldson's words, "predominates over the ear when there is a clash between the two." But there was no such clash that night, for Donaldson's piece also included national security adviser Robert McFarlane's delivery of the de facto line of the day: "From the scale of things that have been discovered, we got there just in time."

After President Reagan took to the airwaves that evening to repeat the "We got there just in time" incantation to the entire nation, citing as his evidence the same "secret documents" and weapons warehouses, the friendly press coverage continued. Although journalists had yet to see, much less examine, these documents and warehouses for themselves, that did not deter them from full-throated endorsement of the administration's case. One particularly striking example was Hedrick Smith's front-page account of the speech in The New York Times. Not a hint of skepticism disturbed the Washington correspondent's recitation of

Reagan's claims on Friday morning. Paragraph after paragraph simply quoted or summarized the President's charges that Grenada was "a Soviet-Cuban colony" being readied to "export terrorism and undermine democracy."

The disinformation barrage continued on Friday evening. All three networks led their broadcasts with U.S. Navy admiral Wesley McDonald's claim that the secret documents also revealed that the Cubans planned to expand their military presence on Grenada dramatically and eventually to take it over. Ample airtime was then spent showing U.S. government-supplied videotapes of the warehouses containing the weapons by which said takeover would be accomplished.

Not one of the network reports exposed what an utter fraud the warehouse gambit was, even though journalists earlier that day had finally been allowed to examine the warehouses and their contents for themselves. Writing in the next morning's *Washington Post*, veteran foreign correspondent Loren Jenkins was the first to disclose that the warehouses, which Reagan had ominously claimed "contained weapons and ammunition stacked almost to the ceiling, enough to supply thousands of terrorists," were in fact largely empty of weapons. "The principal arms storage shed," wrote Jenkins, ". . . was probably a quarter full." And while it did contain some modern Soviet-made infantry weapons, many of the arms were antiquated, with some dating back as far as 1870. Remarkably, not one of the network evening broadcasts picked up on Jenkins's story that night, or the next night, or ever, for that matter. Cheerleading had by then become the order of the day; President Reagan's bogus claims and self-serving distortions would stand unchallenged.

Stressing the alleged Cuban connection was crucial to the Reagan administration's strategy of portraying the invasion as a simple story of Good Guys versus Bad Guys. Once that connection was implanted in the public consciousness, all else followed. As it happened, subsequent reporting revealed little foundation for most of Reagan's justifications for the invasion. A *New York Times* editorial entitled "The Grenada High," for example, later ridiculed "the yarn that an invasion was needed to rescue a few hundred medical students," dismissed the "urgent request" from neighboring islanders with which Reagan had initially justified the attack as having been "plainly encouraged, if not indeed written, in Washington" and declared that "there was more ignorance than evidence" behind the administration's charge that Cubans planned to "export terror" from Grenada. But this mattered little to the White House. By the time such rebukes appeared, it had already achieved its military and political objectives, and successfully sold its version of the operation to the American people.

"They realize that first impressions are lasting impressions; that's part of their public relations genius," Jack Nelson of the *Los Angeles Times* said of the Reagan media strategists. "Grenada is the perfect example. There are still people who think that place was crawling with Cubans. It doesn't matter how often you go back and say that the fact is there were only five or six hundred Cubans, that you got the truth out of Havana and lies out of Washington, people just say, 'Aw, that's just the press.' "

• • •

THE U.S. news media's reporting of the Grenada invasion was a veritable triumph of faith over reason. In retrospect, it is remarkable how credulous leading American journalists were of information given them by a government which had both lied to them about whether an invasion was planned and then censored them by preventing them from covering it. But it was a trust built into the way most journalists approached the task of reporting on their government.

"Most of the inaccurate stuff came out of the press conferences [held in Washington by Defense Secretary Weinberger and various military officials]. But we took it hook, line and sinker," conceded ABC's John McWethy. "When you are in a situation where your primary source of information is the United States government—and for three days basically your only source of information, except Radio Havana—you are totally at their mercy. And you have to make an assumption that the U.S. government is telling the truth."

Asked why he gave Reagan's claims about Grenada such credence after the administration had first misled him about the impending invasion and later refused to allow him or other reporters the chance to independently verify those claims, McWethy asked rhetorically, "Do you report nothing? What you do is say, 'Administration officials say.' You report that Weinberger *says* the fighting was heaviest here, or Weinberger *says* the barracks are under siege. Well, shit, he's the fucking Secretary of Defense. What are you going to do? You report what he says."

McWethy was one of the most knowledgeable reporters on the foreign and military policy beat in Washington. His conservative politics and heavy reliance on U.S. military and diplomatic officials as news sources earned him the derisive nickname of "General McWethy" among some ABC colleagues, but he was too skilled and thoughtful a reporter to be dismissed so easily. Having been investigated more than once by the FBI and other U.S. security agencies for reporting information which allegedly damaged "national security," McWethy was quite aware that governments play games with the truth and, in the process, with reporters as well. Noting that while "major chunks" of the Reagan administration's story about Grenada were wrong, McWethy maintained that the administration nevertheless by and large had to tell the truth if it hoped to sway public opinion.

"If you are a government and want to construct a situation that will go down with the public, you make sure the basic elements of your story are *not* bullshit," said McWethy. "They did take over that island. They did find x number of Cubans. They did find Soviet stuff on that island. They did rescue students who got off the plane and kissed the ground and proclaimed Ronald Reagan a savior. That's what happened and that's what they wanted reported."

The crucial question, of course, was whether all those individual facts truly added up to the big picture U.S. officials said they did. But then the American press rarely questioned the basic premises or perspective of U.S. foreign policy, especially in moments of presumed crisis. Nor did it see much reason to; by a curious sort of osmosis, most Washington reporters had long ago absorbed the same basic worldview favored and articulated by the officials they covered. And after two years during which President Reagan had whipped up anti-Communist hysteria to a pitch not reached since the 1950s, and in the immediate aftermath of the KAL 007 incident, the average mainstream journalist was particularly disinclined to raise doubts about his ideological bona fides by raising too many challenging questions about whether the administration's story made intellectual or moral sense.

It was far easier just to join in the applause, as the *NBC Nightly News* did in its Friday, October 28, broadcast at the end of Grenada week. Because of the Beirut disaster, there had been more American combat deaths that week than in any since the end of the Vietnam War. But that somber note was not allowed to intrude upon the festive mood as NBC concluded its Grenada segment that evening with a marvelously flattering shot of President Reagan strolling through the sunshine across the South Lawn of the White House en route to his Camp David retreat. As viewers watched hundreds of White House staffers and visitors cheering the President and holding up signs proclaiming "Your Finest Hour," anchor Tom Brokaw seconded the motion, quoting an unidentified senior White House aide that the past week had been Reagan's toughest since taking office, but also "his finest hour."

There remained one final scene in the Grenada docudrama scripted by the Reagan propaganda apparatus: a White House reunion, hosted by the President and Mrs. Reagan, and featuring as guests of honor the evacuated medical students and the military men who rescued them. The gala celebration took place on Monday, November 7, two weeks to the day after ABC reporters Mark Potter and Sharon Sakson spotted U.S. military forces on their way to Grenada and inquiring White House reporters were told a U.S. invasion was "preposterous." Product of Hollywood that he was, President Reagan loved happy endings, and it was precisely that message the reception was designed to convey to the public at large.

The television networks could hardly have been more accommodating. Unobtrusively performing the middleman role assigned them, they turned a blind eye to the event's obvious public relations benefits and pretended it really did boast the genuine news value White House officials claimed. Colleagues of hers at CBS later recalled that Lesley Stahl did try to convince her bosses in New York that her story should emphasize how staged the whole affair was, but on this occasion, like many before and after it, the correspondent was overruled, allegedly after heated argument. As a result, Stahl's report, like those of her ABC and NBC competitors, was just what the White House was hoping for: filled with flattering photos of President Reagan surrounded by adoring young Americans waving flags and cheering, empty of any images or rhetoric that might disturb the upbeat, patriotic mood of the moment.

"It was," as ABC's Sam Donaldson declared in his report, "a

love-in at the White House today," and the press was only too glad to join in. Whatever bitterness reporters had once felt at having been barred from covering the invasion, whatever skepticism had been trained on the government's justifications for the intervention, whatever small gestures toward an adversarial posture had been attempted, all that was gone now, vanished like a spark in the darkness. Actual surrender terms were never negotiated, but, for the Reagan team, the triumph over the press was total.

Not everyone in the administration was crowing about having licked the press, however. Barring the media from covering the fighting in Grenada had been a major coup for the "bad cop" faction within the administration, who favored taking a hard line against the press, but it sufficiently offended moderate Gergen so that he resigned his post as White House communications director soon after. At the time of his resignation, Gergen claimed that he was leaving for personal and family reasons, but in a 1986 interview for this book he conceded that the Grenada press ban "was a major break for me. . . . You fight a certain number of these battles, and after a while I found that I was losing some. The pressures build up over time to restrict information, to use polygraphs. The resentment builds up against the press. And it becomes harder and harder to maintain the kind of standards that we were committed to when I came in. In that sense I thought I was less effective internally, and I found it more difficult to justify and defend."

But disappointment over the Grenada blackout did not sour Gergen on the overall value of the time he spent in the Reagan White House. Gergen's allegiance had always been more to the institution of the presidency than to the individual who occupied the Oval Office at a given moment, and in that regard this last tour of duty had been quite fulfilling. He had first gone to work for Ronald Reagan in 1980, a time when the incumbent President seemed all but powerless to defend himself against relentlessly critical press coverage. In three short years, he had helped to reverse that equation. Now the President was back on top, and sailing toward re-election. All things considered, Gergen was proud of what he had accomplished.

Shortly after leaving the White House in January 1984, Gergen published an article in *The Washington Post* assessing the achievements and shortcomings of Reagan's first three years. During a subsequent interview, a section of the article dealing with foreign policy was read back to him with the suggestion that if "the press" were substituted for "the Soviet Union" and "the White House" were substituted for "the United States," the passage accurately described what he and his colleagues had achieved during the Reagan years. The altered version read as follows:

> The central thrust of the administration's approach to the world these past three years has been clear: to correct the imbalance of power with the press so that the White House will once again achieve a "margin of safety." . . . Most of his advisers and the President himself now believe the basic goal has been achieved. They were willing to accept some risks along the way—they knew, for example, that the press would storm and shout—but they sincerely think that the White House is at last safer and more secure.

Before the passage was completely read, a grin flashed across Gergen's often solemn face and he broke in to say, "Yeah, I agree, that's a good point. It's a very relevant analogy."

11

THE NEW PARTY BOSSES

T HE YEAR 1984 turned out to be an astonishingly easy one for Ronald Reagan. He was supposed to be running for President, normally an arduous task for a man also in charge of running the government, but then Reagan had never believed in working hard if he didn't have to, and in 1984 he didn't have to. From the moment he announced his candidacy in late January, the press portrayed him as all but unbeatable and directed its gaze instead at the more entertaining struggle to select his challenger. The Democrats obligingly squabbled among themselves, shrank away from forcefully challenging Reagan or his policies and in general did all they could to confirm the press's complacent expectations.

Michael Deaver had expected—and prepared for—a real battle in 1984. In consultation with James Baker, Richard Darman and Reagan-Bush campaign director Edward Rollins, he had plotted an aggressive plan of attack, empty of substance but brimming with symbolism, designed to portray Reagan as the embodiment of America and make his re-election seem as inevitable as tomorrow's sunrise. In retrospect, he was amazed that he and his colleagues got away with such an easy ride.

"We started off with what was going to be our May-June strategy, which was 'America Is Back,' " explained Deaver. "We knew what the negatives were on the President, but the Mondale people could never get their act together. So we kept apple pie and the flag going for the whole time. I never thought we'd be able to do that. But yes, it was a conscious effort to portray the President['s re-election] as inevitable."

Certainly press coverage alone did not decide who won and lost in 1984, but just as certainly it played a dominant role in shaping what happened. The press was central to Deaver's battle plan, and he was not disappointed by its performance. In fact, he said he was downright "pleased" with it. It's not hard to see why; the press played into the Reagan campaign's hands in at least three major ways in 1984.

First, because of its appalling addiction to horse-race journalism, it focused more on opinion polls than on political issues and ended up conveying the clear impression that President Reagan's re-election was just as "inevitable" as Deaver hoped to make it seem. Second, in a reprise of its jelly-bean journalism approach to covering Reagan in 1981, television chose time and again to broadcast virtually whatever flattering pictures the Reagan apparatus staged on a given day, even as (along with the print press) it largely refrained from pressuring the President to step beyond what Mondale campaign director Robert Beckel called Reagan's "question-free zone" and respond to questions about his record and future plans. The combined effect was to allow the Reagan apparatus virtually complete control over what Americans saw and heard of their candidate on television, thus transforming supposedly objective news stories into virtual campaign commercials.

Still, it is doubtful the press would have conducted itself so servilely were it not for a third and final factor: the news media's eagerness to endorse the "America Is Back" mentality that animated the Reagan campaign. The press's ideological and political center of gravity had begun shifting rightward before Ronald Reagan even arrived in Washington, but over the last four years the trend had sharply accelerated to where, by 1984, there was widespread approval within the press of the job Reagan had done as President. As Jeff Gralnick, the news division vice president who directed ABC's campaign coverage in 1984 (and again in 1988), declared, "Carter was hostage to the Iranian situation, but Reagan is hostage to nothing."

• • •

"CONTROL THE AGENDA" was one of the Ten Commandments of presidential politics in the media age. Like the closely related principles of "stay on the offensive," "talk about the issues *you* want to talk about" and "speak in one voice," it had been a central tenet of the Reagan approach to news management throughout the first term, and Mike Deaver made sure the rule continued to be applied during the 1984 campaign. Walter Mondale's campaign strategists also recognized the importance of controlling the agenda, but they rarely succeeded in doing so. Doubtless they themselves were partly to blame, but they did labor under an enormous disadvantage. As Richard Leone, senior adviser to the Mondale campaign, explained: "I think we had a potential to set the agenda that we tried to exploit, but it was always in a context in which the inevitability of the Reagan victory was something we had to dispute, day in and day out. Most of the questions we got from reporters reflected that angle, most of the stories did."

Leone added that the widespread presumption of Reagan's inevitability made it difficult not only to get the Mondale message out but to raise money. He noted that while the Reagan campaign raised all of the $7 million permitted by federal election law, the Mondale campaign managed to raise only $2 million. "The $5 million we might have had, I don't think our fund-raising people are blind, their difficulty in raising money has been because of the drumbeat of polls that say it's hopeless," said Leone. "People don't want to contribute money to a hopeless cause."

There was a certain poetic justice in all this. Back when he was still seeking the Democratic presidential nomination, Walter Mondale had benefited enormously from the tendency of the political-journalistic establishment to emphasize the horse race and anoint "can't lose" front-runners. (His erstwhile rivals for the nomination had frequently complained in the months leading up to the actual primary contests about the Catch-22 they faced: because they were so far behind in the polls, the press refused to treat them seriously; without media visibility, they found it impossible to raise the money needed to pursue the campaign vigorously enough to make a dent in the polls.)

"We correctly saw that front-loading [of delegate selection] was going to make 1984 different and that a lot of things were going to be settled probably much earlier," said Robert Kaiser of *The Washington Post*. "And then we looked out there and saw that only one candidate was organized in every state, only one candidate had double-digit millions, only one had endorsements— obviously that's the guy!"

Who gave the press the right to decide who "the guy" was? Wasn't that supposed to be the voters' prerogative? It was, but as John Sears, who ran Reagan's 1976 (and, briefly, his 1980) campaign, pointed out, "the voters have to take most of their impressions [of the candidates] from what they see in the press and on television." It was Sears's view that the news media had become the contemporary equivalent of the old party bosses who used to meet behind closed doors to select a party's presidential nominee.

"Originally people were nominated for President basically as a result of what some group of party leaders thought," Sears explained. "There were primaries, but they were basically a chance to show how you could perform under game conditions, rather than anything that really affected the nomination. . . . Now we have a system where the nomination is actually decided in the primaries, and the people who do that are those who choose to vote in the primaries. . . . Now the press is actually the ones who are advising the voters in some ways about these races and who has a chance and who doesn't."

And the press was virtually unanimous in the months leading up to the Democratic primaries that no one (except perhaps Ohio senator John Glenn) had a chance to win the Democratic nomination except Walter Mondale. As *Time*'s chief of correspondents, Richard Duncan, recalled: "I expected, as I think most of us did in the early fall, that it was going to be Mondale in a quick kill." Mondale's victory with 49 percent of the vote in the February 20 Iowa caucuses was treated as further evidence that he would soon be the Democratic standard-bearer; indeed, some journalists seemed ready to name him the official nominee right then and there. As NBC's chief political correspondent, Roger Mudd, declared on the next day's evening newscast, "This victory makes his nomination seem inevitable." Never mind that Iowa was merely one state, that the total number of Democrats participating in its caucuses numbered less than 90,000, that the millions of Democrats yet to vote in other states might have very different preferences; the clear message from the national media was: Mondale's the one.

It is true that Gary Hart eventually gave Mondale a real race, but again, only after receiving the media's implicit blessing. The Colorado senator finished a distant second in Iowa with 16 percent of the vote. Barely five thousand votes separated him from third-place finisher George McGovern, but that difference was enough to make Hart the chief alternative to Mondale in the eyes of the press corps. Immediately Hart was showered with extra media coverage, raising his profile across the country and positioning him for a successful challenge to Mondale in New Hampshire.

The media continued to predict victory for Mondale—a page-one *New York Times* story the morning of the New Hampshire primary announced that he boasted the largest lead of any non-incumbent in history—but the voters refused to follow the script. Hart's triumph in New Hampshire ended talk of Mondale's inevitability; a three-month battle between the two men for the party's nomination began. But things could have worked out quite differently had the voters of New Hampshire not shown the independence of mind to think for themselves. As it was, Hart's challenge still failed, at least in part because his underfinanced campaign infrastructure lacked the staying power to overcome the huge initial fund-raising and organizational advantages the Mondale camp derived from its early front-runner status.

As certain as they were about Mondale, the national news media were, if anything, even more convinced of Ronald Reagan's invincibility come November 1984. "The fact is, there was never any question about the outcome," NBC News president Lawrence Grossman observed in retrospect. "Everybody knew what was going to happen in this election." Brit Hume, who covered Mondale for ABC News, never thought his candidate had a chance: "If Walter Mondale had done everything perfectly, he probably would have won four states. I can't think of a candidate who could have beaten Reagan. The public was going to re-elect Ronald Reagan come hell or high water. Historically, look at how many times a popular incumbent was voted out in the midst of an economic boom and when there were no U.S. troops posted anywhere in the world firing shots in anger." Hume's colleague Stan Opotowsky, ABC's director of political operations, said, "We knew throughout [the campaign] there was no way Walter Mondale was going to get a majority of the electoral votes. We kept monitoring it because it could have changed, but Reagan was so solid in the South and West that he only needed one or two states east of the Mississippi River to assure the election."

President Reagan's presumed inevitability was reflected in campaign news coverage not because America's journalists were trying to throw the election but because their definition of how to cover it emphasized the horse race above all else. Simply put, the press paid far less attention to where a candidate stood on the issues than to where he or she stood in the polls.

The stress on polls helped Reagan because it meant that less attention was paid to the issues, which reinforced in the public mind the separation between Reagan the man, who was undeniably popular, and his policies, which often were not. But leading journalists argued that issues were simply not very important to the average American voter. "People care about issues last," asserted *Newsweek* editor Maynard Parker, who oversaw both national and foreign news coverage during 1984. Parker saw no reason to apologize for the magazine's emphasis on the horse race. "When I walk into a bar or a party," he added, "people don't ask about how Hart is versus Mondale on a certain issue. They ask who's ahead, what's he really like as a person, what kind of executive ability does he have."

"I happen to think . . . that when people are judging an election, personality and character—leadership—is undoubtedly the most critical factor," said Grossman of NBC. "And in any event, that is the aspect of it that television is particularly suited to bring."

If Mr. Grossman's last line unwittingly suggested he was perhaps making a political virtue of what was, for television, a commercial necessity, there were a number of print journalists who quite openly blamed television for the paucity of issues coverage in 1984. For example, when I told *Time*'s Richard Duncan that I'd been surprised, after reading through the magazine's campaign coverage from July 1983 to November 1984, by the overwhelming stress on the horse race rather than on the candidates' records and positions on issues, he replied, "It wasn't that kind of an election. . . . It was all sloganeering—the twenty-second, four-sentence [sound] bite. I don't think we're irresponsible at all in not dignifying that with in-depth coverage." Yet even Duncan ended up defending the horse-race emphasis: "Isn't it important," he asked, "beyond any of the half-assed swipes at the issues they made, who is going to be the next President of the United States? Dammit, isn't that the story—who is going to be President?"

Serious journalists recognized there were dangers in poll-driven coverage—not least of which was its potential to shape the public opinion it was supposed to be measuring—but they rarely prevailed in the internal arguments on the issue that took place within most of the nation's major news organizations in 1984. Merrill Shiels, *Newsweek*'s national news editor in 1984, confirmed that issues versus horse race was "a huge internal argument" at her shop. The reason horse race usually won, she ventured, was "maybe because the political junkies who put this together find the horse race simply more interesting." After all, a candidate's position on a given issue was unlikely to change radically very often in the course of a campaign, but his or her standing in the polls could change several times in the course of a month. That was a powerful enticement for a press which, for commercial reasons, treasured the new above all else.

Perhaps because he was not a journalist, ex-Reagan campaign manager Sears was able to recognize the profit motives behind the media's horse-race preference. "Once the [election] process starts," he said, "you don't get many questions about what your stands on the issues are because the interest of the press becomes much more pronounced on the question of who is winning and who is losing, and which part of the press can indicate that first. That particularly is the influence of television." Sears, a campaign analyst on NBC's *Today* show in 1984 (and again in 1988), added, "Television is still essentially an entertainment medium, not a journalistic medium. Ratings mean *so* much, even in the news departments, that it's inevitable that the horse race is going to be the more entertaining story. So they rush to cover that, and that puts a lot of pressure on the newspapers."

Not surprisingly, the horse-race approach to campaign coverage drew criticism from Mondale officials. "People say that issues don't matter in a campaign, and it's a self-fulfilling prophecy," said Mondale campaign director Robert Beckel. "Issues don't matter if you don't raise them. It's wrong that people don't care about issues. If you present them with a controversy, they do care. They'll listen to it. But if you don't give it to them, if you give them balloons and happy talk and bullshit every night, and the next ad they see is a couple of farmers clapping as [the Olympic] torch goes down the road and Schlitz beer saying 'America Is Back,' shit, there's no controversy there. The only controversy the press found during the entire campaign was Geraldine Ferraro; it was the only significant, major, sustained issue in that campaign. Except, for a very brief period of time, Reagan's age."

The age issue did not arise until late in the campaign, during the first of Reagan's two nationally televised debates with Mr. Mondale. The President was so far ahead in the polls by then—anywhere from fifteen to twenty-five points, depending on the pollster—that most of the nation's political and journalistic establishment saw the debates as little more than a formality, interesting enough as spectacle but unlikely to change enough votes to cost Reagan the election. But as he had so many times before, the Gipper confounded the experts. His answers to reporters' questions on domestic policy during the October 7 debate in Louisville were rambling, disjointed mixtures of fact, fiction and bravado. In contrast to Mondale's crisp, informed aggressiveness, Reagan seemed hesitant and confused; more than once, he lost his train of thought entirely. Speaking of the poverty rate, he opined that it "has begun to decline, but it is still going up." It was a performance that left political observers shocked, Mondale supporters newly optimistic and the Reagan campaign staff at each other's throats, with campaign chairman Senator Paul Laxalt publicly lashing out at unnamed White House aides for a briefing process that had "brutalized" the President.

For the first time in the 1984 campaign Reagan the man, rather than the myth, had become the issue. And adding insult to injury, it was the great magician himself who had broken the spell. Appropriately enough for a man who had such difficulty distinguishing between the movies and real life, Reagan's debate performance was reminiscent of nothing so much as the scene near the end of *The Wizard of Oz*, where Toto the dog pulls aside the curtain and reveals to Dorothy and her companions the well-intentioned but hapless old man who calls himself the Wizard. Dorothy calls him "a very bad man" for foisting such a deception upon her and his adoring subjects. "No, I'm a very good man," the Wizard replies in a sad, weary voice. "I'm just a very bad wizard." For ninety minutes that night from Louisville, Americans saw the real, curtainless Reagan, rather than the usual prepackaged version. For the White House, that inevitably meant trouble on the public relations front.

That Reagan's faltering performance came as such a shock to so many people was itself evidence of a twin dynamic: the continuing success of Deaver and the rest of the propaganda apparatus at showing the world the Reagan they wanted it to see, and the corresponding failure of the press to resist those efforts and remind the public of the true nature of the President hiding behind the curtain. Surely, by 1984 White House reporters did not have to see daily evidence of Reagan's simplemindedness to know it existed, but they shrank back from raising that issue on their own;

to avoid charges of unfairness to the President, they believed that they had to wait until Reagan raised it himself, in public. "The point is," *Washington Post* reporter David Hoffman said about the debate, "the American people saw something for the first time that we've been waiting to tell them, and it was right before their eyes."

Yet the press still held back from stating the obvious. Embarrassing as the President's Sunday-night showing had been, the next day's news coverage gave it remarkably short shrift. The reluctance that *Time* magazine national news editor Steve Smith expressed earlier in this book about saying that the President of the United States was out to lunch was everywhere in evidence. It was as if the men and women of the press felt they needed permission before they could truthfully describe what they had seen the night before.

Instead, the focus was on how momentum had now shifted to Mondale after his upset victory. Thus all three network evening newscasts featured virtually identical stories showing a jubilant Mondale greeting wildly cheering crowds while a subdued Reagan appeared before supporters in North Carolina. Conspicuous by its absence was any analysis of what the two men had actually said the night before in Louisville, and therefore any suggestion of just how substantively ill informed the President had been. That Mr. Reagan had done poorly was implicit in the reports, but just how poorly was left unsaid; the received impression was that the President had merely had a bad night.

The competency issue might never have been raised at all had *The Wall Street Journal* not run a front-page article the next day asking, "Is Oldest U.S. President Now Showing His Age?" Beneath a subheadline asserting that "Reagan Debate Performance Invites Open Speculation on His Ability to Serve," the Tuesday-morning article by Rich Jaroslovsky and James M. Parry quoted medical professors, politicians and pollsters on the implications of Reagan's advanced age. Although it studiously eschewed alarmism, the article inevitably raised the question of whether Reagan was fit to serve an additional four years as President. Its fifth paragraph quoted Michigan State University management expert Eugene Jennings, who had voted for Reagan in 1980: "I am very concerned, as a psychologist, about his inability to think on his feet, the disjointedness of his sentences and his use of the security blanket of redundancy. . . . I'd be concerned to put him in a corporate presidency. I'd be all the more concerned to put him into the U.S. presidency."

It was an extremely important story, for it effectively legitimated discussion of the age issue, a topic the rest of the press had thus far cautiously avoided. The *Journal* article (which actually had been in development for some months) provoked the second spasm of aggressive coverage of the President during the 1984 campaign. (The first occurred right after the Democratic convention and was sparked by Mondale's challenge to Reagan on the tax and deficit issue.) On Tuesday night both CBS and ABC ran their own stories about Mr. Reagan's age, and by Wednesday it was the hot new story that the entire press corps was talking and writing about. That night, CBS noted that the Reagan campaign was engaged in "another day of damage control" and released a poll that charted Mondale gaining six points on Reagan in the three days since the debate. With the Reagan campaign suddenly on the defensive and another debate with Mondale on the horizon, there was a definite shift in the tone and assumptions underlying coverage of the campaign. Suddenly the press seemed to think the 1984 election might be a contest after all.

What was ironic about all this was that the age issue, the cause of Mr. Reagan's temporary reversal, was actually something of a false alarm. Senility had not been Reagan's problem in Louisville; under similar circumstances, he could well have appeared equally muddled at any time during the preceding four years of his presidency; his misstatements and non sequiturs were less a function of aging than of being deprived of his teleprompter and having to think for himself.

But in the absence of any such alternative analysis in the rest of the mainstream press, the *Journal* article ended up setting the terms of subsequent discussion. The resulting distortion was less the fault of the *Journal* than of the rest of the press, for the Jaroslovsky–Parry article was a muscular, well-crafted piece of journalism that would have been a valuable contribution within a broader mosaic of coverage. The problem was that there was no broader mosaic. Rather than analyze Reagan's debate performance for themselves, the rest of the press took the cowardly way out, poaching off the *Journal* article and framing the issue not as a question of whether Reagan knew what he was talking about but whether he was too old to be President.

While damaging to the Reagan campaign in the short term, that news frame ended up working in its favor by the time the second debate, on foreign policy, rolled around ten days later. As Mike Deaver's counterpart, Richard Leone, later commented: "The media played the dominant role in deciding what the second debate would be about and what the test would be—which was whether Reagan was mentally fit to serve, which is the easiest test any candidate ever had to pass. And when he appeared reasonably mentally competent for most of the night, he was declared the winner, that night, by the networks, and the winner of the election for that reason."

Perhaps the most disturbing consequence of the press's horse-race obsession was that it meant that President Reagan was all but ignored *as a political candidate* for the bulk of the election year. For the first six months of 1984, the press was utterly fixated on the immediate and continuing horse-race story of who would be the Democratic nominee. Ronald Reagan was running for re-election during this period just as surely as he was after Labor Day, but in news coverage Reagan was treated as not so much a politician as the President. Although Reagan had much to answer for in his conduct of the presidency over the past three-plus years, the press essentially looked the other way for much of 1984, focusing attention instead on the competition among the Democrats to decide who would be his challenger, a news frame that implicitly suggested that it was they, not Reagan, who had to prove themselves.

"I'll agree that Reagan had an easier ride than Mondale did, and I'll accept some of the responsibility for that," conceded NBC News political assignment editor Andrew Franklin. "But the circumstances helped create that. Reagan was unchallenged, and didn't have to subject himself to attacks from within his own party every week. He could consolidate his base, raise money and prepare for the fall campaign. Sure, he should have faced tough questioning from the press. But the problem was that the Democrats were an ongoing story generating a new lead every week. More was at stake [journalistically] on a short-term basis than with Reagan, so more resources were targeted toward that."

In accordance with their protestations of exercising no great influence over public opinion, most journalists and news executives interviewed for this book rejected the idea that their emphasis on the horse race had the effect of declaring the 1984 election over long before it was held. ABC's Jeff Gralnick, for example, said, "It was apparent in the polling from the end of the [Republican] convention on that the country wanted four more years of Ronald Reagan. The polls and our understanding of them have become good enough that by mid-September we could understand Reagan was going to win two to one. We didn't declare it over; the public declared it over."

Others offered the more sophisticated argument that opinion polls, after all, were merely snapshots of public opinion, and therefore possessed no great predictive power in themselves. Which was true, but ignored the fact that the polls were turned into more than snapshots by the manner in which the press reported them. For the polls did not shape public opinion so much as they shaped how journalists themselves perceived the campaign and therefore how they reported on it. As Mondale campaign director Robert Beckel pointed out: "If you go back and listen to the coverage—the wrap-ups on our stories compared to Reagan's—ours was always 'Way behind, downbeat, very tough,' it projected pessimism. It didn't say the race was over, but it projected pessimism. And on the other side it was 'And Reagan's aides continue to be optimistic about the potential for a landslide.' "

The most that anyone in the press would accept—and this was a minority position—was partial responsibility for Reagan's aura of inevitability. "Did we contribute to a sense of Reagan's inevitability?" asked *The Wall Street Journal*'s Rich Jaroslovsky rhetorically. "Yes. But it was already there. We did not create it." Likewise, NBC News president Grossman asked, "Do polls affect the outcome particularly? I think on television if there is any effect, what they do is accelerate trends somehow, by definition. It's like the wind pushing a wave. The wave is coming in anyhow, and it just makes it higher and go faster."

Two of Ronald Reagan's previous campaign managers, however, went considerably further. When John Sears was asked whether he thought the news media had declared the 1984 election over well before it was held, he coughed out one of his characteristic nervous chuckles and answered, "Yeah, that's absolutely true. But I don't know what anybody can do about it. The press will say, 'Well, we can't avoid the facts, and look at all these polls.' " Longtime Reagan aide Lyn Nofziger agreed with Sears: "Sure," he responded, "I think that's pretty accurate. The press, through osmosis pretty much, mostly wind up with the same thought."

The "same thought" of 1984, communicated with tranquilizing regularity for nearly a year and a half prior to the actual casting of ballots, was that Walter Mondale had the Democratic nomination virtually sewed up while Ronald Reagan was all but certain to be re-elected President in November. Behind this reporting was no media conspiracy. It was simply a consequence of the way the press worked. But the effect of such coverage was to limit the real choices available to American voters, and thereby to violate the spirit of democracy and the integrity of the electoral process.

(The same thing has happened in 1988. The press declared numerous candidacies over even before all the votes were counted in New Hampshire. The final results among Republicans in New Hampshire contradicted unanimous expectations of a George Bush–Robert Dole photo finish—not *one* of the major pollsters accurately predicted the Vice President's nine-point victory—but did this repudiation lead the press to scrap its reliance on polls or to rethink its campaign coverage? Not at all, any more than similar mishaps produced a journalistic change of heart in 1984. Opinion polls still reigned supreme. News organizations continued to survey some 500-odd Americans in order to tell the other 250 million of us what we thought. Introducing the latest overnight tracking polls, the more conscientious reporters might try to cover themselves with the fig leaves of hurried qualifying phrases about the occasional unreliability of such data, but their gestures were more pathetic than noble. If that is how they felt about it, why bother reporting the polls in the first place? As difficult as it was to imagine, the tyranny of the horse race seemed only to get worse.)

• • •

TALK of his alleged inevitability notwithstanding, Ronald Reagan was always far more vulnerable to defeat in 1984 than commonly supposed. His own advisers, if no one else, keenly appreciated this. As Michael Deaver later recalled: "If Mondale had staked out 'Cares about people' and 'Who is most likely to get us into a war?' he would have cut into Reagan. Those were the two issues that were our biggest negatives all through the campaign. We worked on those and got those negatives down to a safe level by things we did over and over and over again, but Mondale never grasped that."

Reagan's men began working on the President's negatives long before he formally entered the 1984 race. Indeed, the formal re-election campaign was merely the culmination of a three-year nonstop propaganda effort of selling Ronald Reagan to the American public. It was explicitly designed to insulate the President from serious scrutiny on the part of the press and to equate any criticism of him with criticism of America. It relied on the same news management principles that the apparatus had so skillfully applied over the previous three years: devise, on the basis of meticulous opinion polling, a long-term communications plan that emphasizes certain politically favorable themes, such as "America Is Back"; provide one handsomely packaged photo opportunity story per day that reinforces the chosen theme of the day; repeat your message many times and in many ways; and, to assure control of the agenda, restrict reporters' access to the President and avoid whenever possible questions on unfavorable topics.

Deaver recalled one time in 1983 when "they came running into my office and said, 'Housing starts are up. Let's get the President down to the pressroom.' I said, 'That's a dumb idea. Somebody go out and find the three cities where housing starts are going up faster than anyplace else.' And I juxtaposed those cities to key political areas for us and it came down to Fort Worth, Texas. So we flew down there and went up to a framed-up house with a couple of hard hats and Reagan had a sign in front of the house showing the line going up on housing starts. Now, the press can say, 'They brought us all the way down here to Fort Worth, Texas, just to have a show and make the President look good.' But the guy sitting there with his six-pack that night is looking at it and saying [here Deaver imitated the viewer, leaning sideways, cocking his head and squinting at an imaginary television set], 'What's the President doing there with those hard hats? Oh! Housing starts have gone up. Things must be getting better.' "

Convinced that Reagan himself was their best weapon, and that the American people craved stability and reassurance above all, the Reagan men intensified their long-standing practice of promoting the President as the personification of Uncle Sam. One secret of Reagan's popularity had always been his status as an All-American icon; he did not merely believe in the myths of the American past, he somehow seemed to embody them. His aides would exploit this characteristic time and again in 1984, associating the President not so much with the country itself (as was often claimed) as with an idealized, timeless image of what America supposedly used to be—and could be again, if only people believed, and followed.

They accomplished this in large part by repeatedly putting Reagan in visual settings and supplying him with rhetoric that reinforced the "America Is Back" themes of economic recovery and national pride. On the Fourth of July, for example, they had him travel to Florida for the Pepsi Firecracker 400 stock-car race, where he first posed with racing star Richard Petty and later received a serenade and a kiss from country singer Tammy Wynette. Probably the single biggest coup was arranging for Reagan to open the XXIII Olympic Games in Los Angeles, an event which itself contributed mightily to the upbeat chauvinism (often sloppily labeled patriotism) that seemed to overtake the country in 1984. Television and the print media had been reporting for months on the runners transporting the Olympic torch across the country for the July 28 opening of the Games; appearing at the opening ceremonies allowed Reagan to associate himself with and thus capitalize on the red, white and blue sentiments the traveling torch and the Games themselves engendered from sea to shining sea. That Soviet athletes stayed home while their U.S. counterparts won bushels of gold medals only accentuated the mood.

Deaver also scheduled a number of overseas trips during the election year to bolster Reagan's presidential image. In April the President visited China. On June 1 he left on a carefully scripted European trip that included a visit to the bluffs of Normandy on the fortieth anniversary of the Allied invasion of Europe, an event which yielded what Deaver later said were his favorite pictures of Reagan's entire presidency.

Just as important as projecting positive messages about the President was preventing, or at least minimizing, projection of negative messages. Here the central tactic was to intensify the already extreme isolation of Mr. Reagan from reporters. On the road, the small "pool" of reporters allowed to observe Reagan's activities were usually kept so far away from him—sometimes, they later charged, by his Secret Service escort—that a hurried, shouted question (provoking at best a cryptic, one-line response from Reagan) was the most they could manage. Reporters could not, for example, get close enough during Reagan's opening of the International Games for the Disabled to question him about the budget cuts in programs for the handicapped he had pushed through Congress.

Occasionally White House restrictions on access were embarrassingly overt. When the President toured a wildlife refuge on Maryland's Eastern Shore in August to tout his environmental record, Larry Speakes actually stepped between reporters and Reagan to cut off a question about the controversial appointment of former Environmental Protection Agency administrator Anne Burford to an administration advisory panel on oceans and the atmosphere. Meanwhile, other White House aides pulled the plug on the television lights so Reagan could not be filmed. (Evening newscasts showed Reagan standing in semi-darkness, delivering a one-sentence defense of Burford.) Finally, presidential press conferences, always dreaded by Reagan's handlers, were virtually eliminated. After his July 19 conference, the President did not once during the rest of the campaign appear before the press corps to answer questions about his record and policies.

The Reagan propaganda apparatus executed both the defensive and offensive aspects of its re-election strategy with customary skill and efficiency. But it also had the good fortune to be spared stiff resistance from what should have been its two principal adversaries, the Democrats and the press. As Deaver admitted, President Reagan was extremely vulnerable on both the fairness and war-and-peace issues in 1984. Nevertheless, the Mondale campaign selected as its number one issue the federal deficit, a stunningly ill-advised choice that reflected the heavy corporate influence within the campaign but offered little hope of rallying the traditional Democratic constituency. Moreover, the Mondale campaign proved itself to be as inept at using the media as its Reagan counterpart was expert. As Deaver later marveled: "The Mondale people flip-flopped all the time. They could never decide what issue they wanted to deal with, and the press saw this."

Like an army whose generals had prepared for the last war,

the Mondale campaign was all but doomed to defeat by its de facto decision to follow the traditional, pre-Reagan model for dealing with the press. This was admirable on democratic grounds, but fatal strategically. One reason Mondale appeared to flip-flop, for example, was the relative openness of his campaign. "We didn't get our message out," Richard Leone conceded. ". . . Mondale has two or three press comments a day and he and his people are always available, so we generate a lot of leads. It's pretty hard to have a uniform message if you're going to do that." Mondale campaign press secretary Maxine Isaacs likewise conceded error, saying of her opponents, "Because they controlled their story so well, they had a very specific message every night, while we had various different kinds of messages. . . . Reagan always appeared in a pristine setting. Ours were usually a mess, with forty reporters bunched around Mondale. We called it a campaignapede."

Journalists who covered the two campaigns confirmed that the disparity in media expertise translated into sharply different news coverage for Reagan and Mondale. Brit Hume, who covered Mondale for ABC, recalled that the press was often able to focus on what *it* wanted in covering Mondale "because he was available to talk about whatever they wanted. Reagan, on the other hand, was *not* available, so the press tended to talk about whatever he was talking about." Susan Zirinsky, the producer of CBS coverage of President Reagan, agreed that CBS had been "softer on Reagan than Mondale." She added, "Reagan got away with more [access restrictions], and he got on the air more, because my pictures were better [than those of her colleagues who covered Mondale]. Walter Mondale was boring! And so diffused—he talked about four different topics in four different press conferences every day."* In short, as Tom Oliphant of *The Boston Globe*, who covered both candidates, observed: "Yes, the press coverage of Walter Mondale did hurt his effort. Yes, the press coverage of Ronald Reagan did help his effort."

None of this seemed quite fair to the Mondale people. Richard Leone later complained that reporters had "been trained by the

---

* In a subsequent conversation, however, Zirinsky stressed that she had not meant that CBS had been softer *editorially* on Reagan, but rather that it was easier to get Reagan stories on the air "because Ronald Reagan was a sitting President and there were policies of his out there that could be defined and examined."

White House to judge the campaign by standards that are the best criteria for the White House—the picture, the color schemes, how effective the speech is, whether the audience is set up right. One of the things the White House has done the last four years, partly by not providing other news, is gotten people to judge them by their own standards."

Surprisingly enough, Leone was unwittingly joined in this analysis by none other than Michael Deaver. In Deaver's self-interested view, the technical expertise of the Reagan apparatus was the key to the positive press coverage the campaign received. "The mechanics of every stop was perfect," he boasted. "From a visual standpoint, every press member got a perfect angle, perfect position. Our backdrops were always terrific, there was always a new gimmick even though it was the same speech. We'd always try to come up with some human-interest thing, either bringing a person up to see him [onstage] or including it in his remarks. And so the press came to realize it was a very well-oiled machine, and they respected that."

Just how thoroughly the press had internalized the Reagan standards of judgment was made abundantly evident on Labor Day 1984, the official kickoff date of the general election campaign. The impression network evening newscasts conveyed that day of the two opposing candidates was based almost entirely on how impressive they looked at their opening campaign appearances. Needless to say, this worked to Ronald Reagan's advantage. The President opened his campaign with a flawlessly executed rally in his home base of Orange County, California. Viewers were shown fetching pictures of a beaming Reagan standing before a huge, cheering crowd while hundreds of red, white and blue balloons floated up and away and a crew of sky divers drifted to earth trailing red, white and blue smoke streams behind them. As his supporters chanted "Four more years," Mr. Reagan flashed his trademark "Aw, shucks" grin and replied, "Okay, you talked me into it." CBS correspondent Bill Plante, in a comment typical of the day's Reagan coverage, closed his report noting that the Reagan campaign hoped for a "massive victory in November."

The upbeat mood of these reports contrasted sharply with the gloomy defeatism that permeated accompanying stories on Walter Mondale's opening day. Mondale strategists made the fatal logistical error of having their candidate crisscross the entire country on opening day, appearing first in New York City at the annual Labor Day parade, later in Wisconsin for a "Middle America" rally and finally in Long Beach, California. The tightness of the schedule dictated a 9 a.m. starting time for the New York event, which in turn meant that Mondale and his running mate, Geraldine Ferraro, began their day leading a nonexistent parade up New York's largely empty Fifth Avenue. The Wisconsin rally, which Mondale strategists regarded as the day's key event, featured a large and enthusiastic crowd but was marred by rain. The resulting visuals on the evening newscasts portrayed the Mondale campaign as hopelessly inept and headed for defeat, an impression strengthened by correspondents' disparaging references to the "embarrassingly small turnout" that greeted Mondale's "underdog effort."

"The fact is, that's what undid Mondale—[Americans] seeing him every night not being very effective in his communications," argued NBC News president Grossman. Articulating one of the more extreme variations of the media's form-over-substance mind-set, Grossman continued, "It says something about the kind of President he'd [have] been. If you don't pay attention to people who are telling you you've got to learn how to use television, you should get some training, some coaching, you should improve yourself, then maybe [when] he tells you there's a bomb coming over in the middle of the night, what kind of reaction do you have? If you're not willing to train for the requirements of the job, then maybe that has done more to undo him than anything else."

If anything bespoke how poorly Mondale advisers understood the news media, it was their strategic decision to rely on the press to carry the attack to President Reagan for them. There were various reasons why this was bound not to happen, including the aforementioned inability of reporters to get close enough to the President to question him. While reporters groused in private about access restrictions, they rarely did more in public—that is, in their reporting, where it really counted—than complain in passing about the unprecedented inaccessibility of President Reagan. Even *The Washington Post*'s David Hoffman, who claimed of Reagan's isolation that he "wrote about it and wrote about it and wrote about it," acknowledged that the press did not do all it could have to highlight the issue. "I feel like I did a lot," said Hoffman. "The networks did a fair amount. Could we have done more? Sure. Could the papers have played it bigger? Yeah. Maybe we should have led the paper a few times."

Surely the press could have forced President Reagan to step out from behind his protective curtain if it had really wanted to— the White House, after all, needed television as much as vice versa—but it was hardly inclined to apply the necessary pressure when it believed that Reagan was headed for certain victory. And many journalists, beholden to dubious if not impossible notions of objectivity and impartiality, felt constrained from forcing the issue. "To lead the broadcast with [stories about Reagan's isolation] in *order* to smoke him out would be to depart substantially from the canons that govern the way we present the news," said CBS White House correspondent Bill Plante. "It'd look like a calculated effort, some would say a political one."

The failure of the press to highlight the inaccessibility issue amounted to complicity in the mind of Mondale's campaign chairman, James Johnson: "If the major networks had decided to do Day One, Day Two, Day Three since the President has answered a question, since he's had a press conference, Day Forty-eight of totally prepackaged bullshit, if they'd put him off the air—suppose the networks had said, 'We don't consider these made-for-television stage shows news and we will not cover them,' if when [the Reagan campaign] went to Jersey City and the thousand balloons were released every network cameraman had put his camera down and started smoking a cigarette—things would have changed immediately. It's not as though news executives aren't used to making those kinds of judgments. They make those kinds of judgments all the time." Johnson claimed that on dozens of occasions during the Democratic primaries network representatives had refused to broadcast photo opportunity stories boasting at least equal news value to those offered by the Reagan campaign, saying, " 'Uh-uh, we're not playing that game anymore. You did the polluted stream yesterday, you did the B-1 plant the day before that, now let's hear a substantive speech.' Flat out. They'd say, 'We're not covering this shit.' "

Rarely if ever did the networks tell that to the Reagan campaign in 1984. It was not merely that the networks were too intimidated in the aftermath of Grenada to take a tough stand; it was also that Deaver's pictures were simply too visually appealing to pass up. As a result, neither the print nor the electronic media focused sufficient attention on Reagan's inaccessibility to smoke him out and force him to answer real questions about his plans and policies. That failing, along with the pervasiveness of jelly-bean journalism, reduced the press and especially television to virtual accessories to the White House propaganda apparatus. In the words of *The Boston Globe*'s Tom Oliphant: "What the press conveyed was by and large Ronald Reagan's version of reality."

• • •

TELEVISION'S love of pretty pictures and journalists' obsession with the horse race were important, but ultimately there was an even more fundamental reason why the press was unlikely to lead any charge against Reagan: the prevailing mood within the U.S. body politic, as well as the U.S. press, was overwhelmingly pro-Reagan in 1984. Not only had Reagan's poll ratings among average Americans been steadily climbing since early 1983, but he was extremely popular within corporate America (to whose executives mainstream journalists ultimately answered). It was of course well known within the press that Reagan had his shortcomings, but these were generally regarded as less important than his perceived success at getting the country back on the right track, both at home and abroad. As Robert Beckel later charged: "The press covering Reagan got caught up in the very mood that the Reagan people wanted them to get caught up in, the theme of their campaign, which was essentially: keep the country dumb, numb and happy."

The media did more than merely get caught up in the "It's morning again in America" mood; it actively embraced and helped to spread it. Who in the press wanted to interrupt the national orgy of self-congratulation and remind Americans of the downside of the Reagan Revolution? That was no way to sell newspapers. By the time of Reagan's run for re-election, happy talk had been flourishing on local TV news broadcasts for some ten years. Championed by Van Gordon Sauter of CBS, the same approach to reporting the news had now insinuated itself at the network level. The 1982 introduction of the national daily newspaper *USA Today* by Gannett Co., the nation's largest media corporation, had further hastened the trend toward American news organizations producing a journalism of reassuring, simple-minded conformity. Combine all this with journalists' lingering insecurities from the Vietnam and Watergate years and it hardly surprises that the press fell smartly in step with the Reagan parade in 1984.

"The press wanted to be seen as patriotic. Journalists were tired of being blamed for losing Vietnam," said Associated Press reporter Robert Parry. "We also didn't want to be the skunk at the garden party. Everybody's feeling good again, we're finally over that Vietnam malaise, dammit. Do you want to be the guy who comes in and says, Gee, it's not that great? Gee, there are problems here? That the government is doing things that maybe are questionable here? That the government maybe isn't telling you the truth? Who wants to be that guy?"

In fact, few in the press saw any reason to be "that guy" in 1984. Most of the senior journalists and news executives interviewed for this book seemed to think Ronald Reagan had done an admirable job as President and deserved to be re-elected.

"The guy smiles a lot, but substantively he doesn't say or do a lot of controversial things, so there's not much there to grab a hold of and go with," *Time*'s Richard Duncan said by way of explaining what he contended was "fairly evenhanded" coverage of Reagan in 1984. Speaking days after the election, the magazine's chief of correspondents continued, "I think maybe he's gotten off a little light on foreign policy, although he has gotten rapped for failure with the Soviets. But things seem to be working in Central America, and there's been more progress in South Africa than one might think."

That was light praise indeed compared to a *Newsweek* cover story in August 1984 on Reagan that asked "How Good a President?" Readers didn't have to bother with the article itself to discern *Newsweek*'s answer; the cover said it all. Of the hundreds of photos of the President the magazine's editors could have chosen to adorn their cover, they settled on one that national news editor Merrill Shiels later acknowledged was "almost a [campaign] poster": a smashingly flattering shot in which Reagan, wearing a short-sleeved sport shirt and an exuberant yet almost reverential grin, gazed off into the distance and the presumably glorious future he envisioned for his beloved United States of America. The written text of the story struck a similarly congratulatory tone, opining that Reagan's record "must rank, on balance, a success."

"I think he got some good press because he is a very attractive human being who is perceived with a good deal of common sense as restoring the dignity of the country and bringing prosperity and eliminating inflation," commented NBC's Lawrence Grossman. "People don't care whether he falls asleep at cabinet meetings or whether he takes a lot of vacations or doesn't know the nitty-gritty of what's going on. They don't need that in a leader."

While the quasi-official line within the press held that these positive feelings toward Reagan had no undue effect on news coverage, a minority of journalists whom I interviewed contended that Mondale and Reagan were in fact *not* treated equally in 1984. *CBS Evening News* campaign coverage producer Richard Cohen, for example, said, "I think Reagan got away with murder. We played into his hands by taking his pictures exactly as they laid them out. . . . We undercovered Mondale; we weren't fair to him. We thought he was a wimp, we didn't like him and we didn't think he could win." Another high-ranking CBS journalist, who refused to be named, agreed that management "didn't let us be as tough [on Reagan] as I thought we could have." Apparently the previously described tension between the New York "fishbowl" and CBS field journalists over how to cover Ronald Reagan persisted in 1984, with additional instances of scripts being rewritten and criticisms softened. "Nobody ever came right out and said to lighten up, be less critical, get on board and wave the flag," added this source. "That'd be too blatant. But they did often say, 'Enough already, you've already made that point,' about a lot of the Reagan coverage."

The press's generally favorable disposition toward Reagan did not, it should be stressed, spare the President from critical coverage entirely. CBS economics correspondent Ray Brady, to cite but one example, pointed out in a July 20 story that while the nation as a whole was better off than four years earlier, the Reagan administration had accomplished that only by putting the economy through the recessionary wringer of high unemployment. Mondale, Brady concluded, would have to focus the public's attention on that wringer if he hoped to cut into Reagan's lead.

Still, the overall tone of Reagan coverage was decidedly positive. It was not simply that the relatively few news stories that questioned the President's policies were overwhelmed by a vastly larger volume of stories implicitly praising what he had wrought. It was also that the critical stories tended to be scattered, one-shot affairs and thus, from the White House's perspective, relatively harmless. The press seemed to practice a sort of pack journalism in reverse; stories that reflected poorly on Reagan were rarely followed up.

That "bad" stories rarely took root within the press—the age flap after the first debate was an exception—was itself testimony to how indisposed the media in general were to going after President Reagan. Thus could Michael Deaver explain that the reason Reagan's unpopular Central America policies did not hurt him in 1984 was that "the press wasn't interested in that issue other than as a one-day story, and the Mondale people didn't press it." A review of the network evening newscasts of 1984 generally confirmed Deaver's statement. Although President Reagan's government was conducting an undeclared war against Nicaragua that cruelly punished its peasant civilians while at the same time backing brutal military governments in the rest of the region, the Central America issue attracted intense media interest only twice during the election year. Stories about the CIA's secret mining of Nicaragua's harbors and the ensuing political fallout on Capitol Hill dominated broadcasts during the second week of April, after which the issue all but disappeared for six months (except for a brief spasm of extremely friendly coverage following the President's May 9 speech warning of the dangers of Communist subversion of Central America). What brought the issue back was the disclosure, just four days before Reagan's October 21 foreign policy debate with Mondale, that the CIA also had distributed to the Nicaraguan contras a manual advocating the assassination of political opponents. But just as the harbor mining was blamed solely on CIA director William Casey, so did the press play along with White House efforts to distance Reagan from the assassination manual, solemnly reporting national security adviser McFarlane's pledge that the President would fire whoever was responsible for the document and then quickly abandoning the story after the second Reagan-Mondale debate.

Nor did the President encounter much flak on the nuclear issue, despite having twice led with his chin on the subject. President Reagan escaped sustained criticism for his reference on August

24 to supporters of a nuclear weapons freeze between the two superpowers as "jackasses." It was exactly the kind of gaffe Mondale officials had been hoping for, but their glee turned to shock and dismay when the press declined to pursue the remark. Richard Leone said that he and others in the campaign "talked about the jackasses thing for four days running, and only got coverage the first day. . . . The story was dead twenty-four hours later."

"Forty-five percent of the country were hard-core freeze supporters, thought it was a pretty good idea," recalled Robert Beckel. "And I said [to press people] this was a blanket indictment of a strong sentiment in the country. The answer I got was 'Well, that's just Reagan.' If I heard that once, I heard it a thousand times. I'd come back and try to dig up a little guilt and say, 'You know, if Carter'd said that . . . you all would never have let him get away with it. Carter [in 1980] said that Reagan would separate blacks from whites, Christians from Jews, and you jumped all over him as if he'd committed the ultimate sin. And yet here's a guy who is calling almost a majority of the American people jackasses for being thoughtful about something they care about for their children and you say, 'Well, that's Reagan.' It was as if they were anesthetized."

Journalists had been similarly understated in their coverage of Reagan's supposed joke about the end of the world, delivered before a live microphone on August 11: "My fellow Americans, I'm pleased to tell you today that I've signed legislation that will outlaw the Soviet Union forever. We begin bombing in five minutes." Reagan expert Lou Cannon of *The Washington Post* had predicted back in a February interview that "a Goldwaterism like 'Let's lob one into the men's room of the Kremlin' delivered at the wrong time could hurt Ronald Reagan," and sure enough, Richard Wirthlin's private polls showed that the fraction of the American electorate who thought Reagan might get the United States into an unnecessary war shot up fifteen to eighteen points overnight. But once again the damage was limited by the story's rapid departure from the news. ABC's director of political operations, Stan Opotowsky, accurately summarized coverage of the remark: "Day One is when it happens, Day Two the opposition candidate comments, Day Three everyone else and his brother comments and after that television by its very nature is done with the story."

Obviously the remark itself could be reported only so many times, but what was striking about Reagan's "bombing in five minutes" gaffe was how little lasting impact it had on coverage of the broader war-and-peace issue. Here was a President who had launched an unprecedented peacetime military buildup, greatly accelerated the nuclear arms race, advocated its expansion into space, reduced the warning time for nuclear attack to six minutes by installing Euromissiles and repeatedly evidenced a frightful ignorance of nuclear issues, all the while shunning serious negotiations with the Soviets. Yet his Goldwaterism provoked not the slightest bit of sustained questioning from the press about his qualifications to oversee the U.S. nuclear arsenal.

What made the "bombing in five minutes" episode especially peculiar was that this was the same press that six months earlier had relentlessly hounded Democratic presidential candidate Jesse Jackson about an off-the-record reference to Jews as "Hymies." Eventually the Reverend Jackson was forced to acknowledge and apologize for the remark, but the press exerted no such pressure on President Reagan.

Nor was that the only time Reagan seemed to benefit from a journalistic double standard in 1984. Take, for example, the ceaseless repetition of the charge that Walter Mondale was a "special interests" candidate—a reference to his backing from labor, women's, minority and other traditional Democratic groups. From the time Gary Hart first pinned it on him early in the primaries through election day itself, Mondale never managed to escape that derisive label. Ronald Reagan, on the other hand, bore no such cross, even though it would have been at least as accurate for the press to describe *him* as the candidate of "privileged interests." The reason the press did not highlight Reagan's links with the wealthy, ABC's Opotowsky suggested, was that "it's not done in public! Walter Mondale goes begging to the AFL-CIO for support. You don't see Reagan going to the board of the Chase Manhattan Bank and begging for their support."

Likewise, the press focused enormous resources and extensive attention on Geraldine Ferraro's family finances but refrained from making any fuss about the unprecedented number of high Reagan administration officials accused of unethical or illegal conduct in office. In fact, as investigative reporter Mark Dowie later revealed in *Mother Jones* magazine, ABC News in 1984 actually established a journalistic hit squad to pursue Ferraro even as it spiked separate and hard-hitting exposés of three powerful Reagan associates: Nevada senator and Reagan-Bush campaign chairman Paul Laxalt, U.S. Information Agency director and old Reagan friend Charles Wick and Secretary of Labor Raymond Donovan.

The single most important reason for Reagan's high standing in the eyes of the nation's establishment in 1984 was his record on the economy. As he entered the homestretch of his re-election race, the nation was in the midst of one of the most robust economic recoveries of the postwar era. Not only was unemployment steadily falling as investment and production rose, but inflation seemed to have been tamed. In communities across the land, working-class and middle-class Americans were convinced that things were getting better and that the credit belonged to Ronald Reagan.

The improvement was so dramatic and the national political-intellectual climate so insistently pro-Reagan that even those previously skeptical of the President's policies began to sing his praises. Merrill Shiels of *Newsweek* told the following story about one of her staff writers: "Harry Anderson, who wrote the economics section in the 'How Good a President?' issue, is not a Reagan lover, but he worked and worked and wrote and wrote and finally came in with a horrified expression on his face and said, 'I think I just re-elected Ronald Reagan.' He handed me his story and I began to read it and I said, 'Boy, you're right!' It was an extraordinarily positive story, which he was inevitably led to by all the work they had done."

Inevitably? It was an unintentionally revealing choice of words, for it hinted at just how thoroughly the Reagan worldview had come to permeate the consciousness of top U.S. journalists by 1984. Was it truly inevitable that any journalist who examined all the evidence would come to the same extraordinarily positive judgment of Reagan's economic record that *Newsweek* had? True, inflation had fallen dramatically. But was it not just as true that poverty had risen dramatically? And had not the taming of inflation been accomplished by shepherding the economy through a recession-depression that cost millions of Americans their jobs and destroyed countless lives and small businesses? Unemployment was indeed falling by the summer of 1984, but did it not still remain noticeably higher than when Reagan first took office?

And had not the majority of new jobs created been in low-paying service-sector work that offered little hope of advancement or of a middle-class standard of living? Obviously the recovery was welcome, but had it not been purchased on credit, leaving behind a $200 billion deficit that promised to make future economic progress even harder to come by? And what of the deterioration of America's international competitiveness and its skyrocketing trade deficit? The engineering of an election-year recovery gave Americans the illusion of prosperity, but in fact, as New School for Social Research economist David Gordon later pointed out, "the real median income of families in the United States *dropped* by 5.7 percent from 1979 to 1984." (Emphasis added.) In short, Reagan had presided over and greatly encouraged the increasing division of the United States into a two-class society.

Yet the press in 1984 did no more to hold President Reagan's feet to the fire on the fairness issue than it did on the war-and-peace and competence questions. To be sure, that was partly because challenger Mondale declined to press the issue himself until late in the campaign. But it was also because questions of fairness and equity had by 1984 been shunted to the margins of the mainstream political debate in Washington, and the press was not about to buck that tide.

"All of journalism has moved to the right," agreed Maynard Parker. The *Newsweek* editor offered a variety of reasons for the shift, including "the loss of the belief in classical liberal ideology" and the fact that "journalists in Washington are extremely well paid now and they have different interests." But Parker, like other journalists, argued that at base the rightward shift of American journalism during the Reagan era was a natural response to an increasingly conservative political climate. In Parker's view: "News magazines have to be centrists." And because "the center has moved to the right" during the Reagan era, so too had American journalism. Exactly what Parker meant by the center became more clear when I asked him about the striking uniformity of views evidenced by major U.S. news organizations during the Reagan era. He conceded that "there wasn't a great diversity of argument [within the press] on many of [Reagan's] programs," and said that this was "mainly because I didn't see a great number of major arguments going on in the body politics which these news organizations cover."

This was true enough. After all, the body politics that U.S.

news organizations covered most intensely were official Washington, official Washington and official Washington. And for most of the last four years, the political elite in the nation's capital—Democrats and Republicans, elected and unelected alike—had issued precious little dissent from the general thrust of the Reagan agenda. Washington was above all a city of conformity, where political actors, the press included, were forever trimming their ideological sails and modulating their personal opinions in order to remain safely within the bounds of the prevailing consensus—a consensus that had been spinning rightward at an accelerating pace throughout Reagan's tenure. Ideologically, the American press was like a leaf in the current, swept along by forces beyond its control, reflecting not so much its own opinions as those of the governing political class of which it was a member. And within that class, the dominant view in 1984 was not only that Ronald Reagan was bound to defeat Walter Mondale come November 6, but that this was an outcome to be welcomed and applauded.

• • •

I DON'T KNOW how many of my colleagues in the pressroom noticed, but the moment Geraldine Ferraro finished her closing statement against George Bush in the October 11 vice presidential debate, Robert Beckel leaped to his feet and swung his fists forward in two simultaneous uppercuts. Only Beckel knew for sure how genuine his gesture of apparent exultation was. But clearly Beckel knew who else was in the room with him: approximately four hundred print, radio and television journalists whose reports would powerfully shape the public perception and therefore the political impact of the debate.

Beckel and other Mondale-Ferraro campaign spokespersons spent the next hour or so in that pressroom. Like their counterparts from the Reagan-Bush camp, they were trying to convince the journalists that it was their candidate who had won. This was an especially urgent task for the Mondale group. Even after their candidate's resounding victory over the President in the Louisville debate four nights earlier, conventional wisdom still maintained that the Democrats needed an unbroken string of political miracles if they were to overcome the Reagan lead by election day.

The pressroom, located in the basement of the Philadelphia Convention Center, directly beneath the huge, white, sterile auditorium where Bush and Ferraro debated, was about the size of a large university gymnasium. Two large telescreens stood at the front of the room. Stretched below them were more than thirty rows of long white tables, creating an effect something like a cross between a high school cafeteria and a rock concert. There was something bizarre about journalists traveling hundreds of miles to watch a television broadcast of an event taking place one floor above them, but that was how the press covered presidential politics in 1984.

Within seconds of Ferraro's closing statement, dozens of reporters were swarming around Beckel to get his reaction. In theory, the debates were supposed to inform the voters about the candidates and their positions on the issues, but one would hardly have guessed that from the interchanges following the debate. The overriding concern of the pressroom reporters was the same concern the media as a whole had exhibited throughout the entire campaign: picking the winner. Questions focused almost exclusively on the candidates' debating styles and on how their performance would affect the horse race. "Did Bush's stridency surprise you?" Beckel was asked. Didn't Mrs. Ferraro look uncomfortable up there? What was her finest moment? What would this mean in the polls?

Asking a question on substance was pointless in that mob atmosphere. One reporter who did got nowhere. Laughter had rippled through the pressroom earlier when Bush had said that the Reagan administration looked at civil rights "as something like crime in your neighborhood." Beckel was asked why Ferraro had ignored the remark. "I thought she handled it very well," he gamely replied. And before the matter could be pursued, another reporter jumped in with an especially probing query: Had Ferraro spoken slowly and clearly enough?

After a few more minutes, Beckel announced, "Okay, that's all for now," and squirmed his way through the pressing crowd to freedom. His sudden exit brought to mind a point soldiers often make about combat—ten feet or two seconds can make all the difference in the world. The same man who moments before had been surrounded by dozens of anxious reporters now stood a mere five yards away, chatting with a colleague, and none of the reporters followed him. Instead, they hurried off to attach themselves to someone else who appeared to be a quotable source. Observing a small cluster of reporters, they rushed to join the group, even if they could not immediately see or did not recognize the person being surrounded. (More than once I was asked, presumably by reporters from college newspapers or local media, "Who was that guy who just spoke?")

There remained, at this point, ten days before the second, and final, Reagan-Mondale debate. Although polls conducted during this interval showed the challenger gradually cutting into the President's lead, the overwhelming presumption within the press as the second debate approached was that Mondale needed, in the sports jargon favored by television campaign commentators, another "knockout" if he was to have any hope of defeating Mr. Reagan.

"We were hurt by the fact that there were only a couple public polls that week," recalled Richard Leone. "[Pollster Lou] Harris had the race down to nine points, which confirmed our polls, and ABC had it at ten, on the night of the debate. But if you asked reporters on Thursday [three days before the debate], they were still saying fifteen points, because this information hadn't permeated yet. So the assumption during the days leading up to the debate when the terms of engagement were set was that we needed a knockout to close [the gap]. . . . I think that's where the public polls hurt us, is on the perception of what it would take after the second debate."

As they had throughout the 1984 campaign, the media were once again underestimating the vulnerabilities of President Reagan—and thus unwittingly diminishing them. And once again, Reagan's own advisers privately knew better. Two senior Reagan campaign officials separately confirmed that the President was extremely vulnerable on the war-and-peace issue right up through the second debate. "We were all worried that it might be exploited," one of them said, "but it never was."

Michael Deaver, however, did manage to exploit the Mondale camp's video illiteracy and thereby hammer an additional nail into the challenger's rapidly closing coffin. "I remember taking Reagan to the hall where we would debate, and the Mondale people had already signed off on the lighting," Deaver recalled. "The lighting was all bad for Reagan, so I changed the lighting. And one of the producers checked with the Mondale people and they said fine, whatever they want." Grinning at the memory,

Deaver added, "What I was doing was top lighting. Mondale had gotten this big makeup artist from Hollywood, so what he wanted was head-on lighting, and lots of it. But the top lighting meant that he had huge circles under his eyes. . . . The Mondale people didn't have any lighting people with them. They didn't understand how important that was."

Mondale did indeed have huge circles under his eyes that night—a post-debate Harris poll indicated that viewers thought Reagan *looked* better than Mondale by a two-to-one margin—but the President fared pretty poorly himself in the early going. While fending off his first question about the assassination manual the CIA had given the Nicaraguan contras, he committed a security breach by letting it slip that the United States was directing the contras' military effort through a CIA agent stationed in Nicaragua. Answering his next question, he denied ever having asserted that submarine-launched nuclear missiles could be recalled. But he saved himself with his answer to a subsequent question on age and leadership: "I will not make age an issue of this campaign. I am not going to exploit for political purposes my opponent's youth and inexperience."

If Reagan's performance in the first debate had recalled the hapless old man who pretended to be the Wizard of Oz, this carefully scripted line in the second debate apparently succeeded in persuading the press and public alike to "pay no attention to that man behind the curtain!" Journalists repeatedly cited the one-liner after the debate as evidence that the President had disposed of the previously troublesome age issue—and won the debate. In further testimony to their disregard for issues and substance, journalists also (with certain individual exceptions) calmly maintained that no gaffes had been committed by either candidate. This despite the fact that Reagan in particular had uttered a predictable array of misstatements, including his old friend, the claim that the United States had engaged in unilateral nuclear disarmament during the 1970s.

Election day was still a full two weeks away, but for all practical purposes the race was over. Entering the last week of the campaign, the only question in the minds, and copy, of the press was exactly how massive Reagan's victory margin would be. Could he pull off a fifty-state sweep?

Network news operations had been criticized following elections past for projecting winners on election night before the polls had closed out on the West Coast; one month before the 1984 election, network executives were called before congressional hearings and urged in the name of democracy to cease and desist from the practice. (The executives refused, piously rationalizing their position with predictable blather about the public's right to know.) It was a classic case of making a molehill out of a mountain. If the good members of Congress truly wished to restore the integrity of the electoral process, they would have had to do much more than proscribe election-night projections; they would somehow have to rid American journalism of its mindless addiction to horse-race coverage in *all* its varied manifestations. The media had started projecting Ronald Reagan as the winner of the 1984 presidential election long, long before the major networks made it official on election night. In a field replete with strong contenders, there was probably no more egregious example of the offense than *Newsweek*'s cover story during election week. "Landslide?" suggested the headline above a smiling and waving Ronald Reagan. One source later disclosed that there had been sharp disagreement over the cover at that week's editorial meeting, but every senior editor I questioned voiced strong support for the final decision. In the self-effacing words of *Newsweek* editor Maynard Parker: "We were simply reflecting the news at that moment."

12

THE NUCLEAR THUNDER

P ERHAPS the single most impressive accomplishment of the White House public relations apparatus during Reagan's first term was the defense of his nuclear weapons policy. The challenge faced by the President's men was summarized by Reagan pollster Richard Wirthlin: "The concern about nuclear war is very powerful, and this President has to deal with it more sensitively than other Presidents. Some Americans do become nervous when his rhetoric and positioning become more confrontational. The Evil Empire speech, his limited nuclear war statement and his August 1984 comment [about the bombing of Russia beginning in five minutes], for example, all have put some Americans' teeth on edge."

The two-track strategy the Reagan apparatus pursued on the nuclear issue was based on the manipulation of fear. Recognizing that growing numbers of citizens were uneasy about the continuing arms race, the apparatus sought to quiet that fear by having the Great Communicator talk fervently about wanting radical *cuts* in nuclear arsenals. Promising reductions not only helped defuse the President's cowboy image, it diverted attention from the immense military buildup the administration was pursuing. At the same time, Reagan made sure to *encourage* a second fear, the fear of the Soviet Union.

"Pleased" was the word Reagan officials most often used when asked how they felt about press coverage of the administration's nuclear policies. "I think in general I'm pleased with it," said Ambassador Max Kampelman, who was appointed the administration's chief nuclear arms negotiator in January 1985. Former national security adviser Robert McFarlane expressed a similar view, while emphasizing how different coverage of nuclear issues had been from coverage of Central America. McFarlane seemed particularly peeved that while Ronald Reagan had given six full-length speeches on Central America during his presidency, "only three of those carried outside the Beltway"—that is, were broadcast on nationwide television. In other words, on three separate occasions the nation's television networks gave the President direct, unfiltered access to deliver, essentially uncontradicted, his version of the truth about Central America to the entire country, and this was, in Mr. McFarlane's opinion, not enough. "If you're only getting 50 percent of the *President's* word outside the Beltway, you're losing an important quantity of your communicating skills," he complained. "From a policymaker's point of view, it was a frustration that you couldn't *always* get the President's point of view on the air."

Apparently the administration encountered no such problems on the nuclear issue, for McFarlane took a rather more positive view of press coverage of U.S.-Soviet relations. Speaking in the immediate aftermath of the second Reagan-Gorbachev summit, held in Reykjavik, Iceland, in October 1986, the man who would soon disgrace himself with a botched Valium-overdose suicide attempt remarked, "If the total mission is to state your case and then have it accurately portrayed in the press, and finally get results, then I think all three of those were reasonably well done on U.S.-Soviet relations."

Obviously, the United States, as a modern empire of global reach and power, had to worry nearly as much about public opinion abroad as at home. In fact, on the nuclear issue, it was the population of Western Europe, not that of the United States, which was the primary target of the Reagan apparatus throughout much of the first term. The reason was simple: popular opposition to U.S. nuclear policy and to President Reagan personally was significantly stronger, more informed and better organized in Europe than in the United States. "It was never as intense here as it was in Europe," said David Gergen. "That's where the veto could come. We were worried about losing those governments. We thought [British Prime Minister Margaret] Thatcher could fall over an issue like that. . . . Peace movement, [the nuclear] freeze, all these things were played out more in the European context than here."

Millions marched through the streets of Western European capitals during the spring and summer of 1981 demanding an end to the arms race and the creation of a nuclear-free Europe. As a first step, the demonstrators called specifically for the Soviets to withdraw all SS-20s and for the U.S. to cancel Euromissile deployment. To regain the offensive, the Reagan administration that fall moved to co-opt the peace movement's demands with an arms proposal billed as the Zero Option. In essence, the United States would offer to cancel deployment of its cruise missiles and Pershings if the Soviets would dismantle not only their SS-20s but also their SS-4 and SS-5 missiles.

The Zero Option was more a propaganda exercise than a serious arms control proposal. Senior White House officials later confirmed that they did not expect the Soviets to take the proposal seriously. "Zero Option said we *won't* deploy if you take yours out. They clearly weren't going to accept that," said Gergen. Both Michael Deaver and a second senior White House official also admitted that the Zero Option was obviously "non-negotiable." Said Deaver, "The Zero Option, from a public opinion standpoint, I was convinced was perfect. It was the ultimate negotiation. We put it on the table; how could you argue with it? It gave the President and us a clear initiative, and a clear defense against those people talking about the fact we weren't willing to negotiate."

The Reagan apparatus mounted an all-out public relations campaign to sell the Zero Option, particularly in Western Europe. The proposal was unveiled by the President himself in a November 18, 1981, speech at the National Press Club in Washington. The U.S. government paid for live satellite transmission of the speech to the European Broadcasting Union, and the speech itself was deliberately timed to assure maximum exposure in Europe. The President began speaking at 10 a.m., which of course was late afternoon in most NATO countries. Europeans driving or arriving home from work could thus catch Reagan's address live, and then hear about it again later on evening newscasts. "That was the first speech given by an American President timed to coincide with European prime time," recalled Gergen, "and I think those things really worked."

The deployment and its Zero Option cover story certainly got an enthusiastic stamp of approval from the news media in the United States. Reagan's November 1981 kickoff speech received favorable coverage on all three networks, with CBS calling the

Zero Option proposal "a dramatic foreign policy initiative" and NBC White House correspondent John Palmer evincing not the slightest skepticism as he reported that "Mr. Reagan called on the Soviet Union to share the U.S. commitment to arms reduction." It was ABC, however, which once again distinguished itself as the White House's most ardent cheerleader. Casting the Soviets as intransigent warmongers and the Reagan administration as bold and humane visionaries, *World News Tonight* anchor Frank Reynolds led off his broadcast the night of the Zero Option speech by invoking the grandeur of man's first steps on the moon: "The Soviets have already indicated they won't budge. But President Reagan called on the Soviets today to join the U.S. in a giant step for mankind to reduce the dread threat of nuclear war." CBS and NBC at least did not turn a completely blind eye to the public relations aspect of Reagan's address; both made it clear that the White House did not expect the Soviets to accept the proposal. But CBS in particular left the clear impression that it was the Soviets who were to blame for this. Not one of the networks raised the possibility that the fault lay with the Reagan administration for advancing a plainly non-negotiable proposal. And while official Soviet objections to the plan were duly noted on all three networks, only NBC's George Lewis saw fit to depart sufficiently from NATO's highly misleading warhead-counting methods to point out that, in light of the nuclear balance of forces in Europe, the Soviets had little reason to accept Reagan's offer.

I later asked Jeff Gralnick, the executive producer of the ABC broadcast in 1981, how journalists could protect the public from being bamboozled by proposals like Zero Option, proposals which only years later were revealed to be intentionally non-negotiable. His answer: "We don't have two years to do our story. Here's an announcement at three-thirty in the afternoon from the White House. You get Frank Reynolds on the line, Sam Donaldson, your Pentagon and your State Department correspondents on the phone, and you have forty-five minutes of conversation: What do we think about this? What do we think the reality of this story is? Does anybody think it's a crock of shit? In the absence of anybody thinking it's a crock of shit, you report it as it appears to be. And then as you learn what it is, you go back and make it good. . . . You take the best thoughts of a group of seasoned reporters, and out of that you make that day's news."

If Gralnick and his colleagues ever felt a need to "go back and make it good" on the Euromissiles story, the results were not evident in their subsequent coverage. Indeed, the tenor of reporting at all three networks remained substantially the same from the November 1981 speech through to the actual deployment of the Pershing and cruise missiles in November 1983. The Zero Option cover story held up, as did the related fiction that the Euromissiles were needed to balance the unfair advantage the Soviets derived from their SS-20s. And while U.S. journalists, print as well as broadcast, were commendably quick to recognize the propaganda quotient of various missile moratorium and reduction proposals offered by Soviet leaders over the intervening twenty-four months, their critical faculties seemed to be on permanent holiday when it came to analyzing the stream of interim proposals and other ploys that continued to flow out of Washington. And so when the missiles finally were installed and the Soviets foolishly made good on their threat to quit the arms talks then underway in Geneva (thus shooting themselves in the foot in the international propaganda war), the U.S. press uniformly portrayed the Russians as petulant bullies who had not the slightest justification for opposing the new missiles.

That the United States and the U.S.S.R. agreed four years later to withdraw medium-range missiles from Europe under the INF Treaty in no way diminishes the success of the original White House sales job.* "The one place I thought we did an effective job communicating in foreign policy was on the deployment of the missiles to Europe," Gergen recalled in one of our interviews. After he agreed with colleagues that the Zero Option had been "clearly non-negotiable," I asked whether he was pleased with how the media portrayed it. "Sure, I was very pleased. I'm not

---

* The Soviet reversal on Euromissiles seems to have been a consequence of Gorbachev's policy of *perestroika*. Under the terms of INF, the Soviets were still obliged to eliminate far more weapons than the Americans, just as the initial Zero Option had proposed. Apparently Gorbachev was able to accept such a one-sided deal because of his belief, articulated in a February 1987 speech to the Moscow Peace Forum, that "parity" had no meaning in the nuclear age; strict numerical balance between the superpowers' respective arsenals was not only irrelevant but a block to genuine progress toward disarmament.

sure I was surprised. I thought it was a real coup." His one regret, he added, was that "we never did convince the Europeans of Reagan's peaceful intentions—that he wasn't a cowboy and that sort of thing. But we at least got the missiles deployed."

• • •

AT HOME, the adversary was the nuclear freeze movement, which had made astonishingly rapid strides since its founding in 1980. By the end of Reagan's first year in office, opinion polls were finding two-to-one margins of support for a mutual and verifiable nuclear weapons freeze between the superpowers. What made the freeze such a compelling political rallying cry was that it finessed the question that had thwarted disarmament proponents for years: what about the Russians? For if, as the freeze advocated, both sides stopped escalating simultaneously, neither would have an undue advantage, and the stage would be set for negotiations toward actual weapons reductions. It was a bold yet simple idea, and it captured the public imagination in a manner decidedly unwelcome to the Reagan administration.

Over the months to come, Reagan officials would manufacture a whole range of objections to the freeze. The President liked to insist that a freeze would be downright dangerous because it would permanently lock the United States into a position of nuclear inferiority. For its part, the press, whether out of ignorance or its ever-present fear of being judged insufficiently tough-minded about the Soviets, consistently refrained from calling Reagan on this falsehood.

The claim that the United States had "unilaterally disarmed" during the 1970s and fallen dangerously behind the Soviet Union in military might had been one of Reagan's favorites during the 1980 presidential campaign against Jimmy Carter. Of course, the United States had done nothing of the kind. Not only had it modernized and upgraded its existing nuclear arsenal, it had initiated a number of major new weapons projects, including the Trident submarine and the cruise missile. And it increased its stock of strategic nuclear warheads from four thousand to ten thousand. Even Reagan's own military advisers declined to back up their Commander-in-Chief's assertions about the Soviets' alleged nuclear superiority. General David C. Jones, for example, then chairman of the Joint Chiefs of Staff, said that he would not trade the U.S. defense establishment for its Soviet counterpart. Likewise, then Secretary of State Haig affirmed that U.S. military systems were "both more sophisticated and reliable and more technically sound" than the Soviets'. And Reagan's own Defense Department annual report for 1982, submitted by super-hawk Caspar Weinberger, said, "The United States and the Soviet Union are roughly equal in strategic nuclear power."

None of these inconvenient facts, however, deterred Reagan from voicing his favorite departure from truth again and again. Among his first utterances of it as President came in a March 3, 1981, interview with Walter Cronkite, the soon-to-retire anchorman of CBS News. America's most trusted newsman apparently saw no reason to challenge the new President's claim. Nor did any of his colleagues in the rest of the mainstream press.

Indeed, the idea that the United States had fallen behind the Soviet Union in the nuclear arms race held such sway within the American establishment as Reagan came to power that the press did little to alert the public to a military development of vital national significance: under Reagan, the United States was not only striving to regain clear-cut superiority over the Soviet Union (a course of action which if undertaken by the Soviets would have been regarded as highly provocative); it was preparing to fight and win an extended nuclear war against the Soviets. There was nothing especially secret about the administration's plans. During his January 1981 Senate confirmation hearings to become the number two official at the Defense Department, Frank Carlucci declared that the United States needed to develop "a nuclear-war-fighting capability," since that was allegedly what the Soviets were doing. That fall, Weinberger repeatedly testified before congressional committees about the administration's intention to prepare for "the full range of plausible nuclear-war-fighting scenarios" with the Soviet Union. Yet except for a brief, buried mention in an August 14, 1981, *New York Times* story on the administration's plans to expand the U.S. nuclear arsenal, the fact that the United States was actively preparing to prevail in a nuclear war went unreported during Reagan's first year in office. Instead, when his $180 billion weapons program was formally announced on October 2, the *CBS Evening News* described it as "a massive strengthening of America's military muscle." ABC and NBC described the program in similarly approving terms and, like CBS, devoted most of their coverage to analyzing the palace politics the proposal aroused in Congress. The networks never really focused on the issue, even after *The New York Times* published a front-page story on May 30, 1982, headlined "Pentagon Draws Up First Strategy for Fighting a Long Nuclear War," which led other newspapers briefly to pursue the story and fifty members of Congress to call on the President to reassess the policy.

And so it was in keeping with the spirit of the times that when Reagan in the spring of 1982 began invoking the specter of Soviet superiority as the reason he opposed a U.S.-Soviet nuclear freeze, the press for the most part let the distortion pass unremarked. At his March 31, 1982, press conference, for example, UPI's Helen Thomas asked the President why the United States did not seek negotiations toward reducing the number of "doomsday" weapons both superpowers maintained. Mr. Reagan explained that "the truth of the matter is that on balance the Soviet Union does have a definite margin of superiority." Ironically, this was the first Reagan press conference conducted on live, prime-time national television as part of his public relations apparatus's previously mentioned strategy for overcoming the gaffe problem. Now, on the very first question, Reagan had made an egregious misstatement of fact. But no matter. If any of the reporters noticed Reagan's error, they were good enough not to bring it up.

On the next day's *CBS Evening News*, anchor Dan Rather also declined to dispute the President's judgment. Before introducing a report on a briefing U.S. senators would soon receive on "the Soviet threat," Rather noted only that Mr. Reagan had gone "further than any of his predecessors or his top advisers ever have gone in assessing the nuclear balance." In a second story broadcast ten days later, Rather seemed to imply that rough nuclear parity existed between the superpowers, but still shrank from contradicting the President's "stunning statement" directly. Neither of the other two network evening news shows bothered to scrutinize Reagan's assertion at all. Unchastened, Reagan continued to assault the truth about the nuclear equation for the rest of his presidency.

Another of Mr. Reagan's criticisms of the freeze was that it simply wasn't good enough; he wanted to shrink, not freeze, nuclear arsenals. Toward that end, in a May 9, 1982, speech at his alma mater, Eureka College, the President unveiled START, his administration's second nuclear arms initiative. Like the Zero Option proposal, START—for Strategic Arms Reduction Talks—an acronym coined by James Baker, stressed the idea of radical weapons *reductions* as a way of convincing the public of Reagan's sincerity as a peacemaker. And also like the Zero Option, START was believed by senior White House officials to be unacceptable to the Soviets. Both Deaver and another senior White House official confirmed to me that START was regarded inside the administration as "non-negotiable."

With its overwhelming emphasis on dismantling large, land-based missiles, START was obviously biased against the Soviets; such missiles were the *basis* of the Soviet arsenal but only one part of the U.S. nuclear triad. President Reagan, however, as he himself admitted some seventeen months later to a group of congressmen, was unaware of this basic fact about the Soviet arsenal. Thus he had no idea that the Soviets would regard START as an attempt by the United States to gain nuclear superiority. Troubling as that ignorance was, it was nothing compared to an assertion Reagan made while defending START at his May 13 press conference. The reason START had emphasized reductions in land-based missiles, Reagan explained, rather than reductions in submarine-launched missiles (in which the United States enjoyed clear superiority), was that submarine-launched missiles, like bombers, were not as dangerous because they "can be intercepted. They can be recalled."

If ever one of Reagan's errors deserved headline coverage, this was it. For the man with his finger on the nuclear button to believe he could change his mind and call back missiles he had ordered launched was alarming news, and raised the most serious of questions about his fitness to be President. Yet not one of the press conference reporters pursued the issue that night with Reagan. Even more astonishing, Reagan's remark went virtually unmentioned the next day as the press, especially the three network evening newscasts, focused most of its attention on the continuing Falklands war.

As for the START proposal itself, while it did not receive quite the enthusiastic greeting that Zero Option did, neither did the press expose it as the transparently one-sided sham it was. Both Rather of CBS and John Chancellor of NBC praised START for being exactly what White House officials privately knew it was not—"a negotiable proposal," in Chancellor's words—even though both men clearly recognized that, in Rather's words, "the Soviets are being asked to make greater sacrifices." Viewers of the *CBS Evening News* did hear, at the tail end of the coverage, Senator Edward Kennedy call instead for a nuclear freeze. And former Secretary of State Edmund Muskie was heard to suggest that START "may be a secret agenda for sidetracking disarmament while the United States gets on with rearmament, in a hopeless quest for superiority in these things." But the general impression conveyed on all three of the networks and by most of the rest of the press was of President Reagan reaching out to the Soviets in a genuine quest for peace.

Despite the success of its START counteroffensive, however, the administration's battle to subdue the nuclear freeze was only just beginning. At the grass-roots level, pro-freeze sentiment continued to grow. Although Gergen deputy Joanna Bistany had been urging her colleagues in the Reagan apparatus since late 1981 to recognize that "these freeze people were really organized and they were going to run over us before we knew we had been run over," it was summer of 1982 before concrete steps were taken to counter the threat. Bistany and Gergen teamed up with McFarlane to plot and execute a nationwide propaganda campaign against the freeze.

"I got communications and policy people from State, Defense and the White House in a room," recalled McFarlane. "That comes to about thirty people. And we first developed the policy positions: where we stood on the several criticisms of the freeze movement, what were the answers to why a freeze was not in the national interest, and why we could do better." At that point, Bistany and Gergen stepped in to offer guidance on how to get the message out. The approach eventually agreed upon, McFarlane added, was "to go to the fourteen major media markets with your policy officials, and over and over again explain where you stand. So we did that. And there were quotas, even. I said every deputy assistant secretary and above had to spend four days in one of these fourteen media markets in the next sixty days or report to me why not. And at each stop, if you're in Atlanta, in these four days, you had to do a *minimum* of [a] meeting with a [newspaper] editorial board, a drive-time talk show, a meeting with a civic club and a speech in a campus setting. . . . By late

'82 we ended up with about six hundred appearances by somebody at the DAS [deputy assistant secretary] level or above."

Mr. McFarlane concluded that the administration's campaign had "substantially countered the freeze." Yet that very fall, nine states, including political heavyweights California, Illinois, Massachusetts and Wisconsin, passed referenda calling on the federal government to negotiate a nuclear freeze with the Soviet Union, as did forty major cities and localities. For all its access to a receptive media, the government continued to be outflanked by a popular movement that spoke in plain language, appealed to Americans' common sense about the nuclear arms race and actually eschewed media politics.

The peace movement's critique of the nuclear dilemma was never much respected by most journalists, however, much less integrated into news coverage. This stood in sharp contrast to the media's reaction to the Committee on the Present Danger, the lobby group of Washington insiders formed in 1976 that was instrumental in persuading the Senate to reject the second Strategic Arms Limitation Agreement negotiated by the Carter administration. Committee members, many of whom went on to top positions in the Reagan administration, charged that a massive military buildup had given the Soviets the capability of launching a nuclear first strike against the United States. Only a correspondingly robust buildup by the United States, they asserted, could close the so-called "window of vulnerability." These claims ignored basic facts of the nuclear equation. In particular, the unquestioned ability of U.S. submarines to retaliate against any surprise first strike ruled out Soviet attempts at nuclear blackmail. Nevertheless, the Committee's arguments were given a much more receptive hearing by the press than those of the nuclear freeze movement, and, especially when delivered by the President, rarely contradicted.

Consciously or not, mainstream American journalism tended to perpetuate, not challenge, the nuclear status quo. News coverage of the freeze itself illustrated the point. The movement's sudden flowering in the spring of 1982 was too portentous a political development to be ignored; a rash of print and broadcast stories accordingly took notice of the new phenomenon and speculated about its prospects. But the coverage consistently gave short shrift to the *content* of the freeze's message and analysis. It thereby trivialized the movement, treating it as a political spectacle whose existence deserved coverage but whose ideas were naïve to the point of irrelevance. An unmistakable air of condescension permeated much of the coverage. It was as if the freeze were a precocious child who had unexpectedly articulated a piercing insight but who now would be sent on his way with a smile and a pat on the head so that the family elders could get on with actually *solving* the problem at hand.

Typical of the coverage was a report by CBS correspondent Bruce Morton on June 6, 1982, six days before the disarmament rally that brought nearly a million demonstrators to New York's Central Park. Opening with a shot of a winsome canine sporting a "Dogs for Disarmament" sign on its back, the report dismissed the freeze as mere fad, a feel-good collection of trendy celebrities, the 1980s equivalent of "radical chic." Morton gave the freeze some credit—"It got our attention," he said, and helped spur the United Nations special session on disarmament and the U.S.-Soviet arms talks—but ultimately concluded with the put-down that "celebrating serious issues in frivolous fashions just may be the American way."

The freeze was portrayed this way—as a group of sincere, well-meaning but hopelessly simpleminded individuals—largely because that is how the purveyors of American conventional wisdom, both in politics and in journalism, regarded them. While government officials could safely depend on seeing their policy pronouncements respectfully reported on the evening news and in the morning papers, dissenting views on the arms race were only very rarely given a hearing. Rueven Frank, the president of NBC News during the early 1980s, when freeze fever was at its height, remarked in an interview for this book that news coverage during the Reagan years had been largely bereft of controversy because the country was living through "a bland period" then. Asked to square that judgment with the explosion of the nuclear freeze movement, Frank replied, "Nobody gives a shit about disarmament, ever. Nuclear freeze is a gimmick! It's 'Let's end war!' I don't know what you can report seriously in twenty minutes about those things."

• • •

THE RHETORICAL onslaught against the freeze escalated with President Reagan's March 1983 announcement of the Strategic

Defense Initiative. Just as the administration had sought to pacify the European public with its Zero Option proposal in 1981, so now it would try to entrance Americans with visions of a magic nuclear shield. As a means of deflating public pressure for genuine disarmament, SDI went an important step beyond the administration's previous ploys. For rather than proposing mere reductions in nuclear arsenals, it promised to neutralize those arsenals altogether. The Strategic Defense Initiative, the President told the nation, would render nuclear weapons "impotent and obsolete."

Yet unlike the Zero Option, Reagan's promotion of SDI seems not to have been motivated primarily by propaganda concerns—nor by military ones, for that matter. In fact, the announcement of SDI came as a surprise to many top Reagan officials, both in the White House and in the Pentagon. While some Reagan officials did claim to favor SDI for strategic reasons, the available evidence suggests that, more than anything else, SDI was about keeping the U.S. military-industrial complex busy and growing. At a projected end cost of at least $400 billion (and probably much more), SDI represented the next stage in the multibillion-dollar federal subsidy program otherwise known as the arms race. In the words of one Rockwell Corporation promotional booklet, space offered a vast new "Frontier for Growth, Leadership and Freedom."

Which is not to suggest that Reagan and his men were blind to SDI's public relations possibilities. At a time when the nuclear freeze movement was continuing to gain strength across the land, SDI gave the administration a chance to reclaim the initiative, and the moral high ground, in the arms debate. Why bother with a nuclear freeze which would only keep the mutual balance of terror in place? The President shared Americans' fears of these terrible weapons; that was why he wanted to build a peace shield. Never mind that the sort of protective umbrella Reagan had in mind was a technological impossibility; it was the thought that counted.

"I didn't understand SDI," Michael Deaver told me. "All I understood was that it could negate a nuclear war. It was a great idea, a defense that we would give to the Russians. Who could argue with that?" Deaver said news reports questioning whether such a system could work didn't worry him: "I wouldn't know if it worked or didn't work. The *concept* was a great idea." Without a hint of self-consciousness, the PR man added, "Reagan can go out and talk about that as a defensive weapon and a big step toward peace in very esoteric terms. And it's a little bit like the education thing. I mean, what can the President do about education? Nothing. It's all in the hands of the states. But we went out"—he chuckled—"and talked about the three Rs, merit pay for teachers—I mean, those are all great concepts."

This was politics as theater taken beyond the absurd. It had the ring of Hollywood producer talk: a nuclear shield, what a concept! Their eager embrace of SDI illustrated that in the minds of natural-born propagandists like Michael Deaver and Ronald Reagan, whether a concept had any relation to reality was irrelevant. It was a great concept regardless, and would be promoted as such. Probably both men sincerely did believe that SDI could "negate nuclear war" and render nuclear weapons "impotent and obsolete." How much this belief was a function of willful ignorance is impossible for an outsider to say, but willful or not, it was truly ignorance. Had Reagan bothered to ask, he would have found that not one of his senior advisers shared his simpleminded faith that SDI would protect American people and cities from nuclear ruin. Reagan's dream of a leakproof nuclear umbrella was a fantasy, and all the King's men knew it. But rather than come forward with this information and try to enlighten their boss on his mistaken beliefs, they cravenly went along with the program, conceding only grudgingly under subsequent questioning from outsiders in Congress and the press that a 100 percent effective civilian defense was out of the question.

SDI became the centerpiece of Reagan's nuclear policy, and propaganda, for the remainder of his presidency. Gradually but inexorably, SDI officials were forced to scale back projections of what the system would accomplish. It would not replace the Mutual Assured Destruction (MAD) framework of deterrence by protecting people from surprise attack; rather, it would *enhance* deterrence by protecting U.S. missiles instead. (And even *that* protection was envisioned as being quite limited. The Joint Chiefs of Staff, as of early 1988, reportedly expected a deployed SDI system to intercept a mere 30 percent of incoming Soviet warheads.) Nonetheless, SDI soon became the largest single program in the Pentagon's weapons budget. SDI may well have been the most expensive and dangerous boondoggle ever launched in

Washington. But as Congress annually approved billions of dollars in funding and corporate snouts plunged ever more vigorously into the trough of federal largesse, the project gathered enough institutional momentum so that many doubted it could ever be reversed.

Initial news stories by and large relayed Reagan's claims about SDI unskeptically, and the press never did focus on that most basic of all political questions, who gets the money?* Yet over time, major news organizations managed to produce quite a bit of valuable reporting on SDI. Much of it was implicitly critical, if only because it exposed unwelcome truths about the system: most tellingly, that it would not work the way Reagan said it would, and that it would cost a fortune to develop.

The media's performance offered a vivid reminder of how difficult it was for any administration to manage the news when it faced strong opposition within the rest of the governing elite. Although the Reagan apparatus succeeded at the mass level in promoting SDI as a magic nuclear shield, the coverage offered by *The New York Times*, *The Washington Post* and other members of the prestige print media was more skeptical. SDI was such an obviously flawed and perilous idea that it provoked considerable unease among influential members of the American academy, Congress and foreign policy and arms control communities. When men like former Defense Secretary Robert McNamara warned that developing SDI would only lead the Soviets to build more offensive missiles, when such stalwart friends of the Pentagon as Georgia senator Sam Nunn charged that SDI would violate the 1972 Antiballistic Missile Treaty, when prominent scientists like Manhattan Project veteran Hans Bethe said that "Mr. Reagan['s] vision of defending cities against nuclear attack had no basis in scientific knowledge," the press listened.

And yet the press did not do all it might have to resist the Reagan administration's SDI promotional campaign. Above all,

---

* As it turned out, it was the usual suspects: McDonnell Douglas, LTV, Lockheed, Boeing, etc. A study by the Council on Economic Priorities found that 87 percent of the SDI contracts awarded in fiscal years 1983 and 1984 went to a mere ten giant corporations, eight of which ranked among the Pentagon's top twenty overall private contractors. When I asked an ABC News producer why his network had ignored the CEP study, he responded that its findings were too predictable to be newsworthy. A producer at CBS replied simply that such a study didn't make for a compelling television story.

news organizations declined to correct or otherwise contradict Mr. Reagan when he stubbornly kept repeating his discredited claims about SDI ushering in a nuclear-free world. For example, when the President declared, as he did in a March 1985 speech to the National Space Club, that SDI "could render obsolete the balance of terror," his remarks were reported "straight," even though most reporters and editors privately had to know better.

Nor did the press seriously challenge Reagan's fundamental claim, so crucial to SDI's mass appeal, that it was a defensive system that posed a threat to no one. Reagan and his supporters often complained about the media's use of the term "Star Wars" as a shorthand reference to SDI. Yet reporters employed the phrase "the President's space defense program" just as often. It would have been more accurate for journalists to skip the "Star Wars" label altogether and simply describe SDI as "the President's space *weapons* program," as their Western European colleagues often did. For SDI was not, in either meaning of the term, truly a "defensive" system. Not only was it incapable of providing a foolproof defense against a "doomsday" attack, its true military value lay in its offensive capability. What made SDI so dangerous and destabilizing was its potential to enhance the United States' ability to launch a surprise first strike against the Soviet Union. It therefore promised to stimulate, rather than retard, the already overheated arms race.

None of this deterred President Reagan from forging ahead with the program, or from claiming that it was SDI that forced the Soviets to the nuclear negotiating table in January 1985. At which point a subtle but significant change came over press coverage of the space weapons program. To be sure, critical stories continued to appear. *The New York Times*, for example, published an impressive six-part series in March, headlining one installment "Dark Side of 'Star Wars': System Could Also Attack." But once the space weapons system became a central subject of negotiations with the Soviets, Cold War ideology came to the fore. Almost without exception, the press fell into the role of government loyalist. Beginning with the preliminary round of talks in Geneva that spring, SDI was accorded extraordinary respect in mainstream coverage of the negotiations. Apparently fearful of undermining the U.S. bargaining position, journalists rarely reminded their audiences of SDI's doubtful feasibility, its monstrous cost or its first-strike potential. It was as if the press had all but forgotten its own previous reporting on the subject.

Typical of the coverage was a story broadcast on the *CBS Evening News* on March 12, the day of the first formal meeting between U.S. and Soviet negotiators. An estimated fifteen million Americans watched veteran foreign correspondent Tom Fenton conclude his report by saying that "the goal of the United States is to get the Soviets to radically change their thinking—from mutual assured destruction to mutually assured defense." Walking toward the camera across a vacant Geneva courtyard, Fenton added that this was an "ambitious undertaking whose outcome is far from certain."

The White House press office later refused comment on whether this summary of the U.S. position corresponded to the "line of the day" crafted that morning by Reagan officials. But if it was not the line of the day, it may as well have been. Intentionally or not, Mr. Fenton's report attributed moral superiority to the United States by portraying it as favoring defense over destruction. The Soviets, on the other hand, were held to prefer destruction to defense. U.S. negotiators would try to enlighten their Soviet counterparts, but who could blame them if they failed? Perhaps someone who knew that *both* superpowers had been following policies of mutual assured destruction for over twenty years, but Fenton's viewers were not told this. Instead, they were led to believe the key Reagan claim that SDI was truly defensive and peace-minded.

American flexibility in the face of Soviet intransigence was the theme of the media event White House officials organized on March 8, the day U.S. negotiators departed for Geneva. The headline of the lead story in the next day's *New York Times* obligingly conveyed the desired impression, even though the story itself contained information suggesting quite the opposite. The headline—"U.S. Says Its Team Has Wide Latitude in Talks on Arms"—was apparently based on a quote from Robert McFarlane, found in the second paragraph (and featured prominently in most other news stories as well), that he had "never seen instructions that provided any negotiators with greater latitude for serious give-and-take." The story's fourth paragraph noted, with no apparent irony, that the administration considered SDI non-negotiable. In other words, U.S. negotiators had no bargaining room on the issue their Soviet counterparts considered the main point of contention.

Newsweek communicated a similar impression of U.S. goodwill and reasonableness. The caption below its large color picture of Reagan shaking hands with chief negotiator Max Kampelman could hardly have been more approving: "Unyielding conviction, adroit political gamesmanship—and the patience to wait years for results."

But the Reagan administration encountered unexpected trouble when, the day before the Geneva talks began, Konstanin Chernenko died and was succeeded as Soviet General Secretary by Mikhail Gorbachev. Both Robert McFarlane and Max Kampelman later confirmed that Gorbachev's ascension made for tougher competition in the crucial international propaganda war. "This country, including its press, started off being extremely impressed with Gorbachev," remarked Ambassador Kampelman, who added, "In Europe the problem is even greater. The polls there are much more serious. They're much more eager to commend Gorbachev, to think of him favorably, than they are here." Echoing David Gergen, Kampelman concluded, "We are much more worried about Europe than this country, that's a fact."

Gone, with Gorbachev's arrival on the scene, were the days when the Reagan administration could rely on the Soviets to serve as their own worst enemies in public relations. As columnist Meg Greenfield later wistfully remarked in *Newsweek*: "When these people [the Soviets], not so very long ago, were in a kind of premodern political ice age, you did not really have to take them seriously except as to the quality and number of their guns. You did not have to argue. You did not have to think. It was very agreeable and, although internationally harrowing, intellectually restful."

Gorbachev's July 1985 announcement of a unilateral nuclear test ban vividly underscored how much the game of shaping public opinion had suddenly changed. What made the Soviet test ban so extraordinary was that it was unilateral. What made it so important was that if the United States joined in, the arms race would be effectively, if temporarily, halted, since weapons not tested could not be reliably deployed. A test ban would not reduce the size of nuclear arsenals, but many nuclear arms experts believed that the sheer number of warheads in existence was no longer the most urgent problem. Even more crucial was to halt the relentless technology spiral that was turning more and more of the decisions about waging nuclear war over to computers. This a mutual test ban promised to do.

While many outside arms control experts, including former top officials of Republican and Democratic administrations alike, considered a mutual test ban an important step forward, the White House viewed the Soviet moratorium with hostility. Various objections were raised against it, but above all, a test ban would preclude development of space weapons. The Soviet test ban also caused trouble on the PR front. "Any kind of announcement that appears to be a significant unilateral concession has a lot of public appeal to it," explained Kampelman.

"The test ban announcement did not cause consternation [at the White House]," said McFarlane, "but rather a sense that they were more agile now, so we had to become more agile ourselves. It's like being a member of the Notre Dame football team and you're used to playing Davidson. And all of a sudden Davidson recruits some players from the New York Giants. You have to adapt and move quicker yourself."

This the White House did. Having gotten advance warning of Gorbachev's moratorium announcement, the Reagan apparatus had the President hustle down to the pressroom to pre-empt it by issuing a public invitation for the Soviets to send observers to an impending U.S. nuclear test in Nevada. Meanwhile, other White House officials, speaking to reporters on background, condemned the Soviet moratorium on the grounds that a mutual freeze would leave the Soviets well ahead in testing and at any rate could not be verified. Neither of these claims was true, as any number of independent experts could have testified, but they were dutifully swallowed and regurgitated nonetheless as the press hewed to the official Reagan line that the whole thing was one more propaganda ploy.

The Soviet moratorium, which took effect on August 6, 1985, the fortieth anniversary of the Hiroshima massacre, continued for some eighteen months. Gorbachev extended it three separate times before letting it expire in February 1987. According to Max Kampelman, the administration "dealt with it by talking to reporters on background primarily, and by simply remaining stubborn about it." Like McFarlane, who commented that White

House reporters "wrote quite sensible stories," Kampelman applauded U.S. press coverage of the Soviet test ban. "I think they handled it well," he said. "I think they handled it well."

From the time it was first announced, the test ban was portrayed in mainstream U.S. news reports not as the best opportunity to stop the arms race to arise in decades but as an attempt at a sneaky trick. Lesley Stahl described the moratorium as "propaganda" four separate times in her *CBS Evening News* story of July 29, the night of Gorbachev's announcement. In their stories the following morning, *The New York Times*, *The Washington Post* and the *Los Angeles Times* each committed the cardinal journalistic sin of getting a basic fact flat wrong when they downgraded Gorbachev's unilateral action from a policy shift to a mere "proposal." And both the *Los Angeles Times* and *The New York Times* ended up further pleasing the White House by making Reagan's invitation, rather than Gorbachev's moratorium, their headline story.

The press then went on to mimic the White House and ignore the moratorium for several months, which meant that most Americans never heard about it in the first place, much less recognized the opportunity it represented. Activists from the nuclear freeze campaign and other peace groups, however, were determined to make it an issue at the first Reagan-Gorbachev summit, held that November in Geneva. There had been a virtual blackout in national news media coverage of the peace movement for the past two years; the movement had dropped off the media map shortly after a congressional resolution endorsing a freeze with the Soviets had passed the House of Representatives in May 1983. Beginning some two months before Gorbachev's announcement, peace activists had circulated a petition urging the superpowers to negotiate a comprehensive test ban treaty. They ended up with 1.2 million signatures, an impressive display of grass-roots strength and mass appeal that put the lie to charges that the freeze had shriveled up and died following Reagan's re-election.

But when movement leaders took the test ban petitions to Geneva to deliver them to Reagan and Gorbachev personally, they found themselves roundly attacked in the press as unpatriotic. Leading the charge were the three major television networks. In accordance with its commitment to bilateral balance, the peace delegation had requested to meet with both the U.S.

and the Soviet leaders well in advance. This key fact was left unmentioned as network news reports instead portrayed the peace delegation as disloyal meddlers.

The Reagan administration found itself badly outmaneuvered when Gorbachev elected to receive the peace delegation himself, while the United States accepted the petitions through a mid-level State Department official. But the networks obligingly covered for the administration by directing fire at the Reverend Jesse Jackson, who, ironically, had been invited to head the delegation partly in order to attract press attention. Tom Brokaw and Dan Rather each challenged Jackson on whether his meeting with Gorbachev had not embarrassed Reagan and thus harmed the United States. Bill Moyers of CBS, the network commentator usually most critical of the Reagan administration, all but called Jackson a Communist dupe.

Not one of the networks mentioned the following basic facts about the peace movement's appeal: that the petition had been signed by over a million Americans (the reports merely referred to "a petition"); that a comprehensive test ban treaty would effectively halt the nuclear arms race; that the Soviets, unlike the United States, had unilaterally halted testing in August and invited the United States to do likewise; and that the Soviet moratorium was due to expire at year's end. Instead the story was framed in Reaganspeak. The arms control angle was downplayed almost to the vanishing point. Coverage focused instead on the Reverend Jackson's impertinence and on his request to Gorbachev that the Soviets respect human rights and allow Jews easier emigration.

Two nights later, reporting on a CBS News/*New York Times* overnight poll, *CBS Evening News* correspondent Bruce Morton congratulated America for having taken "a realistic view of the summit and what it might mean." Among the findings: by 62 to 27 percent, people disapproved of Jackson's meeting with Gorbachev.

While the peace movement was depicted in relentlessly negative terms, President Reagan emerged triumphant from the Geneva summit. He achieved this without taking a single concrete step toward slowing the arms race. Like so many of his past accomplishments, Reagan could not have managed this one without the help of the news media. The networks in particular trivialized the summit, dutifully broadcasting prepackaged photo opportunity pictures of Reagan's fireside chats and lakeside strolls with Gorbachev while restricting their practice of adversarial journalism to demeaning speculation about a supposed "fashion war" between the two leaders' wives. Thus did Ronald Reagan pacify, at least temporarily, the public anxiety about nuclear war that was never far from the surface throughout his presidency.

• • •

ON DECEMBER 19, 1985, Gorbachev revived the idea of a mutual test ban. Although he sweetened the idea by offering to allow U.S. authorities to visit Soviet underground test sites to see for themselves that the moratorium was being honored, U.S. news stories suggested he was making a demand rather than adding a concession. Each of the network evening broadcasts reported the news from Moscow that night, but only late in the broadcast after a lineup of stories that would have made Rupert Murdoch proud. Senator Edward Kennedy's announcement that he would not run for President was the arguably defensible lead story, and then came a string of fantastic tales: a dramatic helicopter escape from a South Carolina prison, the tragic death of a young Ohio boy who had fallen into an icy pond the day before, the taut drama of pistol-wielding terrorists interrupting a Paris courtroom trial, hopeful news of improvements in the Jarvik-7 artificial heart and finally a cautionary report from the U.S. Surgeon General informing America's workers that cigarettes were their biggest occupational health hazard. Only then were viewers told of Gorbachev's latest announcement.

Only CBS found the time to do more than a mere "tell" on the Gorbachev story, but Dan Rather's introduction was enough to make one wish the supposedly liberal news outfit had just ignored the story altogether. "Well, a little pre-Christmas propaganda in the air, a new arms control offer from Soviet leader Mikhail Gorbachev," intoned Rather before turning the story over to Lesley Stahl. The White House correspondent accurately reported Gorbachev's offer, following it with a quote from Larry Speakes explaining why the United States was rejecting it. Speakes's statement—"U.S. testing is required to ensure the continued credibility and effectiveness of our deterrent"—was dubious in fact and misleading in intent. Testing was needed only for new weapons, not for the existing nuclear arsenal. Indeed, that was precisely why the administration so disliked the notion of a test ban: it would block development of the space weapons system. That Stahl knew this to be true was suggested by her otherwise inexplicable follow-up reference to "a series of important experiments" then underway on SDI, but that cryptic remark in no way challenged the validity of the White House viewpoint.

Gorbachev, however, was clearly determined to continue making disarmament proposals. On January 19, 1986, he announced an ambitious plan to rid the world of nuclear weapons by the year 2000. Not only did the plan contain major concessions on such key questions as missiles in Europe, treaty verification and on-site inspection of Soviet facilities; it extended the Soviet testing moratorium another three months. And it articulated for the first time what would come to be known as the Grand Compromise: a mutual 50 percent cut in long-range offensive weapons in return for U.S. renunciation of space weapons.

The January 19 proposal was harder to discredit, if only because the Soviets borrowed a trick from the Reagan propaganda manual—this time, they informed the White House about the proposal only an hour before telling the press. The evening news reports of ABC and NBC credited the Soviets with making a "dramatic" offer (Rather of CBS wearily noted that the Soviets had made "yet another arms proposal"), and all three accurately summarized its major elements. There were simply too many concessions in the proposal to dismiss it categorically, but the sources quoted by network correspondents found very little positive to say about it. NBC's Chris Wallace cited Reagan officials who called it "a slick propaganda effort." Likewise, ABC's Sam Donaldson closed his report by noting that "one well-known administration hard-liner has already privately dubbed it 'nothing but propaganda.' "

One might say in the networks' defense that the deadline rush prevented them from soliciting a wider range of opinion concerning the Gorbachev proposal. But twenty-four hours later, on their January 20 broadcasts, their choices of experts were remarkably unchanged. Representatives of the peace movement, the organized popular opposition to the government on the issue at hand, were not deemed worthy of a hearing, but that was routine procedure. Less predictable was the absence of even so much as an eight-second sound bite from a liberal member of

Congress or a former high government official who might have offered a "responsible" counter to the White House view. Instead, the administration was given space to expand on the criticisms and reservations it had voiced the day before. The closest the networks came to airing an alternative position was Tom Fenton's mention on CBS that the British government believed the offer should be "investigated carefully." And then, as suddenly as it had appeared, the story of Gorbachev's arms proposal vanished. Gorbachev's plan fell "like a rock to the bottom of a pool," remarked *Washington Post* columnist Mary McGrory three days later in one of the very few pieces of journalism that did not ridicule the plan as a cynical play to Western public opinion. "After one splash a week ago, it disappeared from view."

Nine months passed before it reappeared. At the Iceland summit in October 1986, Gorbachev revived his proposal for nuclear disarmament, thus presenting President Reagan with another chance to reverse the direction of the nuclear arms race and perhaps, eventually, to eliminate such weapons altogether. The catch, of course, was that Reagan had to accept restrictions on SDI; testing and deployment of space weapons would be prohibited during the next ten years under Gorbachev's plan. Faced with a choice between obtaining the massive reductions in nuclear arsenals he had always claimed he wanted and pursuing the fantasy of a nuclear shield, Reagan rejected the Gorbachev proposal.

For the Reagan apparatus, Reykjavik constituted the most severe nuclear-related public relations crisis of the entire presidency. Disappointment at the outcome was immediate and widespread. Now, a summit which had failed had to be portrayed as one which had succeeded. Intransigence had to be portrayed as prudence. Unfortunately for the administration, White House chief of staff Donald Regan and Secretary of State George Shultz had already issued angry or disappointed confessions of failure immediately following the summit. Undeterred, Reagan's handlers began during the flight home from Iceland to outline an ambitious PR offensive. What Regan would later imprudently label "the shovel brigade"* was prepared for action. Top admin-

---

* In comments published in the November 16, 1986, *New York Times*, Regan described recent damage-control efforts of the White House as follows: "Some of us are like a shovel brigade that follow a parade down Main Street cleaning up. We took Reykjavik and turned what was really a sour situation into something that turned out pretty well. Who was it that took this disinformation thing and managed to turn it?"

istration officials would be dispatched to all the major media outlets, and would even be ordered to shed their normal mask of anonymity and allow themselves to be quoted by name. In contrast to their previous downbeat assessments, the officials would rejoice at all the progress that allegedly had been made in Reykjavik and speak positively of future prospects. Deployment of this so-called spin patrol would reinforce the self-congratulatory message that the President himself would deliver in a previously scheduled nationally televised address to Congress the night after his return to Washington.

The news media, especially the television networks, gave the administration ample opportunity to make its case, though not without raising a question or two along the way. In accordance with U.S. officials' initial reactions, the early news frame advanced by print and broadcast media alike was that the Iceland summit had failed. On ABC's *World News Tonight*, for example, Sam Donaldson referred to the "collapse" of the talks, while Peter Jennings remarked that both Gorbachev and Reagan "had some explaining to do back home." Congressional Democrats were heard chiding the President for walking away from "a pretty good deal" (Les Aspin) and for supporting "not arms reductions but an arms race" (Edward Markey).

Moreover, in contrast to their performance at the Geneva summit eleven months earlier, journalists also raised questions of their own about the official U.S. position. SDI in particular came in for scrutiny. NBC's John Chancellor wondered at Reagan's refusal to endorse a practical plan to end the threat of intercontinental nuclear war because of his "insistence on a theory" that many scientists said would not work. The headline of a *Washington Post* news analysis charged: "Nonexistent Weapons Undid Summit." Correspondents at all three networks offered reports on SDI, some including information directly contradicting the official Reagan position. ABC's John McWethy, for example, reported that "even the most ardent supporters now admit that to deploy the President's dream of an impenetrable shield in space, one that could fully protect the U.S and Europe, may never be possible." A second McWethy story noted that a survey of National Academy of Science members found top scientists opposed to SDI development by an eight-to-one margin; and by 67 to 5 percent the scientists also said that the United States, not the Soviet Union, was ahead in space weapons research. Other correspondents took a more agnostic approach. Both NBC's Fred Francis and CBS's David Martin concluded that SDI might work or it might not; it was too early to say.

However, despite the critical content of these television stories, they all featured graphics that depicted SDI working perfectly. This had been standard practice at the networks from the time President Reagan first announced SDI in March 1983. Because the eye took precedence over the ear while watching television, the result amounted to stories that, however carefully worded, implicitly told viewers that SDI would indeed work just as President Reagan promised.

Meanwhile, the relatively critical news frame evident during the first days after the summit was dissolving. Within four days of his return to Washington, the question of whether Reagan had erred by passing up a chance at genuine nuclear disarmament was displaced in news coverage by doubts about whether getting rid of nuclear weapons was such a good idea after all. It turned out that during the Reykjavik negotiations Reagan had assented to Gorbachev's idea of eliminating not just ballistic missiles but *all* nuclear weapons, including those deployed on bombers, cruise missiles and other delivery systems. Audiences roared approval when the President mentioned this while campaigning for Republican candidates in the upcoming congressional elections. Back in Washington, however, the national security establishment reacted with bipartisan horror.

Sam Nunn, Democrat of Georgia, led the charge, taking to the Senate floor to urge the President to withdraw his Iceland proposal before the Soviets accepted it. Journalists at all the major news organizations rushed to endorse Nunn's view that, as White House correspondent Bill Plante paraphrased it on CBS, "without nuclear weapons, the Soviets could overwhelm the West with their far larger conventional forces" in Europe. *The New York Times* unleashed a particularly heavy barrage. Former Pentagon Papers co-author and State Department official Leslie Gelb actually beat Nunn to the punch, asking in an October 16 front-page article how the administration planned to "maintain security for the United States and its allies in a world . . . where Soviet conventional military superiority might then prove decisive?" Former U.S. Army lieutenant general Bernard Trainor, the new military affairs correspondent for the *Times*, followed the next day with an article headlined "Cutting A-Arms: Safer or More Dangerous World?"

In fact, it was by no means clear that the Soviets enjoyed "conventional superiority" in Europe. According to the "Military Balance" report published by London's prestigious International Institute for Strategic Studies, military aggression would be "highly risky" for either side. Nor did superior numbers in some categories of armaments mean that the Soviets inevitably would prevail should they be foolish enough to launch a ground attack against NATO forces. Yet not a single journalist, at the *Times* or elsewhere, thought to challenge the notion of Soviet "conventional superiority" in their reports. Instead, they conveyed, perhaps unwittingly, the impression that it was just as well that the talks in Reykjavik had failed. Thus were Americans led to believe that for the foreseeable future there was simply no alternative to continued deterrence, continued nuclear MADness.

(The bogeyman of Soviet conventional superiority was a major theme in press coverage of the Washington summit in December 1987 as well. Time and again opponents of the INF Treaty were shown or quoted warning that eliminating medium-range missiles would leave the Soviets with an overwhelming advantage on the ground in Europe. Rarely were such claims balanced, challenged or even critically evaluated.)

Nuclear war and peace was the overriding issue of the Reagan era, indeed of the late twentieth century, but most of the time the press treated it like just another news story. It was as if America's leading journalists were deaf to the rolls of nuclear thunder sent rumbling across the heavens by the escalating arms race. No other issue more vividly demonstrated the dangers of the news media's unthinking allegiance to the worldview of officialdom. Media critic Todd Gitlin has observed in this regard that the American press "abdicates an independent point of view on the most urgent question in the history of the human race. It takes the arms race for granted. It speaks the language of those who would manage the arms race, not radically reverse it. It lends credence to the arguments of strategists, not the arguments of those who think the strategic logic of the arms race is itself the heart of the problem."

For example, the press rarely posed such basic questions as: What real meaning does "nuclear superiority" have when both sides boast incomprehensible overkill capacity? Likewise, in covering the Euromissile deployment, news stories routinely cast the issue in a Cold War framework that compared U.S. and Soviet force levels and made it a contest of wills between the two competing superpowers, rather than in an arms race framework that stressed how deployment would reduce the nuclear hair trigger to a mere six minutes. Most serious of all, the press implicitly endorsed the notion that there was no great urgency about reversing the arms race. As press analyst Richard Pollak told a 1983 conference on "War, Peace and the News Media," news organizations usually were "content simply to record the head-on rush of [the U.S. and Soviet] nuclear jalopies, as if their collision would produce nothing more than a couple of unmourned traffic fatalities."

A truly independent press mindful of its social responsibilities would have sounded the alarm loudly and often about the nuclear danger. It would have stood up to Ronald Reagan and exposed the preposterous claims, double-talk logic and outright falsehoods that he and his men employed to fend off the nuclear freeze, a test ban and other first steps toward genuine disarmament. It would have taken the peace movement seriously, recognizing in it an alternative view of the nuclear dilemma that was coherent, persuasive, grounded in both expert analysis and popular sentiment and favored by Republicans and Democrats alike. But instead the press deferred to the authority and worldview of the national security establishment. It worried far more about the Soviet threat than the nuclear threat and ended up defending rather than challenging the nuclear status quo. In short, it adopted a business-as-usual approach to covering the fate of the earth, at a time when business as usual threatened unparalleled catastrophe.

13

IN FRONT OF THEIR NOSES

President Reagan was criticized during the Iran-contra affair for acting as if the January 1985 ceremony ratifying his re-election victory had been a coronation rather than an inauguration, but considering the worshipful press coverage subsequently showered upon him, it is easy to see how he could have gotten the wrong impression. The same press that had patriotically cheered him on to triumph in 1984 continued to run ideological interference for Reagan during his second term. Over and over again, Reagan was praised as a peerless leader who had rekindled the fires of greatness in America's soul.

The source of Reagan's extraordinary appeal was actually simple enough. He told Americans what they wanted to hear, and he did so with enough conviction so that many, including members of the press, found it easy, and reassuring, to believe him. Not for him Jimmy Carter's mistake of admitting that the United States' quarter-century postwar reign as the world's pre-eminent empire had come to an end, that new accommodations had to be reached and new limits respected. Reagan, in effect, stood Carter's so-called malaise speech on its head. The United States was not in decline. It could still be the greatest power on earth, "the shining city on a hill," if only it summoned the necessary will and asserted itself.

"Truth is the enemy of anyone presiding over a nation in decline," Patrick Caddell, the instigator of Carter's malaise speech, later observed. "Anyone who acknowledges the truth [as Carter did] is out, because it is an acknowledgment of failure. The only other option is denial. And that can only be carried off by offering a counter-reality that is further and further removed from the actual reality facing the country."

Reagan's counter-reality during the first term consisted mainly of the 1981 dogfight with Libya and the 1983 invasion of Grenada—proof, as he later told the nation, that the United States was once again "standing tall." Grotesquely exaggerating the threat posed by external demons in order to whip the home population into a belligerent, nationalistic frenzy was an old trick, but it worked. And with Congress and the news media serving as active accomplices, Reagan and his public relations apparatus continued to foster national self-delusion and call it patriotism during the second term as well.

When the June 1985 Beirut hijacking of TWA's flight 847 by Lebanese Shiites showed just how vulnerable America was to forces beyond its control, Reagan responded by exhorting his fellow citizens to join in a crusade against "international terrorism." The press seemed only too happy to enlist in the cause. Even as they virtually taunted Reagan to take the "swift and effective retribution" he had promised against terrorism, the news media reinforced the essential underlying presumption of American innocence. As *New York Times* columnist James Reston plaintively lamented: "We are constantly taken by surprise in a world we are trying to help but don't quite understand."

It implied no approval of the hijackers' actions to point out that the Shiites and many other Lebanese had reason to resent the United States; the indiscriminate shelling of their land in 1984 by the battleship *New Jersey* had caused countless gruesome civilian casualties. But the notion that exposure to terrorism abroad was an unavoidable consequence of how the United States acted around the world apparently never occurred to most journalists. News reports instead sowed anger and vengefulness among the population and reinforced the officially sanctioned view that the United States was being unjustly attacked by fanatics who deserved to be crushed for their impudence.

And so once the United States finally did manage to strike back, the reaction in the press and across the land was jubilant. When U.S. jets in October 1985 forced down an Egyptian commercial airliner carrying the hijackers of the Italian cruise ship *Achille Lauro*, President Reagan proclaimed that the midflight interception had sent a message to terrorists the world over: "You can run but you can't hide." According to one network news report, sentiment among pedestrians in New York's Times Square was that "it's about time" the United States retaliated. *CBS Eve-*

ning News anchor Dan Rather exulted that this was "the day the U.S. took terror, captured it and cut it down to size." ABC correspondent James Wooten concluded his report that day: "So finally the whole country has something for which to stand up and cheer."

News organizations took a similar view of the April 1986 surprise bombing of Tripoli. In fact, in a reprise of its self-censorship prior to the Grenada invasion, ABC withheld news of the impending air strike from its evening broadcast for fear of tipping off the Libyans. NBC apparently did the same. Administration officials described the raid, which claimed the lives of at least fifteen civilians while wounding sixty more and destroyed the French embassy along with a sizable residential area, as retaliation for terrorist actions against the United States, specifically the bombing of a Berlin nightclub frequented by U.S. soldiers. Conclusive proof of Libya's responsibility for the Berlin bombing was never produced, however (West German authorities later concluded that Syrians were the more likely culprits), and the U.S. raid was later exposed as an attempt to assassinate Libyan strongman Muammar al-Qaddafi.

The President's public relations wizards had long promoted Reagan as the flesh-and-blood personification of Uncle Sam, with precious little dissent from the press. But nowhere was the media's complicity more in evidence than during the July 4, 1986, "Liberty Weekend." The three major television networks, and especially ABC (which paid $10 million for exclusive rights to the entire four-day extravaganza), treated viewers to an orgy of sycophantish saturation coverage. Even reporters once critical of the President joined the cheering. CBS correspondent Lesley Stahl, for example, gushed: "Like his leading lady, the Statue of Liberty, the President, after six years in office, has himself become a symbol of pride in America; he has devoted himself to reviving the spirit of patriotism across the country." And Stahl's paean was restrained compared to *Time*'s homage in a cover story titled "Yankee Doodle Magic": "Ronald Reagan is a sort of masterpiece of American magic, apparently one of the simplest, most uncomplicated creatures alive, and yet a character of rich meanings, of complexities that connect him with the myths and powers of his country in an unprecedented way."

By the time these fine words reached *Time*'s readers, the secret arms shipments to Iran that would ultimately prove Reagan's undoing had been underway for some eleven months. But in an environment of such political self-congratulation and cultural xenophobia, which the press itself had done much to foster, was it any wonder that news organizations failed to notice and expose the Reagan administration's secret Iran initiative?

Comparing Iran-contra with Watergate, Ben Bradlee later identified one essential difference in press coverage of the two scandals: "Unlike Watergate, all newspapers were on to this story very quickly." It was true, sort of. News organizations did get onto the Iran-contra story quickly—but only after it was dropped in their laps, courtesy of the small Lebanese weekly *Al Shiraa* and the Reagan administration itself.

Like Watergate, Iran-contra spelled the end of a presidency. But this time around, one could hardly credit or blame the press, which had witlessly stared mounting evidence in the face for months without blowing the whistle on the shady U.S. dealings with Iran and the contras. In fact, while major news organizations did not go out of their way to admit it,* the essentials of the contra story and to some extent the Iran arms sales were known to individual members of the press nearly eighteen months before they became headline news in November 1986. Parts of the stories were even reported in major media outlets, in one case on the front page of *The New York Times*. But the stories were not deemed worthy of vigorous pursuit, were not picked up throughout the rest of the news media, were not accorded a sufficiently high profile to attract the attention of the American public. And so they floated past largely unnoticed, fortifying Reagan administration officials in the conviction that they could conduct whatever illegal or unpopular operations they wished without fear of detection.

Seymour Hersh, a leading investigative reporter of the Reagan era, saw this record of press passivity as the true common denominator between Iran-contra and Watergate. In a June 1987 interview with *Extra!*, the newsletter of Fairness & Accuracy in Reporting, a left-of-center media-watch organization, Hersh said:

---

* *The Washington Post* eventually proved to be an exception. Eleanor Randolph, the paper's media correspondent, published a news analysis a year after the story broke entitled "How News Hounds Blew the Iran-Contra Story."

If you consider Nixon's first term there's an obvious analogy with the first six years of the Reagan administration. Nixon was able to bomb Cambodia relentlessly for fourteen months. He wiretapped seventeen American citizens, including . . . some of his own personal aides, for as long as twenty-one months. He was able to sick the CIA on Salvador Allende in Chile and increase the number of CIA operatives involved in domestic spying. The White House "plumbers"—the precursor of the Ollie North operation—mounted illegal activities against Daniel Ellsberg. If the press had been able to break any of these stories in 1971, we might have saved Nixon from himself. He might have been afraid to do some of the things he did in 1972, and this would have changed the course of history. But the press failed utterly to do anything during Nixon's first term, thereby making it easy for Nixon to walk into his own trap in Watergate. Similarly, I think the media have failed to do real penetrating reporting with respect to Reagan. Consequently, Reagan's people thought they could get away with anything. It took a Beirut newspaper to break the story and crack the Teflon.

Would Reagan administration officials have risked trading arms for hostages had the U.S. press been more of a watchdog in the preceding months and years? There is no way of knowing for sure. What is clear is that the scattered, cryptic references that did appear in the press hinting that the United States might be providing arms to Iran, and perhaps even trading them for hostages, did not deter the administration.

The New York Times, for example, reported as early as March 1982 that Israel, as well as Western European nations, had sold hundreds of millions of dollars' worth of U.S.-made weapons and spare parts to Iran. In July 1983, *Time* said U.S. military equipment was arriving in Iran via Israel. In July and again in September 1985, John Wallach, foreign editor of Hearst Newspapers, reported on a "mutual desire to improve [U.S.-Iran] relations," citing Iran's need for weapons and U.S. hopes for the hostages' return. In January 1986, Wallach wrote that arms had indeed gone to Iran through Israel. The stories triggered no wider press reaction.

On April 28, 1986, Jack Anderson and Dale Van Atta reported in their nationally syndicated column that the administration "has begun a hush-hush, barely perceptible tilt toward Iran." Two days later they disclosed that Israel had sold more than $250 million worth of arms and ammunition to Iran since 1981, "generally with the tacit approval of the CIA," but that now "the administration's mood is to 'regularize' the arms flow, instead of going through Israel." Subsequent columns in May, June and August returned to the theme of a U.S. tilt, albeit without mentioning arms sales.

The Anderson–Van Atta columns did, as it happened, generate interest at other news organizations. "I had calls from April through August from top people at all three networks, from the *Times*, the *Post*, all the news magazines," recalled Van Atta, who acknowledged that he himself delayed publication for some four months out of concern for the hostages.

But when no other reporters managed to confirm the columns, they ended up having no real or lasting impact.

In fairness to the press, there was a second reason beyond news media lethargy why Reagan officials may have felt confident their mission would go undetected: the extraordinary wall of secrecy that the plotters managed to erect around the arms deals. As they had with the invasion of Grenada, the officials directing the Iran operation kept it secret not only from administration press spokespersons but, as later revealed during congressional hearings, from fellow policymakers as well.

"It was scary to me at times," recalled Van Atta. "I had good sources who should have known tell me I was wrong on this story."

"A lot of the people who used to get tips didn't know about this," said Leslie Gelb, who headed a special *New York Times* team established in the spring of 1986 to investigate U.S. covert operations. "I went back over six or seven years of staffers on the Hill oversight committees and gave each guy on our team seven or eight names to contact. We literally left no stone unturned. The few who knew something and were trying to lead me didn't do it anywhere near specifically enough."

According to Gelb, CIA director William Casey himself issued an order forbidding officials in the intelligence bureaucracy from talking to reporters on the *Times* team. "I think Casey was afraid that if he didn't close it down, we would have gotten the whole thing," said Gelb. Both Gelb and Washington bureau chief Bill Kovach appealed to Casey to lift the ban, but the CIA boss refused. (It particularly infuriated the *Times* men that Casey had specifically *not* frozen out *Washington Post* reporter Bob Woodward, whose scoops had been a major motivation for the creation of the *Times* investigative team in the first place. Despite, or more likely because of, Woodward's extraordinary access to Casey and

CIA officials, he too failed to uncover the arms deals to Iran or, for that matter, the contra connection.)

"I don't really believe that if the press doesn't know every covert operation going on around the world, it isn't doing its job. There are other things we do in life," remarked *Times* executive editor A. M. Rosenthal. Yet Rosenthal, who had originated the idea of the special investigative team, did agree that, in regard to the Iran initiative, "somebody missed a clue on it."

"Really, the inductive reasoning needed to break this wasn't all that great," noted team member Stephen Engelberg. "You had an effect here—the hostages coming home—and not a cause."

Beyond competitiveness with Woodward and the *Post*, what had motivated the *Times* investigation, according to Leslie Gelb, "was a feeling on all our parts there was a hell of a lot going on in covert operations we didn't know about. The Reagan Doctrine was essentially a blessing for covert operations." But confronted by effective government stonewalling, the *Times* team soon drifted apart. There were plenty of other stories to pursue, and Gelb, for one, was just as happy to move on. By his own admission, he had resisted heading the team, for fear it would queer relations with sources he relied on for his regular national security stories. In retrospect, some team members questioned whether he had gone about the investigation properly, had conducted it with enough circumspection. In Gelb's view, however, the team's failure simply proved that "there are some things the executive branch can keep secret. . . . We went after these fucking things like a battle campaign. . . . The administration shut the lid down very tightly and effectively on it."

• • •

THE PRESS had still less excuse for its failure to unravel the contra angle of the scandal. As NBC White House correspondent Chris Wallace commented: "I don't have any second thoughts about not knowing about Iranian arms sales. . . . I guess I didn't have a good enough imagination to envision Ronald Reagan selling arms to Khomeini. I do have some regrets about the contra aspect. You couldn't know about the diversion of funds, but there were stories out about the NSC and Ollie North backing the contras, and I don't think I or my colleagues worked that story as hard as we could have."

The first report that the Reagan White House, in the person

of National Security Council aide Lieutenant Colonel Oliver North, was supporting the Nicaraguan contras with more than words appeared in June 1985. Published by the Associated Press, the story was written by Robert Parry, the reporter who the year before had broken the story that the CIA had provided the contras with training manuals advocating the assassination of political opponents. Parry's June 10, 1985, story described North's central role in a "private aid network" that had been keeping the contras alive after Congress, angered by such previous CIA lawbreaking as the mining of Nicaragua's harbors, halted U.S. aid in October 1984. Disclosure of the shadow support system underscored the White House's determination to continue its war against Nicaragua regardless of what Congress said.* Yet the story provoked little reaction. Although virtually every newsroom in the country subscribed to the AP wire service, the press as a whole seemed not to notice Parry's exposé of apparent White House lawbreaking. None of the major dailies picked it up, nor was it mentioned in network newscasts. Two days later, the House reversed itself and voted the contras $27 million of so-called humanitarian aid.

But there was no way fellow journalists could miss the next revelation of dubious activity by Reagan officials. A front-page article in the August 8 *New York Times* reported that Nicaraguan rebels were "receiving direct military advice from White House officials on the National Security Council." Reported by Joel Brinkley and Shirley Christian, the *Times* article marked an important advance beyond Robert Parry's story, for it disclosed that the NSC was not only helping the contras raise money, it was also exercising "tactical influence" on their military operations. In other words, the war on Nicaragua was being run, at least in part, out of the Reagan White House.

---

* It was later learned that Reagan officials had begun preparing for a congressional cutoff even before the harbor-mining controversy erupted in April. CIA director Casey wrote NSC chief McFarlane on March 27 about "other sources" that might substitute for congressional funding. North then outlined a plan for keeping the contras militarily, financially and materially solvent if and when congressional support ended. McFarlane personally briefed President Reagan on the plan, and Reagan approved it in April.

And, according to an April 1988 report on ABC's *World News Tonight*, the Reagan administration also took other steps to guarantee a steady supply of weapons to the contras. From 1983 to 1986, the United States and Israel worked with Panamanian strongman Manuel Noriega and employees of the murderous Medellín cocaine cartel of Colombia on an illegal operation that "provided arms to the contras, and then . . . smuggled drugs into the United States."

White House spokesman Larry Speakes saw no way to deny the story. "The facts were the facts," he later explained, "and we couldn't argue with them." But the White House could argue about what they meant, and this Speakes, and President Reagan, did. Despite the fact that Congress, in passing the Boland Amendment the previous October, had specifically prohibited "any [U.S.] intelligence agency" from assisting the contras in any way, Speakes went before reporters and solemnly declared that "no member of the National Security Council staff has, at any time, acted in violation of either the spirit or the letter of existing legislation." At a photo opportunity while signing the $27 million non-military contra aid bill, the President followed the same script, stating simply, "We're not violating any laws."

That seemed to settle the matter, at least as far as the press was concerned. Television's Nicaragua story that evening concerned the release of U.S. peace activists who had been kidnapped by the contras, clearly a newsworthy event. The White House angle of the story, however, received a total of but eighty seconds of airtime on the three network newscasts, most of which was spent reporting Reagan's approval of the contra aid package and, parenthetically, his denial of any lawbreaking. Incredibly, the *Times* itself downplayed the White House's confirmation of its exposé as well. The paper's story the following day ran a mere ten inches on page A4, and had its explosive import obscured with a headline of eye-glazing blandness: "Role in Nicaragua Described by U.S."

Self-serving interpretation took precedence over fact in all these reports; the White House's tacit admission of having provided direct military advice to the contras got less emphasis than its claim that no laws had been broken. The White House would later defend its position by claiming the Boland Amendment did not apply to the NSC, on the grounds that the NSC was not an "intelligence agency." Although this flew in the face of common sense (one of President Reagan's own executive orders on intelligence described the NSC as "the highest government entity with responsibility for intelligence activities"), none of the members of Congress and former federal officials cited by the *Times* disputed this legalistic fiction. The networks, for their part, did not even bother to question, much less contradict, the President's assertions of innocence.

And so, as Speakes recalled, the story "just went nowhere."

Although a Joel Brinkley story on page A3 the next day reported that some CIA officials feared the NSC's involvement with the contras was illegal, and the *Times*'s lead editorial on August 11 strongly condemned the administration's "evasion and deception" regarding the Nicaraguan war, the controversy never attained the critical mass within the rest of the press required to become a continuing story.

Why not? As Stephen Engelberg observed about the arms-for-hostages dealings, the inductive reasoning needed to fathom the White House–contra connection was not that great. Congress had halted official U.S. funding of the contras the previous October, yet the contras remained intact. There had been a number of news reports revealing that present and former U.S. intelligence officials were channeling aid to the contras. Meanwhile, the President was meeting directly and publicly with contra leaders and assuring them the United States would not abandon them. And finally there had come the evidence—reported in *The New York Times*, no less—that members of the President's own staff were indeed aiding the contras, militarily as well as financially.

Journalists subsequently offered various reasons why they did not more vigorously investigate the gigantic hints dangled before them.

"I can give you my answer," said Ben Bradlee, "which is that I didn't know it. Nobody took an isolated fact and hammered it into my brain, which is what you've got to do. You've got to be prescient [to] sense one of these. It's not as if your plate wasn't already pretty full. There's a lot going on in a newspaper at any given time."

Other journalists blamed corporate-ordered cutbacks in staff and resources for their failure to follow up. There was also the media's tendency to defer to the government on alleged national security matters—which may have swayed editors at the *Times*, the *Post* and other news organizations to accede, at least initially, to White House requests to delete North's name from their news stories, for fear he supposedly would become a target for unnamed terrorists. In addition, many reporters on the national security beat valued North as a source and thus were disinclined to cause trouble for him.

"Everybody knew that Oliver North was all over this town talking to people," acknowledged *CBS Evening News* Washington producer Brian Healy. "A lot of people in this company got briefings from him. A lot of people were aware that the contras were getting some sources of supply. But those were the days we [in the press] were talking about how bad off the contras were. Remember those stories? Are they going to survive? We heard stories being floated that these people had sixteen days of matériel left."

The primary inhibition on the contra story, however, derived from the press's tendency to follow the lead and believe the answers of top Washington officials.

"I don't know why it didn't click," added Healy. "Part of it perhaps was that we were too naïve in taking the [Reagan administration's] responses." Referring to the brief flurry of congressional scrutiny sparked by the North revelations, Healy added, "The Democrats asked the questions, we reported on the questions and on the fairly blanket denials [the administration gave]. So they lied, flat out."

"Of course, Congress is just outrageous on that," said Walter Pincus of *The Washington Post*, who did some of the best reporting on the Iran-contra affair. "That's an irony of [House Intelligence Committee chairman, Democrat] Lee Hamilton. To let them get away with it—to let McFarlane one year and North the next lie to him, and with all the resources the committee has, not to be able to check it out—is unbelievable. There are limits to which they are prepared to go."

As had happened so often during the Reagan years, Congress and the press were a study in mutually reinforcing passivity. Explaining the failure of his August 8 story to provoke an investigative push at the *Times* or elsewhere in the press, Joel Brinkley noted, "This was not the first flouting of congressional intent. They flouted congressional intent with the mining of the harbors in Nicaragua. They flouted congressional intent with the CIA assassination manual. They flouted congressional intent with going around restrictions on how much money they could spend on the contras by using other Agency assets, such as Defense Department mother ships. It was not as if this was an issue full-blown out of the sea with this story. It'd been around a long time. This was another example, a serious example. But I don't believe that at that moment we viewed it as more serious than mining the harbor and blowing up third-nation vessels."

As with the Iran initiative, the simple fact was that the prevailing political climate in Washington at the time did not encourage pursuit of a story critical of Reagan's harassment of Nicaragua. In the summer of 1985, both the President's own popularity and the mood of Rambo nationalism he had helped foster were near their height; in Washington, Sandinista bashing was popular bipartisan sport.

In an effort to restore contra aid, the administration had mounted a propaganda campaign whose intensity and scope were comparable only to the 1981 tax and budget cuts offensive and whose viciousness and disregard for truth were second to none. The administration lambasted Nicaragua as a "totalitarian dungeon," while ignoring the decidedly worse human rights records of such neighboring U.S. client states as El Salvador and Guatemala. It accused Nicaragua of mounting an offensive, Soviet-sponsored military buildup which threatened U.S. security, despite confidential U.S. intelligence reports admitting that "Soviet arms shipments to Nicaragua turned sharply upward only after the Reagan administration launched the contra war." It charged the Sandinistas with drug trafficking, when in fact it was the contras who were involved in cocaine smuggling.

Much of the propaganda was organized by the Office of Public Diplomacy, a State Department body described by one senior U.S. official as "a vast psychological warfare operation of the kind the military conducts to influence a population in enemy territory." The aim, as one Reagan official later explained to *The Miami Herald*, was "to slowly demonize the Sandinista government, in order to turn it into a real enemy and threat in the minds of the American people, thereby eroding their resistance to U.S. support for the contras and, perhaps, to a future U.S. military intervention in the region." The program worked, at least on Capitol Hill. Administration accusations of being soft on Communism frightened fence-sitting Democrats into supporting renewed contra aid; the measure narrowly passed.

The effect of all this on news coverage was predictable. (See Notes section for details.) Coverage of the contra aid debate, in accordance with the Washington press corps's palace court mentality, focused as much on head counting and the vote's impact on the President's standing in the capital as on the arguments pro and con and their supporting evidence. Rarely did journalists question the administration's underlying assumptions, such as the supposed U.S. desire for peace and democracy in Central America or the Sandinistas' untrustworthy nature. White House correspondents' definition of adversarial journalism seemed to be confined to asking the President *whether* he was trying to overthrow the Nicaraguan government, not what right he had to do so.

Meanwhile, the story of White House direction of the contra war went unpursued. As Joel Brinkley observed: "The press and Congress and public interest groups all kind of feed on each other, and it's hard for any one of them to sustain a long investigative effort with none of the others maintaining interest in it. That's not necessarily right, but it's a pragmatic fact. Certainly Reagan's popularity helped dampen interest among a lot of agencies and interest groups, chiefly Congress, in pursuing these sorts of episodes."

Reagan's demonization of Nicaragua, abetted by the press, reached hallucinatory proportions in 1986. Not content with the $27 million in non-military aid Congress approved in 1985, the Reagan administration pushed the following spring for $100 million more in outright military assistance, plus an end to restrictions on CIA involvement in the war on Nicaragua. Once again, the President pressed his case with a catalogue of sinister and unsubstantiated accusations against the Sandinistas. Once again, the press was more a help than a hindrance to the White House.

For example, when the administration dusted off the White Paper ruse it had utilized in 1981 to blame Cuba and Nicaragua for El Salvador's insurgency, mainstream journalists gobbled the bait just as eagerly as they had the first time around. Reagan's May 13 tour of a State Department exhibit of "captured Communist weapons" got extended and respectful play on all three network evening newscasts. The President was given ample time to argue that the arms and documents on display were part of "a sophisticated Communist effort to undermine democracy in this hemisphere and to deceive us in the process." Not one of the network correspondents so much as hinted that the Reagan administration had employed the identical tactic five years earlier in a calculated, and subsequently exposed, attempt to deceive Americans.

Worst of all was ABC. After showing Reagan's remarks, correspondent Jeanne Maeserve broadcast leaked satellite photographs "purported to be pictures of newly constructed Nicaraguan prisons." She added that "intelligence sources report that the Nicaraguans are using attack dogs on prisoners, and are torturing others by applying electric cattle prods to their genitals." As she spoke, the propaganda was reinforced visually. A bright yellow map of Nicaragua was superimposed on a prison fence while below it, in two separate columns of three lines apiece, was written in bold yellow capital letters: NICARAGUA KILL WITH AT-TACK DOGS and NICARAGUA TORTURE WITH CATTLE PRODS—malevolent graphics which, on a subliminal level, said more about U.S. policy toward Nicaragua than anything else. Maeserve, who was new to the State Department beat, later conceded she had not independently verified the intelligence sources' claims.

In the midst of such hysteria, few reporters were willing to raise serious questions about U.S. policy toward Nicaragua. Those who did often were suspected, if not directly accused, of a leftist political bias. "There was a period, and it's still true today to some degree, when the true contra partisans in the administration would greet investigative stories that pointed out fallacies or misstatements in policy as being written by people who must be pro-Sandinista," recalled Joel Brinkley. "It was never expressed directly to me. I'd always hear it through other people in government, sources of mine."

Indirect political pressure, said Brinkley, was one of the reasons he had not done more to follow up his August 1985 story. "I regret not having pushed that story, certainly. In retrospect, you'd be a fool not to regret it, considering what was there. I'd had a long frustrating year of writing stories that were often denounced. I was moving off the beat and was not eager to prolong it."

Experienced colleagues in the *New York Times* Washington bureau, however, said it was less Brinkley than his superiors in New York who were responsible for the lapse. "This was clearly not what they wanted in New York," said one Washington hand. "You couldn't always tell if they were lukewarm about a story, but if they wanted something, you knew it. There would be a phone call, and [bureau chief Bill] Kovach would come barreling out of his office and give us our orders."

The ultimate source of the failure to pursue this story, suggested these journalists, was the political tone and newsroom atmosphere that executive editor Abe Rosenthal had fostered around the *Times*. Justly or not, there was a widespread perception among *Times* staffers in both New York and Washington that Rosenthal was, if not outright pro-contra, at least virulently anti-Communist. Recently he had hired Shirley Christian, a former *Miami Herald* reporter who was well known as a harsh critic of the Sandinistas. Well before Christian's arrival, however, it was apparent that stories that reflected badly on the Reagan administration's support of the contras were not Rosenthal's favorites. That did not mean they never got in the paper—they might even appear on page one—but generally the battles, and compromises, along the way were sizable. And everyone at the *Times* was aware of Rosenthal's 1983 recall of *Times* reporter Ray Bonner from Central America, a move many regarded as politically motivated. Especially in the wake of the Bonner affair, said one *Times* journalist, "it was clear that Central America was a way to get yourself in big trouble here, especially with Abe, who, because of his very personal, hands-on management style, was the only one who mattered." As a result, said this source, referring to Brinkley's August 1985 story, "you almost would have had to have been a crusader to follow that up."

"This is nonsense," responded Rosenthal. "This is the conspiracy theory. This is Salem. I will follow up Sy Hersh['s 1974 exposé] about [domestic spying by] the CIA and investigate the *New York Times*['s connections to the CIA], put my life on the line with the Pentagon Papers, but suddenly when it comes to the contras, I'm a changed person?" Such accusations, Rosenthal argued, revealed more about their makers than about him. "I don't even remember the Brinkley story, and the implication I didn't follow it up because I'm for the contras, I'll tell you something: that's for children, really. . . . It would never occur to me that a reporter who I knew felt that the Sandinistas were good for Nicaragua—and we have plenty of reporters who feel that way—if he got beaten on a story that showed the Sandinistas had tortured somebody, it would never occur to me to say he got beaten on it because [he's] basically pro-Sandinista. That's for children. That's for people on the outside, or those who are themselves perverted. But," he added, "they don't become editors of great newspapers."

Whatever the reasons, the failure of the *Times* to pursue its own story discouraged broader press investigation into the White House–contra connection. As Robert Parry, who had been on the Oliver North trail for months, recalled: "The real effect of *The New York Times* and *The Washington Post* is not only that they can sanctify something, but if they're *not* covering it on anything like a regular basis, if they've decided it's not news, it's very hard to convince your editors at AP and even at *Newsweek* that it *is* news. Because they don't see it in the morning papers that they read. So they think, is this a guy who is off on his own tangent, following something that really isn't a story that's going to get us in trouble?"

Parry nevertheless persisted on the Nicaragua story, along with his partner at AP, Brian Barger. Their efforts yielded some extraordinary disclosures. On October 7, they reported that President Reagan had personally approved formation of the contra support network, thus tying the President himself to efforts to defy the Congress and the law. On December 20, they revealed that several top-ranking contra officials were involved in smuggling cocaine. On April 5 they reported that Nicaraguan exiles in Miami were increasingly angry at the widespread personal corruption among contra leaders. In April they also filed numerous reports on the investigation into contra gun running and drug trafficking being conducted by the U.S. attorney's office in Miami. And on May 22 they told how contra leaders had enriched themselves by trading U.S. aid dollars on the black market.

Reaction from their news business colleagues was less than enthusiastic. In fact, most of Parry and Barger's stories went virtually unnoticed by the nation's major media organizations. The October 1985 report that Reagan had personally approved the plan to establish a private contra aid network, for example, was ignored by all three networks and *The New York Times*, and buried on page A14 in *The Washington Post*.

Meanwhile, Parry and Barger were growing increasingly frustrated by what they perceived as a resistance bordering on hostility to their reporting on the part of their superiors. The reporters believed some stories had been delayed and watered down unnecessarily because AP management was afraid of offending the Reagan administration. (Their December 1985 story on contra cocaine smuggling, for example, was published only by accident, when a Spanish-side editor failed to notice an internal embargo command, translated the story and dispatched it. Only after the story had run on the front pages of most newspapers in Latin America was it released in the United States, three days later.) In particular, they suspected superiors were leery of stories focusing on Oliver North, for North was the AP's chief government contact regarding negotiations to gain the release of kidnapped former AP Beirut bureau chief Terry Anderson.

Parry was later quoted in *Rolling Stone* as saying that when he and Barger proposed follow-up on Oliver North and the drug story in early 1986, Washington bureau chief Charles Lewis "took me aside and said, 'New York doesn't want to hear any more on the drug story. We think you shouldn't be doing any more on this.' " On another occasion, said Parry, Lewis told him that "Nicaragua isn't a story anymore."

Charles Lewis later denied ever making such remarks. He said he "had no doubt that Parry and Barger are pissed off that they didn't get to go everywhere they wanted to go, as often as they wanted, when they wanted." But Lewis said there was "no basis for the idea that we were afraid of offending the administration" and cited as proof the fact that "ultimately the stories made it onto the wire. They were distributed by AP around the world." Lewis did concede Parry's counterclaim that "it was never easy," but declared that "when you're dealing with stories of this magnitude, that rely on information gleaned from Third World gangsters of known unreliability or unknown reliability, it *was* never easy and it *should* never be easy. . . . I don't know what got into Parry. I'm sorry he left us, and I'm sorry he's apparently not as proud of his work as we are."

The departures of Parry and Barger from AP came in mid-1986. Barger joined the CBS news magazine show *West 57th*. Parry landed at *Newsweek*. Before he did, however, he discovered that the Associated Press was not the only news organization cautious about reporting the story behind the U.S. war against Nicaragua. That summer, during conversations with editors at *The Washington Post* and *The New York Times* about possibly coming to work there, Parry elicited absolutely no interest in the story he and Barger were then preparing on the subject. Not until a cargo plane carrying U.S. mercenary Eugene Hasenfus crashed in the Nicaraguan jungle on October 5 did the press as a whole again begin to pay any attention to the Reagan administration's not so secret war. The week of Attorney General Meese's November 25 press conference revealing that Iranian arms sales profits had been diverted to the contras, Parry and Barger published their article in *The New Republic*. Entitled "Reagan's Shadow CIA," it told a story the two reporters had been trying to tell for months—the story of "how the White House ran the secret contra war."

"The contras and Ollie North, that whole business, to have allowed that to go on for two years without anybody really pushing it, I think is a real failure of the press," declared *Washington Post* reporter Walter Pincus. And it should be stressed that the press did not *really* push the contra story until after Meese's stunning diversion announcement. That is, until the Reagan administration itself certified that wrongdoing had taken place, the press was essentially deaf, dumb and blind to its abundantly obvious existence. Which recalls yet another of the lessons of White House–press relations during Ronald Reagan's first term: for the American press, truth was not truth and fact not fact until the government said so.

14

HIGH CRIMES AND MISDEMEANORS

S ERENITY is an elusive thing in a city as possessed by power as Washington, D.C., but Michael Deaver claimed at last to have found it. I went to see him Wednesday afternoon, November 26, the day after Attorney General Meese's astonishing press conference revealing the Iran-contra connection. The President's former image-maker had recently relocated his consulting firm into fresh quarters on the Georgetown waterfront, claiming some of the capital's most expensive office space. Southern-facing windows offered a splendid view of the Potomac as it curled around the western edge of town, past the Kennedy Center and the infamous Watergate complex, beneath the three bridges linking the District with Virginia and on toward the river's headwaters nearly three hundred miles to the northwest in the Allegheny Mountains of West Virginia. In all his life, Deaver said, he had never spent the entire day looking out over water. The river carried more traffic than he'd expected, sculls and other pleasure craft mainly, but it was the natural rhythms of the place that most surprised and pleasured him. Early in the morning red-tailed foxes could be glimpsed scampering through the underbrush on Theodore Roosevelt Island. Through the day, a sandbar would gradually emerge and just as gradually disappear, as the tide from the Chesapeake Bay pushed its way upriver. Between four and four-thirty, two herons would drop in from their afternoon activities to watch the sun go down from a perch outside Deaver's windows. As official Washington lustily gorged itself on the latest crisis, it was comforting to know that, elsewhere, life went on pretty much the same as it always had.

Pronouncing himself a man at peace with the world and himself, Deaver told a story about Ronald Reagan, the man through whom he had risen to power, fame and at least fleeting fortune.

"You know, I always give the President a little note before every press conference. I'm very superstitious and so is he, and wherever I've been—Hong Kong, Delhi or wherever—I always call and dictate a note to him. So [last week] I called Nancy about an hour before and said, 'Jeez, I just remembered he's having a press conference and I haven't got a note to him.' And she said, 'Yes, he *asked* tonight if he'd gotten the note.' So I said I couldn't think of anything very current, but just tell him that serenity is not the absence of problems. Serenity is the presence of God."

Whatever God's involvement, an absence of problems was something neither Reagan nor his surrogate son was blessed with at the moment. Deaver had just been released after a three-week hospital stay for an undisclosed illness. It was a measure of how far he had fallen, and of how vicious Washington gossip could be, that there were whisperings he had contracted AIDS. Deaver himself confessed, months later, to alcoholism. The "hospital" he had visited had actually been a detoxification center in Havre de Grace, Maryland.

Confronting his professed addiction may have calmed Deaver's soul, but it did not end his problems. For months now he had been under investigation—first by a congressional subcommittee, later by a federal grand jury and finally by an independent counsel—for illegally trading on his influence and government contacts after leaving the White House in May 1985 to become a lobbyist. Twelve months earlier, press reports had estimated the worth of Michael K. Deaver and Associates at $18 million. Soon the company would be little more than a telephone-answering machine, and Deaver would be indicted on five counts of perjury for having allegedly lied to Congress and the federal grand jury. (He was later found guilty on three counts, and faced a maximum punishment of fifteen years in prison and a $22,000 fine. At this writing, Deaver's case was on hold. His sentencing was stayed until the Supreme Court ruled on the constitutionality of the appointment of a special prosecutor.)

As for Mr. Reagan, the recent press conference of which Deaver spoke had been perhaps the most important of his presidency, and it had gone badly. Nearly every question had concerned the secret sale of arms to Iran, which had dominated news reports since being disclosed two weeks earlier.

In the month following the Iranian arms disclosures, Mr. Reagan's job performance approval rating fell from 67 to 46 percent, the steepest decline ever recorded for a U.S. President. Press accounts focused no attention on the fact at the time, but an ABC News poll conducted the week after Thanksgiving found that an astonishing 48 percent of the public believed that Reagan should resign were it proven that, contrary to his denials, he had known in advance about the illegal diversion of funds to the contras. And the same poll found that by 49 to 47 percent Americans did not believe that Reagan was telling the truth about the Iran-contra arms scandal. Combined, the two findings suggested that nearly half of the population was prepared to see Reagan leave office.

For all his professed serenity, Michael Deaver recognized as well as anyone just how perilous the situtation was for Reagan. His immediate response was to plunge into action on behalf of his old boss and friend. Like a magician called out of retirement for a last performance, he rummaged through his bag of tricks in search of a remedy, undeterred by his own rapidly approaching criminal indictment. Conferring frequently by telephone with Mrs. Reagan, Stuart Spencer, William French Smith and other loyalists from the early California days, Deaver sought to build support for his proposed purging of White House chief of staff Donald Regan, whom he blamed for the disaster. He was also arranging after-hours White House visits by such Washington gray eminences as Democrat Robert Strauss and Republican William Rogers in an effort to convince the President that this problem was real and would not disappear on its own.

Perhaps because he shared an insider's appreciation of the supreme importance of image to the Reagan presidency, David Gergen also shared Deaver's concern that the present crisis could prove fatal. A week after interviewing Deaver, I visited Gergen at *U.S. News & World Report*, where, in a striking illustration of the revolving-door relationship between Washington journalists and officialdom, he now served as editor. In Gergen's view, the Reagan presidency was effectively over. Having won the Senate in the November elections, the Democrats now controlled both houses of Congress. Even more important, severe and probably irreparable damage had been sustained to the source of Reagan's political strength, his credibility. Like Samson shorn of his locks, Reagan stripped of his nice guy image was a weak and vulnerable creature.

"The four-star general has been wounded, there's no question about that," Gergen affirmed. "In a parliamentary system, he might have resigned. That's why it's so important that you not allow yourself to get that deeply hurt, because you can't resign in this system."

But of course one could resign, as Gergen, a veteran of the Nixon White House, well knew. Indeed, just hours after Meese's November 25 press conference, Gergen had publicly offered an image as vivid and appropriate for the current scandal as John Ehrlichman's famous "twist slowly, slowly in the wind" phrase had been for Watergate. Sharing the podium at the prestigious Frank E. Gannett Lecture with Ben Bradlee, a key player in that earlier scandal, Gergen noted that "the past few weeks have brought a sinking feeling of déjà vu. Yet once again we see an American President in a tailspin, the power of his office slipping away from him with each new revelation, none more astonishing than today's. In the case of Ronald Reagan, one has the sense of watching a great oak falling in the forest. We stand in awe as it begins its descent and wait, many of us hoping against hope there will be no thunderous crash."

For Deaver and Gergen, who had done so much to help it flourish—who had nurtured and watered it, shielded it from woodsman's ax and made it loved throughout the land—the ominous descent of the mighty Reagan oak represented a repudiation of the greatest achievement of their professional lives. There were those who argued that the Iran-contra scandal never would have arisen had President Reagan still been surrounded by his first-term team of political and public relations advisers. This was probably true. James Baker, for example, way back in June 1984, had reportedly warned against soliciting contra aid funds from third countries on the grounds that it was an "impeachable offense." And as Deaver emphasized during our November 26 interview, whatever "differences that Baker, Meese, Clark and I might have had" during the first term, "the bottom line was the President. . . . Particularly Baker and myself had a political sense about things that I don't think anybody over at the White House now has. Baker always looked at things through the legislative and legal standpoint—how is this going to play out on Capitol Hill or in the courts?—if you were suggesting something as risky as this. . . . And I'd look at it from, is this consistent with the

Reagan historical position? And it's amazing to me that there's nobody over there with him who would have said, 'My God, you *campaigned* against dealing for hostages in 1980 against Jimmy Carter. You can't do this now.' "

But even the second-stringers who surrounded Ronald Reagan in 1986 managed, after a disastrous beginning, to execute a passable enough damage-control operation to steer him through the gravest political crisis of his presidency. The essential first step was the November 25 press conference. Attorney General Meese later told me that the conference had been held because the President had told him, "If there is anything you find that's wrong, we want to be sure that we get it out publicly as quickly as possible." But it is hard to believe that honesty was truly what led the administration to volunteer such damaging information, if only because of the many false statements the President, Meese and other top Reagan officials made before, during and after the November 25 press conference. When the Hasenfus flight was shot down, for example, Mr. Reagan assured reporters there was no U.S. government connection to it. When first questioned about the story in *Al Shiraa* disclosing the arms-for-hostages deal, Reagan declared there was "no foundation" to the report. Documents subsequently released by the congressional committees investigating the Iran-contra affair portrayed the President himself leading a November 10 White House discussion aimed at concealing the details of the arms-for-hostages program from the press and the public. Reagan also made numerous false statements during his November 13 speech to the nation and in his November 19 press conference. Likewise, Meese did not tell the truth about at least two of the arms sales to Iran during his November 25 press conference. Nor did the lax internal investigation Meese had conducted the previous weekend inspire much confidence in his determination to uncover the full truth about the administration's Iran-contra dealings.

Was it perhaps mere incompetence that led the administration to tell the world about the contra diversion? Was pollster Patrick Caddell correct in speculating that "one reason Meese panicked and blurted out the contra connection was that they'd never before been under that kind of press attack"—an attack which, in Caddell's view, would not have been mounted at all had a mere fifty thousand votes across the country gone the other way in the

November 4 election, leaving the Republicans still in control of the Senate and the President himself still regarded as politically unassailable?

Tom Griscom, who took over Gergen's old job of White House communications director when former senator Howard Baker was named White House chief of staff in March 1987, lent credence to this hypothesis, albeit somewhat reluctantly. While praising the November 25 press conference for "sending a signal of openness," Griscom said he doubted the President's men had thought through the implications of their announcement. "I think the thing was moving so fast that they may have lost some sense of coordination and control."

It seems most likely, however, that circumstances beyond their control gave Reagan officials little effective choice but to try to pre-empt independent disclosure of the contra diversion. Although Meese claimed in the November 25 press conference that North was "the only person in the United States government that knew precisely about this," this was not true. Not only were other senior Reagan officials aware of the diversion, so were numerous others outside the government, including U.S. covert operatives retired general Richard Secord and businessman Albert Hakim, Iranian middleman Manucher Ghorbanifar and Israeli security official Amiram Nir. Eugene Hasenfus was telling anyone who asked that his ill-fated flight had been a CIA operation, following orders directly from the White House. Perhaps most dangerous of all were the group of Canadian financiers who had already threatened to blow the whistle on the contra diversion if they did not soon get their promised profits from the Iranian arms sales. With so many people of competing interests knowing about it, it was only prudent for White House officials to assume the diversion could not remain secret forever. So why not break the story themselves and thereby shape its initial play and framing?

Meese himself later admitted that he and President Reagan had an ulterior motive in publicizing the diversion: "Both his feeling and my feeling were that we wanted to be sure to get it quickly to the public and to Congress so that there would be no suspicion on the part of the Congress or the public that there was any attempt to cover up or conceal anything." Of course, in the wake of three weeks of obvious White House deceptions, such suspicion already existed, but that only made sending such a signal of goodwill all the more urgent.

This would have been especially true if the administration was indeed simultaneously organizing a cover-up. Some congressional investigators came to believe that Meese's announcement of the diversion was itself a diversion. According to this view, the November 25 press conference was the opening gambit in a damage-control strategy designed to (1) shift attention away from the resoundingly unpopular Iran initiative; (2) insulate the President from blame by pointing the finger at lower-ranking fall guys Oliver North and John Poindexter; (3) impose a narrow definition of wrongdoing, one that focused solely on the diversion of funds (the President's responsibility for which could be plausibly denied); and thus (4) distract attention from the secret and wholly unconstitutional national security apparatus that carried out the diversion, the Iranian arms sales and countless other unknown activities.

It is worth noting that, in planning covert operations, it is standard procedure to build in cover stories whose function it is to limit the damage in the event the operation is exposed. But the most compelling evidence for this explanation of Meese's diversion announcement is that North and Poindexter themselves later admitted as much in their testimony to the House and Senate Select Committees. North even drew laughter from his interrogators when he disclosed that CIA boss Casey had informed him that he was probably not senior enough to carry the whole load; his superior, Poindexter, might also be required to take the fall. Taking his own turn at the witness table, Poindexter coolly and without remorse told the committees about his calculated efforts to provide the President with "future deniability" of knowledge about the contra diversion.*

When Meese formally identified North and Poindexter as the

---

* According to a story by *Washington Post* reporters Dan Morgan and Walter Pincus, some congressional investigators believed that it was actually CIA director Casey who originally activated the cover-up plan. In his testimony to the House Permanent Select Committee on Intelligence on November 21, four days before Meese's White House press conference, Casey, who rarely shared secrets with Congress, "volunteered a startling admission: that the National Security Council staff had been 'guiding and active in the private provision of weapons to the contras,' " wrote Morgan and Pincus. "In case the members missed the point, Casey came back to it three times during his testimony."

officials responsible for the diversion at the White House news conference, he established the damage-control framework the Reagan administration would follow throughout the rest of the scandal: focus attention on the contra diversion; concede that it was wrong; blame it on overly zealous underlings who acted without the President's knowledge or approval; and pledge to do everything possible to find out how it had happened and to make sure it never happened again. Appointment of the Tower Board the next day reinforced this perspective. Asking former Republican senator John Tower, former national security adviser Brent Scowcroft and former Secretary of State Edmund Muskie to investigate the operations of the National Security Council suggested the administration had nothing to hide. Even more important, it again implicitly portrayed the President's staff, rather than Mr. Reagan himself, as the guilty party.

Still, the picture painted of Reagan was little short of humiliating. As CBS's Brian Healy remarked: "This was the first time that dumbness, that lack of control, that disorganization, that stupidity, that naïveté, were defenses" for a President in trouble. But having framed the diversion as the essential issue, the White House was in a box. Besides ignorance, the only other available option was that Reagan did know, which could well have sparked calls for impeachment.

Thus did the White House embark on a damage-control strategy whose essential elements, like so much else in the Iran-contra affair, harked back to Reagan's first term. Once again, for example, the four-star general was protected by having his lieutenants—specifically, a lieutenant colonel and an admiral—give blood and by keeping him out of the line of fire. Once again, reporters' access to the President was restricted. Even as he cast himself as the wronged innocent and repeatedly proclaimed his fervent desire to find out what had happened, Reagan was kept away from reporters who might ask such inconvenient questions as why he did not simply call North and Poindexter into the Oval Office and ask them himself. And once again the Reagan White House applied lessons from the Nixon years. In the spirit of burning the tapes, as Nixon later confessed he wished he had done during Watergate, the Reaganites shredded documents. But they made sure to cover themselves. Rather than Nixon's arrogant combativeness, which only turned the rest of the capital elite against him, they affected a disarming mixture of regret and co-operation. Their approach, in a phrase, was the smiling stonewall.

• • •

HEADING INTO the last month of 1986, official Washington was in the grip of what Mike Deaver called "a Watergate mentality," a fact which cut both ways for the Reagan White House. One consequence, according to *CBS Evening News* senior Washington producer Susan Zirinsky, was that reporters were not "afraid to be aggressive. . . . There was a feeling that there could be a cover-up in the White House. Having been through it once, it's not such a shocker the second time." Such suspicions were only en-couraged when Poindexter, North and Secord invoked their Fifth Amendment right against self-incrimination rather than testify before the Senate Intelligence Committee, and when McFarlane's testimony directly contradicted the official White House story that the President had not authorized the initial arms sales to Iran.

At the same time, however, the Watergate parallel served to restrain the press, to beckon the ever-lurking gremlin of self-censorship to the forefront of journalists' consciousness. Media leaders seemed particularly wary of looking as if they were out to "get" the President. "I like to think I learned from my mistakes during that period," *CBS Evening News* anchor Dan Rather said of the Watergate years, which he spent covering the White House for CBS. Quoted in a December 5 *New York Times* story, Rather noted that he now talked "often" with his staff about the tone of CBS coverage, adding, "I emphasize and keep emphasizing ac-curacy and fairness." Also quoted in the *Times* story was *Chicago Tribune* editor James Squires, who urged his reporters not to repeat the "excesses" of the Watergate days, and *Los Angeles Times* editor William Thomas, who declared, "This time we have to avoid all appearances of being after somebody."

There was a schizophrenic quality to press coverage throughout the Iran-contra scandal. The story was too rich with intrigue, wrongdoing and weighty issues not to get journalistic juices flow-ing, yet it so clearly threatened existing power relations and the stability of the political order that it inevitably triggered the pro-tective, loyalist reflexes of the press as well. Thus from November on, stories containing information damaging to the White House ran side by side with stories fairly pleading with the President simply to admit mistakes had been made, fire those deemed responsible, apologize and move on. In the same vein, countless newspaper column inches and broadcasting minutes were devoted to speculation about whether, when and how White House chief of staff Donald Regan and Secretary of State George Shultz might resign their posts, as if that alone would be an adequate remedy for the assault on constitutional government Reagan had overseen.

This "God Save the King" attitude reached its apogee in the aftermath of the February 26 publication of the Tower Report. Critical as the report was of President Reagan, it saved its harshest words, as the White House doubtless had hoped, for his staff, particularly North, Poindexter and Regan. The board's conclusions—that Mr. Reagan's lax "management style" and his advisers' failure to follow proper procedures were what caused all the difficulties—corresponded nicely with the administration's damage-control strategy. True, the President ended up with a bit of a black eye, but considering the evidence of lying and law-breaking contained in the report—including documentation that Reagan himself had ordered that Congress not be informed of the arms sales to Iran—his injuries could well have been much worse.

For its part, the press by and large endorsed the Tower Board's relatively restrained criticisms. "But the Tower [Board] accuses [Reagan] of no actual crime," commentator John Chancellor incorrectly assured viewers of the *NBC Nightly News*, "only the sin of inattention. And Ronald Reagan, with all his skills, ought to be able to handle that accusation. He has one very big thing going for him. Nobody wants him to fail. Nobody wants another Nixon. He should be able to build on that as he reshapes his image and his administration."

Within a week of receiving the Tower Report, Reagan did indeed replace Donald Regan with Howard Baker and go on national television to acknowledge that the arms-for-hostages deals had been a mistake, thus provoking chorus after cheering chorus from Congress and the press proclaiming that the President had "turned the corner toward political recovery," in the words of one front-page story in *The Washington Post*, and could "consolidate his gains by a strong display of leadership on crucial issues in the weeks ahead." On March 19, Reagan held a press conference in which he claimed that his four separate denials at his previous press conference that another country (read: Israel) had participated in the Iranian arms sales had merely been "a misstatement that I didn't realize that I had made." But to nationally syndicated columnist David Broder of the *Post*, the President's performance "provided the strongest evidence yet that the proprietor of the shop has regained a good measure of his emotional balance and is ready to reclaim his role at the center of government."

Widespread as it was, the tendency of the press to internalize and reflect the perspective of official Washington was not absolute. In fact, despite corporate-ordered cutbacks in staff and resources at the major news organizations, there were some sparkling individual pieces of investigative journalism done during the Iran-contra affair. Michael Wines of the *Los Angeles Times*, who early on helped break the story of North's document shredding, went on to contribute, along with Doyle McManus, some of the best enterprise reporting. On December 4, for example, the two reported that some of the proceeds from the Iranian arms sales had been deposited in a CIA bank account which both the United States and Saudi Arabia used to buy weapons for the rebels fighting the Soviet-backed government of Afghanistan; in other words, the Iran-contra story involved much more than those two countries and a runaway National Security Council. Knight-Ridder reporters Frank Greve and Mark Fazlollah made a similar point with a July 26 story disclosing that "the Iran-contra covert funding effort was merely one of a number of secret military and intelligence operations that the White House directed out of view of the Pentagon, the CIA and Congress." One such operation, they noted, had "led to direct combat between U.S. forces and Sandinista troops inside Nicaragua." At *The New York Times*, Stephen Engelberg and Jeff Gerth teamed up to publish a front-page article on February 15 that revealed the Iran arms deals to be but one episode in a four-year National Security Council covert operations program that Oliver North had christened, with Orwellian accuracy, "Project Democracy."

On television, ABC's Karen Burnes broadcast a number of eye-opening stories, including a February 25 report on a "vest-pocket operation run by CIA director William Casey outside all normal channels" to solicit aid for the contras from the government of South Africa. At CBS, investigative producer Howard Rosenberg and correspondent David Martin also helped widen the story's parameters by revealing that the U.S. Army, working with North and Secord, had established a secret arms pipeline even before Congress banned military aid to the contras in 1984. Leslie Cockburn and Jane Wallace of *West 57th* detailed the contra drug connection, wherein Central America–bound airplanes carrying weapons for the contras would return to the United States filled with cocaine or marijuana. CBS also broadcast a number of stories on the strong circumstantial evidence of Casey's and Vice President Bush's involvement in the Iran-contra dealings.

These and various other investigative breakthroughs seemed to have little influence on the overall development of the Iran-contra story, however. Part of the reason was the competitive jealousy that led one news organization to ignore the scoops of its rivals. "We did a page-one story about the Saudis covertly funding U.S. projects overseas that *The Washington Post* never followed up," recalled *New York Times* Washington bureau chief Craig Whitney. "If the *Post* doesn't pick it up and we have nothing more to say on it, it doesn't become part of the political debate in this town."

Precisely that fate befell perhaps the single most explosive investigative story to appear during the scandal: a July 5 article by *Miami Herald* reporter Alfonso Chardy revealing that Oliver North "helped draw up a controversial plan to suspend the Constitution in the event of a national crisis, such as nuclear war, violent and widespread internal dissent or national opposition to a U.S. military invasion abroad." Appearing two days before North's televised testimony before the Iran-contra Select Committees, the Chardy story might well have made it rather more difficult for the lieutenant colonel to sell himself to the American people as a great patriot—had it been picked up by the rest of the press. Although circulated nationally through the Knight-Ridder newspaper chain, the article was not sanctified by *The Washington Post*, *The New York Times* or the three major networks and thus had virtually no effect within official Washington and, in consequence, limited lasting impact nationwide.

"There's been a lot of good coverage, and a lot of lapses too," independent journalist I. F. Stone said about press coverage of Iran-contra. "The problem is, the good stories never get picked up and chewed over in the talk shows. The party line, what the White House or [Defense Secretary Caspar] Weinberger says, gets all kinds of attention. But stories that don't fit the mainstream preconceptions, while they do appear, don't reverberate through the press like the party line baloney does; they don't have the same resonance."

"I wouldn't strongly disagree," replied Joseph Lelyveld, foreign editor of *The New York Times* and the supervisor of the paper's Iran-contra coverage. "We're all aware of that as a danger. We do our best to offset it, [but] our best is very often not good enough. Your consciousness of it has to be raised all the time, because you fall into the trap of thinking news is what was on the *Today* show, and defined by the AP budget and the first five items on the *CBS Evening News*."

Palace court bulletins, not independently generated exposés, dominated the long-term development of the Iran-contra story. The press devoted far more time and energy to reporting official statements and actions concerning the scandal than to trying to dig out the truth about it on its own. To be sure, this focus was not entirely unwarranted. Clearly it was newsworthy, not to mention entertaining, when high government officials took the Fifth Amendment, contradicted one another in testimony before Congress, attempted suicide, suddenly fell ill and died of brain cancer or were maneuvered out of the White House by the President's wife. Nor did the media's emphasis on the comings and goings of officialdom completely spare the White House from exposure of damaging information. As NBC's Chris Wallace said: "We did lots of stories that reflected poorly on the White House: how Reagan changed his story three times to the Tower Board, his false denial of Israel's involvement [during the November 19 news conference]."

But ultimately news coverage was limited, and softened, by Washington journalists' dependence on official sources. In fact, it was precisely this dependence that made it so hard to counter Reagan's damage-control strategy. For in the minds of most members of Congress, the critical question at hand was the same question that then Senator Howard Baker asked about Nixon during Watergate: what did the President know, and when did he know it? This suited the White House perfectly. From the start, the central aim of its damage-control strategy had been to frame

Reagan's direct personal knowledge of the diversion as the over-riding question of the proceedings and the ultimate arbiter of his guilt or innocence. Some journalists recognized what an absurdly narrow definition of the scandal this was, but conceded that their efforts to resist it fell short.

"What upset the American people most about this whole thing, what made it a national scandal that shook the presidency, were the covert sales to Iran," observed Lelyveld of the *Times*. ". . . On the diversion, it's a matter of real partisan debate, because this country is pretty sharply divided on the contras and Nica-ragua. So by keeping the focus on the diversion issue and con-ceding almost everything else, they did a very effective job of damage control. And to a remarkable degree the committee went along with that, because everybody was fighting the last war and asking the 'what did he know, and when did he know it?' question. When in fact it's answered on the things that most upset the country. You have this intriguing mystery of Reagan's knowledge of resupply of the contras, but that's so much less than the whole story. I think we all got caught out on that to some degree, pursuing that rabbit."

For its part, the White House encouraged the focus on Reagan's knowledge of the contra diversion, explained Joel Brinkley of the *Times*, "by responding to that one question, and not to many other questions." Brinkley recalled that "when the Tower [Board] report came out, a massive document full of an incredible array of embarrassing disclosures, the White House put out a half-page statement on the order of 'We're gratified [the report] proves the President's assertion he did not know about the diversion of funds to the contras.' Well, fine. But that ignores all the things it did show."

Communications director Griscom confirmed that the White House followed the same strategy during the summer congres-sional hearings. Network evening news coverage of the hearings, he noted, was generally handled by Capitol Hill, rather than White House, correspondents. The White House encouraged this by its refusal to comment on the proceedings. "If there's no White House response, there's no reason for the story to be shifted down here," Griscom explained. "It was done in a way that clearly kept the focus on the fact that a large part of the [testimony] supported what the President had been saying—that he did not know about [the diversion], had not been told about certain things. If the story had continually been [reported] out of the White House, I think that might have at some point changed the public perception."

Although Brinkley stressed that the *Times* "tried very hard not to let [Reagan's knowledge of the diversion] be the most important issue," he conceded that it did become "the major issue in the minds of the American people." The problem was, he said, "when President Reagan says something, you more or less have to print it. You can print it critically. But his words get in the newspaper. He's the President of the United States, we're the newspaper of record, and when he makes major statements they end up in the newspaper."

"How do you think we felt when Nixon looked us in the eye in a television speech and said he could not tell us the truth about Watergate because it involved national fucking security? We *knew* that was a lie," thundered Ben Bradlee. "But we have not developed a way to say to the reader, 'The President spoke last night, but he told a lie, so we're not going to tell you what it is.' " There was, of course, no reason why journalists could not print a President's statements and, in the next paragraph, point out how they diverged from the known facts. But even as bold a newspaperman as Bradlee seemed to think such behavior was off-limits. "If the President of the United States has that power to manipulate the press, he's got it," Bradlee concluded. "And he uses it."

• • •

THERE WAS a certain historical synchronicity in the timing of the Iran-contra congressional hearings, coming as they did during the summer of 1987, when Americans were celebrating the two hundredth anniversary of their Constitution. For what was at stake in these hearings went far beyond the question of whether President Ronald Reagan had personally approved of the diversion of funds to the Nicaraguan contras or the sale of missiles to Iran's Ayatollah Khomeini. The real danger lay in the secret national security apparatus—what analyst Theodore Draper argued was actually a military junta, operating with the President's blessing, if not his day-to-day oversight—that had been established to carry out these and untold numbers of other military and intelligence operations. The deeper crime was the undermining of constitutional government, the rule of law and the consent of the governed. The true threat was to the radical democratic vision ratified two hundred summers earlier in Philadelphia—that the common majority of citizens, properly informed, could be trusted to govern best and wisest.

Yet the obsession with finding a so-called smoking gun only intensified during the congressional hearings. With individual exceptions like PBS analyst Elizabeth Drew, who aptly captured the absurdity of this quest in her remark that "people are searching for a smoking gun in a room filled with smoke," the daily press went along with the committees' reduction of a constitutional mountain to a legalistic molehill. In this respect in particular, the hearings recalled a truth so often demonstrated during Reagan's first term—that the Washington press corps was only as critical of the President as the opposition party was. One consequence of this contagious timidity was that the obvious legal remedy for unconstitutional behavior by the executive branch, impeachment, never became a public issue.

While denying that Reagan's knowledge of the diversion was "the only question" that mattered, NBC's Chris Wallace did affirm that "we had a sense of that as the critical question—did he know or didn't he know about the diversion of funds?—because that would settle whether his presidency would be over and he would be impeached, since that would have been a clear violation of the law."

"The reason the question of the President's involvement was so important," remarked CBS Washington producer Brian Healy, "was because if he knew, then the question of impeachment comes up." While acknowledging the extraordinary assault on constitutional government that occurred on Reagan's watch, Healy, like Wallace, believed the question of impeachment could be raised only if Mr. Reagan could be shown to have been personally and directly responsible for the specific act of the contra diversion. "The question is whether he knowingly, knowingly, was aware he was committing a sin, as it were," said Healy. "If you do it by ignorance, I'm not sure, I'm not *sure*, that's an impeachable situation."

Leaving aside former national security adviser McFarlane's testimony that Reagan had indeed known of donations to the contra cause by such "third countries" as Saudi Arabia, had personally approved the mining of Nicaragua's harbors and had himself tele-phoned Honduran President José Azcona to urge the release of arms shipped there for the contras, the question remains: should not the President have borne responsibility for the actions of his most senior officials, even if he was somehow unaware of them? As Scott Armstrong, a former Senate Watergate committee in-vestigator, exclaimed: "If you have to prove that Ronald Reagan knew the details of something that was prima facie a high crime and treasonable act, it's an absurd proposition!"

Yet it was a proposition embraced by congressional leaders as well as journalists; and so the possibility of impeachment went virtually unmentioned throughout the Iran-contra scandal. The one time the *i* word did surface, briefly, was during the middle of June, when congressional investigators found a memo from North, addressed to the President, proposing diversion of some of the Iran arms profits. "If that memo had reached the hands of the President and he had approved it, that would be the smoking gun," stated House Select Committee chairman Lee Hamilton on ABC's *This Week With David Brinkley*. ". . . If that occurred— and let us emphasize the 'if'—that if it occurred, you would have a demand for impeachment proceedings." Hamilton soon re-treated, however, for reasons directly related to lawmakers' nar-row definition of an impeachable offense. It turned out that the diversion proposed in North's memo was not to the contras but to a different covert operation altogether; moreover, it could not be proven that President Reagan had indeed received the memo; so that was that.

Journalists later explained that to raise the question of im-peachment before Congress did would have constituted "advo-cacy" journalism. One who tried, CBS senior Washington producer Susan Zirinsky, recalled that she "brought it up several times" but each time she pushed the idea she "had a fight with the reporters on the beat, who told her that it was inapplicable: It's not being raised by the Congress or by the critics outside, so why should we raise it?"

CBS Evening News executive producer Tom Bettag, who called impeachment "the most logical question that goes through a de-bate like that," said CBS journalists did investigate the issue. But the constitutional law experts CBS relied upon for "an impartial reading" thought impeachment unlikely. "If that's where you're

going to come down [in the story] after talking to everybody,"
said Bettag, "then why did you raise it by putting it on the air in
the first place?"

A second reason offered for not raising the impeachment question was that, in Joel Brinkley's words, "public sentiment wasn't
there to impeach Ronald Reagan." While the evidence on that
question was by no means clear-cut—one-third of Americans
polled by *Newsweek* in March 1987 thought Reagan should resign*—there was a more fundamental flaw in this widely shared
line of reasoning. How could the public be expected to develop
an opinion on a given issue unless that issue was posed for their
consideration. In the American system, that was the responsibility
of the press. Yet the modern ethic of objectivity precluded such
journalism. Only if members of the political elite, in this case the
Congress, actually *did* something about impeachment would it
become "news" and therefore part of the national political debate. (In fact, the fullest and virtually the only expositions of the
impeachment question to appear in *The New York Times* and
The Washington Post during the scandal were opinion articles,
one in each newspaper, explaining why Congress was unlikely to
pursue impeachment.) As *New York Times* Washington bureau
chief Craig Whitney explained: "The press is a captive of things
as they happen."

Yet in fact, Texas Democratic representative Henry Gonzalez
did introduce a resolution impeaching President Reagan on March
5, 1987. It was, however, ignored by major news organizations,
apparently because few other members of Congress endorsed it.
"We were aware of it, and we watched to see how much support
it got and whether it was going someplace, but it didn't," explained CBS's Bettag.

Indeed, Congress seemed determined to avoid not only the
issue of impeachment but also a thoroughgoing examination of
the behavior that recommended it. True, Republican and Democratic members alike gave occasionally eloquent lip service to

---

* Besides the aforementioned November 1986 ABC News poll showing that half
the country was prepared for Reagan to resign if he knew about the contra diversion,
there was the additional finding in the March 1987 *Newsweek* poll that more than half of
the American people disapproved of Reagan's job performance, as well as a July 1987
U.S. News & World Report poll showing that 57 percent thought Reagan was lying when
he said he did not know about the diversion.

the vital democratic principles at stake in the summer hearings, but the actual investigation conducted by the combined House and Senate Select Committees was far more circumscribed. The members of Congress chosen to serve on the committees virtually ensured this outcome. All made a point of declaring their belief in the importance of covert operations. Moreover, a two-thirds majority of them favored contra aid, even though Congress as a whole was split on the issue and the public lopsidedly opposed it. As a result, writer Joe Conason later pointed out, "nobody said bluntly that this contra conspiracy was wrong because it violated the will of the American people."

Following the lead of the Tower Board, the Select Committees treated the Iran-contra dealings as what they were not—an aberrational excess—and concentrated on the details of how they were transacted. Questioning Richard Secord, for instance, the first witness and the man who ran the "Enterprise" that Reagan officials had hired to execute policies Congress would not authorize, the committees seemed most concerned about whether he had profited personally from the Iran-contra dealings.

"Instead of asking about this completely unconstitutional structure that had been set up and being outraged by it, they act like they're prosecuting a traffic ticket," Scott Armstrong complained at the time. "Now, the car may have been parked directly across the street from where a murder took place, but they don't care about that. They're asking about the make of the car, the license plate number and who pays the repair bills."

Oliver North later connected the dots for committee members when he mentioned CIA director Casey's desire for an "off-the-shelf, self-sustaining, stand-alone entity" that could carry out operations too controversial to entrust to normal government procedures. Members seemed shocked by this concept, though it was merely a fuller description of Secord's "Enterprise." Yet awash as they were by then in evidence of unconstitutional behavior, the committees still persisted in their dogged pursuit of whether President Reagan had signed off on the contra diversion. North said he assumed so, but did not know for sure.

The deference of the press to officialdom's version of reality reached almost surreal proportions during the testimony of Rear Admiral Poindexter. Well known by journalists as a man prepared to abuse the truth for political ends—Poindexter was the official who, the day before it happened, labeled a U.S. invasion of Grenada "preposterous," as well as the author of the infamous plan to plant "disinformation" in the American news media in order to frighten Colonel Qaddafi of Libya—Poindexter was nevertheless portrayed as the one man who could tell the nation whether President Reagan knew about the contra diversion. On July 15, he testified that no, he had consciously decided not to tell the President about it.

For the Select Committees and the media alike, that seemed to settle the question. That evening, all three network newscasts led with virtually identical descriptions of the day's testimony: that Poindexter had said he did not tell the President, and the "key question" now appeared to have been answered—Reagan didn't know. This despite the fact that the rear admiral himself had testified that he was providing the President with "plausible deniability." Having just heard the week before from Oliver North about CIA director Casey's fall-guy strategy involving North and Poindexter, committee members were now in the bizarre position of knowing they were being bamboozled even as the scam took place. Still, with the exception of Democratic representative Louis Stokes of Ohio, who went before cameras that day and said he doubted Poindexter's word, most members were unwilling to challenge Poindexter's declaration in public. Only after his testimony was over, two days and one hundred and eighty-four variations on "I don't recall" later, did such men as chairman Inouye raise indirect questions about Poindexter's credibility.

Poindexter's testimony effectively marked the end of the Iran-contra hearings. Ironically, the day after Poindexter claimed not to have told Reagan about the diversion, the three networks stopped providing individual live coverage of the hearings and began rotating the task on a daily basis, evidently for financial reasons. The subsequent testimony of Attorney General Meese, Secretary of State Shultz and Defense Secretary Weinberger was not ignored by the networks or the major newspapers, but there was an unmistakable sense that the energy had gone out of the committees' investigation, and hence the press's interest. As NBC Capitol Hill correspondent John Dancy told viewers on July 16, the hearings were now "like a suspense novel without the suspense."

Why did the news media consider the story over once John Poindexter had spoken? "It was a function of two things," explained NBC's Chris Wallace. "The impeachment issue had been answered as well as it's ever going to be; there's no documentary evidence to refute Poindexter, whether you believe him or not. But also, the key witnesses had spoken, the committees had marshaled their evidence, there wasn't much more to say. Some people say, well, why not keep after it? But we shouldn't take the position of pushing the story beyond what the information is."

Leaving aside the remarkably passive approach to reporting implicit in Mr. Wallace's statement—why *shouldn't* journalists push a story beyond what officialdom tells them?—the fact was that even the officially sanctified body of information was replete with enough implausibilities and inconsistencies to convince all but the most trusting that the truth had yet to be discovered. The real problem was that the press had always been at least as captivated by the drama of the Iran-contra story as by the facts. And once the man widely regarded as the key witness had answered what was widely regarded as the key question and absolved the President, the drama was gone. And so was the press.

• • •

AFTER the hearings ended, it was clear to journalists and congressional investigators alike that the final story did not add up. Lawmakers' concluding statements and postmortem stories in the press blamed the conundrum on the wholesale shredding of documents and the pervasive contradictions in testimony of key witnesses. As *Los Angeles Times* reporter Michael Wines wrote, the committees "found facts in eye-glazing abundance. By common agreement, what is still lacking is the truth."

And yet the nation's major news organizations, manifesting the philosophy articulated by Chris Wallace, by and large did not keep after the story. Commercial considerations argued against it, said some journalists. Editors were convinced that after months of heavy play, readers and viewers were tired of Iran-contra. Reporters were told to move on to new areas. Susan Zirinsky of CBS recalled trying twice to sell her New York colleagues on a story about Assistant Secretary of State Elliott Abrams, for example. Abrams, she said, "is still in his job, and he was absolutely horrid! He lied all over the place." But the American people, she was told, were "saturated" on the issue. And even Zirinsky, one of the more aggressive journalists in Washington, was constrained by the new budget realities of network news. In the course of denying that CBS considered the story over after the hearings, she explained, "We have teams of people who are watching it, loosely. But I am working for CBS News in 1987 after $30 million of cutbacks. We are a business. We are journalists first, but I have to make decisions on what yields stories. If I waste enormous amounts of money, I'm not going to be around tomorrow."

One important exception to this trend was *The Washington Post*. On September 6, the Sunday before Labor Day, the *Post* led the paper with a long, aggressive article whose headline asked: "Are Deeper Secrets Still Hidden?" Written by Dan Morgan and Walter Pincus, the article was extraordinary for several reasons, not least of which were the dozens of questions it raised about the plausibility of the stories told by top administration officials. Morgan and Pincus reviewed the entire Iran-contra affair, focusing particular attention on such key moments as the four days before the November 25 Reagan-Meese White House press conference, identifying contradictions and improbable elements in the story then on the public record and highlighting the frequent instances where administration officials suffered memory lapses concerning critical areas of inquiry. Animated by a healthy skepticism, the article organized the avalanche of available facts into a coherent whole that offered the reader an informed, critical understanding of what the subheadline called "An Unsolved Case."

"[It was] an interim report," Pincus later explained. "It was intended to show people this is serious, and it ain't over. The press in general is now ready to accept that this thing is over because the White House says it's over. John Poindexter says he didn't tell Reagan, and somehow the whole thing is gone. It's crazy."

Although the *Post* had not particularly distinguished itself with investigative reporting during the Iran-contra affair, it made up for it with its aggressive and insightful coverage of the story's day-to-day development, especially during the summer hearings. Like their September 6 article, the stories Morgan and Pincus wrote during the course of the scandal took officials to task for inconsistencies in their public statements or, in the case of Congress,

.for failing to press witnesses on apparent weaknesses in their testimony. The articles posed questions and raised issues. And because of the *Post*'s commanding presence within official Washington, these issues and questions at times became part of the political agenda.

For various reasons, however, the *Post*'s coverage of the Iran-contra story generated wide-ranging criticism among others in the Washington press corps. The most common complaint was that the *Post* overplayed the story. "I remember somebody joking at a dinner back in February, maybe it was the Gridiron, that the *Post* often printed the same story three separate times on the front page in the same day," cracked Craig Whitney of *The New York Times*. "I wouldn't call it dishonest, but it makes them appear to be breaking news when they're not."

Brian Healy of CBS suggested that the September 6 article "came very close to being a made-up front-page story. There was no news in that, there was no new information, no new insight. But it left the impression that there was. And that's the sort of story the *Post* did from time to time during the heavy period of the investigation. . . . I'm not saying those stories were irresponsible, but I question whether the placement on the front page as a lead was proper."

Even *Times* foreign editor Lelyveld, who said he "liked the way they kept raising issues again and again," thought that some of Morgan and Pincus's coverage "was very tendentious. They were reporting their sense of what *must* have happened, rather than their knowledge of what did happen." Lelyveld was "quite struck" by the September 6 piece: "I know why they did the exercise, and we've done those too. But having gone to the brink, we maybe would then decide not to publish. It was an attempt to give all the chaotic information form, but when you commit that much space to it, you are sort of implying there's something new here."

Dan Morgan saw these as legitimate questions, but still strongly defended running the piece. "We did raise questions we didn't have answers for," he said. "That was the whole point of the piece. The committee report was going to give the impression there were loose ends that were being tied up. We wanted to show there were loose ends that *weren't* tied up."

For his part, Walter Pincus made no apologies for what he

called "campaign journalism." The fifty-four-year-old former executive editor of *The New Republic* recognized his was a minority view within the profession, but he criticized the rest of the press for "always looking to someone else to do the work for them. If something's wrong in the country, the press shouldn't wait for Congress to act. A free press can have an agenda and should follow it. But now the press belongs to people who have no agendas other than making money, so they fall into other people's agendas."

What had been leached out of the news business over the past twenty years, according to Pincus, was a sense of commitment; reporters no longer thought it proper to care about or get personally involved in the stories they covered. Not only were they better paid, they now tended to work for corporate conglomerates whose managers were far more interested in achieving a minimum 15 percent annual return on investment than in stirring up controversy. Combined with the right-wing pressure campaigns of the 1970s spearheaded by Vice President Spiro Agnew, the effect had been to blind journalists to the inevitably political character of their work and to convince them that to do anything other than recount the daily ebb and flow of events was somehow irresponsible. "The notion you should have no feelings about the stories you cover is now the standard," Pincus observed. "I sometimes think a paper that did a story on a street corner needing a traffic light might stop after printing one story."

Perhaps Pincus exaggerated, but it was true that modern American news organizations placed an extraordinary premium on what was *new*. Recall the criticisms of the Morgan-Pincus article of September 6: if information was not new, it was simply not considered news, regardless of its intrinsic value. Though this was said to be done for the sake of the reader, it actually had more to do with journalists' competitive impulses. How good a job a news organization did on a given story was measured, within the business, largely by how many exclusives it boasted. The scoop mentality dictated a value system wherein it was more important to report something twenty-four hours, or even twenty-four minutes, before the competition did than to offer a report of depth and intelligence. Indeed, stories attempting to provide perspective, such as the September 6 *Post* article, were almost frowned upon. Not because journalists were against perspective, of course, but because that process inevitably involved dredging up "old" information and, worse, making judgments and expressing at least an implicit point of view. That was discouraged for the same reason that asking questions without answering them was considered to border on irresponsibility. It violated not only the objectivity ethic but also the commercial imperatives from which that ethic stemmed.

"We do raise questions in a tentative, crabbed sort of way," said Whitney of the *Times*. "But once you've raised the question and nobody picks it up and you keep raising it and raising it, you're trying to force the public to accept your opinion. And that's not what the press in this country thinks is its role." Moreover, added Whitney, "if you go about the process [of raising issues] more raucously, you risk losing the trust of people who hold differing views. We sell a million copies of this paper every day. You want people on both sides of the question to keep reading you and not feel that you're shading the information one way or the other." This was "a very different philosophy than the guiding philosophy of the press laid out by the Founding Fathers in the eighteenth century," conceded Whitney, "but it's a more complex society today."

The Iran-contra affair was widely regarded as a vindication of the American press, but this interpretation owed more to the remarkable passivity of the press during Reagan's first six years in office than to any valiant behavior on its part during the scandal that shook his presidency. In fact, the press all but missed the Iran-contra story, in three separate ways—by coming to it too late, leaving it too soon and failing to convey its full significance along the way. But let it be emphasized: If journalists turned a blind eye to evidence of the unfolding Iran-contra dealings for some eighteen months before the story was finally handed to them in November 1986, it was not because there were no reliable sources from whom they could have heard the truth. If America's major news organizations did not do a particularly good job of helping citizens see the constitutional forest for the trees during the Iran-contra affair, it was not because they lacked the time, space or resources to tell the story. And if the press abandoned the story too soon, it was not because Washington journalists were gullible fools who swallowed John Poindexter's assurances that he did not tell President Reagan about the contra diversion.

Logistical and financial constraints on journalists were genuine but of secondary importance; they did not fully explain the shortcomings of the American press on the Iran-contra story or, for that matter, throughout the Reagan era.

The real explanation, I believe, is hinted at in a remark Abe Rosenthal made to me. Discussing why his newspaper had not followed up its August 1985 revelation concerning White House military assistance to the contras, the former executive editor concluded a voluble soliloquy with a piercing observation: "For a paper with the resources and intelligence of *The New York Times*, there are no excuses. The only things there are, are values—what we think it's important to do."

15

WITLESS MALEVOLENCE

THE Reagan years seem destined to be regarded as one of the most fantastic eras in American history, a time when the national political debate was dominated by a bundle of ideas that almost without exception were contradicted by objective facts, common sense or both. In economic policy, there was the President's confident assertion that the government could slash taxes and escalate military spending without bloating the deficit, and that it could cut social spending without ravaging the poor. In foreign policy, there was the notion that Nicaragua, a country of some three million impoverished peasants, posed a sufficiently grave threat to U.S. national security to justify the waging of an illegal war that made a mockery of America's claim to global moral leadership. Similarly shallow-brained views prevailed across the entire spectrum of public policy, from civil rights and the environment to nuclear weapons, drugs and terrorism.

The American news media remained remarkably blasé in the face of the seemingly endless stream of irrational or otherwise baseless claims flowing from Washington. Upon Reagan's ascension to power in 1981, the press quickly settled into a posture of accommodating passivity from which it never completely arose. Relieved by the departure of Jimmy Carter, gulled by false claims of a right-wing popular mandate, impressed by Reagan's recovery after being shot and seduced by his sunny personality and his propaganda apparatus's talent for providing prepackaged stories boasting attractive visuals, the Washington press corps favored the newly elected President with coverage that even his own advisers considered extremely positive. Few in the press remarked on how biased Reagan's 1981 tax and budget cuts were in favor of the rich over the poor, for example. And not a soul noticed that, thanks to a bookkeeping trick eventually disclosed by David

Stockman, the Pentagon managed to increase its budget by some $80 billion *per year* above what even Reagan and his peace-through-strength 1980 campaign advisers had advocated.

Criticism did begin to be heard as the economy shuddered to a halt late in 1981 amid growing evidence that Reagan was, as journalists so gently phrased it, "disengaged" from the realities of governance, and things were touch and go for much of 1982. The bad economic news kept coming, and the press sometimes blamed the President. But once the first feeble signs of recovery appeared in the spring of 1983, the danger passed. So-called Reagan gaffe stories mysteriously disappeared. News reports began speculating that Mr. Reagan would be a hard man to beat come next year's elections.

The August 1983 Korean airliner tragedy was exploited to heighten the anti-Communist hysteria that had already done so much to preclude criticism of Reagan's foreign and military policies. Conquering Grenada ratcheted the mood of self-congratulatory nationalism up yet another notch while distracting attention from the 241 marines killed in the Beirut bombing days earlier. Despite the censorship imposed by the administration, the press played the Caribbean invasion as the President's "finest hour" and held no lasting grudge. As James Baker later recalled: "We had a difference of opinion with the press with respect to Grenada, of course, but it didn't carry over into generally negative reporting."

It certainly did not. When the economy kept expanding in 1984, the press saw little reason to resist Michael Deaver's attempt to portray Reagan's re-election as inevitable; campaign coverage obligingly conveyed the White House version of reality. While Walter Mondale was ridiculed as a wimp beholden to special interests, Ronald Reagan was saluted as a great patriot who made Americans proud of their country again. Thus did news organizations in the world's greatest democracy fulfill their self-proclaimed ideal of objective journalism in the fateful year of 1984.

"You ain't seen nothing yet," Mr. Reagan crowed as he began his second term. And it was true—not just of him but of the press, whose exaltations of the President as a leader of unique gifts and moral standing now reached a fever pitch. Reagan's April 1985 visit to a West German cemetery containing the graves of Nazi

SS members, which occasioned the one spasm of hard-edged coverage he encountered in the second term prior to Iran-contra, provoked no tempering of this judgment. Nor did his cheerful disregard for the millions of hungry and homeless people haunting the nation's streets. Nor did the steadily growing list of top administration officials accused of illegal or unethical conduct. Even as he championed the values of individualism and material gain that gave rise to these developments, Ronald Reagan was treated as somehow separate and apart from them.

And then came the Iran-contra affair. David Gergen, who believed the early Reagan years had witnessed a return to the traditional deference that the press had exhibited toward the government in the days before Watergate and Vietnam, expressed the fear early in the scandal that Iran-contra marked the end of deference. At the time, it seemed a plausible conjecture. But as the scandal played itself out over the ensuing months, it became increasingly clear that this climactic episode in the relationship between the Reagan White House and the American press constituted less a departure from the patterns of the past six years than a reaffirmation of them.

After all, it took wrongdoing on the scale of Watergate— wrongdoing judged as such by some 90 percent of the American people and, crucially, by Reagan's own right-wing allies in Washington—along with the Democrats' regaining control of both houses of Congress, before the nation's major news organizations subjected Reagan to the kind of sustained and aggressive coverage that should be the norm in a properly functioning democratic system of checks and balances. And even then, the press delivered a less than stellar performance. It was astonishingly late coming to the Iran-contra story, easily diverted from the fundamental issues and all too willing to give up the chase.

Still, it would be foolish to blame the press alone for the extraordinary political successes of the Reagan administration, or to hold it solely accountable for the shameful deterioration in the honesty and vitality of the nation's political life that took place during the Reagan years. Surely the President himself should also be held responsible for what happened, as should Michael Deaver, James Baker, David Gergen, Richard Darman, Larry Speakes, Richard Wirthlin and all the others who labored so intensively in his service. Together they sold the official myths of

Reagan's presidency to the American public by developing a so-phisticated new model for manipulating the press. Many of the techniques they applied—such as the virtual elimination of regular press conferences and the stage-managed emotional appeals de-signed to distract attention from Reagan's actual policies—be-spoke a fear of open government and accountable democracy, not to mention contempt for people's intelligence. Others, such as packaging and promoting the President as if he were a new brand of automobile, debased the nation's political process in subtler though no less dangerous ways.

Faced with the challenge of implementing policies which, as Gergen conceded after the fact, were directly at odds with mass sentiment, Reagan's men made the presentation of issues, rather than their substance, the pre-eminent consideration. This strategy meshed perfectly with the sort of television-dominated, bottom-line-oriented journalism increasingly being practiced by the major national news organizations in the 1980s. And these organizations responded in kind with gentle, jelly-bean journalism that elevated surface over substance and obfuscated the real issues at stake; it was a perfect symbiosis.

The animating mentality of the Reagan propaganda apparatus was revealed in all its witless malevolence by Michael Deaver's cheerful confession that he didn't know or care whether SDI would actually work; speaking of the weapons system that might someday end life on the planet, he said he supported it because it was "a great concept." Yet the Reagan model and the value system it embodies now threaten to become a permanent feature of American politics. For that alone, the men of the Reagan apparatus deserve censure of the highest order.

But they never could have achieved so much had the rest of official Washington not acquiesced, in word and deed, to so much of their agenda. Cowed by exaggerated impressions of Reagan's popularity, Congress, and the Democrats in particular, repeatedly shrank back from challenging Reagan's basic assumptions and directions. Indeed, throughout the Reagan era, the Democrats were a pathetic excuse for an opposition party—timid, divided, utterly lacking in passion, principle and vision, a paler version of Reaganism but without the Reagan.

Nor can the American people escape all responsibility for what was done in their name during the Reagan years. True, they were frequently deprived of plain-spoken explanations of what was going on around them. But what I. F. Stone once said about the bureaucracy in Washington applies equally well to the U.S. news media: it puts out so much information every day that it can't help but let the truth slip from time to time. To anyone paying the minimum amount of attention required of a concerned citizen, the basic thrust of Reagan's policies was clear. And there were plenty of opportunities for resisting them. For all the power wielded by preservers of the status quo, citizens of the United States had more freedom to challenge government policy than did citizens anywhere else in the world.

To be sure, they were hardly encouraged in this direction by the press (or by most mainstream political leaders, for that matter). Indeed, the political effect of most news coverage was to fill people's heads with officially sanctioned truth and thus to encourage among them a sense of isolation, confusion and apathy bordering on despair. This was to be expected; after all, the press took its definition of what constituted political news from the political governing class in Washington. Thus while the press *shaped* mass opinion, it *reflected* elite opinion; indeed, it effectively functioned as a mechanism by which the latter was transformed, albeit imperfectly, into the former.

It is tempting to dismiss the Reagan years as aberrational, a time when a feverish madness temporarily overtook the country, causing otherwise sensible people in the press and elsewhere to forsake reason, lose the courage of their convictions and drift into smug self-delusion. Alas, all this did happen. But this explanation mistakes symptoms for causes. Most of the salient characteristics of the relationship between the press and the White House predated the Reagan years; the excesses of those years simply made their existence, and their consequences, much more apparent.

The fundamental problem was that the press was part of, and beholden to, the structure of power and privilege in the United States. That did not mean it never challenged a President. The corporate counteroffensive of the 1970s, for example, was eventually reflected in press coverage sharply critical of President Carter. And even Ronald Reagan, a rich man's President if there ever was one, was attacked in the aftermath of the October 1987 stock-market crash. (In a display of breathtaking hypocrisy after the Wall Street debacle, *Time* ridiculed the President it had so vigorously applauded throughout his first term as "befuddled," "dodder[ing]" and "embarrassingly irrelevant," and went on to declare that he had "stayed a term too long.") But for the most part, Reagan was spared from genuinely adversarial coverage. As a member of Washington palace court society and a creature of the establishment, the press simply was constitutionally disinclined to offer fundamental criticisms of a presidency that above all else articulated and advanced the interests of corporate America. Journalists allowed loyalty to their executive superiors and official sources to take precedence over their obligations to the public and the country.

One need only consider the 1988 presidential campaign to see what lessons the press, and the politicians, have drawn from the Reagan experience. Both George Bush and Michael Dukakis have run campaigns modeled on the 1984 Reagan effort: control one's message by staging photo-opportunity events that boast all the spontaneity of May Day parades in Moscow; keep reporters at a distance; and avoid being drawn into meaningful give-and-take about one's record or future plans. Meanwhile, the nation's journalists are once again gripped by horse-race mania. Once again, citizens are told far more about where the candidates stand in the polls than where they stand on the issues. Once again, ratings prevail over responsibility, news is treated as a commodity to be sold rather than an educational trust to be fulfilled and fundamental questions about the nation's direction are neglected in favor of the six-second sound bite.

When Abe Rosenthal said that for a paper like *The New York Times* there are no excuses, there are only values, he could just as easily have been speaking of any of the major newspapers, television networks, magazines and other large news organizations that in their seamless totality exercise such enormous influence over the national political discussion in late-twentieth-century America. The news media have become the single most influential actor on the stage of American politics. Their power is only increasing, and there exist precious few checks and balances upon them.

The press's failure during the Reagan years suggests that the time has come for a fresh debate on its role within American society. For no matter who is elected President in 1988, the quality of press coverage and therefore of the nation's political debate and its democratic process promises only to get worse unless the men and women of the press return to first principles and live up to the concept of a free and independent press first upheld some two hundred years ago by the American Revolution. Perhaps this is too much to expect from employees of the profit-obsessed corporations that now own America's news organizations. But in a land that once produced the likes of Adams, Paine and Jefferson, that is a bitter thought indeed.

Acknowledgments

I AM INDEBTED first of all to the scores of journalists, news executives and government officials who took the time to answer my questions about the relationship between the press and the White House during the Reagan years. For career reasons, some of these individuals had to remain anonymous, but most spoke on the record; a complete listing can be found in Appendix A.

It was an honor and pleasure to work with William Shawn and David Reiff, my editors, and with everyone else at Farrar, Straus & Giroux. Thanks also to my agent, Gail Ross. Van Metaxas did a splendid job of reviewing hundreds of network news stories. Financial support was provided by the Fund for Investigative Journalism, the Samuel Rubin Foundation, the Center for Investigative Reporting, W. H. and Carol Ferry, Philip M. Stern, Leonard and Rhoda Dreyfus and the Institute for Policy Studies. A fellowship at the Breadloaf Writers Conference was much appreciated.

In addition, I would especially like to thank Shoon Murray, as well as William Adams, John Alves, Lisa Bain, Pam Barry, Jack Beatty, Dave Bollier, Robert Borosage, Jill Bullitt, John Clewett, Mark Cohen, Gloria Cooper, Susan Coyle, Tom Devine, Mark Dowie, David Fenton, Bill Finnegan, Max Forseter, Philip Frazer, Patrice Gallagher, Wendy Goldwyn, Tom Keagy, Jonathan King, Spencer Klaw, Howard Kohn, Constance Matthieson, Denny May, Ric Pfeffer, Annie Posthuma, Bob Reiss, Mark Schapiro, Stephanos Stephanides, David Talbot, Betsy Taylor, Mark Uretsky, Roger Wilkins, Kit Wood, and of course all of my family, especially my grandfather, who made it all possible.

Appendix A

The following lists include the names of the individuals interviewed for this book, as well as some of those who refused to be interviewed. Some have since moved on to new jobs; the affiliations listed here were current as of the date of the interview or the time of service covered in the interview. Not listed are approximately two dozen anonymous sources from within both the government and the press.

THE REAGAN ADMINISTRATION
James Baker, White House chief of staff
Aram Bakshian, chief White House speechwriter
Joanna Bistany, deputy assistant to the President
Joseph Canzeri, deputy assistant to the President
Richard Darman, assistant to the President
Michael Deaver, White House deputy chief of staff
Frank Donatelli, White House public liaison office deputy director
Kenneth Duberstein, deputy assistant to the President
David Gergen, White House director of communications
Tom Griscom, White House director of communications
Leslie Janka, deputy White House press secretary
Kenneth Khachigian, White House speechwriter
James Lake, Reagan-Bush '84 campaign press secretary
Robert McFarlane, national security adviser
Edwin Meese III, Attorney General
Lyn Nofziger, special assistant to the President
Nancy Reynolds, former aide to Mr. and Mrs. Reagan
William Russell, Federal Communications Commission press officer
Robert Sims, deputy White House press secretary
Karna Small, deputy White House press secretary
Larry Speakes, deputy White House press secretary
Wayne Vallis, deputy assistant to the President
Richard Wirthlin, White House pollster (Republican National Committee)
    Interviews refused by:
Elliott Abrams, Assistant Secretary of State for Inter-American Affairs
Patrick Buchanan, White House director of communications
Marlin Fitzwater, deputy White House press secretary
Alexander Haig, Secretary of State

Ronald Reagan, President
Donald Regan, White House chief of staff
Edward Rollins, Reagan-Bush '84 campaign director
David Stockman, director of Office of Management and Budget

ABC NEWS

John Arrowsmith, Washington senior producer
David Burke, news division executive vice president
Karen Burnes, correspondent
Sam Donaldson, White House correspondent
Robert Frye, *World News Tonight* executive producer
Jeff Gralnick, *World News Tonight* executive producer
Brit Hume, Capitol Hill correspondent
David Kaplan, producer
Peter Lance, investigative correspondent
Jeanne Maeserve, State Department correspondent
Frank Manitzas, Miami bureau chief
John McWethy, national security correspondent
Robert Murphy, chief of correspondents
Stan Opotowsky, director of political affairs
Mark Potter, correspondent
Richard O'Reagan, producer
Bill Redeker, correspondent
Sharon Sakson, producer
Danny Schecter, producer
Robert Siegenthaler, news division vice president
George Strait, medical correspondent
Charles Stuart, investigative producer
Richard Wald, news division senior vice president
Charles Warner, cameraman
George Watson, Washington bureau chief
Tom Yellin, *Nightline* senior producer
   Interviews refused by:
Roone Arledge, news division president
Peter Jennings, *World News Tonight* anchor
Bill Lord, *World News Tonight* executive producer

CBS NEWS

Tom Bettag, *CBS Evening News* executive producer
Robert Chandler, news division vice president
Leslie Cockburn, producer
Richard Cohen, producer
Brian Healy, producer
Peter Herford, producer

Marty Koughan, producer
Peter Larkin, foreign editor
Ernest Leiser, news division vice president
William Leonard, news division president
Joe Peyronnin, senior Washington producer
Bill Plante, White House correspondent
Marquita Pool, producer
Howard Rosenberg, investigative producer
Van Gordon Sauter, news division president
Jack Smith, Washington bureau chief
Sanford Socolow, *CBS Evening News* executive producer
Jane Wallace, correspondent
Bill Watson, investigative producer
Susan Zirinsky, senior Washington producer
    Interviews refused by:
David Gelber, producer
Gene Jankowski, CBS, Inc., Broadcast Group vice president
Phil Jones, Capitol Hill correspondent
Edward Joyce, news division president
Arden Ostrander, producer
Dan Rather, *CBS Evening News* anchor
Lesley Stahl, White House correspondent
Howard Stringer, *CBS Evening News* executive producer
Lane Venardos, *CBS Evening News* executive producer

NBC NEWS

Percy Arrington, cameraman
Don Bowers, producer
Tom Brokaw, *NBC Nightly News* anchor
Cynthia Burnbach, producer
Lloyd Dobyns, correspondent
Jon Entine, producer
Fred Francis, Pentagon correspondent
Rueven Frank, news division president
Andrew Franklin, producer
James Gannon, producer
Cheryl Gould, *NBC Nightly News* senior producer
Paul Greenberg, *NBC Nightly News* executive producer
Lawrence Grossman, news division president
Emery King, White House correspondent
Mark Kusnetz, producer
Deborah Johnson, foreign producer
Patricia Lynch, producer
Robert McFarland, Washington bureau chief

Andrea Mitchell, White House correspondent
Chris Wallace, White House correspondent
Bill Wheatley, *NBC Nightly News* senior producer
Robert Windrem, producer
Interviews refused by:
John Lane, news division vice president
Tom Pettit, correspondent

NEWSWEEK

Jonathan Alter, writer
Kenneth Auchincloss, managing editor
Eleanor Clift, White House correspondent
Maynard Parker, editor
Robert Rivard, chief of correspondents
Merrill Shiels, national affairs editor
Interviews refused by:
Howard Fineman, White House correspondent
Richard Smith, editor-in-chief

THE NEW YORK TIMES

R. W. Apple, London bureau chief
Gerald Boyd, White House correspondent
Raymond Bonner, reporter
Joel Brinkley, reporter
Stephen Engelberg, reporter
Leslie Gelb, reporter
Jeff Gerth, reporter
Warren Hoge, foreign editor
David Jones, national news editor
Joseph Lelyveld, foreign editor
James Reston, columnist
A. M. Rosenthal, executive editor
Bernard Weinraub, White House correspondent
Craig Whitney, Washington bureau chief
Interviews refused by:
Bill Kovach, Washington bureau chief
John Lee, assistant managing editor
Seymour Topping, managing editor

TIME

Richard Duncan, chief of correspondents
Ronald Kriss, executive editor
Steve Smith, national affairs editor

THE WALL STREET JOURNAL

David Ingatius, reporter
Rich Jaroslovsky, reporter
Jonathan Kwitney, reporter

THE WASHINGTON POST

Benjamin Bradlee, executive editor
Lou Cannon, White House correspondent
Karen DeYoung, foreign editor
Thomas Edsall, reporter
Meg Greenfield, editorial-page editor
William Greider, assistant managing editor
Fred Hiatt, reporter
David Hoffman, White House correspondent
Robert Kaiser, associate editor
Lee Lescaze, White House correspondent
Peter Milius, assistant national news editor
Dan Morgan, reporter
Walter Pincus, reporter
Tom Shales, television critic
Juan Williams, White House correspondent

MISCELLANEOUS

Scott Armstrong, former *Washington Post* reporter and Senate Watergate committee investigator
Vicki Barker, UPI Radio, White House correspondent
Robert Beckel, Mondale-Ferraro '84 campaign manager
Alexander Cockburn, independent media critic
Saul Friedman, Knight-Ridder, White House correspondent
Peter Hannaford, former Reagan public relations adviser
Maxine Isaacs, Mondale-Ferraro '84 campaign press secretary
James Johnson, Mondale-Ferraro '84 campaign chairman
Martin Kaplan, Mondale-Ferraro '84 chief speechwriter
Richard Leone, Mondale-Ferraro '84 campaign senior adviser
Charles Lewis, Associated Press, Washington bureau chief
Christopher Matthews, press secretary to Speaker of the House Thomas "Tip" O'Neill
Victor Navasky, *The Nation*, editor
Jack Nelson, *Los Angeles Times*, Washington bureau chief
Tom Oliphant, *The Boston Globe*, White House correspondent
Robert Parry, Associated Press, reporter
Jody Powell, Carter White House, press secretary
Gerald Rafshoon, Carter White House, assistant to the President

Dean Reynolds, UPI, White House correspondent
Walter Robinson, *The Boston Globe*, White House correspondent
Andrew Schwartzman, Public Media Access project
John Sears, former Reagan presidential campaign manager
George Skelton, *Los Angeles Times*, White House correspondent
I. F. Stone, independent journalist
Dale Van Atta, nationally syndicated columnist
Roger Wilkins, former *Washington Post* and *New York Times* editorialist

Appendix B

NEWSPAPER, MAGAZINE AND
TELEVISION NEWS COVERAGE
RESEARCH METHODOLOGY

THE BASIC APPROACH to researching this book was to study the coverage
of the Reagan administration provided by the major national news organizations—especially ABC News, CBS News, NBC News, *The Washington Post* and *The New York Times*, but also the Public Broadcasting
System, the *Los Angeles Times*, *The Wall Street Journal*, *Newsweek* and
Time—critique it and then question both administration officials and
journalists and news executives about why the coverage turned out the
way it did. Because the Reagan model of news management depended
so heavily on the use of television, and because television increasingly
came to dominate not only Washington journalism but the news business
generally during the Reagan era, the primary focus of the research was
on network news coverage.

The Vanderbilt University Television Archives are the indispensable
tool for researching network coverage. Although located in Nashville,
the archives are subscribed to by various universities around the country;
the author studied them at the George Washington University in Washington, D.C. The archives consist of printed summaries of the three
major networks' evening newscasts dating back to 1976. The order of
stories, their length, their content (visual and verbal), their featured
experts and their remarks and the correspondents who reported them
are all recounted.

With the help of researcher Van Metaxas, the author read through
the archives, beginning in January 1981 and ending in June 1984. The
author himself viewed, recorded and summarized all three network
newscasts on a nightly basis from April 1984 through February 1988.
On the basis of this general survey, specific stories were selected for
closer scrutiny. These stories were chosen either because they covered
events of historic significance (such as the November 1981 announcement of President Reagan's Zero Option nuclear weapons proposal) or
because they seemed to illustrate broader trends within the coverage
(such as the networks' tendency to practice so-called jelly-bean journalism). These specific stories were then viewed and summarized by

Mr. Metaxas, mainly in the Library of Congress in Washington, D.C., which maintains a fairly complete collection of the ABC and CBS newscasts during the Reagan years; copies of the necessary NBC stories were purchased from Vanderbilt and viewed at the Library of Congress as well.

It was important actually to view these stories—rather than simply to read their printed scripts—because most of the message of a TV news story is not in the words that are spoken but in the images that are shown. The first-term stories that were analyzed can be divided into five separate categories: the economy; Central America; nuclear arms; Grenada; and miscellaneous, which includes stories on President Reagan himself, on freedom of information policies and on other relevant issues. A total of 959 television news stories were analyzed closely. On the economy, 136 ABC stories were viewed, 141 CBS and 85 NBC; on Central America, 114 from ABC, 95 from CBS and 94 from NBC; on nuclear arms, 59 from ABC, 64 from CBS and 35 from NBC; on Grenada, 34 from ABC, 40 from CBS and 43 from NBC. Note that these figures do not include stories beginning in April 1984, by which time all three evening newscasts were being watched and analyzed on a daily basis by the author.

The Washington Post and *The New York Times* are the two newspapers whose coverage was most intensively analyzed. The *Post*'s and the *Times*'s own indexes were reviewed in the major subject areas covered in this book for the years 1981 through 1987 in order to obtain a general sense of the tone and direction of each paper's coverage. Specific stories were then selected for closer scrutiny according to the criteria described above. Once research on the book began in earnest in the spring of 1984, the author personally clipped and filed the *Post* and the *Times* on a daily basis as well.

Essentially the same approach was followed in analyzing the coverage offered by *Time* and *Newsweek*, except that the period of time studied was shorter. Every presidential-campaign-related story published in both magazines from July 1983 through November 1984—the duration of the 1984 campaign coverage—was read and analyzed.

Notes

The Orwell quote is found in *As I Please: The Collected Essays, Journalism and Letters of George Orwell*, Volume III, edited by Sonia Orwell and Ian Angus, Harcourt Brace Jovanovich, Inc. (New York: 1968), p. 180.

CHAPTER 1

3   "We have been kinder . . .": Remark made at June 28, 1984, panel discussion sponsored by the American Enterprise Institute in Washington, D.C., titled "Is There a Liberal Media Elite in America?"

3   "all totally subconscious . . .": Author's interview.

3   "Politicians always say . . .": Author's interview.

4   "There were days and times . . .": Author's interview.

4   "to correct the imbalance of power . . .": Author's interview.

4   "Ronald Reagan enjoyed . . .": *Behind the Scenes*, by Michael Deaver, with Mickey Herskowitz, William Morrow (New York: 1987), p. 144.

4   Gallup poll reported in *The New York Times*, January 16, 1987.

4   "I don't know how to explain . . .": Author's interview.

5   "In part it goes back to who he is. . . .": Author's interview.

5   Gergen's remark about "get the right story out" was reported in *Broadcasting*, January 9, 1984.

6   "the ultimate presidential commodity . . .": Author's interview.

6   "There's no question . . .": Author's interview.

6   "The whole thing was PR. . . ." Author's interview.

7   Ferguson and Rogers's documentation was included in Chapter 1 of their book *Right Turn: The Decline of the Democrats and the Future of American Politics*, Hill and Wang (New York: 1986).

7   "worthwhile to institutionalize . . .": Author's interview.

7   "a lot of people going to school . . .": Author's interview.

8   "I can't point my finger . . .": Author's interview.

8   "the Teflon came because . . .": Author's interview.

CHAPTER 2

10   Deaver's cave dwellers story: Author's interview.

11   "Because I could never achieve in athletics . . .": Author's interview.

11   All piano stories: Author's interview.

12   Biographical information on Deaver's early years with Reagan drawn from *Gambling with History: Reagan in the White House*, by Laurence I. Barrett, Doubleday (Garden City, N.Y.: 1983), pp. 259–60.

12   "Reagan became Deaver and Hannaford's meal ticket . . .": *Reagan*, by Lou Cannon, Putnam (New York: 1982), p. 196.

12   "Nobody taught me. . . .": Author's interview.

12   "I never understood . . .": Author's interview.

13   "you probably have a friend . . .": Author's interview.

13   Deaver's Jody Powell story: Author's interview.

14   Story of Gergen's meeting with Ray Price: Author's interview.

14 The biographical information on Ray Price and his strategy memo were reported in *The Selling of the President 1968*, by Joe McGinniss, Pocket Books (New York: 1970).

15 Gergen's 1972 Republican convention story: Author's interview.

15 Those who observed a mellowing of Gergen's views on the press included White House colleagues Robert Meade and Leslie Janka and former CBS News producer Don Bowers. All expressed their views in interviews with the author.

A televised exchange with his old mentor Ray Price during the first month of the Iran-contra scandal illustrated the contrast between Gergen's more evolved view and the embattled paranoia that characterized the Nixon White House's attitude toward the press. Appearing on the December 3, 1986, edition of the *MacNeil-Lehrer Newshour*, Price, once again a newspaper columnist, remained true to the Nixon tradition of blaming the press for the President's problems. Charging that news organizations were blowing the Iran-contra story vastly out of proportion, he sought to brush the scandal away by portraying the entire operation as the doings of misguided middle-level bureaucrats. Invited to comment, Gergen began by emphasizing that he "hate[d] to disagree with Ray Price—a friend, a mentor, the man who first brought me into government." But Gergen refused to join in blaming the messenger. Part of what had made him such an effective media strategist in the Reagan White House was his apparent belief that outright denial of unpleasant truths was self-defeating. It led to self-delusion about the true nature of a developing crisis, and thus prevented the administration from taking the offensive, recasting the issue in a less damaging light and eventually talking its way out of the controversy. The truth could only be finessed if it first was confronted, and the truth, as Gergen pointed out in his reply to Price, was that it was not the press but the government which had sent weapons to Iran and diverted funds to the contras. In fact, added Gergen, in a closing twist that subtly implied Reagan's innocence, the White House would not have learned what was going on in its own government in the first place without help from the press.

15 "I don't think anybody . . .": Author's interview.

16 "All of us came out of the Watergate years . . .": Author's interview.

16 Gergen's "knew would be a cauldron" quote and the related sentiments regarding breaking the string of failed presidencies: Author's interview.

17 The definition of "propaganda" comes from the unabridged edition of *The Random House Dictionary of the English Language*, Random House (New York: 1967).

17 "Television elects Presidents": *The National Journal*, January 28, 1984.

18 "Jim Baker trusted him. . . .": Author's interview.

19 "One of my strongest beliefs . . .": *Washington Journalism Review*, April 1982.

20 Biographical information on Larry Speakes contained in *The Washington Post*, January 5, 1984. *Speaking Out* was published in April 1988 by Charles Scribner's Sons. In it, Speakes wrote that he made up presidential quotations on two occasions: during the 1985 Reagan–Gorbachev summit meeting in Geneva, and after the Korean Air Lines flight 007 was shot down by a Soviet jet in 1983. His $400,000-a-year salary was reported in *The Washington Post*, April 18, 1988.

20 Information on Wirthlin's relationship with Reagan, and on the workings

of his polling system, found in *Hidden Power: The Programming of the President*, by Roland Perry, Beaufort Books (New York: 1984), especially Chapter 17.

21 "If you get numbers back . . .": Author's interview.
21 "Where would you put Dick Darman . . .": Author's interview.
21 "The key to success . . .": Author's interview.
21 "felt it beneath him": Author's interview.
22 "That's what happened to the Carter administration . . .": Author's interview.
22 Biographical information on James Baker: Barrett, op. cit., Chapter 21.
22 "I thought he had the street smarts . . .": Author's interview.
22 "the maestro . . .": Author's interview.
23 "Implementing policy depends on . . .": Author's interview.
23 "The President, Deaver, Baker and those guys . . .": Author's interview. Not everyone in the Reagan White House applauded the emphasis on public relations, however. In *The Triumph of Politics*, David Stockman argued that excessive concern over political fallout kept White House officials from pursuing the radical pruning of the American welfare state implied by Reagan's campaign rhetoric. Stockman had only contempt for "the California crowd." Men like Deaver and Nofziger he ridiculed as political hacks who knew nothing about policy and were interested only in keeping bad news off the tube. It particularly infuriated Stockman that, to men such as Deaver, nothing mattered more than how "the nets" portrayed the President and his policies. The elevation of imagery over substance that so offended ideologue Stockman was symbolized by the fact that policy meetings in James Baker's office were known to be interrupted at 6:30 p.m., when attention shifted from the business at hand to a special multi-screen television set that allowed officials to monitor the three major networks' news shows (besides Cable News Network's continuous news) at once.
23 "total control of the body": Author's interview.
23 For background on Deaver's relationship with Mrs. Reagan, and on Mrs. Reagan's behind-the-scenes power in the White House, see Deaver, op. cit.
24 "One day Dick Powell died . . .": Author's interview.
25 "I saw the toe marks . . .": Author's interview.
25 "It was great television. . . .": *Broadcasting*, January 9, 1984.
25 "a simple truism . . .": Author's interview.
25 "Exactly. Oh, exactly. . . .": Author's interview.
26 "It may sound cynical . . .": Author's interview.
26 "They have managed to create . . .": Author's interview.
26 "You don't tell us how to stage the news . . .": *The Washington Post*, January 5, 1984, as well as personal observation.
27 "They are very good at directing . . .": Author's interview.
27 "This administration, more than any other . . .": Author's interview.
27 "he displays abysmal ignorance . . .": Author's interview.
28 "I will take as much blame . . .": Author's interview.
28 "There was nothing that gave them a better reason . . .": Author's interview.
28 "I didn't have to yell . . .": Author's interview.
29 "While Gergen was there . . .": Author's interview.
29 "I tried to call them back . . .": Author's interview.

29   "called all three major networks . . .": *The National Journal*, January 28, 1984.

29   Gralnick denied: Author's interview.

30   "Gergen would call . . .": Author's interview.

30   Dan Rather's remarks appeared in the November 14, 1983, issue of *The New York Times*.

30   "Gergen made a very conscious effort . . .": Author's interview.

30   "The phone calls more often . . .": Author's interview.

31   "Dan's views were taken . . .": Author's interview.

CHAPTER 3

32   Gergen's remarks about his experience as a naval damage-control officer, about emulating James Hagerty and about the lightning-rod theory: Author's interviews.

33   "If you ask the Reagan people . . .": Author's interview.

34   "Gergen was very much of the mind . . .": Author's interview.

34   "The two things always uppermost . . .": Author's interview.

34   "the big-picture meeting . . .": Author's interview.

34   "may see the smoke . . .": Author's interview.

35   The description of the morning schedule of White House meetings is based on "Communications Reshuffling Intended to Help Reagan Do What He Does Best," by Dick Kirschten, *The National Journal*, January 28, 1984; and on "Presidential Newsmaking," by Juan Williams, *The Washington Post*, February 13, 1983; and was confirmed in interviews with Deaver, Gergen and three other White House officials who regularly attended the meetings.

35   "What are we going to do . . .": Author's interview.

35   "They do do that . . .": Author's interview.

35   "it seems to believe it has a divine right . . .": Author's interview.

35   "Sam never fraternized . . .": Author's interview.

36   "It's to make sure . . .": *The National Journal*, January 28, 1984.

36   Transmission of the line of the day via computer mail and morning conference calls, as well as the weekly policy seminars for administration press officials, were described in interviews with the author by Gergen and Joanna Bistany, among others.

36   "Okay, what do we say about Lebanon . . .": Author's interview.

36   The function of the 9:15 press briefings and the behavior of reporters there were described in numerous interviews with reporters, as well as with Speakes.

37   "How do you get your message out . . .": Author's interview.

37   "You'd bring in eighty or ninety . . .": Author's interview.

38   The many similarities between the news management techniques used by the Nixon and Reagan White Houses were noted in author's interviews with Gergen, Les Janka, Larry Speakes and others who served in both administrations. For fuller descriptions of the workings of the Nixon apparatus, see *Straight Stuff: The Reporters, the White House and the Truth*, by James Deakin, William Morrow (New York: 1984), especially Chapter 9; and also *Presidents and the Press*, by Joseph C. Spear, MIT (Cambridge: 1984).

38   "The difference between Reagan and Carter . . .": Author's interview.

38   "at the [Reagan] White House there is one voice . . .": Author's interview.

39   The differing perspectives of the hard-liners and pragmatists were de-

scribed in author's interviews with Deaver, Gergen, Darman, Bistany and Janka, among others.

39 "Don't get paranoid . . .": "The President and the Press Corps," by John Herbers, *The New York Times Magazine*, May 9, 1982.
39 "I felt you should deal openly . . .": Author's interview.
40 "The only time Jim and I . . .": Author's interview.
40 "That surrogates of the public stuff . . .": Author's interview.
40 "I don't agree with that . . .": Author's interview.
40 Nofziger's "co-opted" accusation: Author's interview.
40 "I never, ever lied . . .": Author's interview.
41 "I remember one Sunday afternoon . . .": Author's interview.
41 "discouraged from talking . . .": Author's interview.
41 The March 11, 1983, Reagan executive order was described that night in the NBC and CBS evening broadcasts, and in the major dailies the following morning.
41 "I still think the greatest mistake . . .": Author's interview.
41 "If you give somebody . . .": Author's interview.
42 "The Democrats would never talk . . .": Author's interview.
42 "but [I] learned during Reagan's . . .": Author's interview.
42 "There is a remarkable lack . . .": Author's interview.
42 "Haldeman didn't like the press . . .": Author's interview.
43 "Frank was loved . . .": Author's interview.
43 "The idea of making the press . . .": Author's interview.
43 "It was a very smart move . . .": Author's interview.
44 Biographical information on Nancy Reynolds and her quoted statements: Author's interview.
44 "I think we were conscious . . .": Author's interview.
44 "In a previous time . . .": Author's interview.
45 "This used to drive me nuts . . .": Author's interview.
45 Dan Rather's theory about presidential news management was reported in "Nixon and the Press," by James R. Dickerson, *National Observer*, October 28, 1972, and cited in Spear, op. cit. For information on Kennedy's private pressures on the press, see *The Powers That Be*, by David Halberstam, Knopf (New York: 1977), and Deakin, op. cit.
46 "sense of humor and smile . . .": *The National Journal*, January 28, 1984.
46 "He's an actor. . . .": Author's interview.
46 "He wasn't well prepared . . .": Author's interview.
47 "A lot of what we've done . . .": Author's interview.
47 "He thinks of the press . . .": Author's interview.
47 "Jimmy Carter you felt sorry for . . .": Author's interview.
47 "I would agree that Reagan has gotten the breaks . . .": Author's interview.
47 "If Jimmy Carter were making these mistakes . . .": quoted in *Ronald Reagan's Reign of Error*, by Mark Green and Gail MacColl, Pantheon (New York: 1983), p. 17.
47 "I don't [think] the White House press apparatus . . .": Author's interview.
48 "One reason we were so good . . .": Author's interview.
48 "90 percent of Reagan's success . . .": Author's interview.
48 The administration's education PR blitz was described in author's interviews with Deaver and Gergen, and in *The Wall Street Journal*, January 5, 1984.
49 "The President himself made . . .": Author's interview.

49 "It used to drive the President crazy . . .": Author's interview.
49 Chris Wallace's story aired on the *NBC Nightly News* on June 9, 1983.
49 Deaver's reaction to Wallace's story and description of the goals of the PR campaign: Author's interview.
50 "It is potentially a very sinister . . .": Author's interview.
50 "This is the only time in history . . .": Author's interview.
51 "Five years ago . . .": Author's interview.
51 "They understand the mechanics . . .": Author's interview.
51 "They had to take what we were . . .": Author's interview.
51 "kind of a mutual back-scratching . . .": Author's interview.
52 "TV becomes a witting . . .": Author's interview.
52 "As opposed to Kissinger . . .": Author's interview.
52 "I think that's true . . .": Author's interview.

CHAPTER 4
54 "If there is anything deficient . . .": Author's interview.
54 "The odds against us . . .": Author's interview.
55 "There are only six or seven . . .": Author's interview.
55 "Anybody else can whistle . . .": Author's interview.
55 "I think by temperament . . .": Author's interview.
56 "What the Reagan White House does . . .": Author's interview.
56 "The reason this can go on . . .": Author's interview.
56 "A lot of reporters recognized . . .": Author's interview.
56 "We aren't consciously sitting around saying . . .": Author's interview. In 1985, however, Sam Donaldson offered a provocative proposal for how the press could flush President Reagan out of his self-imposed isolation from reporters. Addressing a June 4 seminar in Washington sponsored by Ralph Nader's Center for Responsive Law, Donaldson suggested that the major networks (1) not run every possible White House story but only those with "real news" in them; (2) apply the same criterion to the President's speeches to the nation; and (3) make thirty minutes of prime time available every month for a presidential news conference, and if the White House declined to use the time, make it available to a serious alternative voice. The catch, as Donaldson himself acknowledged, was that his proposal was "utopian, because we live in a commercial society."
57 "distortion of the news . . .": Author's interview.
57 "You know, they'd be much better . . .": Author's interview.
58 "What Lou lives for . . .": Author's interview.
58 Lee Lescaze's comments about Lou Cannon: Author's interview.
58 "As all my former and present editors know . . .": Author's interview.
58 "It's hard to avoid the analogy . . .": Author's interview.
59 "So what if you can't get Don . . .": Author's interview.
59 "the most pampered press corps . . .": Author's interview.
59 "There are no whores . . .": Author's interview.
60 Opotowsky's view of Donaldson: Author's interview.
60 The full citation for Donaldson's autobiography is *Hold On, Mr. President!*, by Sam Donaldson, Random House (New York: 1987).
60 Gergen, Deaver, Baker and Darman all expressed the same view about Donaldson's fairness.
61 "you need to be on speaking terms . . .": Author's interview.
61 Elliott Abrams's remarks to the *Columbia Journalism Review* were reported in the September–October 1986 issue.

61 "How do you develop sources . . .": Author's interview.
62 The story of Walter Cronkite's reporting from Vietnam, and of his high regard for Gralnick, were reported in Halberstam, op. cit., pp. 512–14. Gralnick's remark about "in front of the camera or behind it" came in an interview with the author.
62 Gralnick confirmed the dates of his tenure as *World News Tonight* executive producer in an interview with the author; the twelve million nightly audience figure was supplied by Sam Donaldson, on the basis of ABC research.
62 "It's not my job . . .": Author's interview.
63 Lou Cannon's judgment about Reagan's press coverage was confirmed in an interview with the author.
63 "I wouldn't consider talking . . .": Author's interview.
63 "He is either very naïve . . .": Author's interview.
63 *The New York Times* is a very good . . .": Author's interview.
63 " 'Objectivity' contradict[s] . . .": *The Media Monopoly*, by Ben Bagdikian, Beacon Press (Boston: 1983), pp. 181–82.
64 "Despite all the fine talk . . .": Quoted in *Ithaca New Times*, February 29, 1976; cited in *Inventing Reality: The Politics of the Mass Media*, by Michael Parenti, St. Martin's (New York: 1986), pp. 52–53.
64 "Do you lead your newscast . . .": Author's interview.
64 "Even as an objective journalist . . .": Author's interview.
65 "And he ultimately falls back on . . .": Author's interview.
65 "the biggest, most thorough . . .": Author's interview.
65 "Objectivity is fine if it's real. . . .": Author's interview.
66 "What you see are the people . . .": Author's interview.
66 "we really are a transmission belt . . .": Author's interview.
66 "Serving as a stenographer . . .": Author's interview.
67 "more conduit than critic . . .": Author's interview.
67 "In the media at large . . .": Author's interview.
67 "It doesn't ever say this explicitly . . .": Author's interview.
68 Stahl's remarks on *The MacNeil-Lehrer Newshour* aired on February 11, 1987.
68 "It's a little harder for the boys in the White House . . .": Public lecture at the Institute for Policy Studies in Washington, May 20, 1987.
68 "Look at defense . . .": Author's interview.
69 "I don't think the coverage . . .": Author's interview.
70 "To come back from Europe . . .": Author's interview.
70 "As a working journalist . . .": Author's interview.
71 For a comparison of the amount of U.S. press coverage given to dissidents from the Soviet and the U.S. spheres of influence, see *The Real Terror Network: Terrorism in Fact and Propaganda*, by Edward S. Herman, South End Press (Boston: 1982), p. 197.
72 "You're supposed to see El Salvador . . .": Author's interview.
72 The interviews with the two reporters to whom Lagana tried to discredit Parry were conducted by the author.
72 "There is a palpable range . . .": Author's interview.
73 "It isn't very easy . . .": Author's interview.
73 "conveyed Reagan's version of reality . . .": Author's interview.
73 "I have the feeling . . .": Author's interview.
74 The complete text of President Reagan's speech was printed in *The New York Times*, May 10, 1984. Of all the misinformation it contained, the

pious assurance that "we will never be the aggressor" was perhaps the most brazen. The United States had secretly initiated the war against Nicaragua in 1981; for three years, mercenaries financed and directed by the CIA had been attacking Nicaragua from base camps in Honduras and Costa Rica. A mere three weeks before Reagan's speech, it had been discovered that the CIA had mined Nicaraguan harbors, an operation described by conservative Senator Barry Goldwater as an "act of war." Mr. Reagan's charge of a "Communist reign of terror" was equally fallacious. Amnesty International and other human rights organizations had actually given Nicaragua relatively high marks, in marked contrast to the U.S.-supported government in El Salvador (which Reagan praised as having made "great progress toward democracy"), which they had labeled a gross violator of human rights. As for global Communism's alleged plan to subvert the entire Central American region, the administration had never produced evidence of significant arms shipments via Nicaragua to the Salvadoran guerrillas or of the presence of "thousands" of Cuban military advisers in Nicaragua.

75   "it would be very dangerous . . .": Author's interview.
75   "My mission is not to blow . . .": Author's interview.
76   "are members of this class . . .": Author's interview.

CHAPTER 5

77   "freedom of the press . . .": *The Press*, by A. J. Liebling, Pantheon (New York: 1981), p. 32.
77   "The press, myself included . . .": Donaldson, op. cit., p. 238.
77   Pages 20–21 of the 1983 edition of Bagdikian's *Media Monopoly* (previously cited) are the source for all facts regarding the fifty large corporations dominating the news business, their size, interlocking directorates and so forth. His 1987 update was excerpted in the September 1987 issue of *Multinational Monitor*.
78   Information on newspaper chain expansion, sales, revenues, monopoly status, and on network profits: *Columbia Journalism Review*, November–December 1986 (hereafter *CJR*).
78   "I don't know anybody . . .": *Viewpoint*, ABC News, May 6, 1985.
78   "The introduction of mass circulation . . .": Author's interview.
79   *Time* and *Newsweek* covers: *CJR*.
79   *Achille Lauro* story: Author's interview.
79   "No matter what editors say . . .": *CJR*.
80   "They have a less broad interest . . .": Ibid.
80   "Compared to twenty years ago . . .": Author's interview.
80   "The political sensibilities . . .": Author's interview.
80   Anchors' reported salaries: *The Washington Post*, February 9, 1987, except for Peter Jennings's, which was reported in *People* magazine, February 1, 1988. Other salaries: Author's interviews with numerous journalists, including R. W. Apple of *The New York Times*, Thomas Edsall of *The Washington Post*, Robert Chandler of CBS News, Cheryl Gould of NBC News, among others.
81   United States income stratification: *The American Profile Poster*, by Stephen J. Rose, with Dennis Livingston and Kathryn Shagas, Pantheon (New York: 1986).
81   The identities of Tom Dooley and of his creator, turn-of-the-century Chicago newspaperman Finley Peter Dunne, are reported in *The Great Amer-*

ican Video Game, by Martin Schram, William Morrow (New York: 1987), p. 15.

81 "It's not that these guys . . .": Author's interview.
81 "They don't know people . . .": *CJR*.
82 "Oh, why not just tax . . .": Author's interview.
82 The study for the American Society of Newspaper Editors was reported in *The New York Times*, April 12, 1985.
82 David Shaw's survey was published in the *Los Angeles Times*, March 24, 1985.
82 "It's an awful struggle . . .": Author's interview.
82 The actions of the ABC News minority caucus, its arguments to management and the data on black employment at ABC News: Author's interview with George Strait. Richard Wald's response: Author's interview.
83 "Until blacks get in the editorial decision-making . . .": Author's interview.
84 The best summary of the Nixon campaign against the press is in Deakin, op. cit., pp. 284–86.
84 "the complaints aired by the public . . .": *The Washington Post*, August 16, 1981.
85 The full title of the Times Mirror study is "People and the Press." The phrase "a sheep in wolf's clothing" was included, astonishingly, in full-page ads run in major newspapers around the country promoting the study, including *The New York Times*, January 14, 1986.
85 The full citations for the Rothman-Lichters studies are: "Media and Business Elites," by S. Robert Lichter and Stanley Rothman, *Public Opinion*, October–November 1981; and "The Once and Future Journalists," by Linda Lichter, S. Robert Lichter and Stanley Rothman, *Washington Journalism Review*, December 1982. The counter-response by Herbert Gans appeared in the *Columbia Journalism Review*, November–December 1985. The Hess study is cited in Bagdikian 1983, op. cit., p. 58.
86 Information on corporate taxes from "Keep the Bite on Corporations," by Philip M. Stern, *The New York Times*, March 17, 1986.
86 "Clearly, the people who run . . .": Author's interview.
86 "People ask, Do your bosses . . ." and firing story: Donaldson, op. cit., p. 154.
87 "Some intervention . . .": Bagdikian, op. cit., p. 47.
87 The Cronkite article was published in the July–September 1977 issue.
87 "I've heard of cases . . .": Author's interview.
88 "Most newspaper publishers . . .": Deakin, op. cit., p. 28.
88 "It is a rare corporation . . .": Bagdikian, op. cit., p. 21.
89 "As president of the news . . .": Author's interview.
89 The *New York Times* report was published on April 14, 1985.
89 "the publisher was constantly . . .": *My Life and Times*, by Turner Catledge, quoted in *The Whole World Is Watching*, by Todd Gitlin, University of California (Berkeley: 1980), p. 39.
90 "You get to know . . .": Author's interview.
90 "They don't tell you directly . . .": Author's interview.
91 "A good editor . . .": Author's interview.
91 "Reporters and editors, because . . .": Author's interview.
91 The freedom of the press issues raised in the aftermath of the flight 847 story are discussed in "TV, Terrorism and the White House," by Mark Hertsgaard, *American Film*, December 1985.

93   The full citation for Professor Hallin's book is: *The "Uncensored War": The Media and Vietnam*, by Daniel C. Hallin, Oxford University (New York: 1986). See especially pp. 116–18.

95   The networks' choices not to break the Pentagon Papers story are described in Spear, op. cit., p. 175.

96   "Woodward and Bernstein would have died . . .": Author's interview.

96   "The most important new source . . .": quoted in "The Myth of the Adversary Press," by Dan Hallin, *The Quill*, November 1983.

97   Kampelman's article was published in *Policy Review* in 1977. His 1987 remark came in an interview with the author.

97   Katharine Graham's retreat was reported in *CJR*, p. 42.

97   Gergen's remarks were published in *Public Opinion*, December 1981–January 1982.

98   The two best descriptions of Carter's retreat are in Ferguson and Rogers, op. cit., and *Peddlers of Crisis, The Committee on the Present Danger and the Politics of Containment*, by Jerry W. Sanders, South End Press (Boston: 1983).

98   The 1981 defense budget figures were reported in Stockman, op. cit., p. 108.

98   Boylan's article was published in *CJR*.

99   Carter's 1980 aid cuts reported in Ferguson and Rogers, op. cit., p. 111.

99   "I was sitting in the stands . . .": Author's interview. Mr. Rosenthal's response: Author's interview.

99   "quite traumatic for the press . . .": Author's interview.

100   Keith Fuller's speech was delivered in Worcester, Massachusetts, on January 28, 1981.

100   "They're powerful institutions . . .": Author's interview.

CHAPTER 6

101   "there was a consensus . . .": Author's interview.

101   "The return to deference . . .": Author's interview.

102   Again, the best description of the gathering elite consensus of the 1970s is Ferguson and Rogers, op. cit.

102   Three top Reagan campaign foreign policy advisers, including future national security advisers Robert McFarlane and Richard Allen, admitted meeting with a self-proclaimed emissary of Iran in October 1980, but denied making any deal with him. However, the President of Iran at the time, Abolhassan Bani-Sadr, later told *Miami Herald* reporter Alfonso Chardy that two of the Ayatollah Khomeini's closest advisers had indeed arranged with the Reagan campaign to delay release of the hostages until after Reagan was sworn in as President. Moreover, within a month of the Reagan inaugural, Iran began to receive U.S.-made weapons via Israel, reportedly with the acquiescence of the Reagan administration. "I don't know why the timing of the release was so important to the Reagan apparatus," Bani-Sadr told Chardy. "But it seems to me that his aides were trying to prepare the American public psychologically and symbolically for the era of Reaganism." Chardy's story was published by Knight-Ridder on April 12, 1987.

102   Ronald Reagan actually received votes from only 26.7 percent of the total eligible U.S. electorate, according to Curtis B. Gans of the Committee for the Study of the American Electorate in Washington, D.C.

103   "I brought it up in various conversations . . .": Author's interview.

103 Rich Cohen's "jelly-bean journalism" phrase and subsequent remarks: Author's interview.

104 The Reagan finger monster story: Author's interview.

105 Gergen's and Deaver's estimations of the first six months of press coverage: Author's interview.

106 That Reagan's votes in the 1980 election were more anti-Carter than pro-Reagan is suggested by a CBS/*New York Times* poll, conducted from November 7 through 12 and confirmed to the author by John Benson of the Roper Center at the University of Connecticut, the data center and repository for public opinion polling in the United States. When asked by the CBS/*New York Times* surveyors why they voted for Reagan, the single largest category of Reagan voters—21 percent—responded that it was simply "time for a change." Seventeen percent said their votes were "anti-Carter," and another 17 percent cited "the economy." Only 6 percent said they voted for Reagan because they thought he would "do a good job," and a mere 5 percent explained their vote by saying Reagan was the "best candidate."

106 "I always believed that if . . .": Author's interview.

107 "The whole theory . . .": Author's interview.

107 "The key to a successful presidency . . .": Author's interview.

107 "One of the critical . . .": Author's interview.

107 "In 1981 and through . . .": Author's interview.

108 "The linkage between legislative . . .": Author's interview.

108 "The critical element . . .": Author's interview.

108 "A high degree of coordination . . .": Author's interview.

109 "When I looked at what Ronald Reagan . . .": Author's interview.

109 The Haig campaign on El Salvador is described in "Operation El Salvador," by Jonathan Evan Maslow and Ana Arana, *Columbia Journalism Review*, May–June 1981.

110 The two best descriptions of the White Paper campaign are in *Weakness and Deceit: U.S. Policy and El Salvador*, by Raymond Bonner, Times Books (New York: 1984); and *Endless Enemies: The Making of an Unfriendly World*, by Jonathan Kwitney, Penguin (New York: 1986).

111 The description of El Salvador is drawn from Bonner, op. cit.; *Turning the Tide*, by Noam Chomsky, South End Press (Boston: 1985); and Herman, op. cit.

113 "Baker and I tried constantly . . .": Author's interview.

114 White House efforts to downplay the White Paper: *Los Angeles Times*, February 24, 1981.

114 The White House decision to "low-key" El Salvador was described by Gergen in an author's interview.

114 "This is tough for us . . .": Author's interview.

114 "I was personally as well as . . .": Author's interview.

115 The numerical breakdown of network El Salvador stories is reported in "Television and Crisis: Ten Years of Network News Coverage of Central America, 1972–1981," by Emile G. McAnany, *Media, Culture, & Society*, April 1983; summarized in *Columbia Journalism Review*, November–December 1983.

115 "I was very worried . . .": Author's interview.

116 "gave us a second life . . .": Author's interview.

116 "saw a side of him . . .": Author's interview.

116 "There is a theory out there . . .": Author's interview.

116   Donaldson's *Playboy* interview was published in June.

116   "the March shooting . . .": Author's interview.

117   "was framing the question . . .": Stockman, op. cit., p. 174.

117   The Blair House group's endorsement is reported in *The Permanent Campaign*, by Sidney Blumenthal, Touchstone (New York: 1982), Chapter 15.

118   "Most reporters thought the 1980 vote . . .": Author's interview.

119   "one of the times it worked . . .": Author's interview.

120   "a staggeringly dumb political blunder": Stockman, op. cit., p. 218.

120   "Congress called [the vote] . . .": Author's interview.

120   "Within 24 hours . . .": Blumenthal, op. cit., p. 295.

122   "pretty much dictated . . .": Stockman, op. cit., p. 226.

122   "had to have come . . .": Stockman, op. cit., p. 307–8.

122   "a kind of supply-side . . .": Stockman, op. cit., pp. 156, 249.

122   "the Lemming Principle . . .": Author's interview. Lou Cannon confirmed the process described by Anderson in an interview with the author.

123   "a print guy could . . .": Author's interview.

123   Press coverage of the Federal Reserve Bank is decribed in "Club Fed," by Mark Hertsgaard, *Columbia Journalism Review*, May 1988, a review of *Secrets of the Temple: How the Federal Reserve Runs the Country*, by William Greider, Simon & Schuster (New York: 1988).

123   "They focused the press . . .": Author's interview.

124   "This was a program . . .": Author's interview.

125   "Cares about people" as a Reagan negative: Author's interview with Deaver.

125   "Reporters armed with their . . .": Author's interview.

126   "When you've got a good story . . .": Author's interview.

127   The bookkeeping trick is described in Stockman, op. cit., pp. 105–9. Candidate Reagan, Stockman recalled, had called for a 5 percent annual spending increase (in "real," non-inflated dollars) in President Carter's defense budget; Reagan campaign hawks had advocated 9 percent. At a crucial January 30, 1981, meeting among Stockman, Weinberger and Carlucci, a compromise of 7 percent was agreed upon. The sleight of hand came when Carlucci proposed that the 7 percent growth begin with the 1982 budget. Stockman wrote that he accepted the proposal because, having been up since 4:30 that morning after working eighteen-hour days for weeks, he "wasn't listening very well" by the time of the 7:30 p.m. meeting. The catch, as Stockman discovered a few days later, was that the 1982 budget was a whopping $80 billion larger than the 1980 Carter budget that Reagan and his advisers had railed against. In Stockman's words: "We had taken an already-raised defense budget and raised that by 7 percent. Instead of starting from a defense budget of $142 billion, we'd started with one of $222 billion."

127   "There's a symbiotic relationship . . .": Author's interview.

129   The $75,000 per year income calculation is included in *The New Politics of Inequality*, by Thomas Byrne Edsall, Norton (New York: 1984), pp. 204–7.

129   The corporate tax changes are noted in Ferguson and Rogers, op. cit., pp. 122–23.

129   "the hogs were really feeding . . .": "The Education of David Stockman," by William Greider, *The Atlantic Monthly*, December 1981.

129   "The tax bill wasn't challenged . . .": Author's interview.

130   "What it really comes down to . . .": Author's interview.

130 "it's not being anti-Reagan . . .": Author's interview.
130 "It was pretty well known . . .": Author's interview.
131 "They didn't *need* us": Author's interview.
131 Donaldson expressed his regrets in his *Playboy* interview, June 1982.
131 "The real issues . . .": Stockman, op. cit., p. 177.

CHAPTER 7
132 King of the Hill: Author's interview.
132 "The whole theory going in . . .": Author's interview.
132 "he was so far up . . .": Author's interview.
132 The original July date for the Gulf of Sidra action is reported in Barrett, op. cit., p. 212.
133 "And the White House [had] . . .": Author's interview.
133 "how in charge he really is . . .": Author's interview.
133 "a lot of the story was budget cuts . . .": Author's interview.
133 The stock-market decline was reported on the *CBS Evening News*, September 25, 1981.
133 Reagan made his remark about the Soviets at his January 29, 1981, press conference.
134 Reagan's remark about limited nuclear war was delivered at the White House on October 17, 1981.
134 "It was late that year . . .": Author's interview.
135 "It is very easy . . .": Author's interview.
135 Mr. Perfect: Author's interviews.
136 "bold, especially for a mainstream . . .": Author's interview. The *Time* story was published on December 13, 1982. Smith later stunned colleagues by accepting an offer to become the number three editor at archrival *Newsweek* in 1986.
137 *Newsweek*'s "disengaged" reference was in the September 7, 1981, issue. Trillin's satire was published in *The Nation*, March 10, 1984.
137 Brian Healy's remark about "liar": Author's interview.
138 "More disquieting than Reagan's performance . . .": *The Washington Post*, January 20, 1982.

The impression that Reagan knew little about his own policies was strengthened by his performance on the Bob Jones University case. On January 8, the Justice Department had announced that it would intercede in a court case to obtain tax-exempt status for both Bob Jones, which expelled students for interracial dating or marriage, and the Goldsboro Christian Schools, which barred blacks on the grounds that God had separated the races. If successful, the Justice Department initiative would have meant tax breaks for some one hundred additional institutions as well, and quite likely would have encouraged formation of countless other racist schools. It was a position that had been endorsed in the 1980 Republican party platform, but it flew in the face of a 1971 Supreme Court ruling which the Justice Department had faithfully upheld throughout the Nixon, Ford and Carter administrations and in essense amounted to advocating a federal subsidy for racially discriminatory schools, according to Ronnie Dugger in *On Reagan: The Man and His Presidency*, McGraw-Hill (New York: 1983), pp. 212–14.

Liberals, blacks and other minorities had long doubted Reagan's commitment to civil rights, and this move only confirmed their suspicions. The Justice announcement came on a Friday; the storm of protest gathered and grew over the weekend; by Monday, Deaver was convinced that something had to be done. "He was listening to the lawyers, the Justice Department and Meese," Deaver recalled of Reagan in an interview with the author, "and constitutionally what he was saying was right. From a human standpoint, it was wrong." Deaver quickly moved to protect Reagan from the consequences of his own ideology by appealing to his friend on that same human level. Knowing that Reagan worked alone in the Oval Office every morning between 9:30 and 10 a.m., Deaver "got three blacks who worked in the White House into my office . . . and I said, 'I want you to level with him. Tell him how a black feels about this.' And *they were tough*. And *emotional*. One guy told a story about being in church that Sunday when the minister prayed against that devil Reagan. And Reagan called the lawyers in and changed his position."

(On p. 416 of *Gambling with History*, Barrett quoted one of the black officials, Thaddeus A. Garrett, Jr., of Vice President Bush's staff, telling a different but no more flattering story. Garrett's minister had apparently told the parable of a woman who finds and nurses back to health an injured snake, only to be repaid for her kindness by having the snake bite her. "Reagan," the preacher thundered to his flock, "is that snake!")

139 Reagan's remark about trees and air pollution was reported in *Sierra*, September 10, 1980, and cited in Green and MacColl, op. cit., p. 99.

139 Anthony Lewis's column was published in *The New York Times* on February 21, 1982.

139 "I was deeply worried . . .": Author's interview.

140 Reagan's January 12 executive order was reported in the *Washington Journalism Review*, April 1982, p. 37.

140 "but I thought it might be a way . . .": Author's interview.

141 Deaver described his and Baker's effort to dissuade the President in an interview with the author; the intimidating effect on other administration officials was reported in the *Washington Journalism Review*, April 1982.

141 "insulting to bring in a head of state . . .": Author's interview.

141 "It was an attempt to stop . . .": Author's interview.

141 Donaldson related the story of the Deaver rule confrontation in his *Playboy* interview, June 1983.

142 "We expected there to be . . .": Author's interview.

142 "It couldn't last forever . . .": Author's interview.

142 NBC's McFarland's confirmation that ABC and CBS had wanted to continue to boycott came in an interview with the author.

143 "it would have been easier . . .": Author's interview.

143 "not only blinked [first] . . .": Author's interview.

143 "it's their White House . . .": Author's interview.

144 "The situation we've gotten . . .": Quoted in "The White House Press Takes a Stand," by Mark Hertsgaard, *Columbia Journalism Review*, January–February 1986.

144 Clifford's "amiable dunce" phrase is quoted in Donaldson, op. cit., p. 90.

144 Reagan's slumberous activities in Europe and the incident at the Chicago school were described in "The President as Comic-Kaze," by Curtis Wilkie, *Playboy*, June 1983.

144 "I've had my problems with Larry . . .": Author's interview.

145 "We finally just decided . . .": Author's interview.

145 "The President has a honeymoon . . .": Author's interview.

146 "for about six weeks . . .": Author's interview.

146 "Meese used to go in . . .": Author's interview.
147 "We tried to control it . . .": Author's interview.
147 "A lot of people . . .": Author's interview.
147 "If all that was true . . .": Author's interview.
147 "I think we got past . . .": Author's interview.
147 "It is very obvious . . .": Author's interview.
148 "I used to spend a lot of time . . .": Author's interview.
148 "I think everybody in the press . . .": Author's interview.
149 "I think people buy the philosophy . . .": Author's interview.
149 "People don't care. . . .": Author's interview.
149 "Ronald Reagan is the first . . .": *The New York Times*, November 7, 1982.
149 "the kind of mistakes . . .": Author's interview.
150 "They do show Reagan . . .": Author's interview.
150 "It may be accurate . . .": Author's interview.
150 Jaroslovsky's story was published in *The Wall Street Journal* on January 5, 1984.
151 "They [in the White House] have now got us . . .": Author's interview.

CHAPTER 8
152 "The most important thing . . .": Author's interview.
152 Reagan's January 1983 poll ratings: Data supplied by Richard Wirthlin.
152 "Baker, Deaver and Wirthlin . . .": Author's interview.
152 Ferguson and Rogers, op. cit., pp. 24–26.
153 "A look at press coverage . . .": "The Myth of the Great Communicator," by Elliot King and Michael Schudson, *Columbia Journalism Review*, November–December 1987.
153 "I remember going to meetings . . .": Author's interview.
154 "from the very first . . .": Author's interview.
154 "The process of the presidency . . .": Author's interview.
155 "No, it wasn't damage control. . . .": Author's interview.
155 "One would think . . .": Author's interview. Stockman's own recounting of the woodshed metaphor is found on pp. 1–8 of his memoirs.
156 Broder's column, "The Dishonor of David Stockman," was published in *The Washington Post* on April 16, 1986.
156 George Will's remark was reported in the Baltimore *Sun*, April 27, 1986, p. 6H.
157 "The fairness issue was . . .": Author's interview.
157 "inevitably we had to go ahead . . .": Author's interview.
157 Chancellor's "a budget for the rich" was from the February 8, 1982, broadcast of the *NBC Nightly News*. CBS and ABC analyzed the new budget proposals the same evening.
158 The date, subject and purpose of the February 5 Camp David meeting were described by Deaver in an interview with the author.
158 "a structured way for people to say . . .": Reported in *The Washington Post*, May 9, 1987.
158 Mrs. Reagan's appearance at the 1982 Gridiron dinner and the White House enlistment of a writer for her are reported in Barrett, op. cit., pp. 475–76.
159 The Phoenix House story was related in an interview with the author.
159 "it suddenly became clear . . .": Author's interview.
159 Deaver's switching of Blair House meetings: Author's interview.

160 "His personal popularity . . .": Author's interview.

160 "there was a sense we were spinning . . .": Author's interview.

160 "the Baker group, the pragmatists . . .": Author's interview.

160 "I would say '82 . . .": Author's interview.

161 The description of Gergen's counterattack on the fairness issue is based on "Reagan Seeks a New and Improved Image, But It May Not Play in South Succotash," by Dick Kirschten, *The National Journal*, April 17, 1982, and on author's interview.

161 "Frankly, we thought if we asked . . .": Author's interview.

162 "we made a decision . . .": Author's interview.

162 "I know Darman thought . . .": Author's interview.

162 "there was a sense in the air . . .": Author's interview.

162 Gergen shared his views of CBS's and Lesley Stahl's coverage in an interview with the author.

163 "Well, all that happened . . .": Telephone conversation with the author.

163 "The managers of CBS News . . .": Author's interview.

164 "He said, you know . . .": Author's interview.

164 "There was real tension . . .": Author's interview.

164 "Tension between some in the Washington bureau . . .": Letter to the author.

164 "I don't know of any journalist . . .": Author's interview.

165 The description of Howard Stringer is based on "The Troubled Times of Howard Stringer," by Eric Mink, *Washington Journalism Review*, September 1986; "CBS News in Search of Itself," by Peter J. Boyer, *The New York Times Magazine*, December 28, 1986; and author's interviews with CBS sources.

165 "made him sound about four thousand times . . .": Author's interview.

165 "It was very direct . . .": Author's interview.

165 "They'd troop in . . .": Author's interview.

165 "Van started a marking system . . .": Author's interview.

166 "We had discussions . . .": Author's interview.

166 "When you're talking about changing . . .": Author's interview.

166 "No one said to me . . .": Author's interview.

166 "There was a particular feeling . . .": Author's interview.

167 Rather's question came during President Reagan's December 3 interview session with the four network anchors; a transcript was published the next day in *The Washington Post*.

168 "There came a point . . .": Author's interview.

168 "manifested itself in the editing . . .": Author's interview.

168 "Howard felt we had a knee-jerk need . . .": Author's interview.

169 The article by Fred Barnes, "Network Coverage of the Recession," was published in the *Washington Journalism Review*, June 1982.

170 "We were trying in our coverage . . .": Author's interview.

170 "There is that line . . .": Author's interview.

171 Baker denied ever discussing: Author's interview.

171 "I wasn't aware that much . . .": Author's interview.

171 The money figures for CBS: *The Evening Stars: The Making of the Network News Anchor*, by Barbara Matusow, Houghton Mifflin (Boston: 1983), pp. 37, 265.

172 Mr. Sauter's job history was reported in "CBS: Sauterizing the News," by Michael Massing, *Columbia Journalism Review*, March–April 1986 (hereafter *CJR*) and confirmed in an interview with the author.

172   "to go to one cocktail . . .": Author's interview. Sauter, in an interview with the author, initially denied having played hooky. When confronted with Herford's firsthand contradictory account, however, he backed down slightly, conceding he had in fact "tagged a day or two" of fishing onto the front or back end of the occasional meeting. But he claimed—again falsely, according to Herford—that these were company, not affiliate, meetings.

173   The description of Edward Joyce is based on interviews with various CBS sources. Mr. Joyce's refusal to be interviewed prevented obtaining his response.

173   Mr. Herford's description of the Sauter-Joyce team was confirmed by numerous CBS sources in interviews with the author.

173   "Van is essentially an amoral . . .": Author's interview.

173   The best description of the revamping of the CBS evening broadcast is by Massing, *CJR*.

174   "a national agenda . . .": *CJR*. In an interview with the author, Mr. Sauter stressed that setting such an agenda should not be the *intention* of those broadcasts; rather, this was simply an undeniable consequence of their reach and power.

174   "social bio-engineering . . .": Author's interview.

174   "There were periods when I thought . . .": *Newsweek*, September 15, 1986.

175   "Ratings became part . . .": Author's interview.

175   "They don't have to go to a meeting . . .": Author's interview.

175   A useful description of Murdoch's entrance to New York journalism is found in *Arrogant Aussie: The Rupert Murdoch Story*, by Michael Leapman, Lyle Stuart (Secaucus, N.J.: 1985).

176   The facts concerning Sauter's work at KTTV were confirmed in an interview with the author.

176   The 150 weeks figure and related information were provided by the CBS research department.

176   "The values transformation . . .": Author's interview.

176   "All the things that happened . . .": Author's interview. The biographical information on Mr. Frank was reported in the *Columbia Journalism Review*, November–December 1986, pp. 53–55.

177   Mr. Grossman's authorship of the United Negro College Fund slogan was reported privately by a former close associate and confirmed by an NBC public affairs spokesperson. The other biographical information, as well as Tinker's quoted admission, is found in "Larry Grossman's Program for NBC News," by Eric Mink, *Washington Journalism Review*, May 1985.

178   "There was a significant . . .": Author's interview.

178   "there was a bigger fix . . .": Author's interview.

178   "Under the . . . Salant administration . . .": Author's interview.

179   The White House and Sauter denials: Author's interviews.

179   The actions of the FCC were reported in Dugger, op. cit., pp. 149–51, and confirmed in interviews with FCC officials.

179   The 87 percent figure was reported in *The New York Times*, September 12, 1986. The 75.6 percent figure was reported in *The Washington Post*, April 24, 1987.

180   "there was a sense . . .": Author's interview.

180   Chairman Fowler's background was reported in *The Washington Post*, July 21, 1985.

180 "a philanthropy . . .": Author's interview.
180 The discussion of the networks' relationship to the FCC is informed by *News from Nowhere: Television and the News*, by Edward Jay Epstein, Random House (New York: 1973).
180 "pull the plug": *The Washington Post*, July 21, 1985.
180 "News isn't the main business . . .": Author's interview.
181 "I can remember . . .": Author's interview.
181 The figures on documentary programming are based on author's interviews and on a story in the December 5, 1985, *New York Times*.
181 Discussion of the 1934 Communications Act is based on Epstein, op. cit., especially p. 48.
181 Russell described Fowler's 7-7-7 activities in an interview with the author.
182 Discussion of the network-affiliate relationship is based on author's interviews with numerous network officials.
182 The Nixon White House's relationship to *The Washington Post* is described in Halberstam, op. cit., especially pp. 646, 661.
183 Gergen's characterization of CBS News came in an interview with the author.

CHAPTER 9
184 Reagan's Vietnam statement is reported in Cannon, op. cit., p. 271. His Soviet Union statement is noted in Dugger, op. cit., p. 396.
184 The conclusions of Wirthlin's polling data were described by Wirthlin and Deaver in interviews with the author.
185 "I spent a couple of years . . .": Author's interview.
186 The March 1981 date is reported in the best summary of U.S. policy toward Nicaragua in the Reagan era, *Nicaragua: The Price of Intervention*, by Peter Kornbluh, edited by Shoon Murray, Institute for Policy Studies (Washington: 1987).
187 Biographical information on Raymond Bonner: Bonner, op. cit., and author's interviews.
187 "pulled the string . . .": Author's interview.
188 "there was no competition . . .": Author's interview.
190 Bonner's FOIA findings are reported in Bonner, op. cit., pp. 337–64.
190 Herbert Matthews told his own story in *The Cuban Story*, George Braziller (New York: 1961).
191 "we've got to take extra care . . .": Author's interview.
191 Bonner's regret was expressed in Bonner, op. cit., pp. 316–17.
191 "There was more latitude . . .": Author's interview.
192 Regarding television's reporting on the March 28 elections, the Threlkeld quotes were independently discovered; those of Rather, Reynolds, Sheppard and Brown were originally reported in "The Media Go to War," *NACLA Report on the Americas*, July–August 1983, especially pp. 11–15, and independently confirmed.
193 "To get the stories . . .": Author's interview.
193 The National Federation of Lawyers' position was reported in Bonner, op. cit., p. 291.
193 Ambassador Hinton's solution was reported in Bonner, op. cit., p. 298.
195 "feel clean about our handling . . .": Author's interview.
195 The effect of the air war on the Salvadoran peasantry was documented and reported by various church and human rights groups and Western European newspapers, cited in Chomsky, op. cit., pp. 21, 122–23.

196 "We didn't do well . . .": Author's interview.
196 Details of Bonner's recall and departure dates from *The New York Times*: Author's interview with Bonner.
196 "I've had other Central America reporters . . .": Author's interview.
197 Michael Massing's article on El Salvador, "About-face on El Salvador," was published in the November–December 1983 issue.
197 Waghelstein's wishes were reported in Bonner, op. cit., p. 316.
197 "He was not brought back . . .": Author's interview.
197 "wasn't yanked back and punished . . .": Author's interview.
197 *Without Fear or Favor: An Uncompromising Look at The New York Times*, by Harrison Salisbury, Times Books (New York: 1980), p. 93.
198 "What I believed . . ." and subsequent Rosenthal quotes: Author's interviews.
200 Rosenthal's April 1982 trip was reported in Massing's November–December 1983 *Columbia Journalism Review* story.
200 "The way the top . . .": Author's interview.
200 The best article on the rightward drift of the *Times* under Rosenthal is "Fear and Favor at 'The New York Times,' " by Pete Hamill, *The Village Voice*, October 1, 1985. The rise and fall of Claire Sterling's thesis is described in *The Rise and Fall of the Bulgarian Connection*, by Edward E. Herman and Frank Brodhead, Sheridan Square (New York: 1986).
202 "I always say, very lawyerlike . . .": Author's interview.
202 "It did. Not intentionally. . . .": Author's interview.
203 "I think a lot of the Teflon . . .": Author's interview.
204 Gergen's blessing from Baker was described in an author's interview with Gergen.

CHAPTER 10
205 The airport stakeout story is based on author's interviews with Sakson and Potter.
206 "We had pictures . . .": Author's interview.
207 "The desk called me . . .": Author's interview.
207 ABC's errors regarding Franco and Brady were recalled in author's interviews with various ABC sources.
207 "He was very concerned . . .": Author's interview. Although Frye was often criticized by colleagues for an alleged inability to make the snap decisions demanded in daily television journalism, the available evidence suggests that the lateness of the hour was not what kept him from broadcasting the pictures of U.S. military forces on their way to Grenada. Moreover, whatever one thought of his management style, it was simply inaccurate to claim that Frye was incapable of quick and decisive news judgments. When the Reagan administration in February 1984 suddenly reversed policy and ordered the withdrawal of U.S. troops from Lebanon, for example, it sought to lessen negative public relations fallout by not announcing the order until 6:15 eastern standard time, a scant fifteen minutes before the network's evening newscasts. Nevertheless, Frye elected to lead his broadcast with the Lebanon news, something neither of his counterparts at CBS or NBC did.
208 "They said that was wrong . . ." and subsequent quotes from Potter and Sakson: Author's interviews. Potter and Sakson took the unusual step of sending a telex to New York in order to be on record with their information. "I could just foresee a situation like had happened before," said

Sakson, "where the next day there'd be an invasion and Roone Arledge would say, 'Why didn't we have this?' And what they all tend to do in New York is run for cover and say our man in the field didn't push this to us strongly enough." The telex, dispatched at 8:45 p.m., read in part: "We are told we may see evacuation today [Tuesday] of Americans from Grenada. Embassy says marines and three helicopters we taped yesterday will carry out operation. . . . Embassy denies report that marines joining task force headed for Lebanon."

208   Kennedy administration pressure on the *Times* on the Bay of Pigs story is recounted in Salisbury, op. cit.

208   Frye's denial of contacting superiors: Author's interview.

209   "If McWethy gets a wave-off . . .": Author's interview.

209   "I took the line on Grenada . . .": Author's interview.

210   "clearly snookered": Author's interview.

210   The October 20 go-ahead from Washington and the OECS decision were reported in "In Wake of Invasion, Much Official Misinformation by U.S. Comes to Light," by Stuart Taylor, Jr., *The New York Times*, November 6, 1983.

211   "there were a lot of discussions . . .": Author's interview.

211   "it was obvious to me . . .": Author's interview.

212   "they didn't have to watch . . .": Author's interview.

212   "a profound impact . . .": Author's interview.

212   The figures on public opinion regarding Reagan's handling of foreign policy were confirmed by John Benson of the Roper Center. (See Chapter 6 footnote regarding 1980 election totals.)

213   "I was personally told . . .": Author's interview.

214   The back-and-forth among White House press officials and reporters is based on author's interviews with the interested parties.

214   "He said that report . . .": Author's interview.

214   "I had Mike Putzel . . .": Author's interview.

214   "I never, ever ordered . . .": Author's interview.

214   "not that big a surprise . . .": Author's interview.

214   Knight-Ridder reported on October 27, 1983, that the ruling Revolutionary Military Council of Grenada had cabled the U.S. embassy in Barbados more than twenty-four hours before the landing that it believed an invasion was about to be launched. For additional information on happenings in the Caribbean and Castro's pre-invasion actions, see *Grenada: An Eyewitness Account of the U.S. Invasion and the Caribbean History That Provoked It*, by Hugh O'Shaughnessy, Dodd, Mead (New York: 1985).

215   The description of the six o'clock breakfast meeting is based on interviews with Speakes, Janka, Gergen, Deaver and Baker. When Les Janka pressed Baker about why even he and the other spokesmen had been told nothing in advance, the meeting turned nasty as Baker, renowned in official Washington as the consummate gentleman, the epitome of aplomb, lost his temper. "I said to Baker, 'I want to know why we were kept out of the planning for this, and why you told people we had to be kept out of the congressional briefing even last night,' " recalled Janka. "And Baker just exploded at me: 'I want to know who told you that! Who told you that?' I said, 'I just know it, and I want to know why.' And he shouted back at me again, really shouted, 'Whoever told you that is a goddamn liar, and I want to know it. If you won't tell me, then you're a goddamn liar.' " Baker declined to comment on Janka's recollection.

215   "If you've got an invasion . . .": Author's interview.

216   "Later that morning I was . . .": Author's interview.

216   The description of the White House press conference is based on a transcript of the conference and on author's interviews.

216   "I worked through Watergate . . .": Author's interview. Larry Speakes insisted in an interview with the author that it was he who fired Janka, not Janka who resigned.

216   Government secrecy was apparently not one of the story angles discussed at a special editorial meeting ABC News president Arledge called and chaired in his office at 10:30 a.m. the morning of the invasion. Joining Arledge to plot ABC's coverage, according to author's interviews, were David Burke, Richard Wald, Robert Frye, chief of correspondents Robert Murphy and his deputies John Terenzio and Walter Porges, and vice president Steven Tello. Arledge's chief concern was apparently that ABC did not have one of its big-name correspondents on the scene to cover the story. Informed that Richard Threlkeld was presently in Lebanon covering *that* major story, Arledge is said to have snapped, "Dammit, let's get him a Lear jet then, let's get him in there!" Repeated attempts to interview Mr. Arledge were rebuffed.

218   Watson's and Burke's astonishment were expressed in author's interviews.

219   A copy of Ed Fouhy's telegram was provided to the author by George Watson.

219   The November 2 congressional testimony of Brinkley et al. was reported on the *NBC Nightly News*. The ANPA statement was issued on October 27, 1983.

220   "Oh yeah. We raised . . .": Author's interview.

220   "We should have done more . . .": Author's interview.

220   "got an interesting response . . .": Author's interview.

220   The *Los Angeles Times* poll was reported on November 20, 1983. The Harris poll was reported in *Time*, February 27, 1984.

221   Walter Karp's article was titled "Liberty Under Siege."

222   The description of executive order 12356 is based on *The New Yorker*, October 5, 1987.

222   Jack Nelson provided a copy of his speech to the author.

222   The Reporters Committee report was entitled "The Reagan Administration and the News Media" and was provided to the author by the Committee.

223   The description of the Morison case is based primarily on Karp's *Harper's* article; on "Leakers Beware," by Tom Wicker, *The New York Times*, December 6, 1985; on "Public Scrutiny Suffers a Setback," by Walter Karp, *The New York Times*, October 26, 1985; on "Can the CIA Spook the Press?" by Jay Peterzell, *Columbia Journalism Review*, September–October 1986; and on "The Administration's Long Knives and the Hazards of Nationalism," by Ronnie Dugger, *Deadline*, September–October 1986.

225   "There wasn't even lip service . . .": Author's interview.

225   The space shuttle controversy is described in Karp's *Harper's* article. The story of the TWA flight 847 aftermath is told in more detail in "TV, Terrorism and the White House," by Mark Hertsgaard, *American Film*, December 1985.

226   The Posner and Pelton incidents are best described in Dugger's *Deadline* article.

227   "I didn't. If the invasion . . .": Author's interview.
227   White House hopes for "Students Rescued" stories were revealed by Les Janka in an interview with the author.
230   The dates of John Chancellor's tenure at the Voice of America were confirmed by a VOA spokesperson.
230   ABC's March stories on Grenada were reported—ironically, in light of subsequent events—by Mark Potter, the first on March 25 and the second on March 28.
232   The best single piece of dissenting reporting in the mainstream press about Grenada was Stuart Taylor, Jr.'s November 6 article in *The New York Times* (see above). The *Times* editorial, "The Grenada High," was published on November 2, 1983.
233   "They realize that first impressions . . .": Author's interview.
233   "Most of the inaccurate . . .": Author's interview.
234   McWethy's nickname was revealed in author's interviews with other ABC sources. McWethy himself described various FBI and other official investigations of his stories in an interview with the author.
234   "If you are a government . . .": Author's interview.
235   The record number of combat deaths was reported by James Wooten on ABC's *World News Tonight*, October 28, 1983.
235   The CBS fights over Stahl's spot were described in interviews with the author.
236   Gergen's initial explanation was offered in numerous news reports and in an interview with the author; his 1986 admission of additional factors came in an interview with the author.
236   Gergen's article was published in the *Post* on February 19, 1984. The subsequent interview was with the author.

CHAPTER 11

238   "We started off with what . . .": Author's interview.
239   Deaver confirmed he was "pleased" in an interview with the author.
239   Beckel described the "question-free zone" in an interview with the author.
239   "Carter was hostage . . .": Author's interview.
240   "I think we had a potential . . .": Author's interview.
240   "We correctly saw . . .": Author's interview.
240   The biographical information on, and quotes from, John Sears: Author's interview.
241   "I expected, as I think . . .": Author's interview.
241   The 49 percent Mondale vote, the less than 90,000 caucus participants and the Hart and McGovern figures were reported in *The New York Times*, February 22, 1984.
242   "The fact is, there was . . .": Author's interview.
242   "If Walter Mondale had done . . .": Author's interview.
242   "We knew throughout . . .": Author's interview.
243   "People care about issues . . .": Author's interview.
243   "I happen to think . . .": Author's interview.
243   "It wasn't that kind of an . . .": Author's interview.
243   "a huge internal argument . . .": Author's interview.
244   "Once the [election] process . . .": Author's interview.
244   "People say that issues . . .": Author's interview.
244   The figures on the poll differentials were provided by Mondale campaign chairman James Johnson.

245 "has begun to decline . . .": The complete transcript of the debate was published in *The Presidential Election Show: Campaign '84 and Beyond on the Nightly News*, by Keith Blume, Bergin & Garvey (South Hadley, Mass.: 1985). See p. 265.

246 "The point is . . .": Author's interview.

246 The *Wall Street Journal* article was published on October 9, 1984. Its background and development were described by Rich Jaroslovsky in an interview with the author. Once the article was published, said Jaroslovsky, "the other journalists [in town] were glad somebody said it, so they could say it themselves. The networks that night [Tuesday] were able to present the story not as we, ABC, are questioning the President's age, but *The Wall Street Journal* did. I was amused at how it got picked up. I had lots of people come up later and say, 'Thank God you guys said something.' "

248 "The media played the dominant . . .": Author's interview.

248 "I'll agree that Reagan . . .": Author's interview.

249 "It was apparent . . .": Author's interview.

249 "If you go back and listen . . .": Author's interview.

249 "Did we contribute . . .": Author's interview.

249 "Do polls affect the outcome . . .": Author's interview.

249 "Yeah, that's absolutely true. . . .": Author's interview.

250 "Sure, I think that's pretty . . .": Author's interview.

250 "If Mondale had staked out . . .": Author's interview.

251 "they came running into my . . .": Author's interview.

252 Reagan's Fourth of July activities are reported in Schram, op. cit., Chapter 2.

252 Deaver's affection for the Normandy pictures was expressed in an interview with the author.

253 White House reporters' complaints about Secret Service interference were reported in the *Washington Journalism Review*, March 1985. The inability of reporters to question him at the games for the disabled and the Eastern Shore incident were reported in "At Home: The Candidate, Packaged and Protected," by David Hoffman, *Washington Journalism Review*, September 1984.

253 "The Mondale people . . .": Author's interview.

254 "We didn't get our message . . .": Author's interview.

254 "Because they controlled their . . .": Author's interview.

254 "because he was available . . .": Author's interview.

254 "softer on Reagan . . .": Author's interview.

254 "Yes, the press coverage . . .": Author's interview.

254 "been trained by the White House . . .": Author's interview.

255 "The mechanics of every . . .": Author's interview.

255 The comparison of Labor Day coverage was informed by Schram, op. cit., and independently confirmed.

256 "The fact is, that's what . . .": Author's interview.

256 "wrote about it and wrote . . .": Author's interview.

257 "To lead the broadcast . . .": Author's interview.

257 "If the major networks . . .": Author's interview.

258 "What the press conveyed . . .": Author's interview.

258 "The press covering Reagan . . .": Author's interview.

259 "The press wanted to be seen . . .": Author's interview.

259 "The guy smiles a lot . . .": Author's interview.

259 *Newsweek*'s "How Good a President?" issue was published on August 27.

260 "I think he got some good . . .": Author's interview.

260 "I think Reagan got away with murder. . . .": Author's interview.

260 "didn't let us be as tough . . .": Author's interview.

261 "the press wasn't interested . . .": Author's interview.

262 The "jackasses" remark got coverage in *The New York Times*, the *Los Angeles Times* and *The Washington Post* for two days and then disappeared; the story lasted three nights on the evening newscasts of ABC, CBS and NBC.

262 "talked about the jackasses thing . . .": Author's interview.

262 "Forty-five percent of the country . . .": Author's interview.

262 "a Goldwaterism like . . .": Author's interview.

262 Wirthlin's poll findings were reported in *The Quest for the Presidency*, by Peter Goldman and Tony Fuller, Bantam Books (New York: 1985), p. 261.

262 "Day One is when . . .": Author's interview.

263 "it's not done in public! . . .": Author's interview.

263 Mark Dowie's *Mother Jones* article was published in November–December 1985.

264 "Harry Anderson, who wrote . . .": Author's interview.

265 "the real median income . . .": *The Washington Post*, October 26, 1986.

265 "All of journalism has moved . . .": Author's interview.

266 Beckel's gesture was witnessed by the author; the same is true about the rest of the activities in the pressroom reported here.

268 "We were hurt . . .": Author's interview.

268 "We were all worried . . .": Author's interviews.

268 "I remember taking Reagan . . .": Author's interview.

269 The polls regarding Reagan's appearance at the debate were reported in Blume, op. cit., p. 162.

269 Network executives were lectured about early reporting of election results at a Joint Hearing of the Communications Subcommittee of the House Energy and Commerce Committee with the Task Force on Elections of the House Administration Committee, held on October 3, 1984.

270 *Newsweek*'s "Landslide?" cover issue was published on November 5, 1984.

270 "We were simply reflecting . . .": Author's interview.

CHAPTER 12

271 "The concern about nuclear . . .": Author's interview.

271 "I think in general I'm . . .": Author's interview.

272 "only three of those carried . . .": Author's interview.

272 "If the total mission . . .": Author's interview.

272 "It was never as intense . . .": Author's interview.

273 "Zero Option said we *won't* . . .": Author's interview.

273 Zero Option "non-negotiable": Author's interviews.

273 The logistics and objectives of the Zero Option speech were described in author's interviews with Gergen and White House press aide Karna Small.

274 "We don't have two years . . .": Author's interview.

275 "The one place I thought . . .": Author's interview.

275 The discussion of Gorbachev's speech to the Moscow Peace Forum is based on "Whose 'Zero Option' Is It Anyway?" by Mary Kaldor, *The New Statesman*, March 13, 1987.

276 The counter-evidence to Reagan's "unilaterally disarmed" argument is

cited in Green and MacColl, op. cit., pp. 38–39, 44, and in Dugger, op. cit., p. 395.

277   The discussion of Reagan administration plans to fight protracted nuclear wars is based on *With Enough Shovels: Reagan, Bush and Nuclear War*, by Robert Scheer, Vintage (New York: 1983), pp. 129–34.

279   "non-negotiable": Author's interviews.

279   Reagan's admission of ignorance is reported in *Deadly Gambits*, by Strobe Talbott, Knopf (New York: 1984), p. 263.

280   "these freeze people . . .": Author's interview.

280   "I got communications and policy . . .": Author's interview.

281   The discussion of the Committee on the Present Danger is based on Scheer, op. cit.

282   "Nobody gives a shit . . .": Author's interview.

283   "impotent and obsolete": President Reagan's Star Wars speech, March 23, 1983.

283   That senior Reagan officials were surprised by the SDI announcement was reported by George Ball in *The New York Review of Books*, April 11, 1985. Robert McFarlane was one of the officials who claimed to favor SDI on strategic grounds; he outlined the strategic rationale for the system in an interview with the author, saying he supported SDI as a way "to deal with a military imbalance that I saw coming." The $400 billion figure (an extremely conservative one—other estimates ran as high as $1 trillion) and the Rockwell pamphlet were cited in "Look Who's Really Behind Star Wars," by E. P. Thompson, *The Nation*, March 1, 1986.

283   "I didn't understand SDI . . .": Author's interview.

284   The discussion of the SDI program is based on *Star Warriors: A Penetrating Look into the Lives of the Young Scientists Behind Our Space Age Weaponry*, by William J. Broad, Simon & Schuster (New York: 1985); "The Wonders of Star Wars," by Lord Zuckerman, *The New York Review of Books*, January 30, 1986; "Star Wars: The Leaky Shield," by Carl Sagan, *Parade*, December 8, 1985; and numerous news stories, including especially two *New York Times* articles from February 5, 1986 (p. A1) and May 27, 1986 (p. A16). The 30 percent figure used by the Joint Chiefs of Staff was reported in *The Washington Post*, March 27, 1988.

285   The Council on Economic Priorities study, "The Strategic Defense Initiative: Costs, Contractors & Consequences," was released on April 1, 1985.

285   "Mr. Reagan['s] vision . . .": *The New York Times*, May 17, 1986.

286   The President's March 29, 1985, speech was quoted in Paul Warnke's foreword to the CEP study cited above.

286   The *New York Times* articles were published from March 3, through March 8, 1985.

288   The *Newsweek* article appeared in the March 18, 1985, issue.

288   "This country, including its press . . .": Author's interview.

288   Greenfield's column appeared in the December 14, 1987, issue.

289   Among many other examples of elite support for a test ban, see an April 4, 1986, *New York Times* story, p. A3, reporting the agreement of such former officials as Gerard C. Smith, chief U.S. negotiator at the 1972 SALT talks; James Schlesinger, former CIA director and Secretary of Defense; and Lieutenant General Brent Scowcroft, former national security adviser, among others.

289   "Any kind of announcement . . .": Author's interview.

289 "The test ban announcement . . .": Author's interview.
289 "dealt with it by talking . . .": Author's interview.
290 The peace movement's petition drive was described by movement activists in interviews with the author.
291 The Brokaw and Rather interviews with Jackson, the Moyers commentary and the news stories concerning Jackson's meeting with Gorbachev were broadcast on November 19, 1985; the Bruce Morton report on November 21, 1985.
295 The Donaldson, Jennings, Markey and Aspin statements were made during the October 13, 1986, *World News Tonight* broadcast. Chancellor's commentary appeared the same evening on NBC. The McWethy SDI pieces ran on October 16 and 21. The Francis piece ran on October 13, the Martin on October 15.
296 Plante's report was broadcast on October 17.
297 The IISS study's findings were summarized in *The Washington Post*, November 11, 1987.
297 "abdicates an independent point of view . . .": *Mother Jones*, June–July 1987.
298 The "War, Peace and the News Media" conference was held March 18–19, 1983, at New York University, under the sponsorship of the Department of Journalism and Mass Communication.

CHAPTER 13
299 Reagan was criticized by John B. Oakes on *The New York Times*'s Op-Ed page on December 17, 1986.
299 "Truth is the enemy . . .": Author's interview.
300 "We are constantly taken . . .": *The New York Times*, June 23, 1985.
300 Reagan's "You can run . . ." quote and the Rather and Wooten remarks were broadcast on October 11, 1985.
301 ABC's decision to delay broadcast of the Tripoli story was confirmed in an author's interview with John McWethy. NBC's action was apparent from the difference between what was reported on the initial 6:30 p.m. (eastern time) feed—that there had been reports of U.S. military planes departing from bases in Britain—and what was reported at 7 p.m.—that U.S. planes were at that moment attacking Tripoli.
301 The Tripoli casualty figures were reported in *The New York Times* on April 16, 1986. The conclusion of West German authorities was reported on ABC's *World News Tonight*, October 29, 1986. The assassination strategy of the Tripoli raid was reported in Seymour Hersh's article in *The New York Times Magazine* published on February 22, 1987.
301 ABC's $10 million purchase price was reported in the September–October 1986 issue of the *Columbia Journalism Review*.
301 Lesley Stahl's story was broadcast July 4, 1986.
301 The *Time* story was published July 7, 1986.
301 "Unlike Watergate, all newspapers . . .": Author's interview.
302 Eleanor Randolph's story was published November 15, 1987. *Newsweek* was also an exception. In a January 19, 1987, story, *Newsweek*'s Jonathan Alter speculated that one reason the story had gone unreported was that certain reporters in Washington (some of whom he named) depended on North as a source.
303 The early reports of U.S. and Israeli arms dealings with Iran were orig-

inally reported by Eleanor Randolph (see above) and were independently confirmed by the author.

303 The subsequent Van Atta–Anderson columns were published in *The Washington Post* on May 11, 1986, June 29, 1986, August 11, 1986, and May 20, 1987.

304 "I had calls . . .": Author's interview.

304 "It was scary to me . . .": Author's interview.

304 "A lot of the people . . .": Author's interview.

304 "I think Casey was . . ." and the appeal to Casey by Gelb and Kovach: Author's interview with Gelb.

305 "I don't really believe . . .": Author's interview.

305 "Really, the inductive reasoning . . .": Author's interview.

305 "was a feeling on all our . . .": Author's interview.

305 Criticisms of Gelb's leadership were expressed by more than one team member in interviews with the author.

305 "there are some things . . .": Author's interview.

305 "I don't have any second . . .": Author's interview.

306 Robert Parry's story was run by the AP on June 10, 1985.

306 The Reagan contra funding contingency plan is described in Kornbluh, op. cit., p. 62.

306 The *World News Tonight* report about the US–Israeli guns-and-drugs operation was broadcast on April 7. The rest of the press paid scarcely any attention to the story, as described in an article by the author in the April 25 issue of *The New Yorker*.

307 "The facts were the facts . . .": Author's interview.

307 Reagan's assertion of not breaking the law was reported in *The New York Times* on August 9, 1985.

307 The executive order describing the NSC's intelligence functions is described in Kornbluh, op. cit., p. 234.

307 "just went nowhere": Author's interview.

308 "I can give you my answer . . .": Author's interview. The other explanations for failure were offered by various journalists in interviews with the author.

308 "Everybody knew that Oliver . . .": Author's interview.

309 "Of course, Congress is just . . .": Author's interview.

309 "This was not the first . . .": Author's interview.

310 The administration's campaign to demonize the Sandinistas is described in Kornbluh, op. cit., Chapter 4.

310 "Soviet arms shipments to Nicaragua . . .": *The Wall Street Journal*, April 3, 1985.

310 "a vast psychological warfare . . .": *The Miami Herald*, July 19, 1987.

310 "to slowly demonize . . .": quoted in Kornbluh, op. cit., p. 166.

When President Reagan imposed economic sanctions on Nicaragua on May 1, for example, news organizations respectfully reported his accompanying (and legally required) declaration that a "national emergency" existed. Veteran *New York Times* correspondent Bernard Gwertzman apparently saw no reason in his May 5 story to balance Reagan's claim— that Nicaragua's actions and policies "constitute an unusual and extraordinary threat to the national security and foreign policy of the United States"—by pointing out that the administration had yet to produce evidence that Nicaragua was subverting U.S. allies in the region. Nor did Gwertzman note, as his colleague Joel Brinkley had recently reported, that Nicaragua's military was smaller than those of its Central American neighbors combined and that Reagan's own military analysts doubted it would ever invade them.

With congressional Democrats by and large lauding the sanctions, the debate as posed in the media centered on whether sanctions would work, not whether they were justified. As *Newsweek* so objectively phrased it, would an embargo "persuade the Sandinista regime to revive democracy at home [and] stop assisting leftist insurgents elsewhere in Central America" or merely "drive the Sandinistas deeper into the embrace of the Soviet bloc"?

Likewise, news organizations could hardly have been more accommodating when Reagan in a July 8 speech termed Nicaragua, Cuba, North Korea, Iran and Libya "a confederation of terrorist states" and "a new, international version of Murder, Inc." All three networks, as well as the *Post* and the *Times*, made it their top news story. Coming from a man whose own mercenary army routinely terrorized Nicaraguan peasants, Reagan's charge could well have backfired on him. But the press seemed uninterested in this paradox. Denials from the accused governments, when included at all, were truncated or buried in news stories. Instead, the major points of criticism in the eyes of most reporters were why Syria, a prime terrorism suspect, had been left off the list, and why the President was talking so tough about terrorism but doing so little.

Which is not to say that mainstream news coverage never included information injurious to the administration's cause. The truth about the contras was too obvious and widely known, and the administration's exaggerations about the Sandinistas too gross, for that.

In the April 29, 1985, issue of *Newsweek*, for example, grisly color photos of a contra executing a prisoner of war by cutting his throat were published. In the March 30 *New York Times*, Joel Brinkley offered a comprehensive analysis of Nicaragua's military strength that put the lie to much administration hype. When Nicaragua's World Court case against the United States was tried in August, the *Times* (in, for example, an August 18, 1985, story) and other papers reported the testimony of former CIA analyst David MacMichael—that Nicaragua had not helped arm El Salvador's rebels for at least the last four years—and of former contra leader Edgard Charmorro—that the contras, with CIA acquiescence, routinely forcibly recruited new fighters by publicly killing Sandinista officials and their sympathizers (*The New York Times*, September 12, 1985). Reports by human rights organizations on contra atrocities also were covered, though, like the World Court stories, they were invariably tucked away inside the paper, as with the March 7, 1985, *Washington Post* story on the so-called Brody report that ran on p. 14.

"It's like Hitler's Big Lie," argued reporter Vicki Barker of UPI Radio in an interview with the author. "Tell the same lie often enough and people will believe it's the truth. You can have total [journalistic] freedom, you can have the power of Dan Rather, you can go get perfect documentation that the contras are using terror tactics, and it doesn't matter. Because Reagan and his people say twenty times a day the contras are freedom fighters, and that becomes the news."

311 "The press and Congress . . .": Author's interview.
312 Maeserve's concession came in an interview with the author.
312 "There was a period . . .": Author's interview.

312   "I regret not having pushed . . .": Author's interview.
312   "This was clearly not what . . .": Author's interview.
313   "it was clear that . . .": Author's interview.
313   "This is nonsense . . .": Author's interview.
314   "The real effect of . . .": Author's interview.
314   Parry and Barger's frustration was first reported in "The Real Heroes of Contragate," by Jefferson Morley and Tina Rosenberg, *Rolling Stone*, September 10, 1987, and reconfirmed in interviews with the author.
315   "had no doubt that Parry and . . .": Author's interview.
315   Parry's failure to attract interest in his contra supply story was related in an interview with the author. The *New Republic* article was published in the November 24, 1986, issue.
316   "The contras and Ollie North . . .": Author's interview.

CHAPTER 14

318   The AIDS rumors were recounted by a former White House staff member in an interview with the author.
318   Deaver wrote of his alcoholism and his visit to a detoxification center in his memoirs, op. cit.
318   The $18 million figure is cited in Deaver, op. cit., p. 219. For the details of Deaver's trial, see "Deaver Is Found Guilty of Lying about Lobbying," by Bill McAllister, *The Washington Post*, December 17, 1987.
319   The ABC polling figures were confirmed by John Benson of the Roper Center.
319   Deaver's behind-the-scenes damage-control efforts were reported in the press at the time and confirmed in an interview with the author.
320   "The four-star general . . .": Author's interview.
320   A copy of his Gannett speech was provided to the author by Gergen's office.
320   Baker's judgment, relayed to the President by Secretary of State Shultz, was cited by Walter Karp in *Harper's*, February 1988, p. 56. The original citation in the *Report of the Congressional Committees Investigating the Iran-Contra Affair* is on p. 39.
320   "differences that Baker, Meese . . .": Author's interview.
321   "If there is anything . . .": Author's interview.
321   The false statements of Reagan and Meese are documented in the Iran-contra report (see above).
321   "one reason Meese panicked . . .": Author's interview.
322   "sending a signal . . .": Author's interview.
322   "Both his feeling and my . . .": Author's interview.
323   The Morgan-Pincus story was published on September 6, 1987.
324   "This was the first time . . .": Author's interview.
325   "a Watergate mentality": Author's interview.
325   "afraid to be aggressive . . .": Author's interview.
326   John Chancellor's commentary was broadcast on February 26, 1987.
326   "turned the corner . . ." *The Washington Post*, March 5, 1987.
328   "We did a page-one story . . .": Author's interview.
328   "There's been a lot of good . . .": Author's interview.
329   "I wouldn't strongly disagree . . .": Author's interview.
329   "We did lots of stories . . .": Author's interview.
330   "What upset the American people . . .": Author's interview.
330   "by responding to that one . . .": Author's interview.

330 "If there's no White House . . .": Author's interview.
331 "tried very hard not to . . .": Author's interview.
331 "How do you think we felt . . .": Author's interview.
331 Draper's point was made in "The Rise of the American Junta," *The New York Review of Books*, October 8, 1987. To be sure, the Reagan administration was hardly the first to seek to elude democratic accountability for its actions abroad. From the time the United States graduated to full-fledged imperial status in the wake of World War II, American Presidents, urged on by ambitious national security planners, had chafed at constitutional requirements that they notify and obtain the consent of Congress before launching adventurous policies overseas. Actions thought necessary to maintain and expand the empire clashed with such principles of democracy at home, and as often as not, it was democracy that gave way. The CIA, originally mandated by the 1947 National Security Act only to gather and evaluate intelligence, soon became the primary means of conducting such covert policies as the overthrow of governments (in Iran and Guatemala, for example) and the waging of secret wars (in Angola and Nicaragua). The National Security Council, charged in the same act with mere coordination of policy options for the President, became an instrument for actually making and implementing policy, as with the secret bombing of Cambodia overseen by President Nixon and his national security adviser, Henry Kissinger.
332 "people are searching . . .": Originally made during Drew's on-air commentary for PBS, the remark was reconfirmed with Drew's office by the author.
332 "we had a sense of that . . .": Author's interview.
332 "The reason the question . . .": Author's interview.
332 McFarlane's testimony is noted in the previously cited Iran-contra report.
333 "If you have to prove . . .": Armstrong made this remark during a May 13, 1987, lecture at the Institute for Policy Studies in Washington, D.C.
333 Hamilton appeared on ABC on June 14, 1987.
333 "brought it up several times": Author's interview.
333 "the most logical question . . .": Author's interview.
334 "public sentiment wasn't there . . .": Author's interview.
334 The article in the *Post*, for example, was "Ollie's Last Laugh," by David Ignatius, July 12, 1987.
334 "The press is a captive . . .": Author's interview.
334 The *Newsweek* poll was published on March 9, 1987; the *U.S. News & World Report* poll on July 13, 1987.
334 "We were aware of it . . .": Author's interview.
335 "nobody said bluntly . . .": *Harper's*, February 1988.
335 "Instead of asking about . . .": Armstrong's IPS lecture, cited above.
336 The 184 tally was reported in the *Los Angeles Times* on August 5, 1987.
337 "It was a function of two . . .": Author's interview.
337 "found facts in eye-glazing . . ." August 5, 1987.
337 "is still in his job . . .": Author's interview. Zirinsky mentioned in a subsequent conversation with the author that CBS did note Abrams's role in the Iran-contra affair in the course of four subsequent stories.
338 "[It was] an interim report . . .": Author's interview.
339 "I remember somebody joking . . .": Author's interview.
339 "came very close to being . . .": Author's interview.
339 "liked the way they kept . . .": Author's interview.

339 "We did raise questions . . .": Author's interview.

340 "always looking to someone . . .": Author's interview.

341 "We do raise questions . . .": Author's interview.

342 "For a paper with the resources . . .": Author's interview.

CHAPTER 15

344 "We had a difference of opinion . . .": Author's interview.

345 Gergen's fear of an end to deference was expressed in an interview with the author.

346 Gergen's concession came in an interview with the author.

347 I. F. Stone's remark is recounted on p. 18 of *I. F. Stone: A Portrait*, by Andrew Patner, Pantheon (New York: 1988).

347 *Time*'s attack on Reagan was published on November 2, 1987. And in an unmistakable indication of Reagan's new vulnerability to criticism in the aftermath of the crash, the magazine then built a nationally distributed television commercial around it.

Index